HENKE'S
California
Law Guide

Seventh Edition

**Revised and Edited
by**

Daniel W. Martin

*Associate Dean, Library and Information
Services and Professor of Law
Pepperdine University School of Law*

LexisNexis™
Matthew Bender®

QUESTIONS ABOUT THIS PUBLICATION?

For questions about the **Editorial Content** appearing in these volumes or reprint permission, please call:

Valri Nesbit, J.D. .... 1-800-424-0651 (ext. 3343)
Bonnie Akimoto .... 1-800-424-0651 (ext. 3311)
Originally Published in 1976
Outside the United States and Canada please call .... (415) 908-3200

For assistance with replacement pages, shipments, billing or other customer service matters, please call:

Customer Services Department at .... (800) 833-9844
Outside the United States and Canada, please call   .... (518) 487-3000
Fax number .... (518) 487-3584
Customer Service Website .... http://www.lexisnexis.com/custserv/

For information on other Matthew Bender publications, please call:
Your account manager .... (800) 223-1940
Outside the United States and Canada, please call .... (518) 487-3000

ISBN 0–327–16390–9

MATTHEW◆BENDER

Editorial Offices
744 Broad Street, Newark, NJ 07102 (973) 820-2000
201 Mission St., San Francisco, CA 94105-1831 (415) 908-3200
www.lexis.com

(Pub. 64620)

Statement on Fair Use

LexisNexis Matthew Bender recognizes the balance that must be achieved between the operation of the fair use doctrine, whose basis is to avoid the rigid application of the copyright statute, and the protection of the creative rights and economic interests of authors, publishers and other copyright holders.

We are also aware of the countervailing forces that exist between the ever greater technological advances for making both print and electronic copies and the reduction in the value of copyrighted works that must result from a consistent and pervasive reliance on these new copying technologies. It is LexisNexis Matthew Bender's position that if the "progress of science and useful arts" is promoted by granting copyright protection to authors, such progress may well be impeded if copyright protection is diminished in the name of fair use. (See *Nimmer on Copyright* § 13.05[E][1].) This holds true whether the parameters of the fair use doctrine are considered in either the print or the electronic environment as it is the integrity of the copyright that is at issue, not the media under which the protected work may become available. Therefore, the fair use guidelines we propose apply equally to our print and electronic information, and apply, within §§ 107 and 108 of the Copyright Act, regardless of the professional status of the user.

Our draft guidelines would allow for the copying of limited materials, which would include synopses and tables of contents, primary source and government materials that may have a minimal amount of editorial enhancements, individual forms to aid in the drafting of applications and pleadings, and miscellaneous pages from any of our newsletters, treatises and practice guides. This copying would be permitted provided it is performed for internal use and solely for the purpose of facilitating individual research or for creating documents produced in the course of the user's professional practice, and the original from which the copy is made has been purchased or licensed as part of the user's existing in-house collection.

LexisNexis Matthew Bender fully supports educational awareness programs designed to increase the public's recognition of its fair use rights. We also support the operation of collective licensing organizations with regard to our print and electronic information.

(Pub. 64620)

DEDICATION

For my Family
Kathi Jean Stafford
Andrew Stafford Martin
Elizabeth Stafford Martin

(Pub. 64620)

Summary of Contents

Contents

(Pub. 64620)

Contents

Chapter 2. California Constitution

 (Pub. 64620)

Contents

Chapter 3. California Statutes

Chapter 4. Legislative Intent

Contents

(Pub. 64620)

Contents

Chapter 5. Ballot Measure Research

(Pub. 64620)

Contents

Chapter 7. Judicial Administration

Contents

(Pub. 64620)

Contents

xv

Contents

Contents

Chapter 13. Legal Ethics and Discipline

Chapter 14. Law Libraries

(Pub. 64620)

Contents

Chapter 15. Electronic Legal Databases

Chapter 16. Legal Education

Contents

(Pub. 64620)

Foreword

"You can have speed or you can have tradition, but you can't have both."[1] In early 2003, I published an article about the adoption of standard time in the United States,[2] a topic I have been studying for years, and one which I can honestly say has taken up permanent residence in one corner of my brain. I am now at work on the very strange history of daylight saving time and its adoption in the United States in the twentieth century. (Since I am very traditional, this article will not appear speedily.) Time is the lens through which I now look at everything, and as I am writing yet another foreword for HENKE'S CALIFORNIA LAW GUIDE, I find myself pondering several aspects of time as it relates to this book.

The popularity of LEXIS, WESTLAW and now the internet for legal researchers has been about the triumph of speed over tradition. Long gone are the days when judges rode their circuit on horseback and carried their "library" in their saddle bags. Today the law is so voluminous and so complex it simply would be unmanageable without the organizational capability provided by technology. And yet, in his introduction, Dan Martin makes a convincing case for the continued existence of hardcopy. He states: "In spite of all these obvious advantages [of computer databases], print materials are here to stay and print collections in libraries will continue to grow." In some contexts you can have both speed and tradition.

"Now that we have progress so rapid that it can change from year to year, no one calls it progress. People call it change, and rather than yearn for it, they brace themselves against its force."[3] Why should one pick up a book like HENKE'S CALIFORNIA LAW GUIDE? It is simply because the law is evolving ever more rapidly and the researcher must stay on top of this change or progress or whatever it is called. The seventh edition, like several of its predecessors, is organized on the contributor model, i.e., reliance on authors who are experts in specific

---

[1] CLARK BLAISE, TIME LORD: SIR SANDFORD FLEMING AND THE CREATION OF STANDARD TIME 235 (2000).

[2] Jenni Parrish, *Litigating Time in America at the Turn of the Twentieth Century,* 36 AKRON L. REV. 1 (2002).

[3] STEWART BRAND, THE CLOCK OF THE LONG NOW 15–16 (1999).

(Pub. 64620)

areas of legal research to write about the latest materials and methods in that area. Two contributors have been added to the extraordinary group assembled for the sixth edition. The newcomers are Brian Raphael from the University of Southern California School of Law who has updated the chapter on California case law, and David McFadden of Southwestern University School of Law who has updated the chapter on statutes and codes.

"If one is mentally out of breath all the time from dealing with the present, there is no energy left for imaging the future."[4] This is the definition of "temporal exhaustion" given by the sociologist Elise Boulding. She could have been talking specifically about legal researchers in the early 21st century. Law is huge, interdisciplinary, and often uncertain as to its outcome. The guide that helps tame the monster is most welcome. Researching California law, which is on the cutting edge and which regulates the world's sixth largest economy, is a herculean task. The one assigned to it can undoubtedly use the best help available. If you are reading this, you have found the best help available.

And finally, just to drive home the value of this tome in the time-pressed business of legal research, this foreword ends on a cautionary note about the value of time (as in billable minutes) from William Shakespeare's play, *Richard II*:

How sour sweet music is
When time is broke and no proportion kept!
So is it in the music of men's lives.
I wasted time, and now doth time waste me;
For now hath time made me his numbering clock;
My thoughts are minutes.[5]

Jenni Parrish
Director of the Law Library
Professor of Law
University of California
Hastings College
of the Law

---

[4] *Id.* at 29, *quoting* Elise Boulding, *The Dynamics of Imaging Futures*, WORLD FUTURE SOCIETY BULLETIN 7 (Sept. 1978).

[5] WILLIAM SHAKESPEARE, THE TRAGEDY OF KING RICHARD II, Act 5, Sc. 5, lines 42–44, 49–51 (Cambridge Ed. 1936).

 (Pub. 64620)

Acknowledgments

As it was stated in the 3rd, 4th, 5th, and 6th editions of this book, the person who deserves the most credit for Henke's California Law Guide is Professor Dan Henke. He came up with the original idea for an in-depth sourcebook on California law. He authored the first two editions and the later cumulative supplements. Material from those earliest editions still remains intact in this edition.

Writer Richard Foster has said that "books are best written in community."[1] I think that this is especially true in the world of California legal research. I have discussed the 3rd, 4th, 5th, 6th, and 7th editions of this publication project with many law librarians, state government employees, lawyers, law students, library school students, and legal information vendors. I have received much help and some great ideas from friends and colleagues around the state. I am grateful for the help I received from Vahn C. Babigian, Metropolitan News Company; Lucy Barber, California State Archives; Michael Beaird, University of Arkansas; William E. Behnk, California Department of Information Technology; Marcia Bell, San Francisco Law Library; Laura Cadra, UCLA Law Library; Maggie Cimino, Administrative Office of the Courts; Janet Coles, California State Library; Hillary Crandall, Seaver College; Wil Davies, Legislative Analyst's Office; Susan DeBoer, BMI Imaging Systems; Tina Dumas, Nixon Peabody; Charles Dyer, San Diego County Public Library; Jane Evans, Administrative Office of the Courts; Nell Fields, Daily Journal Corp.; Kristen Flanagan, LexisNexis; Nanna Frye, California Courts of Appeal; Scott Giordano, LexisNexis; Melissa Hagar, West Group; Avelino J. Halagao, Jr., West Group; Linda Heatherly, Office of the Legislative Counsel; Valerie Henderson, LexisNexis; Fay Henexson, California Attorney General's Office; Jennifer Hill, Keller Rohrback LLP; Nancy Hoebelheinrich, University of San Francisco; Heather Cline Hoganson, Office of Administrative Hearings; Rita Grobman Howard, Matthew Bender; Richard Iamele, Los Angeles County Law Library; Mike Ibold, California Office of Administrative Law from 1987 to 2003; Jennifer Lentz, UCLA Law Library; Tobe Liebert, University of Texas at Austin; David McFadden,

---

[1] Foster, Richard J., *Celebration of Discipline*, rev. ed. San Francisco: Harper, 1988, 228 p.

(Pub. 64620)

Acknowledgments

Southwestern University School of Law Library; Nancy McGinnis, Pepperdine University School of Law; Anthony Miller, Pepperdine University School of Law; Dan Mitchell, California State Library; Erin Murphy, UC Davis Law Library; Stan Nishimura, Building Standards Commission; Greg Ogden, Pepperdine University School of Law; Jenni Parrish, Hastings College of the Law; Janet Raffalow, California Attorney General's Office; Brian Raphael, USC; George Relles, Consultant; Diane Reynolds, Los Angeles County Law Library; Jimmy Rimonte, Daily Journal Corp.; Carolina Rose, Legislative Research, Inc.; Myra Saunders, UCLA; Deanna Loy Schuler, Independent Consultant; Ellen St. John, Los Angeles District Attorney's Office; Kathi Stafford, Sun Microsystems, Inc.; Tom Stallard, Legislative Intent Service; Dan Taysom, Hastings College of the Law; Dorothy Thomson, Legislative Intent Service; Genevieve Troka, Archivist at the California State Archives; and Justice Paul A. Turner, California Courts of Appeal. Several of the members of the library staff at Pepperdine University School of Law have assisted me on this project. Former employees who were helpful are Hennie Vander Meyden, John Peele, B.J. Segel, Mona Stahl, and Joy Humphrey. I would also like to thank current staff members Katie Kerr, Phillip Bohl, Donald Buffaloe, Barbara Hicks, Felicia Curtis Fields, David Dickens, Daryl Fisher-Ogden, Martha Huggins, Judith Hsu, and Paul Moorman. I am especially grateful to my past and present research assistants Milena Kogan, Timothy Hix, Jacinda Denison, Kevin Slattum, John Hur, Paul Neil, Taylor Nguyen, John Ostler, Trevor Kaufman, Adriana Dulic, Michael Cernovich, and Eric Johnston. Finally, I want to thank J.T. Hardin, who patiently worked with me on the last four editions of this title, and Valri Nesbit and Bonnie Akimoto, who worked with me on this new edition.

All selections from the California Constitution, Rules of Court, and Code are reprinted with permission from LexisNexis.

Daniel W. Martin

Introduction to the Seventh Edition

In the introduction to the sixth edition I mentioned that I believed that nothing in academic law libraries would be considered too unimportant to automatically escape digitization. I still believe this. Information vendors like Thomson, Reed Elsevier, and Wolters Kluwer will continue to offer products in the digital format. Organizations like the Library of Congress, HeinOnline, JSTOR, OCLC, and LLMC-Digital will continue to build full text and/or image databases from materials not originally published in the electronic format. Governments, small publishers, colleges and universities, and even individuals are adding and will continue to add valuable legal information to the World Wide Web.

All of this data in a digital format has some tremendous advantages over print materials in the world of legal research. The databases of the major vendors and organizations should be distinguished from the free or very low cost web resources because of the differences in quality, reliability, search engine strength, historical depth, and updating capabilities, so I'll address them separately below as I compare them to the traditional print (and archival microfilm and fiche) format.

Databases are easier to update than print material. The vendor can make one change in a database and every customer will have immediate access to the new material. This is a huge improvement over the pocketpart, paper supplement, or looseleaf updating processes used with print materials.

Databases are more easily corrected. The vendor can make a database change instead of sending out errata sheets to be glued into a volume or printing a correction in the next issue of a periodical.

Databases can serve more than one user at a time. The larger legal research services can handle thousands of simultaneous users. All of them could theoretically be looking at the same document. A single item in print format in a library can only be easily used by one person at a time.

Databases can put tens of thousands of volumes of material at your fingertips, as long as you are in a location with electrical power and internet access. This is the equivalent of putting those tens of thousands

 (Pub. 64620)

of bound volumes in a lawyer's home library or a law student's dormitory room. It's a virtual library.

In spite of all these obvious advantages, print materials are here to stay and print collections in libraries will continue to grow. Books, journals, and newspapers have their own advantages over digitized materials.

First, even though LexisNexis and Westlaw have the equivalent of tens of thousands of volumes in their online collections, they still carry only a small fraction of the print and fiche materials in most large academic law libraries. In 1998 Penny Hazelton compared the two largest legal information vendors' holdings against the holdings at the University of Washington's law library. She found that there was only a 13% overlap. 87% of the University of Washington's collection was not on LexisNexis or Westlaw.[1]

Even allowing for the added materials LexisNexis and Westlaw have added in the past six years and the additional materials that have been scanned into HeinOnline, JSTOR, LLMC-Digital, and all the other legal information databases, there is still a substantial amount of a typical law library's collection that is not duplicated online.

In addition, there are other legitimate reasons to demand legal materials in print. Print materials can be read in locations without power or internet access. Print materials can be read in areas where lighting may not be ideal for viewing a computer screen. Print materials can be read in areas too hot or too cold or too dusty for a computer to work properly.

However, the strongest argument for the print format is the fact that it is permanent. If the information is printed with good ink on good paper it can last for centuries. We have good examples of this in public and private libraries around the world. The next best permanent format is probably microfiche or microfilm. We know that these two formats can last for decades. But no one knows much about the physical permanence of computer data. Experts have argued for years that data may be lost as the equipment on which it resides breaks down and becomes obsolete. But the question may not be, Will most of the digital

---

[1] Hazelton, Penny A. How Much of Your Print Collection Is Really on WESTLAW or LEXIS-NEXIS? 18 (1) Legal Reference Services Quarterly 3–22 (1999).

data be transferred from format to format as computers move from generation to generation? This will probably happen. The two more important questions to ask are: 1) Is the data complete to begin with? and 2) Is the data inviolable—can it be intentionally deleted or changed?

Is the database complete to begin with? The answer is no. For example, look at the photos, drawings, graphs, charts, diagrams, tables, or other types of illustrations in printed legal materials. Lexis and Westlaw for years have carried reported cases, codes, journals, and other materials that have illustrations in them. Because these databases started out as text-only databases they were unable to handle graphic images. Now that both vendors are on the web they are adding more images to their databases, but not all of the images are online yet.

A second example addresses the completeness of material apart from graphic images. In the 1980s and early 1990s when Westlaw began adding journals to its databases, it only added articles selectively. Not all articles in a journal issue were necessarily included. For instance selected coverage of the Pepperdine law review began with 1982 (v. 10) and full coverage began with 1993 (v. 20 no. 4). Westlaw isn't the only vendor to do this. Third, when a researcher looks at any database version of a newspaper or any other periodical, he or she may find that illustrations, advertisements, and certain articles are missing from the online version. The New York Law Journal on LexisNexis has this disclaimer in that title's Source Information file: "Access to certain freelance articles and other features within this publication (i.e. photographs, classifieds, etc . . .) may not be available."

The bigger question may be, Is the data inviolable? Or phrased another way, once the document is in the database, will it always be there and will it look the same? Again, the answer is no. If you have a copy of a book, it is in a fixed medium. It will always look the same. The information in it will always be there. With a database, that is not true.

Contractual arrangements between the database vendors and the original content suppliers are periodically renegotiated. The original content supplier may decide to pull its data out of a vendor's database, changing the value of that database for all customers. The original content supplier may then move the data to another database vendor or start supplying the data directly to the consumer. This happened with the Bureau of National Affairs' (BNA) products on LexisNexis and Westlaw.

Introduction

Copyright suits can affect what the database vendors can include. The New York Times v. Tasini decision in June 2001[2] gave freelance writers the electronic rights to their articles. Some publishers immediately asked electronic database vendors to remove the articles posted without permission. An LA Times article about the Tasini decision[3] said that LexisNexis was asked to remove over 200,000 articles from its databases.

Embarrassing mistakes can cause a database vendor to remove or change data. When errors are pointed out to the vendors, they can easily make corrections that change the data immediately for all future users. Only users who downloaded the data earlier (or have a hard copy version of the same data) will be in a position to notice the difference. West accidentally published an opinion that was an April Fool's Day joke by Arkansas Supreme Court Justice George Rose Smith. West removed the case, Catt v. State, 691 S.W. 2nd 120 (Ark. 1985), from the database and also deleted any references to it in later cases. LexisNexis doesn't include the original decision in its database, but does include at least one later reference to it (see State v. Willis, 673 A. 2d 1233 (Del. Super. 1995)). Lexis includes this note for the Catt case: "The opinion reported at this cite is not an official opinion of the Supreme Court of Arkansas and is, therefore, not published on the LEXIS-NEXIS services."

Disputes over the accuracy of facts in articles can cause cautious institutions to withdraw those articles from databases. The Chronicle of Higher Education on September 7, 2001 reported that Boise Cascade Corporation had contacted the University of Denver and asked them to withdraw from all databases (Westlaw and LexisNexis) an article that was critical of the corporation's activities in Mexico. The university did as Boise Cascade asked. The article's authors then sued the university in federal court for defamation. The suit was settled, but the article is still not online in either Westlaw or LexisNexis. You can find the article in hard copy in any large law library in the country however.[4] Westlaw

---

[2] New York Times Co., Inc. v. Tasini. 533 U.S. 483, 121 S.Ct. 2381, 150 L.Ed.2d 500 (June 25, 2001)

[3] Richardson, Lisa. Victory for Freelancers Leaves Librarians at a Loss. Los Angeles Times, Tuesday, July 10, 2001. Section E, pp. 1, 4.

[4] See William A. Wines, Mark A. Buchanan, and Donald J. Smith. The Critical Need for Law Reform to Regulate the Abusive Practices of Transnational Corporations: The Illustrative Case of Boise Cascade Corporation in Mexico's Costa Grande and Elsewhere. 26 Denv. J. Int'l L. & Pol'y 453–515 (1998).

 (Pub. 64620)

carries this note: "26 Denv. J. Int'l L. & Pol'y 453 is a valid citation; however, we cannot process this FIND request because this full text document is not included in any Westlaw database." This note on Westlaw is followed by the full citation for the article and links to its entries in the index databases, Current Law Index and Index to Legal Periodicals and Books.

The previous examples all involved the major database vendors. Information on the web itself is much more fragile and ephemeral than information in the major legal databases. LexisNexis and Westlaw are going to be much better about keeping data available in their databases than anyone else. They are information companies that deal with information professionals. They know the importance of the integrity of their databases. They know that their customers want to have some feeling of permanence about their databases. But web information generally is much less permanent. Law firms publish articles by lawyers within their firms, but those articles are removed as the information becomes outdated or the attorney moves on to another firm. Government offices post information on their web site for a fixed period of time and periodically clear out the older material to make room for the latest articles.

There has been at least one attempt made at archiving the web. The Internet Archive WayBack Machine is at: *http://www.archive.org/web/web.php*. This site isn't perfect. It doesn't cover the entire web, but you might be surprised at what it does include. It might give a researcher some help if he or she wanted to look at what a web site looked like last year or four years ago. For example: What did the law firm site look like before the firm-wide reorganization?

This is all a long way of saying that online data is not sacred. There is no perfect, virtual library yet. Large parts of law libraries have not yet been converted into the digital format. Existing databases may not be complete to begin with and seemingly permanent data can certainly be changed or deleted. Web information outside the commercial databases can be so hard to find, so ephemeral, and so unreliable that it is not worth trying to use. Knowing this about online resources gives us one more reason to appreciate the stability, permanence, and accessibility of the print and fiche materials in our law libraries.

As with the previous editions, this legal research guide is California-specific and intentionally does not include a lot of information about

Introduction

basic research strategy. Rather, it is expected that this guide should be used in conjunction with a basic research text such as Mersky and Dunn's Fundamentals of Legal Research, 8th edition, Foundation Press (2002) or Berring & Edinger's Finding the Law, 11th edition, West (1999). These two books thoroughly cover federal research and basic research strategy.

Readers should feel free to send an email message to me at dmartin@pepperdine.edu with new subjects to cover, appendices to include, sources that may have been missed, or text corrections to be made.

Daniel Martin
Malibu, CA
May 17, 2004

(Pub. 64620)

Chapter 1

Law Finding in Perspective

(Pub. 64620)

[i]　Questions to Ask

[ii]　Cases

[iii]　Codes

[iv]　Other Materials

[v]　Some Finding Tools are Citable

[c]　Sources to Read Folder

[i]　Cases

[ii]　Codes

[d]　Sources Rejected Folder

[e]　Sources Read and Noted Folder

[f]　Sources Updated Folder

§ 1.01　The Anglo-American Legal System

Law is an ever-changing discipline. If it is to serve justice it must keep pace with social change and meet the needs of the people from which it springs. The common-law system in the United States has proved to be remarkably adaptable in preserving order during a period of tremendous industrial expansion flowing from the significant scientific achievements of the past century.

Our system of legal precedents is founded upon the maxim, "stare decisis et non quieta movere"— "to adhere to precedent and not unsettle things which are settled." This does not mean that the law is static, for it is not. Old holdings will be modified, reshaped and, at times, overruled by courts of competent jurisdiction when there is sufficient justification for change. Because we rely on precedent, law reports dating back hundreds of years are maintained for the use of lawyers. All of this law is readily available through the use of finding tools described in this guide.

On the one hand, judge-made law at times has been slow in meeting current challenges, and legislative enactments have been brought into play to speed the legal process. On the other hand, legislative bodies have sometimes lagged behind the courts in acting upon vital social issues. The interplay between common or judge-made law and statutes is one of the distinctive features of American jurisprudence. Although judges recognize the supremacy of statutory law, they have the power to interpret the meaning of statutory language. While courts sometimes have tended to be too narrow in their interpretation of the goals of the legislative bodies in enacting remedial statutes for social problems, they now seem to have adapted to the rapidity of modern life.

The distinctions between common or judge-made law and statutes must be recognized in legal research, but the intertwining of the vines of both systems should never be forgotten. For this and other reasons, interpretive, descriptive, and analytical treatises on specific legal subjects prepared by experts have sprung into popularity. They explore the legal topic in-depth and provide a means by which the lawyer may quickly find where his or her problem falls within the subject domain. The overview the expert provides is an aid to identifying the relevant law and directing the researcher to its sources.

§ 1.02   Authority

[1]   Types of Authority

When a lawyer goes to a law library or a legal database, he or she is in search of authority. Legal authority is either mandatory or persuasive. This distinction is important and warrants the following discussion, which is necessarily general and descriptive. The following flow chart provides an overview of legal authority.

[2]   Mandatory Authority

Mandatory authority is the law (case, statute, regulation, etc.) in force in a specific jurisdiction. Legislation in effect in California is mandatory authority in California. California legislation is not mandatory in any other state and no other state's legislation is mandatory in California. However, if Nevada has a statute similar to California's, a Nevada case construing the Nevada statute could be persuasive authority in California. Judicial decisions squarely on point are mandatory authority when issued from a higher court in the same jurisdiction.

Examples of Mandatory Authority include:

1. Constitutions
2. Statutes and Codes
3. Treaties
4. Interstate Compacts
5. Regulations of Administrative Agencies
6. Executive Orders

Types of Authority

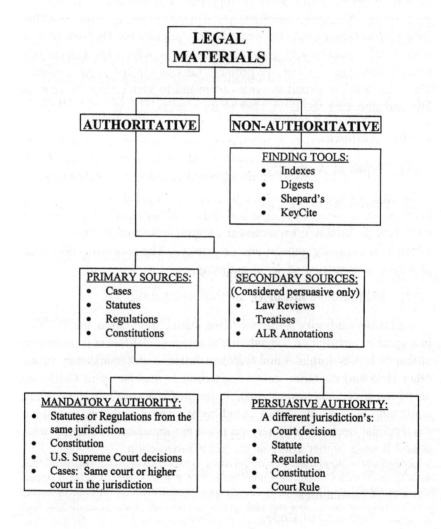

7. Ordinances

8. Charters

9. Court Rules

10. Cases—

a. Decisions, within the same jurisdiction, of same or higher court[1]

b. U.S. Supreme Court decision interpreting federal legislation or federal constitution are binding on all courts

c. U.S. Supreme Court decision on state law is binding on federal courts

d. State court decision on state law binding on federal courts unless federal constitutional question is involved (Note: Unpublished or depublished decision is not binding.)

[3] Persuasive Authority

Persuasive authority may consist of decisions from:

1. Coordinate courts of the same jurisdiction, e.g., U.S. Courts of Appeals for the several circuits; or

2. Those from courts of another jurisdiction; and

3. Those involving dicta[2] from any court in any jurisdiction.

The principal reason for considering decisions from other jurisdictions is that all courts in the United States (Louisiana excepted) embrace the common-law system.

A U.S. Supreme Court decision may be mandatory or persuasive in California. If it interprets federal legislation or the U.S. Constitution, it is mandatory on state and federal courts; otherwise, it is mandatory

---

[1] The editors of Witkin, *California Procedure,* Fourth Edition (San Francisco: Witkin Legal Institute/West Group, 1997) point out in v. 9 at p. 971 that if Courts of Appeal have issued conflicting decisions, trial courts are not bound to follow the Court of Appeal in their division or district, but may pick and choose between or among conflicting lines of authority. (*McCallum v. McCallum* (1987) 190 Cal.App.3d 308, 315, 235 Cal. Rptr. 396, footnote 4.)

[2] Dictum is "an observation or remark made by a judge in pronouncing an opinion upon a cause, concerning some rule, principle, or application of law, or the solution of a question suggested by the case at bar, but not necessarily involved in the case or essential to its determination." *Black's Law Dictionary* (6th ed. 1994). Dictum is never mandatory authority, but, depending upon who has written it, can be highly persuasive.

on federal courts, but only persuasive on California courts. The rulings of the California Supreme Court on matters of a California state law are binding on federal courts in California. If a California Court of Appeal has ruled on a question in the absence of a California Supreme Court decision, the ruling is at least persuasive authority in the federal courts.

Proposals from governmental bodies, legislative background material, attorney general opinions, and many other types of law-related documents may be considered to be persuasive authority.

Commentary on the law in the form of treatises or law review articles may also be persuasive authority. For this reason, many prominent legal authors are cited in state and federal court decisions.

Types of persuasive authority include:

1. Legislation of other states (Courts of the originating state have ruled it constitutional)

2. Legislative history documents to show intent

3. Law Revision Commission's publications

4. Judicial Council's publications

5. Opinions of the Attorney General

6. Decisions interpreting similar legislation (Nevada copies statute from California. Nevada case interpreting it is persuasive in California.)

7. Decisions of coordinate courts of same jurisdiction (Courts of Appeal)

8. Dictum

9. U.S. Supreme Court decision on state law

10. Treatises

11. Encyclopedias

12. Restatements

13. Legal Periodicals

§ 1.03   Types of Legal Sources

[1]   Categories Similar to Authority

Legal materials fall into categories similar to some of those covered in the authority discussion in § 1.02.

[2] Primary Sources

Primary sources are constitutions, treaties, court decisions, statutes, administrative regulations, administrative decisions, interstate compacts, ordinances, and court rules. Primary sources may be either mandatory authority or persuasive authority, depending on the jurisdiction of the legislating body, the level of the court, or the location of the comment in the decision.

[3] Secondary Sources

Secondary sources are commentaries on the law. These sources analyze, interpret, predict, critique, or in other ways describe the law (the primary source). Secondary sources may be treatises, restatements, law review articles, American Law Reports (A.L.R.) annotations, and legal encyclopedia annotations. Secondary sources are never mandatory authority. Even the persuasiveness of these sources may vary greatly. The level of persuasiveness depends on many things, including the reputation of the author, the reputation of the journal or publisher, and the frequency of citing by courts or other scholars.

[4] Finding Tools

Finding tools are the indexes, tables, digests, and citators that are used to locate sources. They are neither primary sources nor secondary sources. They cannot be considered mandatory or persuasive authority and are never to be cited as precedent.

[5] Combined Sources

Many publishers combine in a single volume or set the two or three types of legal materials mentioned here. Looseleaf sets, reporter volumes, and code volumes may contain finding tools, commentary (secondary source), and the primary source material (the law).

§ 1.04 Traditional Legal Research Procedure

[1] Overview

Samuel Johnson once wrote, "Knowledge is of two kinds. We know a subject ourselves, or we know where we can find information upon it."[3] Substantive courses in law school provide the lawyer with a sound

---

[3] Samuel Johnson, 1707–1784. From letter of Tuesday, 18 April 1775 in *Life of Johnson,* by James Boswell. London: Oxford University Press, 1969 [1953]. 1491 p., at p. 627.

knowledge of the principles of fundamental law. As the lawyer progresses, he or she learns how to apply such legal principles to factual situations. If the lawyer then adds to this knowledge and skill an awareness of legal information sources, law-finding tools, and the technique of their use, he or she will have the equipment for legal research.

This legal research handbook describes individual sources and techniques. Legal research problems are rarely solved through the use of one tool. A method of using many research tools in a coordinated fashion is essential.

[2] Begin with Secondary Sources

[a] Factors to Consider

Before a lawyer "looks the law," as Voelker expresses it in the *Anatomy of a Murder,*[4] he or she should have a rough idea of the substantive legal issues that may be involved, know something of the procedural rules that may apply, and be cognizant of the legal status of the litigating parties. With these factors in mind, he or she can make an estimate of the legal situation and consult secondary sources such as restatements, encyclopedias, treatises, or legal periodicals for a review of the general principles that may have a bearing upon his or her case. From these sources the lawyer may be able to readily determine the basic issues that must be resolved and whether statutory law, common law, administrative law, or all three are involved. Also from these sources the lawyer may be directed to specific citations in pertinent primary sources.

[b] Encyclopedia

One starting point for profitable legal research is likely to be the state legal encyclopedia, CalJur 3d (in print or CAJUR on Westlaw). A print encyclopedia will be kept current by periodic supplementation in the form of pocket parts, or separately issued supplement books or pamphlets. It is important to realize at the outset that to a greater degree than perhaps any other field, the legal profession depends upon a complete record of the past and still requires that all essential sources of law be current. The legal researcher cannot accept the data found in a bound law volume without also consulting available pocket parts

---

[4] Traver, Robert, *Anatomy of a Murder*, New York: St. Martin's Press, 1958. 437 p. at page 78.

or supplements, and online sources. In reverse, the derivation of law, particularly that which is statutory, may prove to be vital. The explanatory matter contained in legal treatises helps the searcher obtain a perspective of the law. Often the historical development of given principles will be indicated, distinctions between legal topics emphasized, and attitudes of courts revealed in such commentary.

[c]   Treatises

Another good starting point is a major treatise on the subject.[5] The searcher might want to consult a treatise to refresh his or her memory on the framework and substance of legal principles involved in his or her case. From such a book one may obtain the benefits of prior research by a person possessing expertise in a particular legal specialty. Such an author's view as to the trend of the law may be extremely valuable. However, the searcher should not accept a commentary as the final word. One must find the latest law on point to have authority for any contention.

Treatises of all kinds may be located by using a library's public catalog and by browsing the shelves in a library arranged by subject. The library's catalog may be a card catalog or a computerized catalog. Either type will provide access to a library's collection by author, title, and subject. If the desired book is in the local library's catalog, the user can locate the book on the shelf by using the call number assigned to it according to the classification scheme the library is using. That book should be surrounded on the shelf by other books on the same subject. If the book desired is not in the local library's catalog, the user might use the internet to search another local library's catalog or ask a librarian to check shared catalog holdings lists, such as OCLC or RLIN, the two international bibliographic databases.[6] Libraries participating in OCLC or RLIN interlibrary loan programs will be able to borrow items from other member libraries.

The advantage of a classification system is that once a researcher has found one book on a topic, he or she can browse the shelves in that immediate area for additional books on the topic. Smaller libraries will

---

[5] Treatises are discussed in Chapter 10 *Secondary Legal Sources*.

[6] OCLC is the Online Computer Library Center in Dublin, Ohio. RLIN is the Research Libraries Information Network in Mountain View, California. Both of these companies have bibliographic databases with millions of records. By using these databases, researchers can locate individual records for books and identify the holding libraries.

sometimes not have any classification system at all. Books may be arranged on a few shelves, easily visible, and available to all users. There is no need for a subject classification system and spine labels. However, the larger the library, the more there is a need for a classification system that provides for a subject arrangement of the library materials.

As one walks into any larger law library it is apparent immediately that the books have call number labels on their spines. The most common classification system for legal materials in the U.S. is the Library of Congress (LC) system. [7] Under this system all materials in a single U.S. jurisdiction like California are arranged in a pattern, which is common to all other U.S. jurisdictions. KF is the letter designation for American law. KFC is the letter designation for California law. The classification "schedule" for California (and federal law and the laws of all other states) begins with legislative materials followed by administrative regulations, and then by court reports. These primary materials (KFC 1–KFC 52) are followed by research tools (KFC 57–KFC 70) such as digests, citators, law dictionaries, form books, periodicals, yearbooks, and directories. After the tools, one will find treatises (KFC 74–KFC 1199) on all legal subjects including research, writing, professional responsibility, law office management, legal history, conflict of laws, law relating to persons (capacity, family law), law relating to property, trusts, testate succession, contracts, torts, corporations, bankruptcy, industry/trade regulation, intellectual property, labor law, welfare, public health, public safety, education, constitutional law, municipal law, administrative law, public property, public finance, and the courts (evidence, procedure, etc.).

Librarians may make exceptions to the LC system any time they think they can improve patron service by those exceptions. Some materials that are common exceptions in many libraries are law journals, reference materials (like dictionaries and directories), and materials on microfiche or microfilm (e.g., administrative regulations, A.G. Opinions, newspapers, constitutional documents, and ballot pamphlets). These materials will be pulled out of the regular classification order and shelved or housed in a special section to provide more efficient patron service.

---

[7] A second classification system is the Los Angeles County Law Library (LACLL) Class K-Law. The first edition of LACLL Class K-Law was published in 1951 and predates the LC classification scheme for American law. Both LC and LACLL Class K-Law are subject classification systems and arrange the materials in clear subject categories.

Treatises may possibly be located by searching full text databases like *lexis.com*® and Westlaw. Both of these legal database companies carry many law titles in full text, so they are searchable like the cases and statutes.

IndexMaster, *www.indexmaster.com*, is yet another way to locate the right treatise. This company, for a fee, provides access to thousands of current legal treatises, but not in full text. They supply the table of contents and indexes of these books. This permits the user to decide if the book is the correct one, even before starting to search the catalog or shelves of a particular library. Some libraries are linking the Index-Master detailed records directly to the public catalog record, permitting the user to combine these two steps, evaluating and locating the right source.

[d] Articles from Law Reviews and Bar Journals

Legal periodical articles may be accessed through one of two indexes, *Current Law Index* or *Index to Legal Periodicals*, produced by the two major legal periodical index publishers, Gale and H.W. Wilson.[8] Both companies provide complete access to articles, indexing them by author, title, and subject. In addition, users may be able to access book reviews and articles referencing specific cases and statutes. Both companies also provide the same data in a variety of formats: printed, online, and cd.

Many articles may also be accessed without going through an index. Many journals are available in full-text format on LexisNexis and Westlaw. The articles can be located by using the sophisticated search software from these two information providers. Some law reviews have placed their most recent full-text articles on their own web pages. Law review access is more fully discussed in the secondary sources chapter.

[3] Continue to Statutes, Regulations, or Ordinances

Next it is advisable to search for statutes, regulations, or ordinances that may be applicable. Annotated statutes will cite cases construing them. If administrative authority has been delegated by the legislature to an agency, the agency's regulations must be consulted.

In dealing with statutory law, legislative intent must often be re-searched, because for various reasons, the language and meaning of

---

[8] H.W. Wilson also includes some treatises in its Index to Legal Periodicals. Law review access is discussed in the Secondary Sources chapter. Appendix P is a listing of all law reviews published by the ABA accredited California law schools.

statutes are often unclear. For this reason, legislative histories are important. They are used extensively in federal and state appellate court work today, often being produced at the direction of the court.

[4]   Continue to Cases

[a]   Starting Information

In searching for cases on point, the lawyer will most likely read those cases found in annotated statutes or treatises first. From these, he or she will move on to find more cases through digests, using a variety of methods. The information the attorney is starting with will determine the method.

[b]   *Words and Phrases* Method

Sometimes, the researcher will have no more than a word, in which case, he or she will use the *Words and Phrases* approach. This enables him or her to determine the meaning of a term that has been judicially considered and defined by the courts and to see citations to the cases that include the definition. The *Words and Phrases* multi-volume set is essentially a digest, published by West Group. It contains the definition headnotes from cases out of the National Reporter System, of which West's California Reporter and Pacific Reporter are a part.

[c]   Descriptive Word Method

If certain facts are apparent and unusual, the practitioner may approach the problem factually, using the descriptive-word index of the digest to find a case or cases on point.

[d]   Topic Method

When the legal subject matter is easily determined by analysis, the more experienced lawyer may want to use the topic approach and look to one of the hundreds of topics listed in the front of each digest volume. After determining the proper topic, the user should find the appropriate topic in the digest set, examine the scope note and analysis outline, and proceed to find the applicable subdivision listing cases on point.

It should be noted that finding a case on point is usually a key objective in legal research. This is so because the judicial interpretation of a statute controls the meaning of the statute. Once such a case is found, it is usually easy to find other cases through annotations, digests, citators, and online sources.

[5]   Check Looseleaf Services

Looseleaf services (which combine primary and secondary sources and finding tools) are most useful in administrative law, especially taxation and labor law. They incorporate the principal finding aids found in digests and other finding tools.

[6]   Citator Check

After all cases, statutes, regulations, and ordinances on point are found, they should be checked with citators (Shepard's on LexisNexis or KeyCite on Westlaw) to determine their current status (are they still good law?) and find out how the cited sources have been treated by later courts and by authors of subsequent law review articles. Citators for the different types of California authority are discussed in this text in the chapters on constitution, statutes, cases, administrative law, and attorney general opinions.

§ 1.05   Organizing and Tracking Research

[1]   Major Challenges

There are two major challenges that the lawyer or law student must face when doing legal research. First, he or she must avoid duplication of effort, and second, he or she must not miss any important authorities. Both of these challenges will lessen for legal researchers as they become more experienced in research and more familiar with the sources.

The first challenge is overcome by devising a good method of recording the research path. The White King in *Through the Looking-Glass*, after a particularly alarming encounter with Alice (a giant Alice had picked him up and dusted him off, before placing him on a table), exclaimed: "The horror of that moment," the King went on, "I shall never, *never* forget!" "You will, though," the Queen said, "if you don't make a memorandum of it."[9] The Queen knew that the King needed some type of written document to remind him of what had happened. A written record of the research path will remind the researcher exactly where he or she has been and help him or her avoid looking at any sources a second time. This record will also help an instructor find out where law students got stuck or sidetracked and get them on the right path again.

---

[9] Carroll, Lewis, *Alice's Adventures in Wonderland and Through the Looking-Glass and What Alice Found There*, New York: Oxford University Press, 1971. 277 p. at 133.

The second challenge—not missing a key authority—is important in that it involves the competence with which attorneys serve their clients. There are both California and Federal cases that point out that there is no excuse for performing sloppy or incomplete research and missing important sources.[10] A systematic research plan will help the researcher avoid this pitfall.

[2] The Five-Folder System

[a] Getting Started

The system proposed below, loosely adapted from *A Management Approach to Legal Research,*[11] by Professor Anthony Miller, requires the researcher to record the research path and to proceed through the research process in an orderly fashion. Readers should note that there is no single perfect research method; research techniques vary with both the individual and the problem.

When starting research, one full size lined tablet, five file folders, a stapler, and a pencil are all that is necessary. The system is built around a cover sheet for each source and five file folders to organize research materials. The cover sheet is simply a sheet of notebook paper that contains detailed tracking and filing information.

Label the five file folders:

1. Finding Tools

2. Sources to Read

3. Sources Rejected

4. Sources Read and Noted

5. Sources Updated

Analysis of each of these folders is discussed below.

---

[10] *Smith v. Lewis,* 13 Cal.3d 349, 118 Cal.Rptr. 621, 530 P.2d 589 (1975), overruled on other grounds, *In re Marriage of Brown,* 15 Cal.3d 838, 126 Cal.Rptr. 633, 544 P.2d 561 (1976); *Horne v. Peckham,* 97 Cal.App. 404 (1979); *McNamara v. United States,* 867 F.Supp. 369 (E.D. Va. 1994).

[11] Miller, H. Anthony, *A Management Approach to Legal Research,* 26 ALI/ABA Practical Lawyer 75 (March 1, 1980). Professor Miller teaches at Pepperdine University School of Law.

[b] Finding Tools Folder

[i] Questions to Ask

The finding tools folder contains your plan. There are no "cover sheets" in this folder, but there still should be a single sheet for each tool you use or expect to use. What finding tools will you use to start out? Periodical indexes? What search terms will you use in the index? (Use the TAP rule.)[12] The public catalog? What words will you look under? Case digests? Code indexes? With every tool, indicate your search terms. With LexisNexis and Westlaw this is simple. You can collect all your past searches for the session by clicking on the History tab in the top right-hand corner of the LexisNexis screen or the Trail tab in the top right-hand corner of the Westlaw screen. Once you have used each source and created a sheet with details of your searches, move on to secondary sources.

[ii] Cases

As the researcher begins in secondary sources (the usual starting place) or anywhere else, at the first sight of a potentially relevant case you should make a cover sheet. You should include the case name, full and correct citation, parallel citations, and the place (source citation) where this new citation was found. Several cover sheets may be created before heading off and looking up cases, statutes, etc. These sheets go into the Sources to Read file.

[iii] Codes

As the researcher comes across the first reference to a statute or code section, a cover sheet should be created. Include the full citation. The section number goes in the top right hand corner (for later sorting). Record where the reference was found (for example: the full citation to a law review article footnote; or the code index, index page number, and subject heading) and place the cover sheet in the Sources to Read file.

---

[12] (T)hing, (A)ction, (P)ersons or Parties. A researcher could also use the TARP Rule from the Fundamentals of Legal Research, 8th ed. at p. 15: (T)hing, Cause of (A)ction, (R)elief, (P)ersons or Parties. The worksheet in *West's Sample Pages* (3d ed. St.Paul: West, 1986. 231 p.), which was used to teach thousands of law students each year for many years, lists at p. 2: Parties, Places & Things, Basis of Action or Issue, Defense, and Relief Sought.

[iv]   Other Materials

All materials should have cover sheets. This includes secondary sources like treatises and law review articles.

[v]   Some Finding Tools are Citable

Witkin, for instance, is a finding tool and a secondary source combined. It should have a sheet in finding tools and cover sheets for each relevant, usable section within it.

[c]   Sources to Read Folder

> **Note: The Sources to Read file can be arranged by importance, by type of material, or by alphabet.**

[i]   Cases

After retrieving the case (in hard copy or from a database), read the headnotes (West reporters and Westlaw) or Core Concepts (LexisNexis) and skim the case to see if it is relevant. Irrelevant cases will go into the "Sources Rejected" folder, but must be retained to avoid looking at the source a second time. If the source seems relevant, read the case thoroughly and write the first meaningful word from the case name in the upper right hand corner (for later sorting) of the cover sheet. Write a three-word issue summary in the top left hand corner (for later sorting). Write the headnote numbers for the relevant legal issues on the cover sheet. Then staple the cover sheet to the case photocopy or printout or your detailed notes on the case and file the packet in the "Sources Read and Noted" file. If you are using printouts or photocopies, be sure to underline the relevant text so you won't need to search for it when you return to the file later on.

[ii]   Codes

Locate the code section and review it for relevance. If irrelevant, it goes into the "Sources Rejected" file. If relevant, copy or print the section (they're usually short) so it can be quoted directly in your written product. File the stapled packet in the "Sources Read and Noted" file.

[d]   Sources Rejected Folder

Write a brief note about why the source was rejected and file it (usually a case) alphabetically, so it can be quickly searched and recalled quickly if the case comes up again.

[e]   Sources Read and Noted Folder

This is simply a holding file until the sources can be checked in one of the citators. After Shepardizing online or KeyCiting, mark the code for that (SH or KC) and date it was done. Then move the packet to the Sources Updated folder.

Note: When to stop researching: You will reach a point where you will not find references to any new sources. Many of the sources you have found will refer to each other. You are finished with your research. After you have read, briefed, and cite-checked all relevant cases and statutes, you are ready to begin writing.

---

[f]   Sources Updated Folder

No primary sources should be in this folder that have not been Shepardized or Keycited. You should arrange the packets by issue, since that is the order you will need them for writing. You should never have to return to the original source once the packet is in this file. Once all the packets are complete with cover sheets and copies/printouts/or notes, you are ready to write.

When the writing project is completed, file a copy of the finished work-product together will all the sources in the Sources Updated file. The work-product becomes a table of contents for them. The file of Sources Rejected will be helpful for future reference.

Chapter 2

California Constitution[1]

---

[1] Jennifer Lentz, Reference Librarian, Hugh & Hazel Darling Law Library, UCLA School of Law, made many suggestions that were helpful in the revision of this chapter for the Sixth Edition.

§ 2.01 California Constitutional Background

[1] Overview

Most Californians are aware of the United States Constitution and many of the rights that they have under it. The United States Constitution is regularly taught in schools, debated in the news media, and treated fictionally in novels and on television. However, the Constitution of the State of California is not so well known. It does not receive the same attention the federal constitution receives. Few Californians probably know the additional rights they have under their state constitution.[2] This chapter will point users to both historical and current sources so they may see the stages of our state's constitutional development.

California has had only two constitutions over the last century and a half. The first document, drafted and ratified by the people in 1849, endured until the late 1870s. During that time the population of the state grew immensely. Mining, agriculture, and commerce increased with the population. However, after the Central Pacific Railroad was completed, there were many people out of work and much labor unrest. There were also charges of gross corruption in government. The people of California were ready for a change. The second constitution was drafted in 1878–1879 and became fully effective in 1880.

In the years since 1879, the constitution has continued to change. It has grown much larger for several reasons, but the most important reason is that the constitution is so easy to amend. With the advent of the initiative in 1911, the people of the state can, by ballot, amend the constitution. Amending the constitution by initiative is almost as simple as passing a law by initiative (amending the constitution simply requires more signatures on the petition to get the measure on the ballot). Another advantage is that a constitutional amendment cannot be changed by the legislature on its own (a change requires voter approval). Therefore, the California Constitution looks unlike most other constitutional documents, in that it appears to be a collection of miscellaneous statutes.

In addition to the seemingly legislative function of the Constitution, it also performs the two basic functions of other constitutions: (1) it sets up the outline of government with the duties and limitations of each

---

[2] Few Californians probably know about or appreciate the fact that the California Constitution gives them the right to fish [Cal. Const., art. 1, § 25]. Additionally, Californians not only have the right to pursue happiness, they have the inalienable right to obtain it [Cal. Const., art. 1, § 1].

branch or office, and (2) it designates citizens' rights, liberties, and protections from government.[3] California's citizens' rights are in some ways broader than under the federal constitution.

[2] The Constitution of 1849

The Constitution of 1849 was drawn up over several weeks in the latter part of 1849. Gold had been discovered, California had become an independent territory, and its people wanted their land to become the thirty-first state of the United States. On June 3, 1849, acting Governor, General Bennett Riley issued a proclamation calling for a constitutional convention in Monterey on September 1, 1849.[4] Delegates, who were chosen at a special election on August 1, met in Colton Hall in Monterey from September 1 until October 10, adjourning with a completed constitution. The constitution was printed[5] and circulated and ratified at an election held on November 13, 1849. Much of the new constitution came from the constitutions of Iowa and New York.[6]

   California. San Francisco, 1849.

> Constitution. *Constitution of the State of California.* 19 p. "Address to the people of California": p. [17]–19. Microfiche copy in Congressional Information Services (CIS) State Constitutional Conventions set.

   California. Constitutional Convention, 1849.

> *Report of the Debates in the Convention of California, on the Formation of the State Constitution, in September and October, 1849.* By J. Ross Browne. Washington: Printed by John T. Towers, 1850. 479, xlvi p. This work provides the background for provisions dating back to the time of original

---

[3] Palmer, William J. and Selvin, Paul P., *The Development of Law in California*, St. Paul, MN: West, 1983. 64 p. at 24. This book is reprinted from v. 1 of the 1954 edition of the Constitution volume of West's Annotated California Code.

[4] Hansen, Woodrow James, *The Search for Authority in California*, Oakland, CA: Biobooks, 1960. 192 p. at 94.

[5] The printing of the constitution included 8,000 copies in English and 2,000 copies in Spanish. See Browne, J. Ross. Report of the Debates in the Convention of California, on the Formation of the State Constitution, in September and October, 1849. Washington: Printed by John T. Towers, 1850. 479, xlvi p. at 462.

[6] Wilson, E. Dotson, *California's Legislature 1994*, Sacramento: California Assembly, 1994. 250 p. at 8. See also Morrow, William W., *Introduction to California Jurisprudence 2d.*, San Francisco: Bancroft-Whitney, 1952. xix–lvii p. at xxx. (Reprinted from California Jurisprudence.)

statehood. For each member of the Convention it lists the age, profession, length of residency, and the state or country from which the person came (last a resident). The volume also includes Governor Riley's proclamation of June 1849, Recommending the Formation of a State Constitution. Original constitution appears on p. iii–xiii. There is no index.

California. Constitutional Convention, 1849.

Report of the Debates in the Convention of California, on the Formation of the State Constitution, in September and October, 1849. By J. Ross Browne. Washington: Printed by J. Towers, 1850. 479, xlvi p. Reprint. New York, Arno, 1973. 532 p. (Far Western Frontier).

California. Constitutional Convention, 1849.

Report of the Debates in the Convention of California, on the Formation of the State Constitution, in September and October, 1849. By J. Ross Browne. Washington: Printed by John T. Towers, 1850. 479, xlvi p. Microfiche copy in Congressional Information Services (CIS) State Constitutional Conventions set.

California. Constitutional Convention, 1849.

Journal of the Convention, Assembled to Frame a Constitution for the State of California, Sept. 1, 1849.

[3] The Constitution of 1879

Elected delegates to the second constitutional convention met September 28, 1878, and adjourned on March 3, 1879. Voters ratified the new constitution on May 7, 1879. Provisions for the election of officers and the beginning of their terms became effective on July 4, 1879. All remaining provisions became effective on January 1, 1880.

The drafters of the second constitution were attempting to deal with the immediate problems facing the state, including labor unrest, distrust of government, big business, monopolies, and a slump in the economy. The new constitution reflected these attitudes, placing more power in the hands of the people and less in the hands of legislators.

California. Constitutional Convention, 1878–1879.

Debates and proceedings of the Constitutional Convention of the State of California, Convened at the City of Sacramento,

Saturday, September 28, 1878. E.B. Willis and P.K. Stockton, official stenographers. Sacramento, State office, J.D. Young, sup't., 1880–81. 3 v., consecutively paged.

Convention adjourned March 3, 1879. Constitution appears in v.3, p. 1510–1521. Submitted to the vote of the people, May 7, 1879.

California. Constitutional Convention, 1878–1879.

Debates and Proceedings of the Constitutional Convention of the State of California, Convened at the City of Sacramento, Saturday, September 28, 1878. E.B. Willis and P.K. Stockton, official stenographers. Sacramento, State office, J.D. Young, sup't., 1880–81. 3 v., consecutively paged. Microfiche copy in Congressional Information Services (CIS) State Constitutional Conventions set.

California. Constitutional Convention, 1878–1879.

Constitutional Convention. Daily journal, in convention, assembly chamber, state capitol, Sacramento, Wednesday, October 30, 1878-Monday, March 3, 1879. Sacramento, 1879. Each day paged separately.

California. Constitution.

The Constitution of the State of California Adopted in 1879, with References to Similar Provisions in the Constitutions of Other States, and to the Decisions of the Courts of the United States, the Supreme Court of California, and the Supreme Courts of Such Other States as have Constitutional Provisions Similar to Those of California. To which is prefixed the Constitution of the United States and a parallel arrangement of the constitutions of 1863 and 1879. By Robert Desty. San Francisco, 1879. 431 p. Microfiche copy in Congressional Information Services (CIS) State Constitutional Conventions set.

§ 2.02 Changes to the Constitution

[1] History of Changes

The Constitution of 1849 was amended only three times in the thirty years it was in effect: in 1856, 1862, and 1871. However, the

Constitution of 1879 was amended 334 times from 1880 through 1962.[7] These amendments, many of them "legislative" in character and appearance, made the document cumbersome and difficult to use effectively. In 1962 California's constitution was the longest of any in the nation.[8]

As far back as the late 1800s there was dissatisfaction with the "new" 1879 Constitution.[9] However, even then it was understood that there was a distinction between amending the Constitution and revising it. Amendments were focused, specific, and relatively easy to accomplish. Revision was much more major and required both the Legislature and the voters to agree either on a Convention or on a Revision Commission effort. Therefore, there have been many amendments but few revisions.

There was a minor revision when voters and the Legislature adopted proposals of the Joint Interim Committee on Constitutional Revision in 1949. That revision reduced the document by about 14,500 words, but substantively accomplished little.[10]

A major revision was produced by the voters and Legislature between 1966 and 1976, when they adopted many of the recommendations from the California Constitution Revision Commission. The Commission, which was formed in 1963, proposed a series of changes to the Legislature and the voters over the next several years. Many changes were adopted. The Commission issued its final report in 1971, but its recommendations continued to appear on ballots through 1976. The Commission was dissolved by the Legislature in 1974.[11] In all, approximately 40,000 words were removed from the California Constitution.

A New Constitution Revision Commission was created in 1993 by statute.[12] This commission concentrated on state and local relations, the state budget process, and the structure of state government.[13]

The new commission's recommendations were supposed to have been reported to the Legislature in August 1995, but instead were finally

---

[7] The Constitution Revision Commission was established in 1963 with the purpose of making major revisions in the document.

[8] Wilson, *supra* note 21, at 11.

[9] Grodin, Joseph R., Massey, Calvin R., and Cunningham, Richard B., *The California State Constitution: A Reference Guide*, Westport, CT: Greenwood Press, 1993. 372 p. at 18.

[10] *Id.* at 19.

[11] Wilson, *supra* at 16.

[12] Statutes 1993, chapter 1243.

[13] Wilson, *supra* at 16.

reported in 1996. The entire effort was deemed a failure. Among the proposals of the commission were: 1) There should be a two year budget process; 2) There should be a single ticket for governor and lieutenant governor; 3) Let the governor appoint the treasurer, insurance commissioner, and superintendent of education; 4) Local governments could raise taxes by a majority vote; 5) Statutory referenda and initiatives could be amended by the Legislature after six years; 6) Constitutional referenda and initiatives could only be placed on the November ballot; and 7) Term limits could be extended. All of these new ideas died in the Legislature, though some will undoubtedly resurface in future legislative proposals.

[2] Proposed Amendments to the Constitution

Article XVIII governs the way the state can revise or amend the Constitution. The Legislature can put an amendment on the ballot if the measure passes by a 2/3 vote in both houses. An elector-proposed or initiative-proposed amendment can be placed on the ballot if enough signatures of registered voters are acquired (as of 1998 approximately 700,000 are needed). Finally, an amendment can be proposed by a constitutional convention, but this method has not been used since 1878. Once the measure is placed on the ballot, it must pass by a majority vote before it becomes a part of the Constitution. The controlling constitutional passages under Article XVII read:

> 1. Legislative proposals. The Legislature by roll call vote entered in the journal, two-thirds of the membership of each house concurring, may propose an amendment or revision of the Constitution and in the same manner may amend or withdraw its proposal. Each amendment shall be so prepared and submitted that it can be voted on separately.
>
> **HISTORY:** Adopted November 3, 1970.
>
> 2. Constitutional conventions. The Legislature by roll call vote entered in the journal, two-thirds of the membership of each house concurring, may submit at a general election the question whether to call a convention to revise the Constitution. If the majority vote yes on that question, within 6 months the Legislature shall provide for the convention. Delegates to a constitutional convention shall be voters elected from districts as nearly equal in population as may be practicable.
>
> **HISTORY:** Adopted November 3, 1970.

3. Initiative amendments. The electors may amend the Constitution by initiative.

HISTORY: Adopted November 3, 1970.

4. Effective date; Conflicting measures. A proposed amendment or revision shall be submitted to the electors and if approved by a majority of votes thereon takes effect the day after the election unless the measure provides otherwise. If provisions of 2 or more measures approved at the same election conflict, those of the measure receiving the highest affirmative vote shall prevail.

HISTORY: Adopted November 3, 1970.

[3] California Constitution Revision Commission

[a] Reports of the Commission

For a listing of all Commission papers and a summary of its recommendations and activities, see California. Legislature. Joint Rules Committee. *Report on Materials of Constitution Revision Commission Relating to Provisions in California's Constitution Recommended or Endorsed by Commission.* Prepared by J. Gould. December 10, 1974. Sacramento: State Printing Office, 1975. 147 p.[14]

The content of its reports is typified by its publication.

California Constitution Revision Commission.
Proposed revision of the California Constitution. 1970–71, Parts 1–6. San Francisco, 1065 State Building, 1970–71.

Part 1: Introduction
History of the California Constitution
The California Constitution Revision Commission
Members of the California Constitution Revision Commission
Appendix (Legislative resolutions).

Part 2: Articles II (Voting),
XIV (Water),
XV (Harbors),
XXI (Boundaries),
XXIII (Recall),
XXVII (Repeal of Article XXV),
XXXIV (Low Rent Housing).

---

[14] *Id.*

Part 3: Article XVI (State Debt),
XX (Miscellaneous),
XXVI (Motor Vehicle Tax and Revenue).

Part 4: Article IX (Education),
Article X (Convicts & Institutions).

Part 5: Article I (Civil Rights),
Article XX (Alcoholic Beverages and Convict Labor),
Article XXII (Constitutional Amendments).

Part 6: Article XIII (Taxation) and Revised California Constitution.

Recommended revisions in each article of the Constitution are presented as follows:

(1)   Brief summary of recommended changes.

(2)   Comparative sections table indicating the disposition of existing provisions.

(3)   The proposed revisions which are set forth with the existing provisions from which they are derived.

(4)   The deleted provisions.

(5)   The deleted provisions which are recommended for statutory consideration.

(6)   Existing provisions transferred to other articles of the Constitution.

[b]   Program and Progress of the Commission

In 1966 the Commission submitted proposals for revision of Article III (Separation of Powers), Article IV (Legislative), Articles V, VII, and VIII (Executive), Article VI (Judicial), and Article XXIV (Civil Service).

The passage of Proposition 1-A by California voters at the November 1966 general election revised about one-third of the previously existing Constitution and reduced that portion from approximately 22,000 to 6,000 words.

Proposals were submitted in 1968 for revision of Article IX (Education), X (Convicts and Institutions), XI (Local Government), XII (Public Utilities), XVII (Homesteads), and XVIII (Amending and Revising the Constitution).

In 1968 the electors rejected the proposed changes, although many of the provisions were incorporated into an Assembly Constitutional Amendment, which passed.[15]

The passage of Propositions 14–17 at the 1970 November general election revised Articles XXIV (Civil Service), XX (Partial Constitution Revision), and XVIII (Amending and Revising the Constitution) and repealed Article XXVII (Repeal of Article XXV).

[c] Other Publications of the Commission

📖 California. Constitution Revision Commission. *Final Report and Recommendations to the Governor and the Legislature.* Sacramento, 1996.

📖 California. Constitution Revision Commission. *Constitution Revision: History and Perspective.* Sacramento, 1996.

📖 California. Constitution Revision Commission. *Proposed revision of Articles III, IV, V, VI, VII, VIII, XXIV of the California Constitution.* San Francisco, 1966. 212 pages.

📖 California. Constitution Revision Commission. *Proposed revision of Article IX, X, XI, XII, XVII, and XVIII.* San Francisco, 1968.

📖 California. Constitution Revision Commission. *Proposed revision of the California Constitution.* Sacramento, 1971. 61 pages. This revision was to have been the final report of the Commission. The entire Constitution is covered in this proposal. Some of the sections have no recommendations for change; others are only renumbered. These sections are included to give the document continuity. The cross-reference table at the end describes the source of each section in the existing Constitution and the reports of the Commission.

📖 California. Legislature. Assembly. Constitutional Amendments Committee. Special Report, *Constitution Revision, 1969,* provides additional background material.

📖 Previous reports are *Constitutional revision*, Reports of Assembly Interim Committee on Constitutional Amendments, Part I, 1961–63, v.27, No. 2, p.42 v.2 of Appendix to Journal of the Assembly, Regular Session, 1963 and *History and*

---

[15] *Id.*

methods of constitutional revision in California, Report of Assembly Interim Committee on Constitutional Amendments, 1959–61, v.27, No. I v.2 of Appendix to Journal of the Assembly, Regular Session, 1961.

California. Constitution Revision Commission. Processed and printed publications relating to specific articles and sections were released as the Commission worked steadily toward its goal of complete revision. The Los Angeles County Law Library has a complete compilation of these releases in bound form. The documents include background studies, committee and commission recommendations, minutes of meetings, and section drafts for the years 1964–1971.

More information on the California Constitution Revision Commission, as well as the text of their final recommendations, can be found on the California State Library website: *www.library.ca.gov/ccrc/main.html.*

§ 2.03   Researching Constitutional Law

[1]   Necessity of Checking State Constitution

No search for law in California is complete without checking the Constitution. Before its recent revisions, the California Constitution was more than ten times as long as the United States Constitution. Even after the revisions, California's Constitution is longer than most and still includes a great amount of material that would customarily be handled in statutes.

[2]   Index and Digest Sources

LARMAC: Consolidated Index to the Laws, Rules, and Constitution of California. LexisNexis. Annual. This index is named for its early editors, Neil Edwin Larkin and Paul Aloysius McCarthy. It was first published in 1935 by Marnell & Company in San Francisco.[16] For many years it was published by the Recorder Publishing Company, also in San Francisco. In 1989 LARMAC was taken over by Parker & Sons Publications, which was later acquired by LexisNexis.

---

[16] There is a short but positive review of the first edition of LARMAC (then called Larmac Consolidated Code and Court Rules Index) at 9 *Southern California Law Review* 297 (1936).

The current edition indexes all California codes, uncodified acts, court rules, and the Constitution. Constitution references are to article and section. A cd-rom containing the entire index is included in a pocket in the inside back cover of the volume.

📖 *Statutes and Amendments to the Codes* include the following constitutional data.

    a. Text of the Constitution of the State of California as amended and in force on the day following the November General Election of the year previous to the date of publication; index to the Constitution.

    b. Proposed Changes in Constitution.

    c. Measures Submitted to Vote of Electors.

    d. Table of Resolutions and Proposed Constitutional Amendments Adopted (Year of Publication).

    e. Text of Resolutions and Proposed Constitutional Amendments (Year of Publication).

    f. Text of Statutes and Resolutions for Extraordinary Session(s) covered by volume.

The *Chapter Laws* which make up the substantive portion of the *Statutes and Amendments to the Codes* volumes are not included in the Legislative Bill Service but may be subscribed to from the Legislative Bill Room.

📖 *Summary Digest of Statutes Enacted and Resolutions (Including Proposed Constitutional Amendments) Adopted in . . . and . . . Statutory Record.* Sacramento, CA: [s.n.],[year]. Passed Senate and Assembly Constitutional Amendments appear in Resolution Chapters order in the Section entitled Digests of Resolutions and Proposed Constitutional Amendments Adopted in [year]. Cross-Reference Tables are from ACA or SCA to Resolution Chapter. The Statutory Record includes a Section entitled Resolution Chapters Supplemented or Otherwise Affected.

📖 California. Legislative Counsel. *Legislative Index.* Sacramento. Periodically. 1959-date. This publication consists of an index to measures and a table of sections affected. It is cumulative and periodically published. The preface contains the following description:

INDEX

The index indicates the subject of each bill, constitutional amendment, and concurrent or joint resolution as introduced and as amended. Entries are not removed from the index when subject matter is deleted from the measure in course of passage.

TABLE

The table shows each section of the Constitution, codes, and uncodified laws affected by measures introduced in the Legislature. It may be used in two ways:

1. To locate measures where the section of the Constitution, code, or law is known.

2. To locate measures upon a particular subject, by using a published index to the codes and laws, such as Deering's General Index, the Parker's LARMAC Consolidated Index, and West's General Index, to locate the existing sections, and then by using this table to locate the measures which affect those sections.

The table is arranged by codes and the Constitution listed in alphabetical order. Uncodified laws are listed at the end of the table under the heading "Statutes Other Than Codes," and are cited by year and chapter. References to Budget Items appear in a separate section following Statutes Other Than Codes.

Since each bi-weekly issue is cumulative, only the latest need be retained. The final issue should be kept as a permanent library acquisition. This title is part of the Legislative Bill Service available on annual subscription from the Legislative Bill Room, Room B-32, State Capitol, Sacramento, CA 95814.

From 1959–1972 the final edition of this publication was included in the *Final Calendar of Legislative Business*which was discontinued after 1972.

Assembly & Senate Histories. Compiled under the direction of the Chief Clerk of the Assembly and the Secretary of the Senate. Daily, weekly, semi-final, and final editions. Sacramento, Legislative Bill Room. Constitutional amendments are listed in the respective tables of contents. There is a numerical list of amendments with title and author. A chronological table indicates actions taken on the measure. The final edition of the histories was included in the Final Calendar of Legislative Business from 1881–1972. The semi-final edition cumulates the first year of the Legislature and should be kept with the latest weekly and daily issue until the final edition which should be kept as a permanent library acquisition. These publications are part of the Legislative Bill Service available on annual subscription from the Legislative Bill Room, Room B-32, State Capitol, Sacramento, CA 95814.

📖 California. Legislature. Secretary of Senate. Chief Clerk of Assembly. *Final Calendar of Legislative Business.*Sacramento. 1881–1972. Lists Senate Constitutional Amendments numerically following Senate Final History; Assembly Constitutional Amendments following Assembly Final History. Index under "CONSTITUTION, CALIFORNIA, Proposed. Constitutional Amendments," lists by subject with reference to house, number of amendment, and session in parentheses. Amendments are also indexed by subject.

📖 Assembly & Senate *Daily File*. Published separately for each house. Lists order of business, measures to be considered in committee hearings and on the floor. Legislative Counsel's digest of amendments indicates variances from previous version of legislative measure. These publications are part of the Legislative Bill Service available on annual subscription from the Legislative Bill Room, Room B-32, State Capitol, Sacramento, CA 95814.

📖 Assembly & Senate *Journals*. Sacramento, Legislative Bill Room. Provides the official record of proceedings indicating the number and title of each constitutional amendment introduced and the committee to which it was referred; recommendation of the committee; action taken on each measure including roll call votes; and text of amendments to measures.

These publications are available on annual subscription as part of the Legislative Bill Service from the Legislative Bill Room, Room B-32, State Capitol, Sacramento, CA 95814.

[3] Texts of Constitution and Amendments

📖 California. *Constitution* (Title varies). Biennial State Edition. Sacramento CA 95814, Room B-32, State Capitol, Legislative

Bill Room. Constitutions of the United States and California, separately indexed; also Magna Carta (1215), Mayflower Compact (1620), Declaration of Rights (1765 and 1774), Declaration of Independence (1776), Articles of Confederation (1778). Various editions of this paperback publication have contained articles on the constitution and related topics. For instance, the 1941 edition contains an article on "The Legislature of California," by then Chief Clerk Arthur Ohnimus and the 1961 edition contains the following articles: "Constitutional History of California," by Paul Mason, "What is Our Constitution For," by Hon. Nelson S. Dilworth, and "Is the Flag Worth Fighting For," by Joseph Allan Beek.

📖 Assembly Constitutional Amendment (ACA). Senate Constitutional Amendment (SCA). Sacramento, Legislative Bill Room. Constitutional amendments are included in the Legislative Bill Service subscription.

📖 California. Secretary of State. *Statement of Vote*. Records results of the vote on constitutional amendments.

📖 California. Constitution. *Summary of Amendments to the Constitution with Statement of Vote For and Against Amendment, 1883–1920. Initiative and Referendum Measures Submitted to Vote of Electors.* Compiled by Frank C. Jordan, Secretary of State, 1921.

📖 California. *Statutes of California*. Since 1849, the Constitution has been reprinted in the session laws of the state. The 1850 Constitution was included in the editions up until 1878. The 1879 Constitution is in all editions up to the present.

📖 *Deering's California Constitution Annotated*. San Francisco: Matthew Bender & Company, Inc., a member of the Lexis-Nexis Group. Annual pocket parts and paper supplement, 1954-date. In 1981, the former publisher, Bancroft-Whitney, "closed" their existing (1974) three-volume, annotated constitution and sent subscribers a spine label that read "Constitutional Annotations 1849–1973." Pocket parts were discarded. The third volume of this "annotations" set contains the California Constitution of 1849, the United States Constitution, and selected federal legislation affecting California: Admission of California to the Union; Applicability of Federal Laws— Formation of Judicial System; Settlement of Private Land

Claims; Survey of Public Lands—Preemptive Rights; Sale of Desert Lands; and Confirmation of Title to Indemnity School Lands.

The former publisher then started fresh with a new constitution volume that included only the annotations starting with 1974. The current volume is the only one that is now updated annually with a pocket part. It also contains the United States Constitution, which is indexed separately.

The Deering's version includes the history, cross references, editor's notes, collateral references, references to law review articles, references to Attorney General's Opinions, references to ALR annotations, and notes of decisions or case annotations.

West's California Constitution, Annotated. Annual pocket parts. California Constitutions of 1849 and 1879, Treaty of Guadalupe Hidalgo, Act for Admission of the State of California, Extension of U.S. Laws and Judicial System, Settlement of Land Claims, Magna Carta, Articles of Confederation, and Constitution of the United States with its separate index are additional features.

In 1983 West replaced volume one of the 1954 three-volume set. Volume one of the old set contained a sixty-five page article, "The Development of Law in California," by William J. Palmer and Paul P. Selvin. The 1983 volume does not contain the article, but West did reprint it in 1983 as a soft-bound pamphlet, which is available in many libraries.[17]

West's version includes historical notes, cross references, citations to law review commentaries, and notes of decisions or case annotations.

Deering's California Codes Annotated are available in CD-ROM format. The set contains an annotated version of California's Constitution.

West's Annotated California Codes on CD-ROM contain the California Constitution under the code abbreviation CONST.

LexisNexis. LexisNexis, Dayton, OH. Available through *lexis.com*®, LexisNexis contains the Deering's version of the

---

[17] See Appendix J for the full bibliographic description.

current California Constitution in the "CA-California Constitution" Source (CAL; CACNST). The "CA-Deering's California Codes Annotated, Constitution, Court Rules & ALS, Combined" Source (CAL; CACODE). The CACODE file contains the Constitution as well as the code and court rules. Segments which may be searched include: CASENOTES, CITE, HEADING, HISTORY, NOTES, SECTION, TEXT, and UNNANNO. This online format of the code contains everything that is in the hard copy version of Deering's newer volume, but not annotations or other materials that are in the three historical "Constitutional Annotations 1849–1973" volumes. A segment search using UNANNO is the equivalent of searching in an unannotated code.

Westlaw. West Group, Eagan, MN. The CA-ST-ANN database on Westlaw contains West's Annotated California Codes, including the Constitution. Fields available for searching include: CITATION, PRELIM, CAPTION, TEXT, WORD-PHRASES, CREDIT, SUBSTANTIVE-DOC, HISTORICAL NOTES, REFERENCES, and ANNOTATIONS. The CA-ST database contains an unannotated version.

Legislative Counsel of California, *leginfo.ca.gov/const.html.* The full text of the California Constitution is available on the Legislative Counsel's website. One can browse the table of contents to find a particular article and section or search by keyword. [18]

Other Internet providers. The text of the California Constitution is also available through Loislaw, *loislaw.com*; Accesslaw, *accesslaw.com*; and American Legal Net, *americanlegalnet.com*; JuriSearch, *jurisearch.com*; National Law Library, *nationallawlibrary.com*; Netlawlibraries, *netlawlibraries.com*; and VersusLaw, *versuslaw.com.*

[4] Subject Arrangement of California's Constitution

Article
Preamble
   I. Declaration of Rights
  II. Voting, Initiative and Referendum, and Recall
 III. State of California
 IV. Legislative

---

[18] See chapter 15 on legal databases for more information on www sites.

XXIV. State Civil Service [repealed]
XXV. Old Age Security and Security for the Blind [repealed]
XXVI. [Heading renumbered]
XXVII. Repeal of Article XXV Old Age Security and Security for the Blind [repealed]
XXVIII. Open Space Conservation [repealed]
XXIX. Revenue Control and Tax Reduction [rejected]
XXXIV. Public Housing Project Law

[5] Citators for the Constitution

📖 *Shepard's California Citations—Statutes Edition.* 9th edition, 1995, and current supplement are used to Shepardize particular provisions of the California Constitution. Constitutional amendments and cases interpreting particular provisions of the cited article and section appear with the citing material.

🖥 *Shepard's California Citations—Statutes Edition* is also available online on LexisNexis.

🖥 *KeyCite* is available online on Westlaw.

🖥 LexisNexis and Westlaw may also be used as citators, if the search is composed of terms from the Constitution citation.

[6] Constitutional Intent

[a] Constitutional Proceedings

Constitutional Proceedings may be considered in construction of the constitution.

EXAMPLE

State Board of Educ. v. Levit, 5 Cal.2d 441, 343 P.2d 8 (Cal. 1959)

[b] Ballot Proposals and Voters' Arguments

[i] Resources

📖 California. Constitution. *California Voters Pamphlet.* Prepared by the Legislative Counsel, Distributed by the Secretary of State. (Formerly entitled *Proposed amendments to the Constitution:* Propositions together with arguments.) Sacramento, State Printing Office, 1908-date. A Legislative Counsel compilation of the texts of proposed amendments, initiatives, or referendums with the official arguments for and against.

Complete sets of these ballot pamphlets are available in larger law libraries.

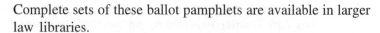 Voters' Arguments are also available in microfiche from Library Microfilms.[19]

California Ballot Propositions Database *www.uchastings.edu/library/ballotprops.htm*. This searchable, full-text database contains all ballot propositions dating back to 1911, including material contained in the ballot pamphlets.

[ii] Case Authorities

The argument in favor of the adoption of a constitutional amendment sent to the electorate in the ballot proposed is evidence to be weighed in determining intent.

EXAMPLE

State v. Superior Court, 208 Cal.App.2d 659, 25 Cal.Rptr. 363 (Cal.Ct.App. 1962)

Selected cases concerned with arguments submitted to the voters include:

EXAMPLES

Story v. Richardson, 186 Cal. 162, 198 P. 1057 (Cal. 1921)

Beneficial Loan Soc'y, Ltd. v. Haight, 215 Cal. 506, 11 P.2d 857 (Cal. 1932)

Kaiser v. Hopkins, 6 Cal.2d 537, 58 P.2d 1278 (Cal. 1936)

People v. Fowler, 32 Cal.App.2d 737, 84 P.2d 326 (Ct.App. 1939)

California Institute of Technology v. Johnson, 55 Cal.App.2d 856, 132 P.2d 61 (Ct.App. 1942)

Warne v. Harkness, 60 Cal.2d 579, 35 Cal.Rptr. 601 (Cal. 1963)

[c] Joint Rules Committee Report

California. Legislature. Joint Rules Committee. *Report on materials of Constitution Revision Commission relating to*

---

[19] Library Microfilms carries Voters Arguments—Amendments to the Constitution and proposed statutes with arguments respecting the same. Microfilm. 1883–1988 with yearly update subscription available for all years with statewide elections.

provisions in California Constitution recommended or endorsed by Commission. Prepared by J. Gould. December 10, 1974. Sacramento, State Printing Office, 1975. 147 p. In attempting to determine Constitutional intent the researcher should examine this publication first. The publication provides a complete history of the development of specific provisions of the Constitution. For each Article and Section there is an origin table and a disposition table indicating the original provision, its disposition in the constitutional scheme, the disposing ballot proposition, and the subject. The drafts in which each section is discussed are indicated by another table.

Appendix A—Constitution Revision Commission Meeting Transcripts.

Appendix B—Constitution Revision Commission Meeting Minutes.

Appendix C—Constitution Revision Commission Committee Meeting Minutes.

Appendix D—Studies, Reports, Drafts and Miscellaneous Materials.

[7] Comparative Constitutional Research—California and Other States

Index Digest of State Constitutions, Second Edition, 1959; Cumulative Supplement, September 1, 1958—December 31, 1967. Richard A. Edwards, Legislative Drafting Research Fund of Columbia University.

Similar provisions in the state constitutions of all United States state jurisdictions may be compared by using this publication.

Constitutions of the United States—National and State. 2d ed. Legislative Drafting Research Fund of Columbia University. Dobbs Ferry, N.Y., Oceana Publications, Inc., 1974.

Sources and Documents of United States Constitutions, edited and annotated by William F. Swindler. Dobbs Ferry, N.Y., Oceana Publications, 1973–1982.

v.1—Alabama, Alaska, Arkansas, California. California coverage includes 1849–1879 provisions table; 1849 & 1879 texts, Governor Riley's 1849 Proclamation, Admission Act; Source notes; description of events.

📖 Poore, Benjamin Perley. *The Federal and State Constitutions, Colonial Charters, and Other Organic Laws of the United States. 2d ed. 2 v. Washington, 1878. Reprint.*

📖 *Thorpe, Frances Newton. The Federal and State Constitutions, Colonial Charters, and Other Organic Laws of the States, Territories and Colonies.*Washington, GPO, 1909. 7 v. Microcard Editions (4337) (4x6).

[8] Constitutional Conventions—California and Other States

Congressional Information Service (CIS) State Constitutional Conventions, Commissions, and Amendments on microfiche. The guides below may be used with the microfiche collection or as an independent reference resource. The microfiche set may be purchased as a whole, covering all 50 states, or broken up by state and period of coverage.

📖 *State Constitutional Conventions: From Independence to the Completion of the Present Union, 1776–1959: A Bibliography.* Compiled by Cynthia E. Brown. Westport, CN: Greenwood Press, 1973. 250 p. This is a printed bibliography/table of contents to Part 1 of the Congressional Information Service (CIS) microfiche collection of State Constitutional Conventions. Twenty-two documents are listed in the California section.

📖 *State Constitutional Conventions, Revisions, and Amendments, 1959–1976: a bibliography, supplement one.* Compiled by Bonnie Canning. Westport, Conn., Greenwood Press. 1977. ca. 48 p. (State constitutional conventions.) A continuation of Greenwood's earlier bibliographies; State constitutional conventions, 1776–1959 and State constitutional conventions, 1959–1975.

📖 *State Constitutional Conventions, Commissions, and Amendments, 1959–1978: An Annotated Bibliography.* Congressional Information Service, Inc., 1981. xviii, 1391 p. (2 v.) This is a printed bibliography to accompany Parts 2, 3, & 4 of the Congressional Information Service (CIS) microfiche collection of State Constitutional Conventions. The first volume is a research bibliography, arranged by the segments of time defined by the state's constitutional revision activity. It contains several hundred listings for California documents. The second volume contains the same material in an alphabetically arranged bibliography. Volume two also contains the index for use with both volumes.

📖 *State Constitutional Conventions, Commissions, and Amendments, 1979–1988: An Annotated Bibliography.* Bethesda, MD: Congressional Information Service, 1989. 284 p. This is a printed bibliography to accompany more recent microfiche from the Congressional Information Service (CIS) microfiche collection of State Constitutional Conventions. Entries are in an alphabetically arranged bibliography.

[9] Bibliography—California Constitution

📖 Babcock, Barbara Allen. "Clara Shortridge Foltz: Constitution-Maker." 66 *Indiana Law Journal* 849 (1991). This article follows the activities and career of Ms. Foltz, the first woman lawyer in California, through the period preceding, during, and after the adoption of the 1879 Constitution.

📖 Cain, Bruce E. and Noll, Roger G., Editors. *Constitutional Reform in California: Making State Government More Effective and Responsive.* Berkeley: Institute of Governmental Studies Press, 1995. 514 p. This volume contains over 20 articles by 26 contributors. All articles are about the structure of the constitution, amending the constitution, the separation of powers, and general issues of constitutional law. The predominant theme is the search for a better method of constitutional reform than the initiative constitutional amendment. One contributor is Joseph R. Grodin, former Associate Justice of the California Supreme Court.

📖 California. State Library, Law Library. *Bibliography of California Constitution Revision Commission Publications.* Sacramento, 1971.

📖 Englebert, Ernest A. *State Constitutional Revisions in California—An Analysis Prepared for the Citizens Legislative Advisory Commission.* Sacramento, 1961.

📖 Erler, Edward J. "Californians and their Constitution: Progressivism, Direct Democracy and the Administrative State." 6 *NEXUS: A Journal of Opinion* 237–253 (Spring 2001). This well-footnoted article addresses the various ways that have been used to update the California Constitution, but concentrates mostly on the initiative process.

📖 Fitzrandolph, John A. "Basic Government Streamlined Through Constitution Reform." 44 *Tax Digest* 106 (1966).

📖 Fritz, Christian G. "More than 'Shreds and Patches:' California's First Bill of Rights." 17 *Hastings Const. L.Q.* 13 (1989).

📖 "From Gold Dust to Silicon Chips: The California Constitution in Transition: A Symposium." 17 *Hastings Const. L.Q.* 1. (1989)

📖 Goldberg, Edward M. "The California Constitution: Will Revision Equal Reform?" 38 *Southern California Law Review* 246 (1965).

📖 Grodin, Joseph R., Massey, Calvin R., and Cunningham, Richard B. *The California State Constitution: A Reference Guide.* Westport, CT: Greenwood Press, 1993. 372 p. This is an excellent state constitutional guide, written by three Hastings College of the Law professors. Part I is a short constitutional history of the state, covering the period from the early 1800s to the present. Part II is the current Constitution with commentary on each article and section. The volume contains many footnotes, a table of cases cited, and a five-page bibliography.

📖 Hansen, Woodrow James. *The Search for Authority in California.* Oakland: Biobooks, 1960. This text, which grew out of the author's PhD. thesis, covers the history of California from the Spanish colonial period through the first Constitutional Convention. The last half of the book is about the Convention, and part of the first half is about the political events and legal circumstances leading up to it. The author gives an issue-by-issue and argument-by-argument description of the Convention's progress. The book is one of a finely printed, limited edition of 750 copies.

📖 Hunt, Rockwell Dennis. *The Genesis of California's First Constitution (1846–49).* Baltimore, Johns Hopkins Press, 1895. New York, Johnson Reprint Corp., 1973.

📖 Lloyd, Gordon. "Nature and Convention in the Creation of the 1849 California Constitution." 6 *NEXUS: A Journal of Opinion* 23–42 (Spring 2001). The author, now a professor in the School of Public Policy of Pepperdine University, covers the delegates to the Monterey constitutional convention in 1849, along with their backgrounds, the events taking place in Europe and elsewhere, and the individual topics addressed in the final document.

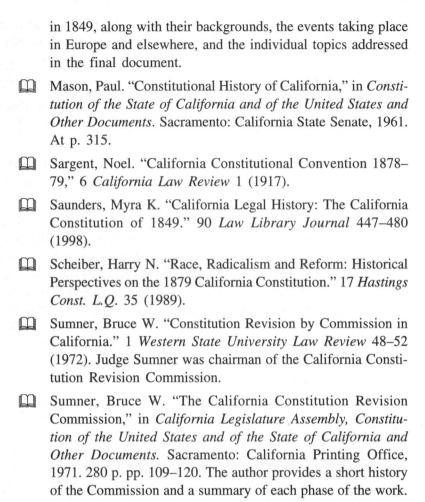 Mason, Paul. "Constitutional History of California," in *Constitution of the State of California and of the United States and Other Documents*. Sacramento: California State Senate, 1961. At p. 315.

Sargent, Noel. "California Constitutional Convention 1878–79," 6 *California Law Review* 1 (1917).

Saunders, Myra K. "California Legal History: The California Constitution of 1849." 90 *Law Library Journal* 447–480 (1998).

Scheiber, Harry N. "Race, Radicalism and Reform: Historical Perspectives on the 1879 California Constitution." 17 *Hastings Const. L.Q.* 35 (1989).

Sumner, Bruce W. "Constitution Revision by Commission in California." 1 *Western State University Law Review* 48–52 (1972). Judge Sumner was chairman of the California Constitution Revision Commission.

Sumner, Bruce W. "The California Constitution Revision Commission," in *California Legislature Assembly, Constitution of the United States and of the State of California and Other Documents*. Sacramento: California Printing Office, 1971. 280 p. pp. 109–120. The author provides a short history of the Commission and a summary of each phase of the work.

Sumner, Bruce W. "The Proposed Revision of the California Constitution: A Summary and Analysis." 9 *Orange County Bar Bulletin* 257 (1966).

Sumner, Bruce W. "Proposition 1: The Second Phase of Constitutional Revision in California." 11 *Orange County Bar Association Bulletin* 241 (1968).

Swisher, Carl Brent. *Motivation and Political Technique in California Constitutional Convention of 1878–79*. Pomona: Claremont, 1930.

Symposium on the California Initiative Process. 31 *Loy. L.A. L. Rev.* 1161 (1998).

Chapter 3

California Statutes[1]

§ 3.01   Statutes and Codes

Statutes are the laws passed either by the Legislature or by the voters through the initiative process [information and references on statutes passed by initiative are found in Chapter 5]. Statutes may be printed individually (slip laws) or posted on the World Wide Web.[2] California

---

[1] This chapter was revised for the seventh edition by David McFadden, Senior Reference Librarian, Southwestern University School of Law Library.

[2] The texts of chaptered bills with the accompanying Legislative Counsel's Digest are available on the Legislative Counsel's web site at: *www.leginfo.ca.gov/index.html.*

(Pub. 64620)

statutes are published by both LexisNexis and West Group periodically throughout the year as part of their current legislative services. At the end of each legislative session, all statutes from that session are assembled in chronological order and published in the Statutes of California. Many libraries in California have collections of the session laws running from the early 1850's to the current date.[3]

Codes are compilations of all the statutes, arranged by subject. Codes bring together the original statute and all later amendments. Codes also delete out-of-date, superseded, or repealed statutes. Printed code sets by LexisNexis and West Group are updated at least annually by pocket-parts, supplemental volumes, and replacement volumes.[4] Codes on the internet may be updated more or less frequently.[5] Printed current legislative services or online legislative services are used to keep the codes up-to-date throughout the year, or until the next code update.

§ 3.02   Historical Development of the California Codes

[1]   The 1872 Codes

California was one of the earliest code states. In 1872, California enacted four codes which in large measure were based upon codifications developed by David Dudley Field for the State of New York.[6]

---

[3] Early statutes were also officially distributed in Spanish. Some law libraries still have on their shelves copies of California session laws in Spanish, for example: Leyes del Estado de California, Decretadas Durante la Decima Octoba Sesion de la Legislatura 1869–70. Thomas R. Eldredge, Traductor del Estado. Sacramento: D.W. Gelwicks, Impresor del Estado, 1870. One of the first actions of the first Legislature (1850) was to create an office of State Translator. This person was charged with correctly translating any laws, decrees, documents, or orders into Spanish. 1850 Cal. Stat. 51. The Spanish session laws are listed at page 47 of Rosamond Parma's and Elizabeth Armstrong's article: The Codes and Statutes of California: A Bibliography. 22 *Law Library Journal* 41–56 (April 1929).

[4] LexisNexis and West Group ship annual pocket parts and replacement volumes each December or very early in January so the sets will reflect the code changes caused by the actions of the previous year's Legislature. Most laws take effect on the January 1st following their passage.

[5] Researchers will need to check with the individual vendors for information on code update frequency. Some internet sites do not give clear information on how current their code products are.

[6] According to Erwin Surrency (History of American Law Publishing. New York: Oceana, 1990. 372 p. at 236) eleven other states adopted the Field Codes. Surrency's list includes Arizona, Colorado, Idaho, Montana, Nevada, North Dakota, Oregon, South Dakota, Utah, Washington, and Wyoming. Two other writers point out that the Field

Those original California Codes, as revised and annotated by Code Commissioners Creed Haymond and John C. Burch, are:

📖 California. Code Commission. *Revised Laws of the State of California in Four Codes.* Sacramento, H.S. Crocker & Company, 1872.

   Civil Code. 2 v.

   Code of Civil Procedure. 2 v.

   Political Code. 2 v.

   Penal Code. 1 v.

   These codes do not appear in *California Statutes and Amendments to the Codes* as they were printed as separate state documents and in commercial versions.

[2] Code Revisions

After their initial enactment, the codes have been often reviewed and revised. Three of the four original codes still exist (Civil, Civil Procedure, and Penal) but the fourth, the political code, has been changed into the Government Code.[7] When the massive code revision of 1929[8]

Codes had more success with the newer states in the west than in the State of New York for which they were designed. Michael Weber, in the introduction to a reprint of the Field Codes (New York Field Codes 1850–1865. Union, NJ: The Lawbook Exchange, 1998. 5 v.), stated that while New York adopted the Code of Civil Procedure in April of 1848, it was not until 1881 that the state adopted the Code of Criminal Procedure and the Penal Code. New York never did adopt the Civil Code or the Political Code. Charles M. Cook observed in his book on codification (The American Codification Movement: A Study of Antebellum Legal Reform. Westport, CT: Greenwood Press, 1981. 234 p.) that only the far western states adopted any of the Field Codes related to substantive law. California adopted parts of all five of the Field Codes, combining the Code of Criminal Procedure and the Penal Code into a single Penal Code volume. Incidentally, New York's David Dudley Field was the brother of Stephen J. Field, a prominent California legal figure and later a justice of the U.S. Supreme Court.

   [7] Fortunately the 34 maxims of jurisprudence have been preserved from the 1872 Civil Code, Part IV, Sections 3509–3543 (Field's code). These are Latin maxims, translated into English, which were earlier adopted by New York (N.Y.C.C., Sections 1964–1998). Examples are: "When the reason of a rule ceases, so should the rule itself;" "He who consents to an act is not wronged by it;" "No one can take advantage of his own wrong;" "No man is responsible for that which no man can control;" and "The law disregards trifles." In today's code, the maxims are in the Civil Code, Part 4, Sections 3509–3548 (four more were added in 1965 from a list of 40 presumptions in the evidence section (Section 1963) of the 1872 Code of Civil Procedure (Field's code)).

was completed in 1953, there were 25 code titles. Since that time four additional code titles have been added: Commercial Code, 1963; Evidence Code, 1965; Public Contract Code, 1981; Family Code, 1994.

During the 1990s, Georgetown University, in conjunction with Book-Lab, Inc. of Austin, Texas, worked on a preservation project to reprint codes from the 50 states. Over 100 volumes of California codes were reprinted on acid-free paper before the project ended. The reprinted codes were a mixture of official codes, unofficial codes, and unofficially "compiled laws" published between 1850 and 1930.

📖 California. Commission to Examine the Codes Adopted by the Nineteenth Legislature. *Report of the examiners of the codes.* Sacramento, T.A. Springer, State Printer, 1874.

📖 California. Commission for Revision and Reform of the Law. 1871–1911. *Reports.* Sacramento: Supt. of State Printing.

📖 California. Law Revision Commission. *Reports, Recommendations, and Studies.* Sacramento. v. 1955/57-present. For more information see the www page: *www.clrc.ca.gov/publications.html.*

§ 3.03 Current California Codes

[1] Titles of the California Codes

There are currently twenty-nine code titles:

Business & Professions
Civil
Civil Procedure
Commercial
Corporations
Education
Elections
Evidence
Family
Financial
Fish and Game
Food and Agriculture

---

8 The code revision was authorized by Statutes of California 1929, Chapter 750, which created the California Code Commission and set out the charge for the nine member group.

Government
Harbors and Navigation
Health and Safety
Insurance
Labor
Military and Veterans
Penal
Probate
Public Contract
Public Resources
Public Utilities
Revenue and Taxation
Streets and Highways
Unemployment Insurance
Vehicle
Water
Welfare and Institutions

[2] Annotated Codes

Although the State of California publishes an official reporter, it does not publish an official code. Most California lawyers rely upon commercially published sets of annotated codes.

   📖   *Deering's California Codes Annotated.*[9] Matthew Bender & Company, Inc., a member of the LexisNexis Group. Annual

---

[9] Deering's California Annotated Codes were named for brothers Frank Prentiss Deering and James Henry Deering, who were the early compilers/editors of the codes. Both men were San Francisco attorneys and were also law librarians. The older brother, Frank (1855–1939, California Bar number 182), was one of the first law librarians of the San Francisco Law Library. He served in that capacity from April 1882 until May of 1888. His name is on the title page of publisher Bancroft-Whitney's 1886 Code of Civil Procedure volume of the *Codes and Statutes of California*: "by F.P. Deering of the San Francisco Bar."

Younger brother James Henry Deering (1858–1953, California Bar number 6332) took the leadership of the San Francisco Law Library in 1888 and served until 1928. James was the librarian in charge of rebuilding the collection after its complete destruction in the 1906 San Francisco earthquake and fire. James Deering also took over the editing/compiling of the California codes from his brother. Early volumes (for example 1893) list his name on the title page: "compiled, annotated and indexed by James H. Deering." His name continued to appear as the compiler/annotator/indexer of the Bancroft-Whitney codes until at least 1930. For more information on the Deering brothers see: San Francisco Law Library Board of Trustees. Crisis at the San Francisco Law Library. 26 *San Francisco Attorney* 21–25 (Oct./Nov. 2000).

pocket parts; Advance legislative service; Advance annotation service. The set contains the California codes, Rules of Court, State Bar Rules, California Constitution, uncodified Water provisions, and selected uncodified initiative measures and statutes. Over 6,000 suggested forms are integrated with the code and rule provisions. Also included are case annotations, legislative history, Code Commissioner's notes, Judicial Committee comments, Advisory Committee comments, drafter's notes, Law Revision Commission comments, Legislative Committee comments, cross references, collateral references, annotations to Attorney General opinions, indexes to individual codes, and a General Index. In addition to the General Index, the index volume contains a New & Noted index covering significant legislation from the current year's session and a Popular Names index which contains entries based on popular or common names of laws.

📖 *Advance Legislative Service* to Deering's California Codes Annotated. Published in successive pamphlets during and after the legislative session. The Advance Legislative Service includes chaptered acts, along with changes to Rules of Court. Cumulative tables are also included:

- Table showing sections added, amended, renumbered, or repealed;

- Table showing Bills and corresponding Chapter numbers;

- Table of Rules of Court changes;

- Table of uncodified acts affected by legislation; and

- Cumulative subject index.

📖 *West's Annotated California Codes.* Eagan, MN: Thomson-West. Pocket parts. Interim pamphlets. This is a comprehensive code with general indexes. It includes historical notes showing the source and tracing the development of the law. It also has law review references, references to Opinions of the Attorney General, references to the California Code of Regulations, cross references to related laws, and library references to the American Digest System, Corpus Juris Secundum, commission recommendations, and committee reports.

📖 *West's California Legislative Service,* supplementing West's Annotated California Codes. Issued from time to time during the legislative session. Features include:

   a. Alphabetical table of laws in each pamphlet

   b. Statutes and Code Amendments

   c. Tables

     (1) Cumulative—West's Annotated California Codes. Sections added, amended, or repealed

     (2) Cumulative Statutes—Sections added, amended, or repealed

     (3) Cumulative Senate and Assembly Bills enacted into law

     (4) Cumulative subject index

📖 *West's Annotated California Codes,* superseded volumes, are available from William S. Hein & Company, from 1954 to date.[10]

💿 *Deering's California Codes Annotated on LexisNexis CD.* Matthew Bender & Company, Inc., a member of the Lexis-Nexis Group. Includes all features of Deering's California Codes Annotated, including case annotations, popular table name, legislative changes, and index.

💿 *West's Annotated California Codes* on CD-ROM. West Group. Includes annotated codes with Constitution, rules of Court, and Local Rules.

🖥 *Deering's California Codes Annotated.* Dayton, OH: Lexis-Nexis. Various files are available on *lexis.com*® and located in the CAL library, including the statutes (CODE), the state constitution (CACNST), state, federal, and local court rules (CARULE), and a group file combining these with recently enacted slip laws (CACODE), all of which can be navigated using the LexisNexis electronic Table of Contents. Online material contains all of the information as the print product listed above. Additional legislative files in the CAL Library include Advance Legislative Service (CAALS).

🖥 *West's Annotated California Codes on WESTLAW.* The database identifier is CA-ST-ANN. Historical materials from 1987

---

10 See Appendix A for Publishers/Vendors list.

are in CA-STANNYY (YY is year, i.e., 1998). The index to the codes is also available on WESTLAW in the CA-ST-IDX databases. The current legislative service is in the CA-LEGIS database. Legislative services for earlier years from 1987 are available in CA-LEGIS-OLD. Codes can be found by search, citation, table of contents, index and popular name. Navigating codes has improved. An entire chapter or sub-chapter can be opened which is more like the books. KeyCite references are contained alongside the annotated codes to allow links directly to past and pending developments and related information.

[3]   Unannotated and Single-Volume Codes

These sets tend to be one-volume compilations of one or a few selected codes. They are not completely unannotated but only have the barest references to secondary authority or perhaps a very brief commentary. They do not contain case notes as do the full annotated sets.

    Matthew Bender's California Desktop Code Sets. Matthew Bender & Company, Inc., a member of the LexisNexis Group. Selected codes and rules of court are combined in different sets. Each volume has an index. Bleed bars delineate different Code topics. Table of sections affected lists the change and the effecting chapter. Statutes and regulations include legislative history and amendments to statutes from year to year are highlighted by printing in boldface type all matter added to a section and indicating by a figure within brackets, such as [1], each point of deletion. The deleted matter is then shown by bracketed footnotes keyed to the corresponding figures.

    Titles include:

    Standard California Codes: 6-in-1®. Matthew Bender & Company, Inc., a member of the LexisNexis Group. Includes complete text of the Civil Code, Code of Civil Procedure, Evidence Code, Family Code, and Probate Code, and Rules of Court, and selected provisions of the Government Code. Selected research references to California Forms of Pleading and Practice (Matthew Bender), Matthew Bender®. Practice Guide: California Civil Discovery, Matthew Bender®. Practice Guide: California Pretrial Civil Procedure, and Judicial Council of California Civil Jury Instructions (Matthew Bender, Official

Publisher), and *Witkin*, West Group, and *Rutter*, West Group. 1 v. Annual.

📖 *Standard California Codes: 4-in-1®*. Matthew Bender & Company, Inc., a member of the LexisNexis Group. Includes complete text of the Civil Code, Code of Civil Procedure, and Evidence Code, and Rules of Court, and selected provisions of the Government Code. Includes selected research references to California Forms of Pleading and Practice (Matthew Bender), Matthew Bender®. Practice Guide: California Civil Discovery, Matthew Bender®. Practice Guide: California Pretrial Civil Procedure, and Judicial Council of California Civil Jury Instructions (Matthew Bender, Official Publisher), and *Witkin*, West Group. 1 v. Annual.

📖 *Standard California Codes: Penal Code with Evidence Code and Selected Penal Provisions of Other Codes*. Matthew Bender & Company, Inc., a member of the LexisNexis Group. Includes complete text of the Penal Code and Evidence Code and selected provisions from 11 other code topics, Rules of Court, and the California and U.S. Constitutions. Includes selected research references to California Forms of Pleading and Practice (Matthew Bender), Matthew Bender®. Practice Guide: California Pretrial Civil Procedure, and Judicial Council of California Civil Jury Instructions (Matthew Bender, Official Publisher). 1 v. Annual.

📖 *California Corporations Code and Commercial Code with Corporate Securities Rules and Releases*. Matthew Bender & Company, Inc., a member of the LexisNexis Group. Includes complete text of the Corporations Code and Commercial Code, selected provisions of other codes, California Code of Regulations, Commissioner's Releases, Delaware Corporation Law, and federal statutes and regulations. Includes selected research references to Matthew Bender®. Practice Guide: California Pretrial Civil Procedure, and Judicial Council of California Civil Jury Instructions (Matthew Bender, Official Publisher), and Miller & Starr, Cal. Real Estate 3d. 1 v. Annual.

📖 *California Intellectual Property Laws.* Matthew Bender & Company, Inc., a member of the LexisNexis Group. Compilation of Codes. 1 v. Annual.

📖 *Workers' Compensation Laws of California.* Matthew Bender & Company, Inc., a member of the LexisNexis Group. Compilation of codes pertaining to workers' compensation statutes, includes regulations and federal statutes. 1 v. Annual.

Other Matthew Bender Publications. Matthew Bender & Company, Inc., a member of the LexisNexis Group. Selected codes in individual volumes or combined in sets. All except California Vehicle with accompanying CD-ROM. Indexed.

- *California Education Laws.* 1 v. Annual.

- *California Penal and Vehicle Codes.* 1 v. Annual.

- *California Real Estate Code.* 1 v. Annual.

- *California Air Pollution Control Laws.* 1 v. Annual.

- *California Vehicle Code.* 1 v. Annual.

- *California Contractors License Law & Reference Book.* 1 v. Annual.

📖 *Deering's California Desktop Code Series.* Matthew Bender & Company, Inc., a member of the LexisNexis Group. Selected codes and rules of court are combined in different sets, also available on CD-ROM. Each volume has an index. Includes the following titles:

📖 *Civil Practice Code.* Matthew Bender & Company, Inc., a member of the LexisNexis Group. Includes Civil, Civil Procedure, Evidence, and Rules of Court, including highlighting of amendments from year to year. Includes selected research references to California Forms of Pleading and Practice, Matthew Bender & Company, Inc., and *Witkin*, West Group. 1 v. Annual.

📖 *Family Code.* Matthew Bender & Company, Inc., a member of the LexisNexis Group. Family Code, along with selected provisions of the Welfare and Institutions Code and Rules of Court, including italicized indication of changes in the text of amended sections, and selected research references to California Forms of Pleading and

Practice, Matthew Bender & Company, Inc., and *Witkin*, West Group. 1 v. Annual.

📖 *Penal Code.* Matthew Bender & Company, Inc., a member of the LexisNexis Group. Penal Code, along with selected provisions from the Health and Safety Code, Vehicle Code, and Rules of Court, including italicized indications of changes in the text of amended sections, and selected research references to California Forms of Pleading and Practice, Matthew Bender & Company, Inc., and *Witkin*, West Group. 1 v. Annual.

📖 *Probate Code.* Matthew Bender & Company, Inc., a member of the LexisNexis Group. Probate Code, including italicized indication of changes in the text of amended sections, and selected research references to California Forms of Pleading and Practice, Matthew Bender & Company, Inc., and *Witkin*, West Group. 1 v. Annual.

📖 *Bernhardt's California Real Estate Laws.* Matthew Bender & Company, Inc., a member of the LexisNexis Group. Compilation of Codes. 1 v. Annual.

📖 *Business and Commercial Code.* Matthew Bender & Company, Inc., a member of the LexisNexis Group. Uniform Commercial Code, including italicized indication of changes in the text of amended sections, and selected sections of the Business and Professions, Civil, Corporations, Finance, and Government Codes. 1 v. Annual.

📖 *Parker's California Codes.* Matthew Bender & Company, Inc., a member of the LexisNexis Group. Selected codes in individual volumes or combined in sets, with accompanying CD-ROM. Includes summary of changes with excerpts from the Legislative Counsel's Digest. Each volume has an index. Bleed bars delineate different Code topics. Table of sections affected lists the change and chapter location.

📖 *Business and Professions Code.* 1 v. Annual.

📖 *Civil Code.* 1 v. Annual.

📖 *Code of Civil Procedure.* 1 v. Annual.

📖 *Corporations Code.* 1 v. Annual.

📖 *Evidence Code*. 1 v. Annual.

📖 *Family Code*. 1 v. Annual.

📖 *Government Code*. 2 v. Bi-Annual with supplement (off years).

📖 *Insurance Code*. 1 v. Annual.

📖 *Labor Code*. 1 v. Annual.

📖 *Probate Code*. 1 v. Annual.

📖 *Uniform Commercial Code*. 1 v. Annual.

📖 *West's California Desktop Codes*. Eagan, MN: Thomson-West. Annual. Current titles are:

📖 *Blumberg California Family Code Annotated*. 1 v. Annual.

📖 *Business Statutes Annotated*. 1 v. Annual.

📖 *Civil Practice Statutes and Rules Annotated*. 1 v. Annual.

📖 *Code of Civil Procedure*. 1v. Annual.

📖 *Commercial Code Annotated*. 1 v. Annual.

📖 *Corporations Code*. 1 v. Annual.

📖 *DiMugno & Glad California Insurance Laws Annotated*. 1 v. Annual.

📖 *Dwyer & Bergsund's California Environmental Laws Annotated*. 1 v. Annual.

📖 *Education Code*. 1 v. Annual.

📖 *Environmental Laws*. 1 v. Annual.

📖 *Evidence Code*. 1 v. Annual.

📖 *Family Laws and Rules*. 1 v. Annual.

📖 *Imwinkelried & Hallahan California Evidence Code Annotated*. 1 v. Annual.

📖 *Insurance Code*. 1 v. Annual.

📖 *Juvenile Laws and Rules*. 1 v. Annual.

📖 *McGovern's California Probate Code Annotated*. 1 v. Annual.

📖 *Miller and Starr's California Real Estate Laws Annotated*. 1 v. Annual.

📖 *Penal Code.* 1 v. Annual.

📖 *Probate Code.* 1 v. Annual.

📖 *Revenue and Taxation Code.* 1 v. Annual.

📖 *Vehicle Code.* 1 v. Annual.

📖 *Water Code.* 1 v. Annual.

📖 Gould Publications. Binghamton, NY: Gould Publications, *www.gouldlaw.com/.* This publisher supplies three California code publications:

📖 *Fish and Game* (includes addenda of other pertinent laws). Looseleaf.

📖 *Penal Code Handbook* (includes Penal Code and Evidence Code, and selected sections from Business and Professions, Family, Health and Safety, Vehicle, Welfare and Institutions, as well as selected sections from the Rules of Court) available in looseleaf or soft-cover binding.

📖 *Vehicle Code* (includes addenda of pertinent related laws) available in looseleaf or soft-cover binding.

📖 Continuing Education of the Bar. Berkeley, CA: California Continuing Education of the Bar. These are not traditional annotated codes. They contain the text of the code with references to CEB publications.

📖 *California Probate Code, annotated to CEB publications.* 1 v. Annual.

📖 *Trial Attorney's Evidence Code Notebook, Annotated. Third Edition.* Annotations printed below most Code sections include reprints of Law Revision Commission and Legislative Commission Comments, cross-references to other relevant Code sections, citations to illustrative cases, and cross-references to *Jefferson's California Evidence Benchbook* and other CEB practice books.1 v. Looseleaf.

💿 *LexisNexis CD.* Matthew Bender & Company, Inc., a member of the LexisNexis Group. Includes all twenty-nine California Codes, as well as the California Constitution, Rules of Court, Rules of the Commission on Judicial Performance, and California Rules of Professional Conduct, the Delaware

Corporation Laws, and Corporate Securities Releases. Updated several times per year.

Parker's California Codes. Matthew Bender & Company, Inc., a member of the LexisNexis Group. Selected codes in individual volumes or combined in sets. Titles include:

Business and Professions Code; Civil Code; Code of Civil Procedure; Corporations Code; Evidence Code; Family Code; Government Code; Insurance Code; Labor Code; Probate Code; Uniform Commercial Code.

Other Matthew Bender Publications. Matthew Bender & Company, Inc., a member of the LexisNexis Group. Selected codes in individual volumes or combined in sets. CD-ROM accompanies the volume. Titles include:

California Education Laws. 1 v. Annual.

California Penal and Vehicle Codes. 1 v. Annual.

California Real Estate Code. 1 v. Annual.

California Air Pollution Control Laws. 1 v. Annual.

California Contractors License Law & Reference Book. 1 v. Annual.

Gould Publications. *California Penal Code Handbook* and *California Vehicle Code Handbook* are available in DiskLaw/P.D.A. Law on CD-ROM and P.D.A. Law is available for Palm Pilots or PocketPCs.

West's California Codes, unannotated version on Westlaw. This database is CA-ST. Westlaw also has the code index online in the CA-ST-IDX database.

AccessLaw, www.accesslaw.com. This is one of the oldest of the upstart companies. In the early 1990s the company was distributing California law on floppy diskettes. Then they moved to cd products containing codes and cases. Today they offer web access, CD-ROM, or DVD.

American LegalNet, www.americanlegalnet.com. This site has the codes viewable through LivePublish software on the internet.

Findlaw. California codes using Findlaw's search engine as well as from California Legislative Counsel.*http://california.lp.findlaw.com/ca01_codes/index.html*

▢ *JuriSearch, www.jurisearch.com.* This site has the California codes.

▢ *Loislaw, www.loislaw.com.* This site has all of the California codes.

▢ *National Law Library, www.nationallawlibrary.com/.* This site carries California codes and acts back to 2000.

▢ *Netlawlibraries, www.netlawlibraries.com.* This site links to the official state California Law page from the California Legislative Counsel.

▢ State of California. Legislative Counsel *www.leginfo.ca.gov.* This state office was the first to put the California codes on the internet.

▢ *VersusLaw, www.versuslaw.com.* This site has the California codes.

§ 3.04 Code Index

📖 LARMAC: Consolidated Index to the Laws, Rules, and Constitution of California. LexisNexis. Annual. This index is named for its early editors, Neil Edwin Larkin and Paul Aloysius McCarthy. It was first published in 1935 by Marnell & Company in San Francisco.[11] For many years it was published by the Recorder Publishing Company, also in San Francisco. In 1989 LARMAC was taken over by Parker & Sons Publications, which was later acquired by LexisNexis. The current edition indexes all California codes, uncodified acts, court rules, and the Constitution. Owners of Deering's California Codes should note that the LARMAC Index is word-for-word identical to their Deering's index. The only differences are the title pages, and there is a cd-rom containing the entire LARMAC Index in a pocket in the inside back cover of the LARMAC printed volume.

§ 3.05 Content of California Codes

The California Code Commission appointed pursuant to Chapter 750, Statutes of 1929, entered upon a revision, compilation, and codification

---

[11] There is a short but positive review of the first edition of LARMAC (then called Larmac Consolidated Code and Court Rules Index) at 9 *Southern California Law Review* 297 (1936).

of the laws of California and completed its work in 1953, being abolished by Chapter 1445, Statutes of 1953. Its Final Report, dated September 1, 1953, states:

> The completed program of the Code Commission consists of twenty-five codes, twenty-two codes prepared by the Commission, and three of the four 1872 codes. Of the 1872 codes, the Political Code has been repealed, and both additions and deletions have been made in the Civil Code, Code of Civil Procedure and Penal Code. The commission believes that this system of codes contains all of the "live" laws of general interest.

The Codes do not include all of the laws of California.[12] The following types of acts have not been codified, because they are of little general interest and because their inclusion would unduly extend the codes:

1. Acts authorizing a change of name.

2. Acts authorizing the sale of specific land by administrators.

3. Acts authorizing the grant, sale, or purchase of specific land by the State, and authorizing quiet title actions against the State as to specifically described property.

4. Acts authorizing the issuance of duplicate land warrants.

5. Acts providing for the refunding of bonds of special districts.

6. Validating acts.

7. Appropriation acts which are effective only during a limited period of time. (Acts making a continuous appropriation, or in addition to making an appropriation, conferring a power, have been codified.)

8. Acts authorizing the issuance of bonds, which will become inoperative upon payment of the bonds.

---

[12] This helpful explanation from the Office of Legislative Counsel appeared on the NOCALL email list on 3/12/04 (used with permission): "The California Legislature has authority over what is to be codified, or to remain uncodified as not of general interest or applicability. The Legislative Counsel advises the Legislature on maintaining the code, preparing an annual report on needed revisions. In preparing draft bills as requested by a legislator, a Legislative Counsel deputy normally incorporates provisions in the existing codes, unless the proposal is for legislation of limited duration or not of general statewide application. The Table of Sections affected (regarding proposed law) and the Statutory Record prepared by Legislative Counsel include information on 'Statutes other than code' so that it's possible to systematically track repeals and modifications of uncodified laws."

9. Acts terminating of their own force by the lapse of a specified period of time.

10. Initiative acts. (These acts cannot be codified by the Legislature because of the constitutional limitations on the powers of the Legislature with reference to them.)

   The commission recommended to the publishers of the Codes that the initiative acts be published as an appendix to the appropriate code, rather than as a separate volume. Deering's carries them in its Uncodified Initiative Measures and Statutes Volume. West includes them as code sections.

11. In addition to the acts referred to above, many statutes that are addressed to existing codes contain sections that stand independently. Some of these sections, which were not originally enacted as part of any code, contain substantive provisions of law, and for this reason they have been added to the appropriate code. Others are of such limited effect that they have not been codified. Sections of acts which fall into this latter category are:

   a. Those relating to the effective or operative date of a statute.

   b. Those making an appropriation limited in time.

   c. Those sections referred to as double-jointing clauses, which operate to repeal a part of an act if a new code is adopted.

   d. Those limiting the length of time during which a statute remains operative.

   e. Those designating the author's name.

   f. Those setting out separability and constitutionality clauses.

Where any of the above mentioned factors may be involved in a given situation, the researcher should consult the appropriate volume of the Statutes and Amendments to the Codes.

The mission of the Code Commission was to prepare a statutory record, codify, consolidate, compile, or revise all statutes in force, repeal all statutes repealed by implication or held unconstitutional, or made obsolete, and to correct errors in form or substance. Its first report covered the Probate Code with notes. During its existence numerous reports on code revision and proposed enactments were issued. Some of the larger law libraries in the state have collections of drafts which include strike outs, rewordings, and notes of changes of previous laws. In some situations, this data may be of help in determining legislative intent. Commission notes are cited in Deering's Codes. Following its demise in 1953, the Code Commission was succeeded by the Law Revision Commission.

§ 3.06 Codification Methodology

Appendix C of Final Report of the California Code Commission lists session law chapters by which each code was enacted. Each code chapter is accompanied by two cross-reference tables, showing the source of each section of the code and also the disposition of each section of the existing law in the code. These cross-reference tables are published in the appendix to the Statutes and Amendments to the Codes of the year in which the chapter was enacted. These tables offer the only official record of the source of each code section and the disposition of each law included in the codes.

> With respect to these codification bills, it is important that they be differentiated from the usual legislative amendments to the codes. As to such codification measures, the decisions of the California courts have established that every presumption is to the effect that no change in the substance of the law was intended. This was true of the work of earlier code commissions.[13]

The policy of codification may be summarized as follows: (1) All general laws and sections appended to code amendments, which are in force, unlimited in duration, and of general interest, will be codified; (2) General laws and sections appended to code amendments, which are of limited application and duration and not of general interest, will not be codified.

_____
[13] See *San Joaquin & Kings River Canal & Irrigation Co., Inc. v. Stevenson,* 164 Cal. 221, 128 P. 924 (Cal. 1942); *People v. Ellis,* 204 Cal. 39, 266 P. 518 (Cal. 1928); *In re Healy's Estate,* 122 Cal. 162, 54 P. 736 (Cal. 1898); *Evans v. Superior Court of Los Angeles,* 215 Cal. 58, 8 P.2d 467 (Cal. 1932); *In re Armstrong's Estate,* 8 Cal.2d 204, 64 P.2d 1093 (Cal. 1937); *Sobey v. Molony,* 40 Cal.App.2d 381, 104 P.2d 868 (Ct.App. 1940); *Speegle v. Board of Fire Underwriters of the Pacific,* 29 Cal.2d 34, 172 P.2d 867 (Cal. 1946); *Ex Parte Trombley,* 31 Cal.2d 801, 193 P.2d 734 (Cal. 1948); *Southern California Jockey Club v. California Horse Racing Bd.,* 36 Cal.2d 167, 223 P.2d 1 (Cal. 1950).

To insure codification without substantive change, the California Code Commission adhered to a policy of circulating among interested persons drafts of all code bills. Where possible, a reprint of the code bill was also circulated. Drafts and Proposed Codes are available arranged chronologically under each code. The Commission operated under drafting rules and principles described in Appendix G of its 1947–48 Report. Researchers should check the public catalog under "California Code Commission" for these materials in the larger California law libraries.

§ 3.07 Keeping the Codes Current

📖 California. Legislative Counsel Bureau. *Report on Legislation Necessary to Maintain the Codes.* 1947–date.

The Legislature recognized that the process of codification was never complete, due to the fact that old sections became obsolete and general laws were enacted that should be placed in the codes. So the Legislature, upon the abolition of the California Code Commission, imposed upon the Legislative Counsel the duty to "advise the Legislature from time to time as to legislation necessary to maintain the codes and legislation necessary to codify such statutes as are enacted from time to time subsequent to the enactment of the codes."

The reports contain acts recommended for codification and corrective legislation necessary to maintain the codes, as well as a summary of prior recommendations for codification. Government Code Section 10242, CAL. STATS. 1945, c.111, p.430, empowers the Legislative Counsel to advise the Legislature on needed revision of the codes and to present to each session a statement calling attention to laws that have been repealed by implication or declared unconstitutional by the courts. CAL. STATS. 1953, c.1445, p.3039 gives the Legislative Counsel the duty of maintaining the codes and codifying the statutes as they are enacted. The duty of recommending express repeal of all statutes repealed by implication or held unconstitutional by the California or U.S. Supreme Court was transferred to the Law Revision Commission.

§ 3.08 Citators for the Codes

📖 *Shepard's California Citations—Statutes.* Colorado Springs, CO: Shepard's, a member of the LexisNexis Group. Includes Shepard's Signals on treatment of case. Used to Shepardize California statutes and codes.

⌨ *Shepard's on LexisNexis.* Dayton, OH: LexisNexis. Available through *lexis.com®*. Includes history of statutes and codes. Citations to opinions and law reviews citing statutes and codes. Statutes searchable by section and subdivision. Links to point pages of cited cases.

⌨ *KeyCite* is a citator service available online from Westlaw.

⌨ *Codes in Cases* is a citator available online on JuriSearch. It is much simpler than *KeyCite* and *Shepard's* and merely lists cases without editorial enhancement.

⌨ *GlobalCite* is a citator service available online from Loislaw. It is much simpler than *KeyCite* and *Shepard's* and merely lists cases without editorial enhancement.

§ 3.09 California Laws Not Included in the Codes—Collected

📖 *Deering's Uncodified Initiative Measures and Statutes, Annotated.* Matthew Bender & Company, Inc., a member of the LexisNexis Group. This publication is part of the subscription to *Deering's California Codes Annotated.* Annotated and indexed, supplemented annually. All statutes of a general and permanent nature, with the exception of certain initiative measures.

📖 *Deering's Water Uncodified Acts.* 4 volumes plus pocket part supplements. Indexed. Contains the complete text as amended of the uncodified water district laws. The acts are arranged chronologically and have been assigned act numbers, along with section headings.

📖 *West's Water Code Appendix,* v.71–72A, plus pocket parts and pamphlet supplement contains the complete text as amended of the uncodified water district laws. The acts, arranged chronologically, have been assigned chapter numbers which are incorporated in a system of section numbering designed for ready identification and maximum ease of citation. To facilitate use of the Appendix, alphabetical and chronological Tables have been inserted following the Foreword, index references have been incorporated in the Index to the Water Code and in the General Index, section headings have been editorially prepared, and a section analysis has been set out at the beginning of each Act.

The supplementary services for *Deering's California Codes Annotated*, *Matthew Bender's California Desktop Code Sets*, and *West's Annotated California Codes* provide a practical and convenient means of determining the changes that have been made in the text of the codes by legislative action. *Deering's California Codes Annotated* indicates additions by bold italics and deletions by asterisks. *Matthew Bender's California Desktop Codes* show additions in bold face text and show deletions by means of numbered footnotes. *West's Annotated California Codes* delineates additions by underlining, while deletions are shown by asterisks. Editorially prepared explanations of legislative amendments affecting personal, property, and vested rights, and procedural matters, cover changes in the text of the law.

§ 3.10 Cross-Checking Code Sections With Statutes

[1] Researching

In dealing with the codified law of the state of California, it is always advisable to check the official Statutes and Amendments to the Codes. As pointed out above, operative dates, separability and constitutionality clauses, and sections of statutes limiting the length of time during which a statute is operative are omitted from the codes. In addition, the California Constitution, article 4, section 9, provides, "Every act shall embrace but one subject, which subject shall be expressed in its title. If any subject be embraced in an act which is not expressed in its title, such act becomes void only as to so much thereof as is not expressed in its title." While the courts have liberally construed this constitutional provision to uphold legislation, there exists the possibility that it may be invoked to void legislation.

[2] *Statutes and Amendments to the Codes*—1850 to present

The *Statutes* contain the Constitution of the State of California and the Constitution of the United States of America, as amended to date of publication, the Chapter Laws and Resolution Chapters, cross-reference tables of code sections amended, and the Statutory Record from 1959. The *Statutes* are available for sale from Publications Section California Office of Procurement, P.O. Box 20191, Sacramento, CA 95820.

Statutes are available from the Assembly Office of the Chief Clerk. Official Publications Archive website from 1850 to

1992 at *http://www.assembly.ca.gov/clerk/ BILLSLEGISLATURE/BILLSLEGISLATURE.HTM* and from the California Legislative Counsel's website from 1993 to present at *http://www.leginfo.ca.gov/statute.html.*

State Session Laws. Microfiche service of officially published laws of all fifty states, Puerto Rico, and the Virgin Islands. Buffalo, NY: William S. Hein & Co., Inc., 1981. California is covered by this service from 1849 to the present. Information Handling Services has discontinued publication of session laws. The William S. Hein Company has a publications program that carries them forward.

[3] Summary Digest of Statutes Enacted

Summary Digest of Statutes Enacted and Resolutions Adopted, including proposed constitutional amendments and table of sections affected. Sacramento: California Legislature, Compiled by Legislative Counsel, 1935–present; Bound with Statutes, 1968–present.

The *Summary Digest* consists of a short summary of each law enacted, and each constitutional amendment, concurrent or joint resolution adopted. Unless otherwise indicated, each digest is the Legislative Counsel's digest which appeared on the face of the legislative measure when placed on final passage by both houses.

The text of the summary is arranged numerically by chapters. Cross-reference tables are included which designate chapter number of each legislative measure enacted by bill number or resolution number.

A subject matter index to all measures including constitutional amendments and resolutions is included. Since 1953 a table of sections affected by laws enacted shows each change made in existing law by listing each code section or general law affected by legislative action. The table cites both bill number and chapter number by which the existing law was affected.

A table of abbreviations appears at the beginning of the volume. There is also a bill-to-chapter reference table.

[4] Indexes to the Statutes of California

Index to the Laws of California, 1850–1920, including the statutes, the codes, and the Constitution of 1879 together with amendments thereto, prepared in accordance with an act of the Legislature approved May 24, 1919. By Legislative Counsel. Sacramento, State Printing Office, 1921. 1288 p. Indexes all statutes, constitutional amendments, and resolutions adopted as they appear in official statute volumes in this period. Pages 78–96 include a list of chapters, which, in the opinion of the Commission on Revision of the Laws, were impliedly repealed by the early codes. The courts have not always followed the list, e.g., see *Needham v. Thresher,* 49 Cal. 392 (Cal. 1874). There is no comprehensive index to the session laws after 1932. However, the Statutory Record described below provides a complete history of every act ever passed by Legislature, and its first edition indexes 1921–1932.

📖 *Statutory Record, Supplement to Index to the Laws of California.* Statutory Record, 1850–1932; index, 1921–1932. Compiled in accordance with Chapter 584, Statutes of 1931, by the Legislative Counsel. Sacramento, California State Printing Office, 1933. 1207 p. Originally prepared by the California Code Commission in connection with its work, the *Statutory Record,* and its supplements, provide a complete history of every act passed by the Legislature from 1850 to the present, showing all sections amended, added, repealed, supplemented, or superseded.

For a description of the origin and uses of the Statutory Record, see 1930, 1933, and 1949 *Reports of the California Code Commission.* Also, Hagar, "Helpful Statute Finders," 16 *Calif. State Bar J.* 325 (1941) and Ridgway, "The Statutory Record," 8 *Calif. State Bar J.* 190 (1933).

- *Statutory Record,* 1850–1932.
- *Statutory Record Supplement,* 1933–48. 539 p.
- *Statutory Record Supplement,* 1949–58. 530 p.
- *Statutory Record Supplement,* 1959–68. 730 p.
- Statutory Record in most recent *Statues and Amendments to the Codes* volume.

Cumulative changes will appear in later session law volumes until such time as an additional separate bound volume supplement is published.

📖 *Statutes & Amendments to the Codes.* Index in individual editions.

⚲ *Legislative Index.* Sacramento: Biweekly. Final edition is permanent. Cumulative subject index to bills, resolutions, and constitutional amendments introduced in the current legislature.

[5] Table of Sections Affected

In a current session of the Legislature the Table of Sections Affected, Part 2 of the Legislative Index, should be referred to in order to determine the enacted legislation affected by pending bills. The table is arranged by codes and the Constitution listed in alphabetical order. Uncodified laws are listed at the end of the table under the heading "Statutes Other Than Codes" and are cited by year and chapter.

§ 3.11 Bibliography on Statutes and Codes

⚲ Aikin, Charles. "The Government of California," Special Feature in West's Annotated California Codes: Government Code Sections 1 to 11999. St. Paul: West, 1955. pp. 1–29.

⚲ Cassidy, Roderick B. "Public Utility Regulation in California," Special Feature in West's Annotated California Codes: Public Utilities Code Sections 1 to 6000. St. Paul: West, 1956. pp. 1-24.

⚲ Davis, J. Allen. "California Motor Vehicle Legislation," Special Feature in West's Annotated California Codes: Vehicle Code Sections 1 to 448. St. Paul: West, 1956. pp. 1–49.

⚲ Gaylord, Edward H. "History of the California Election Laws," Special Article in West's Annotated California Codes: Elections Code Sections 1 to 5999. St. Paul: West, 1955. pp. XXVII-LXIV.

⚲ Gould, J. "The California Tax System," Special Feature in West's Annotated California Codes: Revenue and Taxation Code Sections 1 to 6000. St. Paul: West, 1956. pp. 1–77.

⚲ Grossman, Lewis. Essay: "Codification and the California Mentality." 45 *Hastings Law Journal* 617–639 (March 1994). This author, like Charles Cook and Michael Weber, mentioned in Section 3.02, looks at the motivation of Californians to adopt the Field Codes in 1872.

⚲ Kleps, Ralph N. "The Revision and Codification of California Statutes," 1849–1953, 42 *California Law Review* 766–802 (1954).

📖 Knowles, Joseph L. "The Education Code," Special Feature in West's Annotated California Codes: Education Code Sections 1 to 8000. St. Paul: West, 1955. pp. XLIX to LVIII.

📖 Miller, Justin. "History of the California Code of Civil Procedure," Special Feature in West's Annotated California Codes: Civil Procedure. St. Paul: West, 1954. pp. 1–44.

📖 Palmer, William J. and Selvin, Paul P. "The Development of the Law in California." Special Feature in West's Annotated California Codes: Constitution Articles V to XI. St. Paul: West, 1954. 64 p. This was also reprinted by West in paperback in 1983.

📖 Parma, Rosamond and Armstrong, Elizabeth. "The Codes and Statutes of California: A Bibliography," 22(2) *Law Library Journal* 41–56 (April, 1929).

📖 Parma, Rosamond. "The History of the Adoption of the Codes of California," 22(1) *Law Library Journal* 8–21 (January, 1929).

📖 Strauss, J.D. and Murphy, George H. "California Water Law in Perspective," Special Feature in West's Annotated California Codes: Water Code Sections 1 to 19999. St. Paul: West, 1956. pp. 1–49.

📖 Turrentine, Lowell. "Introduction to the California Probate Code," Special Feature in West's Annotated California Codes: Probate Code Sections 1 to 399. St. Paul: West, 1956. pp. 1–40.

📖 Val Alstyne, Arvo. "The California Civil Code." Special Feature in West's Annotated California Codes: Civil Code Sections 1 to 192. St. Paul: West, 1954. pp. 1–43.

📖 Weinstock, Sidney L. and Maloney, John R. "History and Development of Insurance Law in California," Special Feature in West's Annotated California Codes: Insurance Code Sections 1 to 10109. St. Paul: West, 1954. pp. 1–57.

Chapter 4

Legislative Intent

(Pub. 64620)

§ 4.01   Introduction

[1]   Objective

Legislative intent is concerned with the objective the legislative body had in enacting a statute. California Code of Civil Procedure section 1859 states:

> In the construction of a statute the intention of the Legislature, and in the construction of the instrument the intention of the parties, is to be pursued, if possible; and when a general and [a] particular provision are inconsistent, the latter is paramount to the former. So a particular intent will control a general one that is inconsistent with it.

> HISTORY: Enacted 1872.

Courts increasingly resort to the use of extrinsic aids such as legislative documents in arriving at their findings as to the intent of a statute enacted by the Legislature. A review of recent decisions indicates that the use of legislative history materials in determining legislative intent in California is still prevalent. Because of this, one might find it odd that the State of California does not publish the complete proceedings and debates of its Legislature as does the Congress of the United States. Neither does California make its legislative hearings and reports available on a regular basis. Legislative journals seldom reveal more than the committee which considered the bill, amendments, and the vote. Occasionally, a Legislative Counsel report or a Law Revision Commission recommendation will shed some light on an act later adopted. The compilation of a complete legislative history designed to show the intent of a statute is much more difficult for a California statute than a federal statute. However, since the use of legislative histories by the state courts is increasing, it is important that an attorney know the sources from which legislative intent may be gathered and learn how to use them.

It is not as if the legislature has totally ignored this problem. Action was taken in the early 1960s, the mid-1970s, and again in the mid-1990s to make legislative materials more available to the public. Three examples of legislative action are discussed, below.

[2] 1961 Resolution and Resulting Hearings and Report

The California Assembly passed House Resolution No. 24 at the 1961 legislative session. It reads:

> Relative to a study of means of defining and preserving the intent of the Legislature with respect to legislative enactments
>
> Whereas, The primary rule of statutory construction is to ascertain and declare the intention of the Legislature and to carry such intention into effect to the fullest degree; and
>
> Whereas, it has been suggested that there is need for more effective means by which the Legislature may define and preserve the intent of the Legislature with respect to legislative enactments; now, therefore, be it
>
> Resolved by the Assembly of the State of California, That the Assembly Committee on Rules is hereby directed to assign to an appropriate interim committee the study of the feasibility and desirability of providing means by which the Legislature may define and preserve the intent of the Legislature with respect to legislative enactments, and to direct such committee to report its findings to the Assembly

As a result of this legislative action, hearings were held and published and a report was issued:

📖 California. Legislature. Assembly. Committee on Rules. Subcommittee on Legislative Intent. *Hearings*, November 29, December 6, 1962, Sacramento, 1963. 139 p.

📖 California. Legislature. Assembly. Committee on Rules. Subcommittee on Legislative Intent. *Final Report.* Sacramento, 1964, 59 p.

[3] The Legislative Open Records Act

The Legislative Open Records Act, Cal. Stats. 1975, c.1246 (A.B. 23, 1975),[1] providing for access to legislative records, is described in the Legislative Counsel's digest as follows:

> This bill would enact a Legislative Open Records Act and make the records of the total expenditures and disbursements of the courts, and those of the Governor and the Governor's office, except those prepared on or before January 6, 1975 and specified records in the

---

[1] Codified at Government Code Sections 6250–6268.

custody of or maintained by the Governor's legal affairs secretary, subject to the California Public Records Act. The Legislative Open Records Act would provide that legislative records, as defined, are open to inspection by every citizen at all times during the normal office hours of the Legislature and that each house of the Legislature and the Joint Rules Committee shall adopt written guidelines stating the procedure to be followed when making legislative records available. Excepted from this rule, would be: (1) certain preliminary drafts, notes, or memoranda; (2) records pertaining to pending litigation; (3) personnel, medical, or similar files, if the Assembly, Senate, or Joint Rules Committee determines there would be an unwarranted invasion of privacy, as specified; (4) records of the names and phone numbers of senders and recipients of telephone and telegraph communications; (5) records pertaining to the name and location of recipients of automotive fuel or lubricants expenditures; (6) in the custody of or maintained by the Legislative Counsel; (7) in the custody of or maintained by the majority and minority caucuses and, majority and minority consultants of each house of the Legislature; (8) correspondence of and to Members of the Legislature and their staff; (9) records the disclosure of which is excepted or prohibited pursuant to provisions of federal or state law; (10) communications from private citizens to the Legislature; and (11) records of complaints to or investigations conducted by, or records of security procedures of the Legislature. The Legislative Open Records Act would also authorize actions for injunctive or declaratory court relief to enforce the right to inspect legislative records.

In addition, this bill would, with respect to both the Legislative Open Records Act and the Public Records Act, require the award of court costs and reasonable attorneys' fees to a plaintiff who prevails in the action, and to the public agency when the court finds that the plaintiff's case is clearly frivolous.

This bill would also require that both the Legislature and the Governor issue reports annually containing an itemized statement of expenditures by Members and committees of the Legislature and the Governor.

With respect to the California Public Records Act, the bill would specify that the fee for a copy of a public record shall not exceed 10 cents per page, or the prescribed statutory fee, where applicable.

The Assembly, Senate and Joint Rules Committee would also be required to submit to the Director of Finance each year an itemized statement of proposed expenditures from the contingent funds of the

Legislature for inclusion in the Governor's Budget. In addition, the Governor would be required to submit such a statement concerning the proposed expenditures for support of the Governor and the Governor's office.

[4]   1996 Public Records Retention Legislation (Chapter 928)

Senate Bill No. 1507, according the Legislative Counsel's Digest accomplishes the following:

Existing law provides that the public may inspect legislative records, as defined, but does not require disclosure of preliminary drafts, notes, legislative memoranda, or specified correspondence.

This bill would require each committee of each house of the Legislature, as specified, and each joint committee to maintain legislative records, as defined, relating to legislation assigned to the committee in official committee files. The bill would require each committee to preserve those records that are in its custody or to lodge the records with the State Archives. The bill would require the Rules Committee of the Assembly and the Senate, or the Joint Rules Committee, to provide for storage of official committee files that are not maintained by the committee or lodged with the State Archives. The bill would require each committee, having custody thereof, to adopt written procedures for public access to official committee files not lodged with the State Archives. Records in official committee files, including preliminary drafts, notes, legislative memoranda, or specified correspondence would be open to inspection by the public, other than certain confidential communications.

[5]   Other Reasons to Study the Legislative Process

Aside from the problems of statutory construction and legislative intent, the lawyer, law student, and law librarian often have need to determine quickly the legislative status of a particular bill in which they may have an interest. The sources and finding aids detailed in this chapter should assist them in this task.

§ 4.02 The Legislative Process—A Record of Action

[1] Bills

[a] Constitutional Provisions Governing Bills[2]

A bill is a draft of a proposed law presented by a legislator to the Legislature for enactment. California Constitution, article IV, sections 8–10 govern bills and legislative procedure:

§ 8. Passage of bills; Effective dates; Urgency statutes

---

[2] In spite of the elaborate Constitutional safety measures that are in place, there is still some room for creative legislation in California. USC Law Professor Susan Estrich has written about a hospital industry shell bill, a measure with nothing in it. (Last Impression: A Doctor's Legal Prescription. California Law Week, July 26, 1999 at p. 31.) Shell bills, also called spot bills or skeleton bills, are used by legislators to save a place for important legislation they may want to introduce later. Shell bills begin their lives as very short, insignificant, sometimes pointless bills. In the amendment process the original text is struck and the additions can change the subject quite radically, sometimes only remotely relating to the original bill's purpose. An example of a shell bill is AB 1843 of 1985. The original bill was waiting in place and a new bill was inserted in the remaining shell.

Another more recent example of a shell bill is SB 53, amended and passed by the Senate on June 2, 2003. This was actually a full-bodied bill, the state budget bill, but the Senate democrats stripped it down to a shell to speed it through and avoid an inter-party fight in the Senate about how to actually balance the state budget. The bill was changed from spending legislation into "proposed appropriations for display purposes." This language change, and the removal of the urgency provision, permitted the Senate democrats to pass the bill so it could move more quickly to the Senate-Assembly conference committee for debate. A third shell bill example is SB 1160 introduced by Senator Cedillo on February 2, 2004. The bill was an expression of legislative intent to hold a place for the real bill that Senator Cedillo was negotiating with Governor Schwarzenegger. The text of the shell bill reads: "It is the intent of the Legislature to enact appropriate legislation that improves the safety of all California residents while operating motor vehicles on our highways by ensuring that all drivers of motor vehicles are properly licensed, tested, and maintain proof of financial responsibility."

A second way legislators can be creative with bills is to hijack an existing bill that may not have been waiting around as a nearly empty shell. An example of this is SB 241 of 1987, the tort reform act that was drafted on a napkin in Frank Fat's restaurant in Sacramento. The agreement among several warring factions was drawn up in the closing hours of the legislative session, but still in time to be passed and signed by the Governor. The original bill text was deleted and the new tort reform measure was inserted in its place. There were many articles written about this activity at the time. A Washington Monthly article by Paul Glastris is typical. Glastris, Paul. *Frank Fat's Napkin*. Washington Monthly, December 1987, pp. 19–25.

(a) At regular sessions no bill other than the budget bill may be heard or acted on by committee or either house until the 31st day after the bill is introduced unless the house dispenses with this requirement by rollcall vote entered in the journal, three fourths of the membership concurring.

(b) The Legislature may make no law except by statute and may enact no statute except by bill. No bill may be passed unless it is read by title on 3 days in each house except that the house may dispense with this requirement by rollcall vote entered in the journal, two thirds of the membership concurring. No bill may be passed until the bill with amendments has been printed and distributed to the members. No bill may be passed unless, by rollcall vote entered in the journal, a majority of the membership of each house concurs.

(c)(1) Except as provided in paragraphs (2) and (3) of this subdivision, a statute enacted at a regular session shall go into effect on January 1 next following a 90-day period from the date of enactment of the statute and a statute enacted at a special session shall go into effect on the 91st day after adjournment of the special session at which the bill was passed.

(2) A statute, other than a statute establishing or changing boundaries of any legislative, congressional, or other election district, enacted by a bill passed by the Legislature on or before the date the Legislature adjourns for a joint recess to reconvene in the second calendar year of the biennium of the legislative session, and in the possession of the Governor after that date, shall go into effect on January 1 next following the enactment date of the statute unless, before January 1, a copy of a referendum petition affecting the statute is submitted to the Attorney General pursuant to subdivision (d) of Section 10 of Article II, in which event the statute shall go into effect on the 91st day after the enactment date unless the petition has been presented to the Secretary of State pursuant to subdivision (b) of Section 9 of Article II.

(3) Statutes calling elections, statutes providing for tax levies or appropriations for the usual current expenses of the state, and urgency statutes shall go into effect immediately upon their enactment.

(d) Urgency statutes are those necessary for immediate preservation of the public peace, health, or safety. A statement of facts constituting the necessity shall be set forth in one section of the bill. In each house the section and the bill shall be passed separately, each by rollcall vote entered in the journal, two thirds of the membership concurring. An urgency statute may not create or abolish any office or change the salary, term, or duties of any office, or grant any franchise or special privilege, or create any vested right or interest.

HISTORY: Adopted November 8, 1966; Amended November 7, 1972. Amendment adopted by voters, Prop 109, effective June 6, 1990.

§ 9. Statutory titles; Amendments

A statute shall embrace but one subject, which shall be expressed in its title. If a statute embraces a subject not expressed in its title, only the part not expressed is void. A statute may not be amended by reference to its title. A section of a statute may not be amended unless the section is re-enacted as amended.

HISTORY: Adopted November 8, 1966.

§ 10. Enactment of bills; Governor's veto

(a) Each bill passed by the Legislature shall be presented to the Governor. It becomes a statute if it is signed by the Governor. The Governor may veto it by returning it with any objections to the house of origin, which shall enter the objections in the journal and proceed to reconsider it. If each house then passes the bill by rollcall vote entered in the journal, two thirds of the membership concurring, it becomes a statute.

(b)(1) Any bill, other than a bill which would establish or change boundaries of any legislative, congressional, or other election district, passed by the Legislature on or before the date the Legislature adjourns for a joint recess to reconvene in the second calendar year of the biennium of the legislative session, and in the possession of the Governor after that date, that is not returned within 30 days after that date becomes a statute.

(2) Any bill passed by the Legislature before September 1 of the second calendar year of the biennium of the legislative session and in the possession of the Governor on or after September 1 that is not returned on or before September 30 of that year becomes a statute.

(3) Any other bill presented to the Governor that is not returned within 12 days becomes a statute.

(4) If the Legislature by adjournment of a special session prevents the return of a bill with the veto message, the bill becomes a statute unless the Governor vetoes the bill within 12 days after it is presented by depositing it and the veto message in the office of the Secretary of State.

(5) If the 12th day of the period within which the Governor is required to perform an act pursuant to paragraph (3) or (4) of this

subdivision is a Saturday, Sunday, or holiday, the period is extended to the next day that is not a Saturday, Sunday, or holiday.

(c) Any bill introduced during the first year of the biennium of the legislative session that has not been passed by the house of origin by January 31 of the second calendar year of the biennium may no longer be acted on by the house. No bill may be passed by either house on or after September 1 of an even-numbered year except statutes calling elections, statutes providing for tax levies or appropriations for the usual current expenses of the State, and urgency statutes, and bills passed after being vetoed by the Governor.

(d) The Legislature may not present any bill to the Governor after November 15 of the second calendar year of the biennium of the legislative session.

(e) The Governor may reduce or eliminate one or more items of appropriation while approving other portions of a bill. The Governor shall append to the bill a statement of the items reduced or eliminated with the reasons for the action. The Governor shall transmit to the house originating the bill a copy of the statement and reasons. Items reduced or eliminated shall be separately reconsidered and may be passed over the Governor's veto in the same manner as bills.

HISTORY: Adopted November 8, 1966; Amended November 7, 1972; November 5, 1974. Amendment adopted by voters, Prop 109, effective June 6, 1990.

[b] Drafting Requirements

📖   California. Legislative Counsel. *Legislative Drafting Manual.* Sacramento, 1975. 49 p., A 1–10. The principal objective of this manual is to provide guidance in the preparation of legislative measures and amendments to such measures that are proposed for introduction and consideration by the California Legislature. It is also intended to promote uniformity in the form, style, and language of such measures.

[c] Legislative Rules of Procedure

📖   Mason, Paul. *Manual of Legislative Procedure for Legislative and Other Governmental Bodies.* Sacramento: Senate, California Legislature, 1979. 674 p. Rule 31 of the Temporary Joint Rules in the 1993–94 Handbook states that "All relations between the houses which are not covered by these rules shall be governed by *Mason's Manual*" (1979 edition). This text is a general parliamentary rules reference guide designed for use in state legislatures. It provides parliamentary authority for the Assembly in cases not covered by the Constitution, statute, or Assembly or joint rules.

[d] Legislative Procedure—How a Bill Becomes a Law in California

How a Bill Becomes a Law

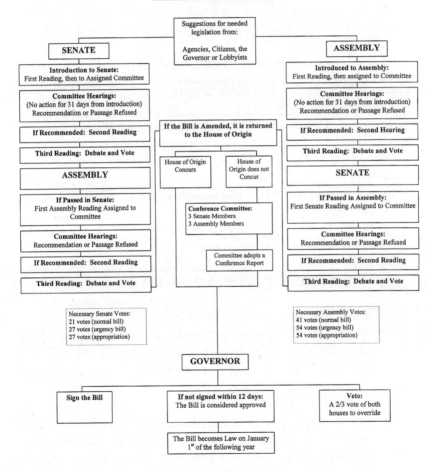

The California Senate

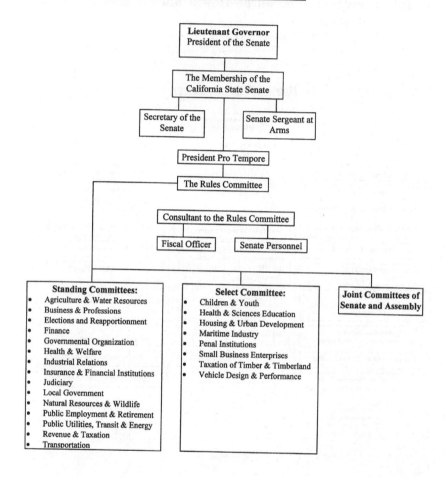

Lieutenant Governor
President of the Senate

The Membership of the
California State Senate

Secretary of the
Senate

Senate Sergeant at
Arms

President Pro Tempore

The Rules Committee

Consultant to the Rules Committee

Fiscal Officer

Senate Personnel

Standing Committees:
- Agriculture & Water Resources
- Business & Professions
- Elections and Reapportionment
- Finance
- Governmental Organization
- Health & Welfare
- Industrial Relations
- Insurance & Financial Institutions
- Judiciary
- Local Government
- Natural Resources & Wildlife
- Public Employment & Retirement
- Public Utilities, Transit & Energy
- Revenue & Taxation
- Transportation

Select Committee:
- Children & Youth
- Health & Sciences Education
- Housing & Urban Development
- Maritime Industry
- Penal Institutions
- Small Business Enterprises
- Taxation of Timber & Timberland
- Vehicle Design & Performance

**Joint Committees of
Senate and Assembly**

The California Assembly

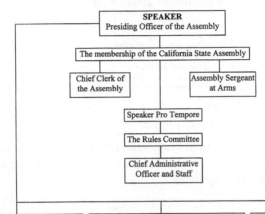

Standing Committees:
- Agriculture
- Criminal Justice
- Education
  - □ Permanent Subcommittee on Post Secondary Education
- Elections & Reapportionment
- Finance, Insurance & Commerce
- Governmental Organizations:
- Health:
  - □ Permanent Subcommittee on Health Personnel
  - □ Permanent Subcommittee on Mental Health & Develpmental Disabilities
- Housing & Community Development
- Intergovernmental Relations
- Judiciary
- Labor Relations:
  - □ Permanent Subcommittee on Industrial Safety
- Local Government
- Public Employees & Retirement
- Resources, Land Use & Energy
- Revenue & Taxation
- Transportation
  - □ Permanent Subcommittee on Air Quality
- Water
- Ways and Means

General Research Committee:
- Select Committee on Fire Services
- Select Committee on Health Sciences Education
- Select Committee on the Implementation of Career Education
- Select Committee on Revision of the Corporations Code
- Select Committee on Western States Forest Industries Task Force
- Special Subcommittee on California's Food and Agricultural Economy

Joint Committees of Senate and Assembly

The California Legislative Process

The following outline and organization provides a method for reviewing the legislative process.[3]

   a. An idea for legislation may originate with

   (1) a legislator

   (2) constituents or an organized group

   (3) the Governor or a state agency.

The Legislative Counsel's staff is available to assist a legislator in drafting legislation.

The bill may have only one subject.

   b. A bill (or resolution or constitutional amendment) is introduced by a legislator, assigned a number, its title read, and assigned to an appropriate standing committee.

Journal and History report introduction. The bill is printed. The digest of the bill is prepared by Legislative Counsel and is printed on the first page of the bill. The digest has been printed on the bill since 1963. Since 1967 the digest has been amended with each bill amendment.

Joint Rule 8.5 (from Handbook) provides that "No bill shall be introduced unless it . . . is accompanied by a digest, prepared and attached to the bill by the Legislative Counsel, showing the changes in the existing law which are proposed by the bill." In addition to providing a summary of the changes in existing law, the digest also contains the number of votes required to pass the bill and indicates if the bill contains an appropriation.

The following initials are used for convenience in referring to measures introduced:

Senate	Assembly	
SB	AB	(Bill)
SCA	ACA	(Constitutional amendment)
SCR	ACR	(Concurrent resolution)
SJR	AJR	(Joint resolution)
SR	HR	(House resolution)

[3] California Legislative Publications Charts, 3d ed. Revised by Richard H. Nicoles and Mary E. Schell. GPS Publication 3. Sacramento: California State Library, 1976. Grateful acknowledgment is expressed to the compilers for the use of the legislative procedure outline, legislative organizational charts, and bibliographic data used in this publication.

Joint resolutions relate to matters connected with the federal government. They are usually used to express approval or disapproval of the Legislature of legislation pending or proposed in Congress.

Concurrent resolutions relate to matters to be treated by both houses of the Legislature. Concurrent resolutions are used to approve amendments to city or county charters, create joint committees, adopt joint rules, and to memorialize the death of a member of the Legislature or other prominent person.

A house resolution (SR or HR) relates to the business of one house only. House resolutions usually request a committee of the house to study a specific problem, amend the house rules, or create interim committees.

SRs and HRs are not printed separately but are printed only in the Journal of the house of origin. Histories give page references to Journal.

In the Assembly the speaker assigns a bill to a legislative committee by the end of the second legislative day following the bill's introduction. In the Senate the bills are assigned by the Rules Committee at the time of their introduction. After committee assignment 2,000 copies of each new bill are printed. The digest is printed at the bottom of the first page of the bill.

c. The Committee schedules the bill for hearing. No bill may be heard until 30 days have elapsed after its introduction unless the house waives the 30-day waiting period by a three-quarters vote.

The *Daily File* contains a schedule of committee meetings with the dates the different bills are scheduled to be heard in committee. Publication in *Daily File* must occur at least four days in advance of a hearing by the first committee and two days in advance by subsequent committees of the same house.

d. The Committee holds hearing (open hearings). Hearings of standing committees are not usually published. There is no requirement that they be recorded.

e. The Committee votes on the bill and the committee chair reports committee recommendations to house, e.g.:

Do pass
Do pass, as amended
Be amended, and referred

The vote on the bill is by roll call. Roll call votes are recorded and published in appendix to the *Journal* of the house. The Committee recommendation is reported in the *Journal* and *History*.

The bill may be referred to another committee of the same house before going to the floor.

If a bill does not get the necessary votes to pass it out of committee and reconsideration is not granted within 15 days, it is returned to the Chief Clerk of the Assembly or the Secretary of the Senate, depending upon its origin, and may not be considered further during the session.

The action is noted in *History* and *Journal.*

There are two deadlines for bills to be acted upon. If a bill has not cleared the house of origin by January 30 of the second year of the biennial session, it may no longer be acted upon and is filed with the Chief Clerk of the Assembly or the Secretary of the Senate. At the end of the second year, following adjournment on November 30, all bills remaining in committee are returned to the Clerk or Secretary.

f. If the bill has been reported from the committee without amendment, it is read a second time.

The *Daily File* contains a list of bills on second reading file. *Journal* and *History* report the second reading. If the bill has been reported out of committee with amendments, and these amendments, or amendments offered from the floor, have been adopted on second reading, the bill is reprinted.

Bills reprinted following amendment show such amendments by the use of strikeout type for matter omitted and italic type for new matter.

In the Assembly, a bill amended on second reading is returned to the second reading file.

Each time the bill is amended, it is reprinted and after each reprinting if the amendments were adopted in the house of origin, it is re-engrossed (see step g). The Legislative Counsel's digest of the bill, printed on the first page of bill, is revised to reflect changes resulting from amendments. This is required by Joint Rule 26.5.

g. After the second reading, a bill is then sent to the engrossing and enrolling clerk who compares the printed bill with the original bill to detect and correct any discrepancies. This comparison of the original and printed bills is called "engrossing."

h. After engrossing, the bill goes on the third reading file. The *Daily File* includes list of bills on third reading file.

i. At the third reading, arguments for and against the measure are presented and a roll call vote is taken. No bill may be considered or acted upon on the floor of the Assembly unless and until a copy of the printed bill as introduced, a printed copy of each amended form of the bill and an analysis of the bill by the Office of Research have been placed upon the desks of the members. (Cal. Const. art. IV, § 8(b); Assembly Rules 64, 68.6)

Bills on third reading may be amended by motion from the floor, and if the motion to amend carries by a majority vote of those present, the bill is sent out to reprint, re-engrossment, and returned to the third reading file.

The Assembly Rules provide in part as follows:

No amendments to a bill offered from the floor, except committee amendments reported with bills, amendments offered with a motion to amend and re-refer a bill to committee, amendments deleting any number of words, amendments adding a total of not more than 25 words, or amendments previously printed in the Journal shall be in order unless and until a copy of the proposed amendments has been placed upon the desks of the members. If a copy of amendments adding a total of 25 words or less is not placed on the desks of the members it shall be made available to the author of the bill, and the amendments shall be read in their entirety by the Chief Clerk prior to debate.

Amendments offered from the floor during a bill's second or third reading shall be prepared by, or approved as to form by, the Legislative Counsel.

Before debate five copies of the proposed amendment to Assembly bills, and five copies of the proposed amendment to Senate bills, must be delivered to the Chief Clerk's desk.

Amendments from the floor during a bill's third reading that would make a substantive change in the bill shall have an analysis prepared by the committee of origin in conjunction with the Assembly Floor Analysis Unit and a copy of that analysis shall be distributed to each member's desk prior to the beginning of debate on adoption of the proposed amendment, unless otherwise ordered by the Speaker. (Assembly Rule 69)

After all debate on the bill has been concluded, a vote is taken by roll call, and the bill is either passed or refused passage. It requires a majority vote of the membership of the Assembly (41 votes) to pass most bills. Certain measures, i.e., urgency bills, bills appropriating money from the General Fund (except money for the public schools), and Constitutional Amendments must receive a two-thirds vote (54 votes). (Cal. Const. art. IV, § 8(d), 12(d), and art. XVIII, § 1)

In the Senate, the vote required is proportionately the same—21 affirmative votes are required to pass most bills, and 27 affirmative votes are necessary to pass the others.

Debates are not published by the State. *Journals* are only a record of proceedings. The Sacramento Union beginning in the late 1850s and continuing for a number of years published debates in its pages. These are not indexed, but by consulting the official records, one can determine on what date a matter was considered and consult the Union for the following day.

Number of affirmative votes required for passage:

Ordinary Bill—Majority Needed
Senate 21 of 40 members
Assembly 41 of 80 members

Urgency Measure or Constitutional Amendment two-thirds vote required:

Senate 27 of 40 members
Assembly 54 of 80 members

The Journals record the vote.

Bills to which no opposition has been expressed may be placed, at the request of the author, upon what is called the consent calendar, and are voted upon without debate.

Daily File contains list of bills on consent calendar. Joint Rules 22.1–22.3 govern the Consent Calendar. To be placed on the calendar a bill must meet these requirements:

(1) It is not a revenue measure or one upon which the waiting period has been waived.

(2) The bill must receive a "do pass" or a "do pass, as amended" recommendation by a unanimous vote of the committee members present.

(3) The bill, in its final version as approved by the committee, cannot have had any opposition expressed to it by anyone present at the committee meeting.

(4) Author of bill must request that the bill be placed on the Consent Calendar.

The bill may be reported out of committee with the recommendation that it be placed on the consent calendar. The bill is read a second time and placed on the calendar. It may not be considered for adoption until the second legislative day following the day of its placement on the calendar.

Should any member object to the bill it is returned to the second reading file. If it is amended from the floor it ceases to be a Consent Calendar bill. Where no objection is made the bill is read a third time and voted upon.

j. Upon passing the house of origin, a bill must then go to the other house where the same procedure is followed.

k. If the bill passes the second house, it is returned to the house of origin with a message that it has been passed.

The action is noted in the *Journal* and *History*.

If the bill has been amended in the second house, the house of origin must vote upon the amendment. If the amendment is approved, the bill is enrolled.

The bill is printed in enrolled form, without use of strike out or italic type and with blanks for signatures of the Secretary, the President of the Senate, the Chief Clerk, and the Speaker of the Assembly on the first page, and blanks for signatures of the Governor and Secretary of State on the last page. The digest is omitted.

If the amendment is not approved, each house appoints a conference committee. These committees meet jointly, discuss the bill, and file reports with both houses, embodying their recommendations.

If the conference committees cannot agree, then new committees are appointed, but not more than three conference committees may be appointed to deal with any one measure.

The bill is reprinted incorporating amendments agreed upon by the conference committee, and if approved by both houses, is printed as enrolled bill. After a bill has passed both houses it is returned to the house of origin for enrollment. Enrollment is the final legislative action taken on a bill by the house of origin, confirming that the bill passed both houses in the identical form. The enrolled bill, which is printed without any amendment symbols, is signed by the Secretary of the Senate and the Chief Clerk of the Assembly then sent to the Governor for his approval or veto.

l. The enrolled bill is sent to the Governor. Joint and concurrent resolutions and constitutional amendments do not require the Governor's signature but go directly to the Secretary of State.

m. The Governor, after receiving a bill, has twelve days in which to sign or veto it. If he or she fails to act within twelve days the measure becomes a law without his or her signature, except that bills passed before September 1 in the second year of the biennium and in his or her possession on or after September 1 must be signed or vetoed by September 30 of that year or they become a law without his or her signature. If vetoed, the bills must also be returned to the house of origin by the deadline, or the bill will become law.[4]

The Governor's action on bills is reported in:

(1) California. Governor. *Press Release.*

(2) California. Legislature. *History.*

Any bill passed by the Legislature at a special session which is in the Governor's possession on or after the adjournment of the session becomes a law unless the Governor vetoes the bill within twelve days by depositing the veto with the office of the Secretary of State.

The Legislature has sixty days to act upon the veto. A two-thirds vote of each house is required to override a Governor's veto. The Governor has privilege of item veto in considering appropriation measures, that is, he may delete or reduce the amount appropriated for a specific purpose.

If the Governor sends a veto message to the house of origin, it is printed in the Journal of that house.

n. After the Governor has signed a bill, he sends it to the Secretary of State, who gives it a number known as the chapter number. Bills are numbered consecutively in the order in which they are received.

Concurrent and joint resolutions and constitutional amendments are numbered consecutively upon receipt in a separate series of resolution chapters.

Laws are printed individually with chapter number in heading and called chapter laws.

Individual chapters are collected usually in multiples of one hundred, given covers, and stapled together.

The sets are entitled Bill Chapters or Resolution Chapters.

Finally, chapters are bound with an index and tables of code sections affected in volumes referred to as session laws or statutes.

o. A law goes into effect on the January first following a ninety-day period from the date of enactment of the statute. A statute enacted at a special session goes into effect on the 91st day after adjournment of the special session at which the bill was passed. Laws calling

---

[4] In 1994 nine bills, which Governor Pete Wilson thought he had vetoed, were not returned by his staff to the houses of origin by the deadline. Although Governor Wilson had already announced that he had killed the bills, all nine of them became law because of the staff mistake. *See* Daniel M. Weintraub, *Waylaid Veto Plans Result in 9 New Laws.* Los Angeles Times, Oct. 5, 1994, section A, page 1, col. 3.

elections, providing for tax levies or appropriations for the usual current expenses of the State, and containing urgency measures go into effect immediately.

p. Below are two sources of charts of California's legislative process.

(1) Roster and Government Guide. Sacramento: California Journal. Includes an illustrated chart on the California legislative process.

(2) California Legislative Publications Charts. 3d ed. Revised by Richard H. Nicoles and Mary E. Schell. GPS Publication 3. Sacramento: California State Library, 1976.

[e] Legislative Intent Cases

California courts frequently consider bills and legislative action thereon in determining legislative intent. A selected list of cases follows:

EXAMPLE

People v. Sterling Refining Co., 86 Cal.App. 558, 261 P. 1080 (Ct.App. 1927)

In re Zadro, 16 Cal.App.2d 398, 60 P.2d 577 (Ct.App. 1936)

Consolidated Rock Products Co. v. State of California, 57 Cal.App.2d 959, 135 P.2d 699 (Ct.App. 1943)

Nutter v. City of Santa Monica, 74 Cal.App.2d 292, 168 P.2d 741 (Ct.App. 1946)

People v. Knowles, 35 Cal.2d 175, 217 P.2d 1 (Cal. 1950)

People v. Brown, 55 Cal.2d 64, 357 P.2d 1072 (Cal. 1960)

Burks v. Poppy Construction Co., 57 Cal.2d 463, 370 P.2d 313 (Cal. 1962)

Di Genova v. State Bd. of Education, 57 Cal.2d 167, 367 P.2d 865 (Cal. 1962)

Don Wilson Builders v. Superior Court of Los Angeles, 220 Cal.App.2d 77, 33 Cal.Rptr. 621 (Ct.App. 1963)

Griffin v. Board of Supervisors of the County of Monterey, 60 Cal.2d 318, 384 P.2d 421 (Cal. 1963)

Rich v. State Board of Optometry, 325 Cal.App.2d 591, 45 Cal.Rptr. 512 (Cal. 1965)

Sanders v. County of Yuba, 247 Cal.App.2d 748, 55 Cal.Rptr. 852 (Ct.App. 1967)

Benor v. Board of Medical Examiners, 8 Cal.App.3d 542, 87 Cal.Rptr. 415 (Ct.App. 1970)

Estate of Wanamaker, 65 Cal.App.3d 587, 135 Cal.Rptr. 333 (Ct.App. 1977)

State Farm Mutual Auto Insurance Co. v. Haight, 205 Cal.App.3d 223, 252 Cal.Rptr. 162 (Ct.App. 1988)

People v. Quattrone, 211 Cal.App.3d 1389, 260 Cal.Rptr. 44 (Ct.App. 1989)

Wiley v. So. Pacific Trans. Co., 220 Cal.App.3d 177, 269 Cal.Rptr. 240 (Ct.App. 1990)

Adoption of Kelsey S., 1 Cal.4th 816, 826, 4 Cal. Rptr. 2d 615, 823 P.2d 1216 (1992)

City of San Jose v. Superior Court, 5 Cal.4th 47, 54, 19 Cal. Rptr. 2d 73, 850 P.2d 621 (1993)

Torres v. Automobile Club of So. California, 15 Cal.4th 771, 779, 63 Cal. Rptr. 2d 859, 937 P.2d 290 (1997)

Bank of America v. Lallana, 19 Cal.4th 203, 212, 77 Cal. Rptr. 2d 910, 960 P.2d 1133 (1998)

California Teachers Assn. v. State of California, 20 Cal.4th 327, 341, 84 Cal. Rptr. 2d 425, 975 P.2d 622 (1999)

StorMedia Inc. v. Superior Court, 20 Cal.4th 449, 459–460, 84 Cal. Rptr. 2d 843, 976 P.2d 214 (1999)

[f]   Where Texts of Bills Are Available[5]

 Legislature Bill Service, Legislative Bill Room. Legislative Bill Room distributes all legislative publications.

Free copies of legislative publications may be obtained under Rule 13 of the Temporary Joint Rules of the Senate and Assembly. Rule 13 states in part that with certain exceptions within state government, "No more than one copy of any bill or other legislative publication, nor more than a total of 100 bills or other legislative publications during a session, shall be distributed free to any person, office, or organization." Current stock is maintained by the Bill Room for one year.

---

[5] *See* Appendix A for the publishers/vendors listing.

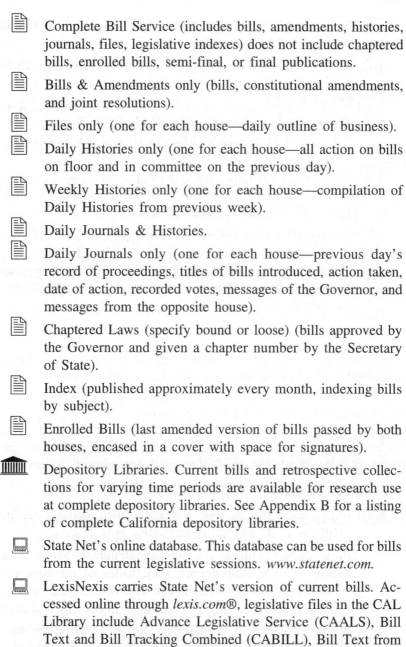

Complete Bill Service (includes bills, amendments, histories, journals, files, legislative indexes) does not include chaptered bills, enrolled bills, semi-final, or final publications.

Bills & Amendments only (bills, constitutional amendments, and joint resolutions).

Files only (one for each house—daily outline of business).

Daily Histories only (one for each house—all action on bills on floor and in committee on the previous day).

Weekly Histories only (one for each house—compilation of Daily Histories from previous week).

Daily Journals & Histories.

Daily Journals only (one for each house—previous day's record of proceedings, titles of bills introduced, action taken, date of action, recorded votes, messages of the Governor, and messages from the opposite house).

Chaptered Laws (specify bound or loose) (bills approved by the Governor and given a chapter number by the Secretary of State).

Index (published approximately every month, indexing bills by subject).

Enrolled Bills (last amended version of bills passed by both houses, encased in a cover with space for signatures).

Depository Libraries. Current bills and retrospective collections for varying time periods are available for research use at complete depository libraries. See Appendix B for a listing of complete California depository libraries.

State Net's online database. This database can be used for bills from the current legislative sessions. *www.statenet.com.*

LexisNexis carries State Net's version of current bills. Accessed online through *lexis.com*®, legislative files in the CAL Library include Advance Legislative Service (CAALS), Bill Text and Bill Tracking Combined (CABILL), Bill Text from the Current Legislative Session (CATEXT), Bill Tracking for the Current Legislative Session (CATRCK), Legislative Committee Analysis of Pending Bills (CACOMM), and Statutes Archive (CAARCH).

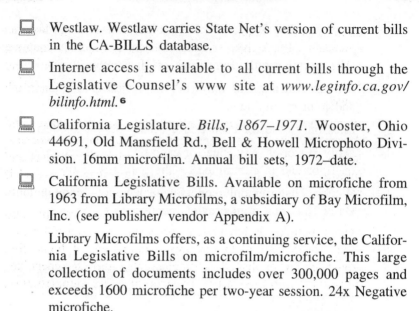

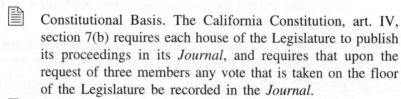

Westlaw. Westlaw carries State Net's version of current bills in the CA-BILLS database.

Internet access is available to all current bills through the Legislative Counsel's www site at *www.leginfo.ca.gov/bilinfo.html.* [6]

California Legislature. *Bills, 1867–1971.* Wooster, Ohio 44691, Old Mansfield Rd., Bell & Howell Microphoto Division. 16mm microfilm. Annual bill sets, 1972–date.

California Legislative Bills. Available on microfiche from 1963 from Library Microfilms, a subsidiary of Bay Microfilm, Inc. (see publisher/ vendor Appendix A).

Library Microfilms offers, as a continuing service, the California Legislative Bills on microfilm/microfiche. This large collection of documents includes over 300,000 pages and exceeds 1600 microfiche per two-year session. 24x Negative microfiche.

[2] Chapter Laws

Chapter Laws (slip laws loose or stapled in groups of 100) are available by subscription from the Legislative Bill Room in the State Capitol. These are the final version of the bills as passed by the Legislature and approved by the Governor with the chapter number assigned by the Secretary of State added. Although many libraries may not have the slip laws, most libraries do have the chapter laws in a bound, annual compilation, the Statutes and Amendments to the Code.

[3] Daily Journals

Constitutional Basis. The California Constitution, art. IV, section 7(b) requires each house of the Legislature to publish its proceedings in its *Journal,* and requires that upon the request of three members any vote that is taken on the floor of the Legislature be recorded in the *Journal.*

Content. The *Daily Journals* contains an accurate account of the proceedings of each house (not a verbatim report of debates), the titles of all measures introduced, considered, or acted upon by the house, the full text of all amendments to any such measures, the text of all house resolutions, roll calls

---

[6] *See* Chapter 15 for more information on www access.

upon all actions requiring a recorded vote, messages from the Governor and the other house, committee reports, motions, acknowledgment of the receipt of all communications, and such other matters as properly come before the respective houses.

In addition, the *Journals* include rules of the Senate and Assembly, lists of press representatives, legislative advocates, letters of transmittal of reports of executive departments and interim committees, and Opinions of Legislative Counsel if printing is requested by the legislator who sought the opinion.

The bound versions of the *Journals* for the Assembly and Senate include an alphabetical subject index and a bill action index. Registration and expense statements of legislative advocates are published in supplements. *Journal* appendixes contained administrative reports of state departments, 1881–1943.

Joint Interim Committee Reports and Senate Committee Reports appeared in *Senate Journal* appendixes, 1947–1970, and Assembly Committee Reports appeared in *Assembly Journal* appendixes, 1957–1970.

 Volumes of the *Journals* are available for sale from the Legislative Bill Room. The *Journals* for the regular sessions are printed with black ink. The *Journals* for the extraordinary sessions are printed in colored ink or on colored paper.[7]

 California Senate and Assembly Daily Journals. Library Microfilms (subsidiary of Bay Microfilm) (see Appendix A, Publishers/Vendors). Available from 1912–present in 4 × 6 negative microfiche.

 Daily Journals are available on the web at *www.leginfo.ca.gov.* They may also be found by going through the government link on the State of California web page (*www.ca.gov*) or by going to the new California Legislative Portal Website, *www.legislature.ca.gov.*

 Legislative Intent Cases. California Courts have referred to legislative journals when considering legislative intent problems. A selected list of cases follows:

---

[7] The January 1995 extraordinary session began with the use of blue paper for the journals.

EXAMPLE

Consolidated Rock Products Co. v. State of California, 57 Cal.App.2d 959, 135 P.2d 699 (Ct.App. 1943)

Hise v. McColgan, 24 Cal.2d 147, 148 P.2d 616 (Cal. 1944)

People v. Santa Fe Federal Savings and Loan Ass'n., 28 Cal.2d 675, 171 P.2d 713 (Cal. 1946)

Pearson v. State Social Welfare Board, 54 Cal.2d 184, 353 P.2d 33 (Cal. 1960)

Bethlehem Pacific Coast Steel Corp. v. Franchise Tax Board, 203 Cal.App.2d 458, 21 Cal.Rptr. 707 (Ct.App. 1962)

County of Los Angeles v. State, 43 Cal.3d 46, 233 Cal.Rptr. 38 (Cal. 1987)

City of Berkeley v. Superior Court, 26 Cal.3d 515, 530, fn. 15, 162 Cal. Rptr. 327, 606 P.2d 362 (1999)

Delaney v. Baker, 20 Cal.4th 23, 33–34, 82 Cal. Rptr. 2d 610, 971 P.2d 986 (1999)

[4] Daily File

[a] Content and Purpose

The *File* is printed daily during the legislative session. It includes the titles of all measures which have been reported out of committee and which are to be considered by the Assembly or the Senate, as well as motions to reconsider, notices of intention to withdraw a bill from committee, and concurrences in amendments of the other house that are pending. Items are printed according to order of business, numbered consecutively, and considered in this order unless special permission be granted to take up an item out of order, or to pass an item on file.

The *File* also contains a table or listing of all bills and constitutional amendments with their dates of introduction and the thirty-first day thereafter, in order to facilitate compliance with the provisions of the Constitution, and a list of any bills upon which the thirty-day waiting period may have been dispensed with. The *Assembly File* shows all bills which have been scheduled for hearing in committees, in order to provide the public with advance notice of what bills will be heard. (Assembly Rule 56.)

[b] Subscription Service

The *Daily File* is available by subscription from the Legislative Bill Room (see publisher/vendor list in Appendix A).

📄 California State Assembly File Analysis, 1975–1988 & Continuing. Library Microfilms (subsidiary of Bay Microfilm) (see Appendix A, Publishers/Vendors). Available 1975–date in 4 × 6 negative microfiche, microfilmed at 24x reduction.

🖥 The Daily Files of the Senate and Assembly are available on the Leginfo webpage at: *http://www.leginfo.ca.gov/dayfile.html*.

[5] Committee Reports and Committee Analyses

[a] Sources

There are no published transcripts of the deliberations of Standing Committees in California. A few Standing Committee reports are published in the Journals and indexed there.

Joint Interim Committee Reports and Senate Committee Reports appeared in *Senate Journal* Appendixes, 1947–1970. *Assembly Journal* Appendixes carried Assembly Committee Reports, 1957–1970.

The text of the *Senate Journal* included committee reports through 1946 and the text of the *Assembly Journal* carried committee reports through 1956. *West's Annotated California Codes* since 1955 includes references to the committee reports published in the legislative journal appendixes.

Examples of committees that perform research and analyze bills are the Senate and Assembly Judiciary Committees. Both of these committees review and analyze hundreds of bills each session, evaluating the bills for their effect on judicial workloads and existing laws and procedures. The analysis is usually prepared just prior to the committee hearing on the bill.

Also, since the mid 1960s, legislative committees have generated analyses of each bill heard. These are available at the State Archives or from the committee itself.

[b] Access to Older Committee Records and Reports

📄 California. Legislature. *Legislative Committee Reports, list of special committees and commissions, 1850–1936, by legislative session.* Berkeley, University of California. Library Documents Department. (Thesis by Christian L. Larsen, appendix.)

 California. Legislature. Joint Budget Committee. *California Legislative Committees and Reports, 1937–1947.* Sacramento. Information relating to each committee includes:

(1) Resolution number providing its legal authority.

(2) Number of members and the chairman.

(3) Statement of scope of committee's activities.

(4) Appropriations made available to it.

(5) Listing of its printed reports.

An index of legislative committees lists each separate committee alphabetically according to its title or the name by which it was or is commonly called. There is also a subject index with cross references to other committees reporting on a given subject.

 California. University. Bureau of Public Administration. Standing and Interim Committees of the California Legislature. *Report Prepared for the California Citizens Legislative Advisory Commission.* Berkeley. Legislative practice is reviewed. Committee reports are covered on pp. 65–66, 85–87.

 Some legislative committees preserve letters, reports, and communications of various types from proponents and opponents of legislative measures and place these in the chairman's files. These may eventually be placed in the State Archives.

Committee records for the period 1850–1863 are relatively complete. From 1863–1963 there are few records. Since 1963 the situation has improved and the trend is toward complete placement of committee files in the State Archives.

 California. Legislature. Assembly. Rules Committee. Office of Research. *Hearings and reports of committees of the California Legislature* [years]: a summary and listing. Sacramento. 1961– publication suspended.

(Title adopted when interim committees were discontinued.)

Lists hearings and reports of Assembly, Assembly Select, Senate, Joint Committees. Hearings date, place, general subjects, availability of transcripts. Joint Committee reports were sometimes published in the appendices of the *Senate Journal*.

 California. State Library. *California State Publications*. Sacramento. Monthly with annual cumulation. 1947–present.

Lists committee reports and hearings.

[c] Legislative Intent Cases

Court decisions citing legislative committee reports are not unusual. A selected list follows:

EXAMPLE

Story v. Richardson, 186 Cal. 162, 198 P. 1057 (Cal. 1921)

Koenig v. Johnson, 71 Cal.App.2d 739, 163 P.2d 746 (Ct.App. 1945)

People v. Perkins, 37 Cal.2d 62, 230 P.2d 353 (Cal. 1951)

People v. Brown, 55 Cal.2d 64, 357 P.2d 1072 (Cal. 1960)

Di Genova v. State Board of Education, 57 Cal.2d 167, 367 P.2d 865 (Cal. 1962)

Griffin v. Board of Supervisors of the County of Monterey, 60 Cal.2d 318, 384 P.2d 421 (Cal. 1963)

In re Sheridan, 230 Cal.App.2d 365, 40 Cal.Rptr. 894 (Ct.App. 1964)

Hope v. Contractors State License Board, 228 Cal.App.2d 414, 39 Cal.Rptr.514 (Ct.App. 1964)

Mancini v. Superior Court of Los Angeles, 230 Cal.App.2d 547, 41 Cal.Rptr. 213 (Ct.App. 1964)

People v. Altois, 60 Cal.2d 698, 36 Cal.Rptr. 443 (Cal. 1964)

City of Palo Alto v. Industrial Accident Commission, 232 Cal.App.2d 305, 42 Cal.Rptr. 822 (Ct.App. 1965)

Ne Casek v. City of Los Angeles, 233 Cal.App.2d 131, 43 Cal.Rptr. 294 (Ct.App. 1965)

People v. Arthur Murray Inc., 238 Cal.App.2d 333, 47 Cal.Rptr. 700 (Ct.App. 1965)

People v. Smith, 248 Cal.App.2d 134, 56 Cal.Rptr. 258 (Ct.App. 1967)

Maben v. Superior Court, 255 Cal.App.2d 708, 63 Cal.Rptr. 439 (Ct.App. 1967)

Riebe v. Budget Financial Corp., 264 Cal.App.2d 576, 70 Cal.Rptr. 654 (Ct.App.1968)

People v. Tanner, 24 Cal.3d 514, 156 Cal.Rptr. 450 (Cal. 1979)

Milligan v. City of Laguna Beach, 34 Cal.3d 829, 196 Cal.Rptr. 38 (Cal. 1983)

Hutnick v. U.S. Fidelity and Guaranty Co., 47 Cal.3d 456, 253 Cal.Rptr. 236 (Cal. 1988)

Pacific Bell v. California State Consumer Services Agency, 225 Cal. App. 3d 107, 116, 275 Cal. Rptr. 62 (1990, 2st Dist, Div 3)

Central Pathology Service Medical Clinic v. Superior Court of Los Angeles, 3 Cal.4th 181, 10 Cal.Rptr.2d 208 (Cal. 1992)

National R.V., Inc. v. Foreman, 34 Cal. App.4th 1072, 1083, 40 Cal. Rptr. 2d 672 (1995)

People v. Ledesma, 16 Cal.4th 90, 98, 100, 65 Cal. Rptr. 2d 610, 939 P.2d 1310 (1997)

[6] Legislative Records

[a] Senate Office of Research *http://www.sen.ca.gov/sor/*

a. Prepares analyses of ballot propositions. See, for example: Senate Publication No. 643-S, "Analysis of November 1992 Ballot Propositions" (Analysis). *Californians for Political Reform Foundation v. Fair Political Practices Com.,* 61 Cal. App. 4th 472, 71 Cal. Rptr. 2d 606 (1998)

b. Prepares research papers on topics important to legislature. See *California Senate Office of Research, Drug-Exposed Infants—Summary of Related Legislation. In re Troy D.,* 215 Cal. App. 3d 889, 263 Cal. Rptr. 869 (1989) and "Seclusion and Restraints: A Failure, Not a Treatment," by Laurel Mildred. (An expose of the mistreatment of the mentally ill.) Cited in: Patient deaths propel Senate panel hearings. *The San Francisco Chronicle,* March 21, 2002, Thursday, p. A20

c. Performs surveys to compile statistics for the Senate. See: A Senate Office of Research survey of a random sample of 113 day care operators, comprised of 80 family day care homes and 33 day care centers. *California Federation of Family Day Care Ass'ns v. Mission Ins. Co.,* 174 Cal. App. 3d 502, 219 Cal. Rptr. 788 (1985).

[b] Assembly Office of Research (AOR)

This office was established in 1967 and died in the early 1990s. The office prepared an analysis of each bill before the Assembly voted on it. The summaries of the bills and the analysis (since 1975) are preserved on microfiche in the State Law Library. Although the California Research Bureau, which serves the entire legislature and the executive branch as well, was not created to replace the Assembly Office of Research, it appears that the new Bureau, which came into being in the early 1990s, has assumed a lot of the research and evaluation responsibilities of the earlier AOR.

📖   *AOR Reporter.* v. 1–? (1975–?). California. Legislature. Assembly. Office of Research. Sacramento. This publication is designed to present Members of the Assembly and staff with articles on current issues before the Legislature, and a summary of some of AOR's ongoing public policy research projects and short-term informational requests on subjects of general interest.

[c] California Research Bureau (CRB)

The CRB is a department of the California State Library. It is staffed by researchers, writers, and librarians who provide support to the state's executive and legislative branches. The staffers write reports and memoranda at the request of the officials or legislators. The resulting publications might be either private or available to the public. The public reports back to 1991 are available on the CRB website: *http:// www.library.ca.gov/html/statseg2a.cfm.* In addition to being based in the California State Library, the Bureau also has a Capitol building office staffed with librarians familiar with current policy issues.

[7] Hearings

    California. Legislature. *Assembly & Senate Committees. Hearings.* Transcripts. Ordinarily, transcripts are published only for investigative hearings and not for bill-hearing sessions.

Assembly Committees: Assembly Publications Office, Sacramento.

Joint Committees: If Chairman is from Assembly, inquire of Assembly Publications.

Senate Committees: Inquire of individual committee.

Hearings are not held on all bills. When they are held, no transcript may be made, or if made, it may be held for office use only.

The Legislature has failed to provide for regular distribution of hearing transcripts to Law Library Depositories throughout the state. It is therefore usually necessary for interested persons to write directly to committee chairmen requesting the transcripts they need. The notice of hearings appearing in the file may be used to determine the subject, date, and place of legislative hearings.

Despite the fact that the Legislature fails to provide for distribution of hearings to depositories which would select them, some law libraries make a true effort to acquire them for their patrons. The expense involved to libraries is far in excess of that which would be entailed in automatic depository distribution because of the search and ordering labor required.

Prior to 1935 few transcripts were published for release outside of the Legislature, and those that were produced usually became the property of the legislators. Few were placed in the State Archives. However, under the leadership of the State Archival personnel the collection is growing, though most of the transcripts are from the years 1945 forward.

 California. Legislature. Assembly and Senate Committees. Hearings. Videotapes. 1989–present. Since 1989–90 all floor sessions have been recorded and committee hearings have been recorded on request and on a rotating basis. The Senate tapes are stored in the State Archives. Researchers may also go to the Senate's web page to find current and past video and audio recordings of hearings: *http://www.senate.ca.gov/ ~newsen/audiotv/audiotv.htp.* (includes a link to the California Channel).The Assembly tapes are stored in the Assembly Office of TV.

An audio-only version of Assembly hearings is available through the Assembly's website: *http://www.assembly.ca.gov/ Committee_hearings/.* Many Senate and a few Assembly hearings may be viewed live on the California Channel. See: *http://www.calchannel.com/aboutus.htm.* This network has been broadcasting since 1991 and is available throughout the state on cable TV or by live webcast. Website users may also search the archives to retrieve and view webcasts of earlier recordings (predominantly Senate).

 California. Legislature. Assembly. Rules Committee. Office of Research. *Hearings and Reports of Committees of the California Legislature During 19____–19____: A listing.* Sacramento. This listing of hearings indicates the study hearings held by each committee. Hearings of standing committees that are scheduled regularly during a session to hear pending legislation are not included in this record. Available hearings may be ordered from the Assembly Publications Office.

 California. Legislature. Assembly Publications Office. Sacramento. This office provides a complete list of all reports and transcripts of hearings currently available for sale in an inventory-like document including description, stock number, unit price. It is suggested that documents not listed be requested directly from the issuing committee or office. When ordering, persons are advised to specify the title of the report or hearing, the city, date, stock number, quantity desired, and the address to which delivery should be made. Users may contact the office by calling (916) 319-3997.

[8] Author File

The legislator carrying a bill collects a file of background information, statements of proponents and opponents, memoranda, correspondence, floor and committee statements, and press releases. Courts do look to this documentation. This material, at the discretion of the author, may be publicly available in whole or part at the office of the author, the California State Archives, or any other institution chosen by the author as a depository for his or her legislative records.

Courts decisions citing authors' files for legislative intent are listed below:

Commodore Home Systems, Inc. v. Superior Court, 32 Cal.3d 211, 219, fn.9, 649 P.2d 912, 185 Cal. Rptr. 270 (1982)

Grupe Development Co. v. Superior Court, 4 Cal.4th 911, 924, fn.2, 844 P.2d 545; 1993 Cal. LEXIS 548; 16 Cal. Rptr. 2d 226 (1993)

Pacific Gas & Electric v. County of Stanislaus, 16 Cal.4th 1143, 947 P.2d 291, 69 Cal. Rptr. 2d 329 (1997)

[9]   Statements of the Bill Author

Lacking official documentation for determining the legislative intent of a state statute, researchers have sometimes resorted to the testimony of individual legislators. The results on the credibility of such evidence in the courts are mixed. Usually such testimony is excluded on the ground that the courts seek the intention of the Legislature as a body and not individual opinion or recollection. However, such testimony has been allowed where the legislator drafted the bill, *Estate of Simoni,* 220 Cal.App.2d 339, 33 Cal.Rptr. 845 (Ct.App. 1963), and as a confirmation of what transpired during committee hearings, *Rich v. State Board of Optometry,* 235 Cal.App.2d 591, 45 Cal.Rptr. 512 (Ct.App. 1965).

[10]   Histories

[a]   Content and Purpose

The *Daily History* shows the actions on all measures considered each day, with cumulative actions for each succeeding day until the end of the week.

At the close of each week, a *Weekly History* is published that contains the titles of all measures introduced during the session, together with all actions taken thereon and showing the dates upon which such actions were taken. Also included are lists of members of house with occupation, party, district, seat, office, telephone number, house mailing address, list of officers of house, seating chart, list of press-radio-TV representatives, standing committees, members, meeting days, list of bill numbers by authors; committee membership by name of legislator. The *Daily History* may be discarded when the following day's issue is received. Each *Weekly History* supersedes its preceding issue. A semi-final History was introduced in the 1973–1974 biennial session. The final edition was included in the *Final Calendar* from 1881–1972. The *Final Edition* is now published separately.

[b]   Subscription Service

The *Daily History* and *Weekly History* are available by subscription from the Legislative Bill Room (see listing of publishers/vendors in Appendix A).

[c] Detailed Contents and Arrangement

The *Assembly Weekly History* indicates all legislative action on all bills and resolutions to date of publication. Arrangement is by bill or resolution number, then by date action was taken on measure.

[11] Legislative Index

📖 *Legislative Index.* Compiled by Legislative Counsel. Available in the Legislative Bill Room in the State Capitol (see publisher/vendor appendix). Cumulative. Published periodically at approximately two-week intervals during the legislative session.

Subject Approach to Legislation

This *Index* indicates the subject of each bill, constitutional amendment and concurrent or joint resolution as introduced and as amended. Entries are not removed from the *Index* when subject matter is deleted from the measure in course of passage.

The *Index* also indicates the subject of each single house resolution as introduced. Single house resolutions are Indexed under "House Resolutions" or "Senate Resolutions."

Section Number Approach to Legislation

Part 2, Table of Sections Affected, is a table of sections of the Constitution, codes, and statutes other than codes affected by Bills and Constitutional Amendments.

[12] Final Calendar of Legislative Business, 1881–1972

History and index of all Senate and Assembly bills; Constitutional amendments; Concurrent, Joint, Senate, and House resolutions introduced; Table of Sections affected. Compiled under the direction of the Secretary of the Senate and the Chief Clerk of the Assembly. Sacramento, 95814, Legislative Bill Room (see publisher/vendor list in Appendix A).

Combination History and Index. Senate Final History, Senate general information; Assembly Final History, Assembly general information; subject matter index, table of sections affected.

The Assembly Final History contains the table entitled "Chapter Numbers of Assembly and Senate Bills."

[13] Governors' Messages and Vetoes

The documents coming out of the current governor's office are easy to locate on the governor's home page on the state's website: *http://www.governor.ca.gov/state/govsite/gov_homepage.jsp.* Some documents from the past administration may still be found on the current governor's page by going to the bottom of the specific page (press releases, proclamations, public notices, or executive orders) to the link for "previous administrations." Both the State Archives and the State Library are working on solutions to the problem of electronic documents and web pages being lost as administrations change.

[a] Journal Coverage

Governors' messages are printed in the Journals. The address to the Joint Convention appears in the Assembly Journal. Veto messages are published in the *Journal* of the house of origin of the bill vetoed.

[b] Archival Coverage

Governor. Chaptered Bill File. 1943–present. This is an arrangement of bill chapters by legislative session in separate file units. The content is listed on the file folder cover and usually includes a copy of the bill as finally passed, a statement by the author of the bill as to the background and legislative intent, analysis by the Legislative Counsel and the Attorney General on the constitutionality of the proposed law and its effect on the then existing laws, and a summary and analysis by the Governor's Legislative Secretary with a recommendation for approval or veto. Additional data such as letters from interested parties supporting or opposing the legislation may also be included. Bill reports by the Attorney General to the Governor are confidential. State agency analyses may also be included.

[c] Vetoes

In the Senate and Assembly Journal subject index, look under the name of the Governor and find "Veto Messages" or "Messages-Vetoing" for page references. If the bill number is known, look in the bill action index for references to the message and legislative action taken thereon. There may also be an index listing "Veto by Governor."

Pocket Vetoes, eliminated by constitutional amendment in 1966, are listed in the Final Calendar of Legislative Business, 1881–1965, under

"Senate Bills—Not Approved by Governor" (Pocket Vetoed) and "Assembly Bills—Pocket Vetoed by Governor."

Veto messages appear in the *Daily File* of the house to which the legislation was returned.

The State Archives maintains a separate file of Vetoed Measures.

State Net, the Legislative Counsel, and the Senate include veto and signing messages in their legislative tracking services.

[d] Proclamations

Proclamations are issued in press release form. When suggested by legislative resolution they may be found in the Journals.

[e] Acts of Executive Clemency

Acts of Executive Clemency also appear in the Journals. Other governor's messages appearing in the Journals include calls for special sessions of the Legislature, inaugural, annual, and special messages, appointments subject to legislative approval.

[f] Governors' Press Releases

Governors' Press Releases often provide the quickest means for determining the meaning or purpose of bills signed into law or vetoed.[8] Governor's press releases are available in the "Press Room" at the Governor's website for the current governor only: *www.governor.ca.gov.*

§ 4.03 Agencies, Departments, Commissions, and Other Organizations Related to the Legislative Process

[1] Key Legislative Analysis

[a] Overview

All of the organizations listed below have ties to California's legislative process. They may analyze legislation, propose legislation, or write opinions about legislation. Some are described at length in a thorough, though now out-of-date study, *Guidelines for Determining the Impact of Legislation on the Courts*, Ralph Andersen & Associates. Sacramento, 1974. 100 p. Chapter III, Current Efforts in Analyzing Court-Related Legislation, describes agencies and organizations analyzing legislation.

---

[8] *But see* footnote 4, in this chapter (governor's announcement of vetoed bills incorrect because bills not returned to Legislature by deadline).

Additional and more current information on these organizations may be found in books listed in Appendix E, California Government Texts, and Appendix L, Legal/Governmental Directories and Almanacs.

[b] Department of Justice[9]

The Attorney General is the head of the Department of Justice. The department regularly reviews all legislation in order to identify any which might relate to its duties or to substantive areas of law in which the department may be involved. The department has a legislative liaison, who pursues any necessary action with the legislature.

[c] Legislative Counsel

The Legislative Counsel is involved in drafting legislation for legislators as well as drafting initiative measures for citizens. The Legislative Counsel is also the primary legal advisor to the Legislature, with responsibility to advise legislators on the legality of proposed laws. The Legislative Counsel prepares a digest for all bills, describing the present state of the law and the changes that would occur if the bill were to pass.

  Legislative Intent Materials: Legislative Counsel.

California. Legislative Counsel. Opinions.[10]

The Opinions are cited in Deering's Codes. Publication of the Opinions in the Journals began in 1927. A variety of index approaches may be required as they are found under entries for subject matter, under the name of the incumbent Legislative Counsel.

Opinions are printed in the Assembly Journal when released by the legislator requesting the opinion. A list of them is included in the Assembly Final History but this may not be complete as the Opinions in Appendixes and Supplements are sometimes ignored.

---

[9] *See also* Chapter 11, Attorney General.

[10] There is a good explanation of the Opinions in the Questions and Answers section of 16 (4) Legal Reference Services Quarterly 81–83. The authors are Laura Cadra and Amy Atchison. The Office of Legislative Counsel is the bill-drafting agency for state government and issues confidential opinions that are not released to the public unless such action is approved by the legislator or committee requesting the opinion. Opinions often appear in the legislative journals and committee reports.

The courts have also considered Legislative Counsel's opinions and digests of bills as evidenced by the following cases.

EXAMPLE

People v. Knowles, 35 Cal.2d 175, 217 P.2d 1 (Cal. 1950)

Yorty v. Anderson, 60 Cal.2d 312, 384 P.2d 417 (Cal. 1963)

Warne v. Harkness, 60 Cal.2d 579, 387 P.2d 377 (Cal. 1963)

Patton v. La Bree, 60 Cal.2d 606, 387 P.2d 398 (Cal. 1963)

Maben v. Superior Court of Los Angeles, 255 Cal.App.2d 708, 713, 63 Cal.Rptr. 439 (Ct.App. 1967)

Rockwell v. Superior Court of Ventura County, 18 Cal.3d 420, 443, 134 Cal.Rptr. 650 (Cal. 1976)

Southland Mechanical Constructors v. Nixen, 119 Cal.App.3d 417, 173 Cal.Rptr. 917 (Ct.App. 1981)

Zipton v. W.C.A.B., 218 Cal. App. 3d 980, 988, 267 Cal. Rptr. 431 (1990, 1st Dist, Div 3)

Five v. Chaffey Joint Union High School District, 225 Cal.App.3d 1548, 1555, 276 Cal.Rptr. 14 (Ct.App. 1990)

People v. Turner, 40 Cal. App.4th 733, 741, 47 Cal. Rptr. 2d 42 (1995, 2nd Dist, Div 5)

North Hollywood Project Area Com. v. City of Los Angeles, 61 Cal. App.4th 719, 724, 71 Cal. Rptr. 2d 675 (1998, 2nd Dist, Div 2)

[d]   Judicial Council[11]

The Judicial Council is the primary administrative agency for the California judicial system. Its main responsibility is to improve the administration of justice. The agency adopts rules for court administration practice and procedure. In addition, the agency may perform other tasks as requested by the Legislature. The Administrative Office of the Courts executes Judicial Council policies. The Office monitors legislation of interest to the courts, advises legislators, and prepares reports for the legislature.

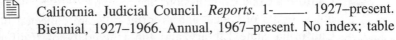 California. Judicial Council. *Reports.* 1-____. 1927–present. Biennial, 1927–1966. Annual, 1967–present. No index; table of contents.

---

[11] *See also* Chapter 7, Judicial Administration.

Recommendations are indexed in the California State Law Library Guide to Legislative History 1963–present. They are not cited in the annotated codes.

Cases referring to Judicial Council reports in legislative intent issues are:

EXAMPLE

Hohreiter v. Garrison, 81 Cal.App.2d 384, 184 P.2d 323 (Ct.App. 1947)

Reimel v. Alcoholic Beverage Control Appeals Board, 254 Cal.App.2d 340, 62 Cal.Rptr. 54 (Ct.App. 1967)

[e]   Commission on Uniform State Laws

The National Conference of Commissioners on Uniform State Laws, established in New York in 1892, is supported by contributions from the fifty states and is comprised of Commissioners from each jurisdiction of the United States. Its objective is to secure uniformity in state law upon all subjects where uniformity is deemed desirable and practicable. The Conference website is: *http://www.law.upenn.edu/bll/ulc/ulc.htm.*

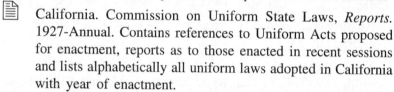

California. Commission on Uniform State Laws, *Reports.* 1927-Annual. Contains references to Uniform Acts proposed for enactment, reports as to those enacted in recent sessions and lists alphabetically all uniform laws adopted in California with year of enactment.

See *Senate Journal,* 1931, P.195; 1933, P.265; the reports for 1938/39, 1945/46, 1954/55 are published as individual documents.

Decisions of other states construing UCC and where they are compelling authority are accepted by the Court of Appeal. See *Needle v. Lasco Industries, Inc.,* 10 Cal.App.3d 1105, 89 Cal.Rptr. 593 (Ct.App. 1970)

[f]   Code Commission

California Code Commission. Sacramento. 1929–53. Reports, notes, drafts of codes, and preprint bills are collected in the California State Library and the University of California, Berkeley, Law Library. The State Library has a 76-volume set with a separate index to the contents of each volume. Code

Commissioners' notes to the practice codes are included in the annotated codes.

The drafts and "Proposed Codes" may yield some helpful data in legislative history problems although the commission did not intend to change the substance of the law in carrying out its codification task.

A selected list of California court cases which have referred to Code Commission and Law Revision Commission reports and notes follows.

EXAMPLE

Suydam v. Los Angeles Railway Co., 27 Cal.App.157, 149 P.55 (Ct.App. 1915)

In re Martinson, 87 Cal.App. 393, 262 P.477 (Ct.App. 1927)

People v. Valentine, 28 Cal.2d 121, 169 P.2d 1 (Cal. 1946)

Wemyss v. Superior Court, 38 Cal.2d 616, 241 P.2d 525 (Cal. 1952)

Schleimer v. Strahl, 219 Cal.App.2d 613, 33 Cal.Rptr. 412 (Ct.App. 1963)

Flournoy v. State of California, 230 Cal.App.2d 520, 41 Cal.Rptr. 190 (Ct.App. 1964)

Ne Casek v. City of Los Angeles, 233 Cal.App.2d 131, 43 Cal.Rptr. 294 (Ct.App. 1965)

Branzel v. City of Concord, 247 Cal.App.2d 68, 55 Cal.Rptr. 167 (Ct.App. 1966)

Sanders v. County of Yuba, 247 Cal.App.2d 748, 55 Cal.Rptr. 852 (Ct.App. 1967)

People v. Wiley, 18 Cal.3d 162, 133 Cal.Rptr. 135 (Cal. 1976)

[g] Law Revision Commission

📖 California. Law Revision Commission. *Reports, Recommendations, and Studies.* Palo Alto: California Law Revision Commission, 1955/57-present. Annual. See also the www page at *www.clrc.ca.gov.* Many of the reports and other publications are available from this web site in pdf format back to 1991. Prior to that date many of the publications are available in print and can be ordered using the information from the web site.

Only the recommendations of the Commission (as distinguished from the research studies) express Commission intent. A legislative history of Commission measures introduced is included and provides reasons for amendment. Cumulative Table of Constitutional and Statutory Provisions affected by Commission Recommendations lists all sections of the Constitution or the codified or uncodified laws that were adopted, enacted, amended, or repeated upon the recommendation of the Commission.

The principal duties of the Law Revision Commission are to: (a) Examine the common law and statutes of the State for the purpose of discovering defects and anachronism therein; (b) Receive and consider suggestions and propose changes in the law from the American Law Institute, the National Conference of Commissioners on Uniform State Laws, bar associations and other learned bodies, judges, public officials, lawyers, and the public generally; and (c) Recommend such changes in the law as it deems necessary to bring the law in California into harmony with modern conditions.

Reports describing the work of the Commission are submitted annually to the Governor and Legislature. As a result of research studies, recommendations are made for revision or elimination of overlapping provisions in the codes. In *Issacson v. City of Oakland,* 263 Cal.App.2d 414, 69 Cal.Rptr. 379 (Ct.App. 1968), the court adopted a recommendation of the Law Revision Commission.

Separate pamphlet reports cumulate into bound volumes of reports. Bound volumes contain cumulative tables of constitutional and statutory provisions affected by recommendations of the Commission, a cumulative table of cases, and a cumulative subject index for volumes 1–3. There is no cumulative index for the set but volume five on sovereign immunity and volume six on the Uniform Rules of Evidence are indexed. The reports are cited by the annotated codes.

Research studies issued prior to the reports are available in the larger law libraries.

[h]   State Bar of California [12]

Today the State Bar is much less involved in promoting legislation and acting as a lobby than it was ten years ago. The bar members very publicly decided that the bar was becoming too political for a state

---

[12] *See also* Chapter 12, State Bar of California. The state bar's internet site is: *www.calbar.ca.org.*

licensing organization. The bar was reorganized in the 1990s and most lobbying efforts were eliminated. In 2002 the Bar's political arm, the Conference of Delegates was officially separated from the State Bar. The Conference of Delegates organization formed a corporation, the Conference of Delegates of California Bar Associations. The group will continue to hold conventions with the State Bar until 2007. The group will also continue to have a voluntary contribution check-off space on the dues renewal forms of State Bar members.

Nevertheless, the Bar continues to play a role in proposing legislation and reviewing all legislation that would affect the practice of law in the state. The Bar's many committees, such as the Administration of Justice, Appellate Courts, and Professional Responsibility, all take a direct interest in promoting and reviewing legislation and rules.

For help with Bar involvement in earlier legislation a researcher can still locate:

> 📖 *Reports of the Committee on Legislation* were published in the Proceedings of the State Bar of California from 1928–1950 and in the Journal of the State Bar of California from 1926. Proposed legislation sponsored and drafted by the State Bar is included in these publications. *Annual Reports of the Board of Governors* provide additional data on Bar legislative activities.

[i] Legislative Analyst

The Legislative Analyst's Office, created in 1941,[13] prepares an annual analysis of the Governor's proposed budget. The staff of approximately fifty members prepares the budget analysis, conducts special studies, and reviews legislation. The review of any legislation is done at the request of the Assembly Committee on Appropriations and Assembly Budget Committee (formerly the Assembly Committee on Ways and Means) and the Senate Appropriations Committee (formerly the Senate Committee on Finance) and and the Senate Budget and Fiscal Review Committees to see how the proposal would affect state or local revenues or expenditures.

The Courts have considered the Legislative Analyst's reports and/or studies in the following cases:

---

[13] The Legislative Analyst's Office was originally called the Legislative Auditor. It retained this title through 1957. Documents coming out of the office in 1958 first used the name, Legislative Analyst.

People v. Ramirez, 33 Cal.App.4th 559, 566, 39 Cal. Rptr. 2d 374 (1995, 2nd Dist, Div 5)

Shippen v. DMV, 161 Cal.App.3d 1119, 208 Cal. Rptr. 13 (1984, 3rd Dist)

Resources for locating Legislative Analyst reports and information include:

📖 California. Legislative Analyst. *Analysis of the Budget Bill.* Available in print or on the Legislative Analyst's website.

💻 Both the Assembly Budget Committee and the Senate Budget and Fiscal Review Committee analyze the budget and issue reports, available on their websites: *www.assembly.ca.gov/acs/ newcomframeset.asp?committee = 4* and *www.sen.ca.gov/ftp/ sen/committee/STANDING/BFR/_home1/PROFILE.HTM.* The staff also conducts special studies in response to legislative inquiries. The Legislative Analyst's www page is: *www.lao.ca.gov/.*

[j] Bureau of State Audits

This office, formerly the Auditor General's Office, was reorganized in mid-1993 by legislation which placed it under the Little Hoover Commission or the Milton Marks Commission on California State Government Organization and Economy. The new office, operating under the auspices of the Joint Legislative Audit Committee, will continue to perform independent audits of various governmental programs. A significant duty of the office is to examine any state contract involving the expenditure of over $10,000 of public funds. The Bureau of State Audits or California State Auditor website is: *http:// www.bsa.ca.gov/bsa/.*

[2] Agency Public Records Access

[a] Overview

The bill-analysis activities of executive agencies might be important to a researcher. All executive agencies from time to time are concerned with legislative proposals. Reference to their files would yield pertinent legislative intent material, especially where they have instigated legislation.

California Government Code sections 6251–6254, California Public Records Act, governs access to many agency public records.

[b] Agencies Active in Legislation

The listed agencies are heavily committed to legislative analysis because of their roles in the administration of justice on a variety of fronts.

- California Department of Finance: *www.dof.ca.gov.*
- California Department of Corrections: *www.corr.ca.gov.*
- California Youth Authority: *www.cya.ca.gov.*
- California Highway Patrol: *www.chp.ca.gov.*
- California Department of Motor Vehicles: *www.dmv.ca.gov.*
- California Department of Consumer Affairs: *www.dca.ca.gov.*
- California Department of Health Services: *www.dhs.cahwnet.gov.*
- California Franchise Tax Board: *www.ftb.ca.gov.*
- California Board of Equalization: *www.boe.ca.gov.*
- California Department of Insurance: *www.insurance.ca.gov.*
- California Department of Corporations: *www.corp.ca.gov.*

[c] Executive Agency and Commission Reports

Executive Agency and Commission Reports including recommended legislative measures were published in the appendices of the legislative *Journals* until 1944. Since then they have been published as separate documents. Some information on recent agency reports can be found on the www at *www.agencyreports.ca.gov/.* This source provides a list of agencies with reports overdue. There is also a search mechanism to search for overdue agency reports on specific subjects. A selected list of cases referring to such reports in legislative intent situations follows:

EXAMPLE

Pearson v. State Social Welfare Board, 54 Cal.2d 184, 5 Cal.Rptr. 553 (Cal. 1960)

Meyer v. Board of Trustees of San Dieguito Union High School District, 195 Cal.App.2d 420, 15 Cal.Rptr. 717 (Ct.App. 1961)

Pacific Employers Insurance Co. v. Industrial Accident Commission, 219 Cal.App.2d 634, 33 Cal.Rptr. 442 (Ct.App. 1963)

Warne v. Harkness, 60 Cal.2d 579, 387 P.2d 377 (Cal. 1963)

[d] Agency References and Resources

📄 "A Look at the California Public Records Act and Its Exemptions." 4 *Golden Gate U. L. Rev.* 203 (1974).

📄 California State Publications lists agency publications which may have a bearing on legislation.

📄 The State Archives maintains some agency legislative files for various periods of time.

[3] The Role of Professional and Trade Associations and Legislative Advocates in the Lawmaking Process

Associations and advocates play a constructive role in the enactment of statutes by representing the interests of their clients and providing legislators with background information on professional and industrial problems. Some indication of the diversity of interests that exists in lawmaking may be gathered from a review of the selected organizations involved in legislation affecting the administration of justice.

Legislative advocates (lobbyists) in California are required to register with the Secretary of State and a directory is issued by that office and located at *www.ss.ca.gov./prd/ld/contents.htm.* In addition, their expense records have been published in Appendixes to the *Journals.*

1. Consumer Attorneys of California (formerly California Trial Lawyers Association): *caoc.com.*

2. California Association of Realtors: *www.car.org.*

3. California District Attorneys Association: *www.cdaa.org.*

4. California Public Defenders Association: *www.cpda.org.*

5. American Civil Liberties Union: *www.aclu.org.*

6. California Peace Officers Association: *www.cpoa.org.*

7. Peace Officers Research Association of California: *www.porac.org.*

8. California Probation, Parole & Correctional Association: *www.cppca.org.*

9. League of California Cities: *www.cacities.org.*

10. California State Association of Counties: *csac.counties.org.*

11. California Court Clerks Association (Municipal Court Clerks Association) *www.courtclerks.org.*

12. California Medical Association: *www.cmanet.org.*

13. California Manufacturers Association: *www.camfg.com.*

14. California Applicants Attorneys Association: *www.caaa.org.*

15. Sierra Club: *www.sierraclub.org.*

16. California Taxpayers Association: *www.caltax.org.*

17. California Land Title Association: *www.clta.org.*

§ 4.04   Research Sources and Techniques

[1]   Sources and Findings Aids: Newspapers, Periodicals, Newsletters, and Indexes

Sacramento Newsletter: Report on California Legislation, Government and Politics. Sacramento, 1943–present. (Titles: MacBride's Newsletter, MacBride-Booe Sacramento Newsletter.) Weekly report on current activities of Legislature, committees, state officials, politics, election campaigns, etc.

California Journal. A monthly digest of state government and politics. Sacramento. 1970–present. Special features are periodic tables of voting records on significant measures and brief checklists of "Selected Government Reports." Supplements include "California Journal Roster and Government Guide," issued annually, and analyses of candidates and propositions, issued prior to each primary and general election.

Survey of California Law. University of Santa Clara, 1948–1955, 7 v.

Southern California Law Review, "The Work of the California Legislature," Biennially, 1939–1949, v.11 (1937), v.13 (1939), v.15 (1941), v.17 (1943), v.19 (1945), v.21 (1947), v.23 (1949).

"Review of Selected (year) California Legislation." *Pacific Law Journal,* McGeorge School of Law, University of the Pacific, 1971–present. (This is the successor publication of the review formerly published by California Continuing Education of the Bar in the *Journal of the State Bar of California* and as a separate publication, 1965–70.)

Journal of the State Bar of California published committee reports with legislative recommendations, legislative program.

Review of selected code legislation, 1957–63. See *People v. Wilson,* 60 Cal.2d 139, 383 P.2d 452 (Cal. 1963).

📖   *Cal Law—Trends and Developments, 1967–1970.* Golden Gate College of Law, San Francisco, Bancroft-Whitney.

[2] Technique for Compiling a California Legislative History

The goal in compiling the legislative history of a law is to find any information which reveals the intent of the legislators who passed the law. Before beginning the search, one should have a good background in statutory construction.[14] Then the researcher should follow the steps listed here.

Code section to be researched: _____

1. Locate the selected code section in the current annotated code (Deering's or West's) (on line, CD-ROM, or hard copy), its pocket part, or the supplementary session law service. Read the selected code section and any others that are referred to in the selected section. Note any references to Law Revision Commission Comments, Attorney General Opinions, Legislative Counsel Opinions, California Code of Regulations, committee reports, and law review articles.

General References: _____

2. Determine the chapter number and the year of the legislative session when the law upon which the code section is based was enacted. Chapter and year information follows the text of the code section in both West's and Deering's codes. Also note chapter numbers and years of any amendments. In the recent annotated codes from both publishers, the bill number follows the year and chapter number.

Chapter:_____Year:_____

3. Locate the statute in *Statutes of California/Statutes and Amendments to the Code.* Read the chapter version or uncodified version of the law. At the beginning or the end there may be an urgency statement or some other message of intent, which may or may not be codified.[15]

---

[14] For example, the researcher could look at Singer, Norman J., *Statutes and Statutory Construction,* Fifth Edition. Deerfield, IL: Clark Boardman Callaghan, 1994. Cite as: Sutherland Stat. Const.

[15] For instance, Stats. 1985, c. 223 ends with clear intent statement, which was not codified.

4. Use the "Table of Laws Enacted,"[16] located at or near the front of the first volume, or the "Summary Digest,"[17] located near the back of the last volume (1967 and later) to find the bill author(s) and bill number corresponding to the chapter and year information from the code. To find the bill numbers for the earliest laws (1850–1864), researchers will need to use the subject index of the Journals. For the period 1881–1972, the *Final Calendar of Legislative Business* may be used for subject access to the bill number. After 1972 the final *Legislative Index* may be used for subject access.

Bill Number: _____

Bill Author(s): _____

5. Locate the bill or bills, which may be in hard copy (bill service from the Legislative Bill Room), in microform (Library Microfilms, 1963–1992 and continuing),[18] or in an on line format.[19] Bills are often the only data a researcher has to work with in attempting to determine legislative intent. All prints of a bill should be compared, particularly when amendments have been adopted or offered and rejected in the course of the legislative process. Because additions and deletions caused by amendments are marked clearly on the bills, one needs to read only the first version thoroughly and then to check all additions and deletions on the subsequent versions.

The Legislative Counsel's Digest of the content of a bill is changed as the bill is amended (since 1967) and the *Daily File* indicates the changes as they take place. This Digest matter may provide good leads to other extrinsic data.

---

[16] "Table of Laws Enacted" is the current title of the table. It has also been published as "Contents" and "Table of Laws." Prior to 1865/66 there were no cross-references in the Statutes to the bill at all. Prior to 1905 there was no cross-reference to the bill author. The Table of Statutes Enacted provides the researcher with names of coauthors. The Summary Digest only lists the first bill author.

[17] The Summary Digest was first added to the Statutes in 1967. It is written by the Legislative Counsel and gives the researcher a brief legislative history of the law. Only the first bill author's name is provided. The legislative services of West's and Deering's codes print the Legislative Counsel's Digest at the beginning of each new law. This digest also gives the bill number and author.

[18] There are earlier bills available in microfilm in some libraries. Bills from 1867/68 through 1971 were filmed in 1971 by then Legislative Counsel, George Murphy.

[19] LexisNexis, Westlaw, State Net, and the Legislative Counsel's web page will only have the most recent years of bills online.

(Pub. 64620)

Since it is common for the author of a bill to include an expression of intent or policy developed by himself or herself or the committee to which he or she belongs, the text of all measures should be reviewed carefully.

6. Check the Legislative Indexes for similar bills in the session of enactment and previous sessions. What did not happen to a piece of legislation may be as important as what did happen. Competing bills on a hot legislative issue should be contrasted to identify proposals that failed to become law. When the bill section you are tracking is inserted into the bill late in the legislative session (August or September), it is possible that it was carried in a competing or companion measure in the same session. The section may also have come from a predecessor measure from an earlier legislative session.

7. Locate the *Assembly File Analysis.* [20] If the selected statute was passed after 1974, the *File Analysis* will be available. The File Analysis is a nonpartisan of each bill presented for final action on the Assembly floor (except for the Consent Calendar). Paper or fiche (from Library Microfilms) versions are available back through 1975.

The *Assembly File Analysis* of an individual bill is divided into four principal parts:

(a) The first section records committee actions and the roll call votes taken on the bill's passage. In the case of Senate Bills and bills returning for concurrence or consideration of a Governor's veto, this section also includes a record of all floor votes.

(b) The digest describes what the bill does and the changes it would make in existing laws. Most often, this section presents a simplified version of the Legislative Counsel's Digest, which appears on the cover of each bill. In the case of complex bills, however, the digest in the analysis will provide a summary of the major provisions of the legislation.

(c) The section on Fiscal Effect reports any impact the bill might have on the state's finances, as determined by the

---

[20] For a descriptive article on the Assembly File Analysis, see Kahrl, Sliced Bread—The Assembly File Analysis in the Legislative Process, 1 *AOR Reporter* 11-35(1975). Printed by California Assembly Reproduction Center.

Legislative Analyst and the staff to the fiscal committees of both houses. Cost estimates prepared by the Department of Finance in the executive branch of government are not currently made available for use in the Assembly File Analysis.

(d) The Comments section provides information on the background of the bill, its intent, and a more detailed treatment of its provisions and effect. Often, this section includes quotations from the analyses prepared for the committees which reviewed the bill.

8. Identify the committee(s) the bill has gone through. The *Final History in the Final Calendar of Legislative Business, 1881–1972,* the *Final History, 1973–present,* or in the case of current legislation, the *Daily, Weekly,* or *Semi-Final History,* provide the history of each bill. The history tells which committees it was assigned to, when the bill was amended, when it was read, when it passed, and when it went to the Governor. The online resources provide this information on bills in the current or most recent sessions.

Committee: _____

9. Once the committee is identified, it may be difficult to find the committee reports or committee hearings, which, if published, were never distributed regularly or widely. Many libraries catalog committee reports as books, so users must check the library public catalogs. Larger libraries will have the best collection of these materials.

10. Check the *Assembly* and *Senate Journals.* The journals contain floor and committee votes, Legislative Counsel Opinions, Governors' veto messages, and legislators' letters of intent. Check for statements of legislators, e.g., 1959 Senate Journal 4222, "This statement is published as an expression of legislative intent relative to Senate Bill No. 1106."

Prior to 1970 journals had many interim reports in the appendix volumes. Appendix to the *Journal of the Senate* includes Senate and Joint Interim Committee Reports, 1947–70; Appendix to the *Journal of the Assembly* includes Assembly Interim Committee Reports, 1957–70.

Find these reports by reference from:

a. California. Legislature. Assembly Rules Committee. Assembly Office of Research. *Hearing and Reports of the*

*Committees of the California Legislature during the interim:
A summary and Listing, 1963–present.* (Indicates if reports
were published in the Journal.)

b. California. State Library. *California State Publications,*
1946–date.

c. *Senate Weekly History*—Reports received and noted in the
Senate Journals of the (_____) regular session. Journal Appendixes published through 1943 contain administrative reports
of State Departments.

11. Check (1) *Opinions of the Attorney General,* (2) *Opinions
of the Legislative Counsel* (released for publication), (3) *Analyses
of the Legislative Analyst.*

12. Check California. Commission on Uniform State Laws.
Reports, 1953–present, for references to Uniform Acts proposed
for enactment, data on those enacted, and list of all uniform acts
adopted in California with date of enactment.

13. Check California. Law Revision Commission. *Reports,
Recommendations and Studies.* 1955/57–present.

14. Check Veto Messages of the Governor, if bill was vetoed.
(These appear in journal of the house of origin of the bill under
the name of the Governor "Veto Messages" or "Messages-
Vetoing" or under heading "Veto by Governor." Where the bill
number is known the bill-action index may be used.) Pocket
Vetoes are listed in the Final Calendar of Legislative Business,
1881–1966, under "Senate Bills—Not approved by Governor
(Pocket Vetoed)" and "Assembly Bills—Pocket Vetoed by Governor." Governor's Messages are printed in the journals. Also
check Governor's Press Releases.

15. For legislation concerned with Administration of Justice,
check California. Judicial Council. *(Annual or Biennial) Reports.*

16. Call or write to the sponsor(s) of the bill.

17. Call the legislator who introduced and carried the bill.

18. Published material containing discussion on bill before and
after its enactment.

19. Newspaper and other accounts may be found through:

a. California. State Library. California Section. Index of *San
Francisco Chronicle.*

b. *Sacramento Union* published legislative debates from the latter part of the 1850s.

c. University of California. Berkeley, Bancroft Library. Clipping files on California political subjects.

d. The *Sacramento Bee*, which is an important source of news on California government, is online on LexisNexis and Westlaw.

e. California Journal: Independent analysis of politics and government. (Information for Public Affairs/StateNet) 1970–present.

f. *Sacramento Newsletter*, 1947–present.

20. Where it can be established that California modeled its bill after that proposed by a legislative service organization, the publications of that organization.

21. Where it can be established that California modeled its bill upon another state's law or another state had an identical law, its legislative history or a court construction of it may prove helpful. Similarly useful are *Legislative Council Reports* on the subject. *Legislative Council Reports* may be located through Council of State Governments. Chicago. Legislative Research Checklist, 1947–present. (The University of California Berkeley, Law Library maintains a complete microset of all the reports listed.)

22. If a California law is a copy of a Model or Uniform Law, that history is pertinent. *Handbook*, National Conference of Commissioners on Uniform State Laws, annual, and *Uniform State Laws* should be consulted. Before final acceptance and proposal of a draft law by the conference, the tentative draft is published together with comments on each section. *Uniform Laws Annotated*, 1930–present, provides a conversion table from ULA sections to the state statute number.

23. Check the *Pacific Law Journal* "Annual Review of Selected California." Check the green pages of the January issue.

[3] Online Bill Tracking/Legislative Databases

To keep up with current or very recent legislation, online bill tracking can be done through several services available in California. State Net, available at *www.statenet.com*, is based in Sacramento and follows the activities of the Legislature closely. It offers a wide range of customized services to clients.

Although less customized than the State Net services, LexisNexis and Westlaw also provide bill-tracking capabilities following bills in the legislature. Both LexisNexis and Westlaw use State Net data from 1991 to date, by agreement with Public Affairs, Inc.

LexisNexis carries bill tracking reports in the "CA Bill Tracking Reports" Source (CAL; CATRACK), accessed through *lexis.com*®. CATRCK has pending bills tracked from introduction to enactment or veto. The "CA Full-Text Bills" Source (CAL; CATEXT) contains the full text of all versions of pending bills. The "CA Legislative Committee Analysis of Pending Bills" Source (CAL; CACOMM) contains the text of legislative committee analyses of pending bills. These two sources are combined in the "CA Bill Tracking & Full-Text Bills, Combined" Source (CAL; CABILL).

The CA-BILLTRK database on Westlaw contains bill summaries and status information. The CA-BILLTXT database contains the full text of bills and resolutions. Both of these Westlaw databases contain information on legislative calendars, such as adjournment dates and action deadlines. The CA-BILLS database combines CA-BILLTRK AND CA-BILLTXT. The CCA (California Committee Analyses) database contains the full text of committee analyses for the current legislative session. CCA-OLD contains analyses from previous sessions. The Scope command in Westlaw will give the researcher a full description of the database as well as search tips.

Researchers in California also have access to limited free bill tracking through the Legislature itself. The indexes of the Assembly and Senate bills are available at *www.leginfo.ca.gov/bilindex.html*. Once the researcher has identified the bill he or she wants to track, it is then a simple matter to subscribe to their email subscription service by following the menu beginning at: *www.leginfo.ca.gov/bilinfo.html*. A second way to subscribe to senate bills is to go to the senate home page: *www.sen.ca.gov*. One can then link to current legislation and from there go to the bill subscription service. Updates are sent to subscribers by email. *See also* the Publishers/Vendors list in Appendix A.

[4] Commercial Services for Legislative Intent Research

Many attorneys and judges, who know their limitations in time, ability, and geography, find it much easier and more economical to have experts do the work for them. As mentioned earlier, state legislative research is not nearly as straightforward as federal legislative research. State research takes more time, requires a certain expertise and familiarity with the legislative process and documents, and is almost impossible to do outside of Sacramento. The companies below have people who are experienced in working with the state legislature and related state offices and officials. They can save the researcher much time, money, and frustration.

 Legislative Intent Service. This service, now over twenty-five years old, has a staff of five attorneys and a staff of twelve research support personnel. Their product consists of research into both intrinsic and extrinsic evidence of legislative intent. Intrinsic evidence is developed from an analysis of the relevant code sections prior to inclusion of the wording in question, and an examination of the bill or bills which carried the wording through the legislative process. Particularly important are the amendments to these bills, adding, subtracting, or varying words and phrases. Often intent can be discerned by seeing what language was included or excluded during the passage of the bill. Extrinsic evidence consists of *Assembly and Senate Committee Analyses, Legislative Analyst's Reports, Legislative Counsel's Opinions,* correspondence, notes, and letters of support and opposition from the author's personal Bill File. If appropriate, affidavits as to the content of legislative debates by the Assemblymen and Senators who participated in them may also be obtained. Legislative Intent has a current inventory of over 30,000 prepared legislative histories. The company has begun moving toward a fully digital product so it is able to deliver legislative histories in any combination of print and/or CD and/or web formats. The Legislative Intent Service home page is *www.legintent.com.*

 Legislative Research Incorporated (LRI) also does legislative intent research in California. The company has been in business since 1983 (first under the name Legislative Research Institute). LRI has over 10,000 prepared legislative histories on file. The LRI www home page is: *www.lrihistory.com.*

 Legislative History & Legislative Intent. This company started in 1997 and has an informative www page at: *www. lhclearinghouse.com.*

Capital Research. This company, based in Citrus Heights, was recently started to compete with the other legislative intent research companies in the Sacramento area. It is the only one that does not have a web page. Contact information is in Appendix A.

(*See also* the Publishers/Vendors list in Appendix A.)

[5] Legislative Source Materials in the California State Archives

The State Archives, which is under the control of the Secretary of State's Office, contains the legislative bill file group (including all paper copies of bills from 1850), original laws record group, legislative papers file record group, modern legislative committee papers, the Governor's chaptered bill file record group, agency legislative files, petitions to the Legislature, and Governor's Office record group. Archive information on the www is located at *www.ss.ca.gov/archives/archives.htm*.

(See also the Publishers/Vendors list in Appendix A.)

[6] Bibliography—The California Legislature

📖 California. Department of General Services. Office of State Printing. *California Blue Book.* Quadrennial. (Although this title is mandated by statute to be published,[21] there has not been a new issue in many years). Brief descriptions of state executive agencies, judiciary, and Legislature; photographs and biographies of Senate and Assembly members and agency secretaries; description of state symbols. Available from Publications Section.

📖 California. Legislature. *California Legislature at Sacramento.* Sacramento: California Legislature. Annual. (Spine title: Handbook.) This pocket-sized book contains biographies and photographs of members and officers of the Legislature; a list of committees with membership; Senate, Assembly, and joint rules; district maps; U. S. representatives; election statistics; and county data. Available from Legislative Bill Room.

📖 California. Legislature. Senate. *California's Legislature.* [Sacramento: California Assembly] 2000. 304 p. A practical guide to the Legislature and state government. Reviews organization

---

[21] Cal. Gov. Code, § 14885.

of the Legislature and the legislative process with special section on legislative printing and publications. Includes chapters on the Constitution, election process, executive and judicial branches, history of the Capitol. Appendixes provide lists of governors, lieutenant governors, Assembly speakers, and official seals, symbols, flags. Footnotes refer chiefly to statutory or constitutional authority or to rules of the Legislature. In the 1998 edition at p. iii there is a note from the editor about the history of the publication:

> "The Legislature of California," by then Chief Clerk Arthur Ohnimus, was first published as an insert in the 1941 "Constitution" booklet published by the California State Assembly. After the article had expanded extensively with each new edition, the Assembly authorized the printing of the document as a separate pamphlet in 1958 (*HR 45, adopted March 13, 1958*). Subsequent revisions dramatically altered the publication from its original format, and the new work was renamed "California's Legislature" in 1969. Revisions were printed approximately every two years, with the exception of 1986–1993, when no new editions were published. Available from Legislative Bill Room or as a PDF file on the web at: *http://leginfo.public.ca.gov/califleg.html*.

California. Legislature. Assembly. *The California State Assembly*. Brief introduction to the Legislature and the Assembly. Includes Assembly seating chart. Available free from Legislative Bill Room.

California. Legislature. Assembly. *California Legislature Roster*. List of members of the Legislature and Congress with mailing addresses. Available free from Legislative Bill Room.

California. Legislature. Senate. *The California Senate*. Brief introduction to the Legislature and the Senate. Senate seating chart; bill process chart. Available free from Legislative Bill Room.

California. Senate. *The Legislative Process: A Citizen's Guide to Participation*. Sacramento: Senate Publications. 32 p. This short publication contains charts and illustrations as it provides an overview of the legislative process in California. The 14 page glossary is better than those usually included in guides of this type. Also available from the website of the California Alliance for Arts Education: *http://www.artsed411.org/ involved/docs/guide.pdf* from the website of the California League of Women Voters: *http://ca.lwv.org/lwvc/pdf/ guide.pdf.*

📖 California. Legislature. Committees: Assembly and Senate. *List of standing committees, permanent subcommittees, general research committees, and select committees.* Includes schedule of meeting and membership. Available free from Legislative Bill Room.

📖 California. Legislature. Assembly. Committee on Elections and Reapportionment. *Legislative Sourcebook; the California Legislature and Reapportionment, 1849–1965,* by Don A. Allen. History of reapportionment of the California Legislature. Historical maps of districts; alphabetical list of members, 1849–1965; sessions of the Legislature; many tables on population, composition of the Legislature, etc.

📖 California. Secretary of State. *Roster, California State, County, City and Township Officials. (California Roster).* Biennial. Includes legislative district maps, historical list of elected executive officials, and city election dates. Available from Publications Section.

📖 Coonjohn, Jeffrey J. *A Brief History of the California Legislative Counsel Bureau and the Growing Precedential Value of Its Digest and Opinions.* 25 Pacific Law Journal 211–235 (1993). The article and its 185 footnote references provide a great reference source on the Legislative Counsel's office.

📖 Delahanty, James. Super Legislators: One Person Amendment of Statutes in California. *L.A. Daily Journal Report,* Sept. 22, 1978 (No. 78-18) pp. 4–15. This article addresses the treatment of post-enactment statements of legislators as legislative history.

📖 Fisher, Joel M. *The Legislative Process in California,* by Joel M. Fisher, Charles M. Price, and Charles G. Bell. Washington, American Political Science Association, 1973. A generalized and abstract survey of the California Legislature, viewed in part in relation to state legislatures generally. Includes discussion of professionalism and effectiveness and reviews the roles of committees, special interest groups, lobbyists, political parties, and the Governor in the legislative process. Some historical background. Extensively footnoted; bibliography.

☐ Hichborn, Franklin. *California Politics, 1891–1939.* 5 v., includes general index, index of persons, table of contents for each volume. [Los Angeles]: Haynes Foundation, 1950. (Limited edition, available in University of California, Berkeley, Law Library.) Based on documents collected by the author during his years as a reporter of legislative session, political conventions, and political campaigns.

☐ Hichborn, Franklin. *Story of the session of the California Legislature of [year].* 1900, 1909, 1911, 1913, 1915, 1921. San Francisco: James H. Barry Company.

☐ Larsen, Christian L. *The Use of Special Committees and Commissions by the California Legislature.* Berkeley: U. of California, 1937.

☐ League of California Cities. *Navigating the Legislative Process: Deadlines, Procedures and Common Terms.* Sacramento: League of California Cities, 2003. 17 p. Although this publication is aimed at city officials who want to better understand the state's legislative process, it is a good guide for almost anyone who shares that goal. The booklet contains a fine glossary of legislative terms, with a frank explanation of terms like spot bill, unbacked bill, and "tombstoning" a bill. The publication is also available at the League's website: *http://www.cacities.org/userfiles/godoc/6600%2ElegGuide%2Epdf.*

☐ Perman, Marc R. Comment: Statutory Interpretation in California: Individual Testimony as an Extrinsic Aid. 15 *University of San Francisco Law Review* 241 (Fall/Winter 1980–1981).

☐ Rose, Carolina C. California Legislative History and Intent: *Research & Practice Guide:* Practical "how to" guidance for improving your advocacy skills when legislative history/intent is at issue. Article posted on Legislative Research Incorporated's website: *www.lrihistory.com/seminar.html.*

☐ Steck, Emil. California Legislation: Sources Unlimited. 6 *Pacific Law Journal* 536 (1975).

☐ University of California, Hastings College of the Law. *Compiling a California Legislative History: Legal Information*

Guidepost #3. On the internet at: *http://www.uchastings.edu/ library/Legal%20Research/Research%20Guides/ calleghist.htm.*

☐ Van Alstyne, Arvo and Ezer, Mitchel J. "Legislative Research in California: The Uncharted Wilderness." 35 *Los Angeles Bar Bulletin* 116, 145 (February and March 1960).

☐ White, Bertha Rothe. "Sources of Legislative Intent in California." 3 *Pacific Law Journal* 63 (1972).

Chapter 5

Ballot Measure Research[1]

---

[1] This chapter is written by Tobe Liebert and adapted from an article originally appearing in the *Law Library Journal*.

(Pub. 64620)

§ 5.01 Introduction

Researching California ballot measures[2] is often a difficult process. Traditional tools and resources do not adequately address this unique area, which is similar to, yet distinct from, statutory research. This is

---

[2] The word "ballot measure" will be used in this chapter. The term ballot measure includes initiatives and referenda. If a ballot measure qualifies for the election, it will receive a "proposition" designation on the ballot, which is the term most familiar to the public.

unfortunate because ballot measures generate intense interest and have produced far-reaching changes in California law.

The purpose of this chapter is therefore to: (1) outline briefly the process of enacting state law[3] through the ballot measure process, (2) discuss the various documents that are produced along the way, (3) give guidance on where to find the text of these documents, whether in print or online, (4) discuss legislative history for law enacted through this process, and (5) review the various types of legal challenges that can be raised to ballot measures.

Researching California ballot measures has been made somewhat easier in recent years by the proliferation of information on the Internet. The State of California is actively using the Internet to increase the accessibility of documents associated with ballot measures.[4] Additionally, proponents and opponents of specific initiatives have discovered that the Internet is a good way of publicizing their causes. These efforts have made it much easier to locate information on ballot measures, especially during the petition stage. The standard caveat about Internet resources applies, however, namely that such information can be ephemeral and (in the case of unofficial sites) sometimes of dubious reliability. It should also be remembered that the Internet will be of limited use for historical research.

§ 5.02 Basics of the Ballot Measure Process

[1] History

While many states permit the crafting of law through the ballot measure process,[5] California has embraced this form of "direct

---

[3] The California Constitution provides in article II, section 11, that the citizens of cities and counties may also exercise the initiative power. This chapter will address research of statewide measures only. When researching local initiatives and referendums, *see* 38 Cal. Jur. 3d *Initiatives and Referendum*, secs. 35-63 (1977). *See also California Commission on Campaign Financing, To Govern Ourselves: Ballot Initiatives in the Los Angeles Area* (1992), and Patrick J. Borchers, "California Local Initiatives and Referenda: An Argument for Keeping the Progressive Flame Burning," 21 *Pac. L.J.* 119 (Oct. 1989).

[4] The California Secretary of State maintains an excellent website for ballot measure research. The address of this site is: *www.ss.ca.gov.*

[5] Only 14 states do not have some form of initiative or referendum, and all states but Delaware require the approval of the electorate to amend the state constitution. *See* Julian N. Eule, "Judicial Review of Direct Democracy," 99 *Yale L.J.* 1503, 1509–10 (1990).

democracy" in a way that consistently attracts the nation's attention. It is often the most divisive and controversial topics that become the subject of ballot measures, thus guaranteeing that these campaigns generate headlines and passionate debate across the country. Further, legal challenges to law created through the ballot measure process have put issues such as affirmative action, immigration policy, and tax reform squarely before the courts.[6]

California's experience with the ballot measure process began in 1911, when the people of the state voted to amend the Constitution to permit the submission of initiatives and referendums to the electorate. The most ardent supporter of the adoption of the ballot measure was Hiram Johnson, whose election as Governor of California in 1910 was the key to putting this issue before the voters. The ballot measure was urged as the antidote to the Southern Pacific Railroad's political machine, which was widely believed to control the state's Legislature.[7] Since this time, the people of California have used the ballot measure process more than any other state to shape the laws by which they are governed.

[2] The Initiative

The initiative is defined by article II, section 8 of the California Constitution as "[t]he power of the electors to propose statutes and amendments to the Constitution and to adopt or reject them." Thus, a *statutory* initiative proposes either a new statute or amends an existing statute, while a *constitutional amendment* initiative proposes an amendment to the California Constitution.

Article II, section 8 of the California Constitution further states that a petition proposing a statutory initiative must be signed by a number equal to 5 percent of the votes for all candidates for Governor at the last gubernatorial election, while a petition proposing a constitutional

---

[6] *See, e.g., Amador Valley Joint Union High School Dist. v. State Bd. of Equalization,* 583 P.2d 1281 (Cal. 1978) (action challenging Proposition 13); League of United Latin American Citizens v. Wilson, 908 F.Supp 755 (C.D. Cal 1995) (action challenging Proposition 187); and Coalition for Economic Equity v. Wilson, 110 F.3d 1431 (9th Cir. 1997) (action challenging Proposition 209).

[7] Joseph R. Grodin et al., *The California State Constitution: A Reference Guide* (1993). For a thorough discussion of the impetus for the initiative procedure in California, please refer to V.O. Key, Jr. & Winston W. Crouch, *The Initiative and Referendum in California* (1939).

amendment must be signed by a number equal to 8 percent of the votes for all candidates for Governor at the last gubernatorial election.[8]

[3] The Referendum

The referendum gives the voters a type of veto power over the Legislature. Article II, section 9 of the California Constitution defines the referendum as "[t]he power of the electors to approve or reject statutes or parts of statutes except urgency statutes, statutes calling elections, and statutes providing for tax levies or appropriations for usual current expenses of the state."[9]

To qualify a referendum for the ballot, article II, section 9 of the Constitution states that a petition must: (1) receive signatures equal to 5 percent of the votes for all candidates for Governor at the last gubernatorial election, and (2) be presented to the Secretary of State within 90 days of the enactment of the statute to be challenged.[10]

The referendum has fallen into disuse in recent years, as no referendums have appeared on the statewide ballot since 1982.

[4] The Recall Election

The recall election permits the voters to remove an elected official from office. The recall election procedure has been available to California voters since 1911, having been added to the Constitution at the same time as the powers of initiative and referendum. The California Constitution provides for the recall of both statewide and local officials. The authority for the recall election is found in article II, sections 13–19 of the California Constitution.

The initial step in a recall effort is the circulation of a petition. A petition for the recall of a statewide officer must be signed by registered voters equal in number to 12% of the vote for that office in the preceding election. This petition must be circulated in a minimum of five California counties. A petition for the recall of a state legislator must be signed by voters equal in number to 20% of the vote for that office in the preceding election. The successful recall petition will result in the recall question being put before the voters, whether statewide or locally. The

---

[8] Originally both the statutory initiative and constitutional amendment initiative required the 8 percent figure, but in 1966, the number required for the statutory initiative was lowered to 5 percent. *See* 1966 Cal. Stat. 960, 971.

[9] Cal. Const., art. II, § 9(a).

[10] Cal. Const., art. II, § 9(b).

statutes controlling the recall election process are found in the Elections Code, sections 11000 to 11386.

The last significant revision of the recall election process was in 1974, as the result of the passage of Proposition Nine. The October 2003 recall election of Governor Gray Davis was the first time a California Governor faced a recall election, although local officials have been recalled many times. The California Secretary of State's office prepared a ballot pamphlet setting forth the official arguments for and against the recall of the Governor and the list of potential replacement candidates.

[5] Citizen-Sponsored Measures

Both the citizens and the Legislature can place ballot measures before the electorate. Measures originating in the Legislature are discussed in the next section.

Citizen-sponsored ballot measures (whether proposing an initiative or referendum) begin their life in the form of a petition. The petition contains the text of the proposed measure and is circulated by the sponsors in hopes of gathering enough signatures to quality for the ballot. The process of qualifying a petition for the ballot is governed by both the California Constitution and sections of the California Elections Code [hereafter the "Elections Code"].

The text of the petition may be drafted by the proponents, but section 10243 of the California Government Code permits the Legislative Counsel to assist in the drafting of a petition, upon request.

Before the petition may be circulated, a draft of the proposed petition must be submitted to the Attorney General. The Attorney General is then responsible for preparing a title and "[a] summary of the chief purposes and points . . ." of the petition, not to exceed 100 words.[11] The petition must then bear this title and summary when circulated. The Attorney General must also determine if the measure would affect the state's revenues or expenditures. If so, the summary must include an estimate of the fiscal impact of the measure.[12]

The Courts have consistently held that the title and summary of a proposed measure must be prepared by the Attorney General as long as the petition is in the proper form and has been presented in accordance

---

[11] Cal. Elec. Code, § 9002.

[12] Cal. Elec. Code, § 9005.

with the law.[13] The Attorney General has no discretion in this matter, even if it is believed that the proposed measure would be unconstitutional or otherwise invalid as a matter of law.

The petition itself must conform to the requirements set forth in sections 9001, 9008, 9009 and 9020 of the Elections Code. These sections discuss the necessary title, summaries, headings, and signature form. While these provisions are mandatory, the courts are reluctant to invalidate an otherwise qualified petition because of failure to strictly follow these provisions [see § 5.05[2], pre-election challenges].

Sections 9030–9035 of the Elections Code set forth the procedures for verifying that a petition has received the requisite number of signatures. Once it is confirmed that the petition has received a sufficient number of signatures, the petition is forwarded to the Secretary of State, where further verification procedures are undertaken.

If a petition receives the required number of signatures, it will appear on the ballot of the next election. Article II of the Constitution specifies that initiatives and referendums will appear on the ballot of the next general election held at least 131 days after the petition qualifies.[14]

[6] Legislatively-Sponsored Measures

Legislatively-sponsored ballot measures are of three types: (1) constitutional amendments, (2) bond proposals, and (3) measures that would amend or repeal a law already established by the initiative process.

Constitutional Amendments—Article XVII, section 1 of the Constitution permits the Legislature to propose an amendment or revision to the Constitution. Two-thirds of each house must pass the proposed amendment, which is then submitted to the voters as a ballot measure.

Bond Proposals—Article XVI, section 1 of the Constitution prohibits the Legislature from creating any debt in excess of $300,000 unless this proposal is first submitted to the voters. Article XVI, section 2 states that such proposal must be submitted in the "form of a bond act or statute."

Amending or Repealing a law established by an initiative—Article II, section 10(c) of the Constitution states that law established through a statutory initiative may not be amended or repealed by the Legislature without approval of the electorate (unless the initiative contained an

---

[13] *Planning and Conservation League v. Lungren,* 45 Cal.Rptr.2d 183 (Cal. App. 1995).
[14] Cal. Const., art. II, § 8(c).

exception). Thus, a subsequent measure must be approved by the voters in order for the Legislature to amend or to repeal a law established through the initiative process.

The procedure for placing a legislatively-sponsored measure on the ballot is essentially the same as passing a statute. That is, the measure begins as a bill (with an AB or SB designation) or constitutional amendment (with an ACA or SCA designation) and then must pass both the Assembly and Senate. In the case of a bill, it must also be signed by the Governor. A successful bill or constitutional amendment proposing that a measure be presented to the electorate does not, however, then become law (despite being chaptered by the Secretary of State and appearing in the *Statutes and Amendments to the Code*). The measure will become effective only if it receives a majority of votes at the next election. [15]

The researcher will use the traditional sources associated with statutory research when researching legislatively-sponsored ballot measures. Please refer to Chapters 3 and 4 for guidance on California statutory research.

§ 5.03 Locating Documents

[1] The Petition

The text of a proposed initiative is drafted by the proponents of the measure. To locate the text of a petition that is in circulation, you may contact the Attorney General or the sponsor of the petition drive.

With the flourishing of World Wide Web sites, it is also possible to locate the text of the petition through the Internet. The Secretary of State maintains an excellent Internet site for information on petitions. The current URL of this site is: *www.ss.ca.gov*. This site provides the following information: (1) a list of petitions that have qualified for the next election; (2) petitions that have been submitted to the Secretary of State for signature verification; (3) petitions that are currently circulating; and (4) petitions that have been submitted to the Attorney

---

[15] It should be noted that the idea of a legislatively-sponsored ballot measure is something of a contradiction in terms. The motivation behind the creation of the initiative process was the belief that the people needed a way to bypass corrupt legislators and directly enact law through the ballot box. Having the legislature pass measures and then place them before the voters is certainly a cumbersome method of enacting law, but one that is provided for as a way of securing the maximum protection of the citizenry in areas judged to be particularly sensitive.

General for summary and title. The information provided for each petition includes a summary of the proposed measure's purpose and the name and phone number of the proponent(s).

[2]   The Ballot Pamphlet

[a]   Composition

The ballot pamphlet is the official publication designed to inform the voters of the proposed ballot measures. The ballot pamphlet is prepared by the Secretary of State and its contents and form are carefully proscribed.[16] The Secretary of State shall mail the ballot pamphlet to the voters not less than 21 days before the election.[17]

By statute, the pamphlet must contain the following:

- A complete copy of each measure, designated as a "proposition;"[18]

- A copy of the specific constitutional or statutory provision, if any, that each measure would repeal or revise;

- A copy of the arguments and rebuttals for and against each measure; and

- A copy of the analysis of each measure prepared by the Legislative Analyst's office.[19]

The ballot pamphlet can be located in many different ways. As mentioned earlier, the pamphlet is mailed to all voters prior to the election. After the election, ballot pamphlets are published in the microfiche set, *Voters Arguments, 1883–1978: Amendments to the Constitution and proposed statutes with arguments respecting the same.*[20] This set reproduces the full-text of the ballot pamphlet and thus contains both the text of the measures and voter arguments.

---

[16] Cal. Elec. Code, § 9084–9090.

[17] Cal. Elec. Code, § 9094.

[18] Upon qualification, the ballot measure receives a "proposition" number. Since November of 1982, all propositions have been numbered sequentially, beginning with "1" and to continue in sequence for 20 years. Cal. Elec. Code, § 13117. Because many people know ballot measures only by their proposition number it is important to remember this system.

[19] Cal. Elec. Code, § 9084.

[20] Library Microfilms, *Voters Arguments, 1883–1978: Amendments to the Constitution and proposed statutes with arguments respecting the same* (1979). This set is produced by Library Microfilms of Palo Alto, California, and is supplemented annually.

Institutions holding collections of ballot pamphlets include the California State Library and the Institute of Governmental Studies Library at the University of California, Berkeley.

Prior to the mailing of the ballot pamphlet, it may be possible to see the text of the propositions on the Internet. As previously mentioned, interested groups often sponsor websites that provide the full-text of the proposed measure, along with other information. These sites are typically very partisan, however, so the commentary and type of information given at any particular site may not be objective or comprehensive.

[b] Voter Arguments

Voter arguments are printed in the ballot pamphlet. The arguments are prepared by the proponents and opponents of the measure. Predictably, they are very partial. Voter arguments are submitted to the Secretary of State, and section 9067 of the Elections Code establishes priority on the ballot pamphlet (although any person is free to submit an argument to the Secretary of State). The following priorities are set by statute: (1) members of the Legislature (in case of a measure submitted by the Legislature); (2) the proponent of an initiative (in case of an initiative or referendum measure); (3) "bona fide" associations of citizens; and (4) individual voters. [21]

After the Secretary of State has received the arguments for and against the ballot measure, copies of the arguments must be sent to the authors of the arguments so that "rebuttal arguments" (not to exceed 250 words) can be prepared and submitted to the Secretary of State. [22]

Voter arguments may be considered as part of the legislative history behind the passage of the ballot measure [*see* § 5.04, legislative history].

[c] Analysis from Legislative Analyst

Every measure has an analysis prepared by the Legislative Analyst's Office. [23] The analysis is an impartial evaluation of the purpose and effects of the proposed measure. This includes a fiscal analysis showing the potential cost of the proposed measure to the government. The

---

[21] Cal. Elec. Code, § 9067.

[22] Cal. Elec. Code, § 9069. The voter arguments for legislatively-sponsored measures follow a separate procedure. Cal. Elec. Code, § 9041–9044.

[23] Cal. Elec. Code, § 9087. The analysis was first prepared in 1949 and was the responsibility of the Legislative Counsel's office.

analysis is included in the ballot pamphlet prepared by the Secretary of State.

California courts have upheld the analyses prepared by the Legislative Analyst's office on the few occasions that they have been challenged.[24]

[3] The Successful Ballot Measure

[a] Locating and Research Techniques

The text of a successful ballot measure (that is, passed by the voters) can be located in a number of sources, in addition to the sources already discussed. The most important action that occurs to the successful ballot measure is its placement in the appropriate section(s) of the California Constitution or Code. Researchers will want to view the text of the successful ballot measure both in its original form and as it was codified.

Viewing the full-text of the ballot measure in its *original form* is indispensable to fully understanding the impact of the measure. This is because the text of the measure precisely states what sections of the Constitution or Code are being added to or amended. This is an essential roadmap because a measure often affects numerous sections of the Constitution and/or Code. For example, 1990's Proposition 115 (the "Crime Victims' Justice Reform Act") amended several provisions of the California Constitution and added to and repealed sections of the Code of Civil Procedure, Evidence Code, and Penal Code.

Likewise, viewing the successful measure *as codified* allows the researcher to see the information contained in the annotations, e.g., case summaries, law review citations, and subsequent history. This information is critical for determining how the courts have interpreted the measure and for following any subsequent amendments that may have occurred in the law.

While there is no comprehensive resource that indexes ballot measures by subject, the California Secretary of State has published a study that categorizes ballot measures by subject through the year 1989.[25]

---

[24] *California Gillnetter's Assoc. v. Dept. of Fish and Game,* 39 Cal.App.4th 1145, 46 Cal.Rptr.2d 338 (Cal.App. 1995) and *Tinsley v. Superior Court of San Mateo,* 150 Cal.App.3d 90, 197 Cal. Rptr. 643 (Cal. App. 1983).

[25] March Fong Eu, *A History of the California Initiative Process* (1989). Additionally, the Los Angeles County Law Library has created a website that holds great promise as an aid to performing ballot measure research. This website currently has a list of all statewide ballot measures, arranged by election, back to the general election of November 1952. Each entry describes the proposition, indicates whether or not it was

[b]   *Statutes and Amendments to the Code*

The *Statutes and Amendments to the Code* is the primary print source for looking at the text of a ballot measure in its original form. It has many drawbacks, however, especially when researching either a very recent ballot measure or older ballot measure. [26]

From 1982, the *Statutes and Amendments to the Code* prints the full-text of every ballot measure adopted or defeated. For example, to see the text of an initiative passed in the primary election of June 3, 1986, go to the first volume in the *1986 Statutes and Amendments to the Code* and, using the Contents page, locate "Measures Submitted to Vote of Electors at Primary Election June 3, 1986." A page reference directs you to a section in the first volume where the text of all ballot measures for that election appear.

Prior to 1982, the *Statutes and Amendments to the Code* did not reprint the text of any citizen-sponsored measure that was defeated. Only the text of successful citizen-sponsored measures were reprinted in full. For ballot measures submitted by the Legislature, the page reference was given for the location in the *Statutes and Amendments to the Code* where the text of the proposed ballot measure could be located, as chaptered.

[c]   Advanced Legislative Services

The annotated codes produced by West and Deering's include a softbound advance legislative service. *West's California Legislative Service* now prints all ballot measures from the current year. For example, to view a proposition appearing on the November general election ballot, locate the next pamphlet appearing after the election and all citizen-sponsored measures will be printed, whether or not they were successful. For legislatively-sponsored measures, this pamphlet provides three pieces of information that will lead to the full-text of the measure: (1) the session law cite of the successful bill or constitutional amendment underlying the ballot measure; (2) the number of the bill or constitutional amendment itself; and (3) a cite to the particular pamphlet in the service that contains the text of the measure. *West's California Legislative*

---

successful, and specifies the code or constitutional section that the proposition proposed to add to or amend. While there is no subject index, the text-searching capabilities of Web browsers allows for keyword searching of this information. The address of this site is: *www.lalaw.lib.ca.us.*

[26] The *Statutes and Amendments to the Code* is currently several years behind in publication. This is a significant hurdle for research on recent ballot measures.

Service also publishes proposed Constitutional Amendments passed by the Legislature throughout the year.

The advance legislative service of *Deering's California Codes Annotated* currently has the full-text of all successful ballot measures. These are printed in the next pamphlet appearing after the election.

[d] The Annotated Codes

As mentioned above, the successful ballot measure will be codified and can be located in *West's Annotated California Codes* or *Deering's California Codes Annotated.*[27] The annotations in the Codes are very valuable for finding cases interpreting the measure and discovering what secondary sources have discussed the measure. Locating the text of a successful measure in the Codes can be very difficult, however, because the indexes to both *West's* and *Deering's* are of limited assistance. These indexes are arranged by subject matter and rarely refer to a proposition number. If the original text of the measure is available, use this text to determine where the measure is codified.

[4] Legislatively-Sponsored Measures

Propositions arising in the Legislature are also printed in the ballot pamphlet, and this resource may be used to locate qualified measures of this type. Additionally, the researcher can locate the bill or constitutional amendment that gave rise to the measure by using traditional print resources for locating legislative documents. The bill will be either an Assembly Bill (AB) or Senate Bill (SB) and a constitutional amendment will be designated as either an Assembly Constitutional Amendment (ACA) or Senate Constitutional Amendment (SCA).

An excellent Internet resource for locating current bills is the Website of the Legislative Counsel of California. The URL of this site is: *www.leginfo.ca.gov/index.html.* This site has an archive of bills going back to the 1993–94 legislative session.

§ 5.04 Legislative History

[1] Overview

Legislative history properly refers to the various steps and proceedings that occur as a bill makes its way through the legislative process.

---

[27] To see the text of the few measures that have not been codified, consult the *Uncodified Initiative Measures and Statutes* volume of *Deering's California Codes Annotated.*

Researchers often delve into a statute's legislative history, primarily for the purpose of discovering the "intent" of the Legislature in enacting that particular law. Legislative history does exist in this traditional sense for legislatively-sponsored ballot measures.[28] Citizen-sponsored measures, however, have been created through a much different process, and thus, it is inaccurate to refer to the "legislative history" of a citizen-sponsored measure. Numerous California cases can be found, however, where a court has looked for the "intent" behind a measure, regardless of whether it arose from the Legislature or a petition drive.[29]

[2] Citizen-Sponsored Measures

[a] Scope of Documents

The documents accorded weight as evidence of the "intent" behind citizen-sponsored measures are different from the type of legislative history documents associated with legislation. The item relied on by courts when looking for the intent of the electorate are the voter arguments contained in the ballot pamphlet. There are numerous other documents that the researcher may locate, however, that arguably shed light on the intent of the ballot measure. The California courts have not, however, looked to any document outside of the ballot pamphlet when searching for intent behind a *citizen-sponsored* ballot measure.[30]

---

[28] For a thorough review of the subject of legislative history for ballot measures, *see* J. Clark Kelso, "California's Constitutional Right to Privacy," 19 *Pepp. L. Rev.* 327 (1992). In this article, Professor Kelso examines the specific legislative history associated with 1972's right of privacy initiative.

[29] *See, e.g., Lungren v. Deukmejian (Roberti)*, 45 Cal.3d 727, 248 Cal.Rptr. 115, 755 P.2d 299 (Cal. 1988). The *Lungren* court stated that "[t]he rule that the ballot pamphlet is an important aid in determining the intent of the voters in adopting a constitutional amendment or statute is too well settled to require extensive citation of authority." It is important to remember, however, that the courts will undertake this search only when it is first determined that the words of the measure are somehow ambiguous. If the text is clear and unambiguous, there will be no resort to the "legislative history." This is consistent with general rules of statutory construction.

[30] In *Evangelatos v. Superior Court*, 44 Cal.3d 1188, 246 Cal.Rptr. 629, 753 P.2d 585 (Cal. 1988), the Supreme Court considered whether "the history of the times and of legislation upon the same subject" should be examined to determine if a proposition should be applied retroactively. Ultimately, the Court held, however, that no retroactive application was permissible where the text of the proposition was silent on the issue and there was no evidence that the electorate intended a retroactive application. *Evangelatos*, at p. 605.

[b] Voter Arguments

California case law holds that the "official argument" accompanying a successful ballot measure may be considered as an aid in interpreting that ballot measure. In *Hill v. NCAA*, the California Supreme Court considered a challenge to a NCAA drug testing policy under the state's constitutional right to privacy, a right established by Proposition 11.[31] The Court found that the word "privacy" had no definitive definition and so looked to the intent behind Proposition 11:

> The Privacy Initiative is to be interpreted and applied in a manner consistent with the probable intent of the body enacting it: the voters of the state of California. [Citations omitted]. When, as here, the language of an initiative statute does not point to a definitive resolution of a question of interpretation, 'it is appropriate to consider indicia of the voters' intent other than the language of the provision itself.' . . . Such indicia include the analysis and arguments contained in the official ballot pamphlet. [Citations omitted].[32]

For citizen-sponsored measures, California courts have looked exclusively at the voter arguments when searching for intent. In a dissenting opinion filed in the *Hill* decision, Judge Mosk noted: "Indeed, they [the voter arguments] offer, in essence, the only such evidence."[33]

[c] Hearings and Reports

While committee hearings and reports should be considered as part of the "history" behind a ballot measure, they are not, however, considered relevant in discovering the intent of the electorate in passing a measure. As the Legislature had no role in drafting a citizen-sponsored measure, the Legislature cannot be said to have had any intent in this matter. In *People v. Castro*, the Supreme Court specifically rejected an argument that language contained in a committee report could shed light on the intent behind a citizen-sponsored measure.[34]

---

[31] *Hill v. NCAA*, 7 Cal.4th 1, 26 Cal.Rptr.2d 834, 865 P.2d 633 (Cal. 1994).

[32] *Id.*

[33] *Id. See also White v. Davis*, 13 Cal.3d 757, 120 Cal.Rptr. 94, 533 P.2d 222 (Cal. 1975). Some commentators have questioned the courts' use of voter arguments as evidence of intent, especially now that the law provides for an objective analysis of the measure from the Legislative Analyst. *See, e.g.*, Professor J. Clark Kelso's article, "California's Constitutional Right to Privacy," 19 *Pepp. L. Rev.* 327 (1992).

[34] People v. Castro, 38 Cal.3d 301, 211 Cal.Rptr. 719, 696 P.2d 111, 117 (Cal. 1985).

It is possible to locate hearings and reports on citizen-sponsored measures as committees of the Assembly and Senate do hold hearings concerning such proposed measures. After the Attorney General has prepared the summary of a initiative petition, the text of the proposed initiative is forwarded to the Legislature where public hearings may be held on the subject of the measure.[35]

Once a measure qualifies for the ballot, the Legislature is required by statute to hold joint legislative hearings concerning the measure.[36] Locating a hearing transcript can yield much valuable information. In addition to the testimony of witnesses, the transcript may contain a staff analysis and other written documentation submitted to the committee concerning the effects of the measure. Committee reports may also contain a useful analysis of the measure.

Locating the text of hearings and reports generated by the California Legislature is, however, often a frustrating experience, as these documents are not distributed to libraries in any systematic manner. The use of an online catalog such as MELVYL[37] may be the best method of locating these items. The Offices of Research for the Assembly and the Senate may also be helpful. Finally, the California State Library publishes *California State Publications*, which may be useful in locating reports concerning ballot measures.

[d]   Analyses from the Senate Office of Research

The Senate Office of Research issues analyses of all statewide ballot measures prior to each election. The analysis is usually a fairly brief document containing a summary of the key provisions, fiscal impacts, legislative history, arguments pro and con and a partial list of supporters and opponents. In print, these publications may be available through the *AOC Reporter* or through the Senate Office of Research. The full-text of these analyses are currently being made available over the California Senate's World Wide Web site: *www.sen.ca.gov*. Again, this can be considered part of the history of a ballot measure, but not a document evidencing the intent of the electorate.

---

[35] Cal. Elec. Code, § 9007.

[36] Cal. Elec. Code, § 9034.

[37] MELVYL is the joint online catalog of the University of California library system. It is searchable over the Internet using the following URL: *merlin.ucop. edu.*

[3] Legislative History for Legislatively-Sponsored Measures

As legislatively-sponsored ballot measures begin their life as either bills or constitutional amendments, there is legislative history in the traditional sense associated with these measures. Legislative history denotes various documents produced during the course of the Legislature's consideration and passage of a bill or constitutional amendment, including various versions of the bill, committee reports, committee hearings, signing statements, and floor debate. In short, you would conduct legislative history as you would for any Senate or Assembly bill. [38]

The *Assembly Final History* and *Senate Final History* volumes are the starting point for discovering the procedural history associated with a legislatively-sponsored ballot measure. For example, to locate the history of a measure originating in the California Assembly, use the *Assembly Final History* volume for the year of the legislative session in which the measure was introduced. Using the "Table of Contents," locate the "Assembly Constitutional Amendments" and then trace the legislative path of the bill or resolution that proposed the amendment to the California Constitution. The *Final History* will set forth committee assignments, votes, and final disposition of the bill or resolution. Conversely, use the *Senate Final History* volume to trace the history of any measure arising in the California Senate.

§ 5.05 Legal Challenges to Ballot Measures

[1] Overview

Ballot measures frequently become the subject of litigation. These challenges may be raised either before or after the election. The parties will vary, depending upon the basis and timing of the challenge. [39]

---

[38] For an example of the type of legislative history material that may exist for a legislatively-sponsored measure, see the Appendix in *California's Constitutional Right to Privacy, supra* note 97. For guidance on conducting legislative history, please consult Chapter Four, Legislative Intent. Justice Mosk, in his dissent in *Hill v. NCAA, supra* note 100, characterizes documents produced by the Assembly and Senate as "secret legislative history" which are very hard to come by. Justice Mosk thus believes that such documents are inappropriate for determining the intent of the electorate, even when the measure is drafted by the Legislature.

[39] For an extensive discussion of case law surrounding ballot measures, see 38 Cal. Jur. 3d *Initiative and Referendum*, §§ 1–68 (1977).

[2] Pre-Election Challenges

[a] Court's Disfavor

California courts generally disfavor pre-election challenges to ballot measures, sensibly preferring to see if the measure is successful before agreeing to review the matter.[40] In *Brosnahan v. March Fong Eu*, the California Supreme Court stated:

> As we have frequently observed, it is usually more appropriate to review constitutional and other challenges to ballot propositions or initiative measures after an election rather than to disrupt the electoral process by preventing the exercise of the people's franchise, in the absence of some clear showing of invalidity.[41]

This general rule favoring post-election review contemplates that no serious harm will result if consideration of the measure's validity is postponed until after the election.[42]

There have been several occasions, however, where the courts have heard pre-election challenges to measures and then removed them from the ballot. Procedurally, anyone seeking to challenge a ballot measure prior to the election must file a writ of mandate requesting that the measure not be placed on the ballot.[43] For a discussion of what entity has standing to challenge a ballot measure, see the discussion in *League of Women Voters v. Eu (Wilson)*.[44]

[b] The Ballot Title or Summary

As might be expected, the title and summary assigned to a ballot measure are often a source of contention. Both sponsors and opponents have objected to either the title or summary prepared by the Attorney

---

[40] Fewer than one-tenth of the measures titled by the Attorney General qualify for the ballot and only one-third of the qualified measures are passed by the voters. California Commission on Campaign Financing, *Democracy by Initiative: Shaping California's Fourth Branch of Government*, 322 (1992). Thus, it would make little sense for the courts to hear pre-election challenges to ballot measures, since only a small percentage will be successful.

[41] *Brosnahan v. March Fong Eu*, 31 Cal.3d 1, 181 Cal.Rptr. 100, 641 P.2d 200, 201 (Cal. 1982).

[42] *Legislature of State of Cal. v. Deukmejian*, 34 Cal.3d 658, 194 Cal.Rptr. 781, 669 P.2d 17 (Cal. 1983).

[43] *See, e.g., Save Stanislaus Area Farm Economy v. Board of Sup'rs of County of Stanislaus (Family Farm Alliance)*, 13 Cal.App.4th 141, 16 Cal.Rptr.2d 408 (Cal. App. 1993).

[44] *League of Women Voters v. Eu (Wilson)*, 9 Cal.Rptr.2d 416 (Cal. App. 1992).

General. To withstand legal challenge, it is sufficient that the title be, as required by statute, a "[s]ummary of the chief purpose and points of the measure."[45]

Proposition 209, the "California Civil Rights Initiative," created a classic battle over a ballot title. Opponents of the measure filed suit to compel the Attorney General to alter the title of the measure, arguing that the title should reflect the fact that the measure would prohibit affirmative action programs. The trial court agreed and entered a judgment compelling the Attorney General to so alter the title. On appeal, the California Court of Appeals vacated the decision of the lower court and let the title stand as written. The Court stated:

> The title and summary need not contain a complete catalogue or index of all the measure's provisions and "if reasonable minds may differ as to the sufficiency of the title, the title should be held sufficient." As a general rule, the title and summary prepared by the Attorney General are presumed accurate, and substantial compliance with the "chiefs purpose and points" provision is sufficient.[46]

Thus, the courts will defer to the Attorney General's judgment, except in rare cases.[47]

[c]   The Form of the Petition

Opponents of ballot measures may attempt to block the measure on the basis of the petition's failure to satisfy some provision of the Elections Code regarding the form of the petition or the manner of its circulation. Ballot measures have occasionally been blocked from appearing on the ballot on this basis, but the courts generally will not intervene as long as there has been "substantial compliance" with the requirements of the law. In *Assembly of State of California v. Deukmejian*, the Supreme Court stated:

> This court has stressed that technical deficiencies in referendum and initiative petitions will not invalidate the petitions if they are in

---

[45] Cal. Elec. Code, § 9002. See *People v. Frierson*, 25 Cal.3d 142, 158 Cal.Rptr. 281, 599 P.2d 587, 614 (Cal. 1979); *Epperson v. Jordan*, 12 Cal.2d 61, 82 P. 445, 448 (Cal. 1938).

[46] *Lungren v. Superior Court (Jones)*, 48 Cal.App.4th 435, 55 Cal.Rptr.2d 690, 692 (Cal. App. 1996) (citations omitted).

[47] For examples of the few instances where the Attorney General's title has been successfully challenged, see *Boyd v. Jordan*, 1 Cal.2d 468, 35 P.2d 533 (1934) and *Clark v. Jordan*, 7 Cal.2d 248, 60 P.2d 457 (1936).

"substantial compliance" with statutory and constitutional requirements [citation].[48]

In *Malick v. Athenour*, the Court of Appeals held that the failure to adhere to the precise language of the Elections Code was not fatal if the intent of the law could still be satisfied (the court finding that verification of signatures was possible through alternate means).[49] Thus, while the courts stress that there are limits to the safety net of the "substantial compliance" doctrine, few measures will be invalidated after an election for a failure to satisfy procedural or formal requirements of the Elections Code.

[d] Constitutionality of the Measure

Another basis for challenging a ballot measure prior to an election goes to the substance of the proposed measure. Opponents may attempt to block a measure from appearing on the ballot if they believe that the proposed measure is unconstitutional or otherwise invalid as a matter of law. In *Legislature of State of Cal. v. Deukmejian*, the California Supreme Court took the reluctant step of removing an initiative measure from consideration by the voters. This litigation was prompted by the Governor's declaration of a special election to consider an initiative measure that would realign Assembly, Senate, and Congressional districts. This action was challenged on the ground that the California Constitution forbade redistricting more than once in a 10-year period following a census. The Supreme Court agreed:

> We conclude, based upon the principle that in the enactment of statutes the constitutional limitations that bind the Legislature apply with equal force to the people's reserved power of initiative, that such an exception cannot be justified. Therefore, the proposed initiative is constitutionally impermissible and may not be submitted to the voters.[50]

---

[48] *Assembly of State of Cal. v. Deukmejian*, 30 Cal. 638, 180 Cal.Rptr. 297, 639 P.2d 939, 948 (Cal. 1982) (citations omitted).

[49] *Malick v. Athenour*, 37 Cal.App.4th 1120, 44 Cal.Rptr.2d 281, 285 (Cal. App. 1995). But see *Nelson v. Carlson*, 17 Cal.App.4th 732, 21 Cal.Rptr.2d 485 (Cal. App. 1993) (holding that failure to attach general plan to petition was fatally defective error). For two early opinions blocking local recall petitions from appearing on the ballot because of technical deficiencies, see *Gerth v. Dominguez*, 1 Cal.2d 239, 34 P.2d 135 (Cal. 1934) and *Muehleisen v. Forward*, 4 Cal.2d 17, 46 P.2d 969 (Cal. 1935).

[50] *Legislature of State of Cal. v. Deukmejian*, 34 Cal.2d 658, 194 Cal.Rptr. 781.

Factors cited by the court for not delaying review until after the election were the tremendous costs of holding a special election and the impracticability of redistricting before the next general election should the measure be successful.[51]

[3] Post-Election Challenges

[a] Overview

Successful ballot measures have been challenged in court on many different grounds. Experience with Propositions 187 and 209 in 1998 demonstrates that opponents may use the judiciary to successfully block the implementation of voter-approved measures.[52] While courts generally give great deference to the will of the electorate, numerous successful measures have been struck down, in whole or part, because of either a procedural or substantive violation of the law.

California courts have repeatedly stated that successful ballot measures should be liberally construed and reasonable doubts resolved in favor of the measure.[53] In *McFadden v. Jordan*, the Supreme Court declared: "The right of initiative is precious to the people and is one which the courts are zealous to preserve to the fullest tenable measure of spirit as well as letter."[54] The deference given to successful measures is founded on the principle that the power of initiative and referendum is not granted to the people, but "reserved" by them.[55] Thus, the courts have endeavored to protect initiatives from attack.

Despite the court's great reluctance to invalidate successful ballot measures, there are a number of reasons why an initiative may be struck down, in whole or part.

---

[51] *Id. See also Amer. Fed. of Labor-Congress v. March Fong Eu*, 36 Cal.3d 687, 686 P.2d 609, 613 (Cal. 1984) (stressing that the presence of an invalid measure on the ballot takes attention away from valid measures); and Note, "Judicial Intervention in the Preelection Stage of the Initiative Process: A Change of Policy by the California Supreme Court," 15 *Pac. L.J.* 1127 (1984).

[52] Opponents of both propositions filed suit in federal district court and obtained injunctions against implementation of the measures.

[53] *See, e.g., Raven v. Deukmejian*, 52 Cal.3d 336, 276 Cal.Rptr. 326, 801 P.2d 1077 (Cal. 1990); *Farley v. Healey*, 67 Cal.2d 325, 62 Cal.Rptr. 26, 431 P.2d 650 (Cal. 1967); and *Estate of Cirone*, 153 Cal.App.3d 199, 200 Cal.Rptr. 511 (Cal. App. 1984).

[54] *McFadden v. Jordan*, 32 Cal.2d 330, 196 P.2d 787, 788 (Cal. 1948).

[55] *Rossi v. Brown*, 9 Cal.4th 688, 38 Cal.Rptr.2d 363, 889 P.2d 557, 560 (Cal. 1995).

[b]   Violation of the "Single-Subject" Rule

One of the express limitations on the exercise of the power of initiative and referendum is the "single-subject" rule of Article II, Section 8, subdivision (d) of the California Constitution.[56] This provision prohibits measures "embracing more than one subject."[57] The purpose of this provision is twofold. First, the single-subject rule is intended to prevent voter confusion. Second, it prevents "logrolling," a practice where less popular provisions are combined with more popular provisions in the hope that voters will support the entire package based upon the popular components.

California courts have rarely struck down a ballot measure for violating the single-subject rule, instead going to great lengths to preserve the measure. In *Raven v. Deukmejian*, the California Supreme Court summarized the law on this subject:

> This Court has recently considered numerous initiative challenges based on the single-subject rule, and the principles that guide our analysis are now well-settled. We have held that "an initiative measure does not violate the single-subject requirement if, despite its varied collateral effects, *all of its parts are reasonably germane* to each other," and to the general purpose or object of the initiative.[58]

The single-subject rule does not require interdependence or interrelationship of the measure's provisions in order to pass scrutiny.[59] One reason why the single-subject rule is so loosely applied is that the voters

---

[56] *See* Daniel H. Lowenstein, *California Initiatives and the Single-Subject Rule*, 30 UCLA L. Rev. 936 (1983). Professor Lowenstein gives a thorough discussion of the sometimes confusing and contradictory caselaw on this topic.

[57] This provision was enacted through a constitutional amendment in 1948, and has been interpreted as imposing the same "single-subject" limitation that applies to acts of the Legislature. *Perry v. Jordan*, 34 Cal.2d 87, 207 P.2d 47 (Cal. 1949). The other express Constitutional limitation on the initiative power is found in article II, section 12, which bars constitutional amendments and statutes which name any individual to office, or identify any private corporation to perform any duty or to have any power or function.

[58] *Raven v. Deukmejian*, 52 Cal.3d 336, 276 Cal.Rptr. 326, 801 P.2d 1077, 1083 (Cal. 1990) (citations omitted).

[59] *Id.* See also: *Manduley v. Superior Court*, 27 Cal.4th 537, 117 Cal.Rptr 168, 41 P.3d 3 (2002).

must be able to deal "comprehensively and in detail with an area of the law."[60]

One of the rare occasions where a successful measure was declared to violate the single-subject rule occurred in *Chemical Specialties Mfrs. v. Deukmejian*. The California Court of Appeals held that the "People's Right to Know Act" violated the single-subject rule because its provisions, ranging from disclosure on household products, to seniors' health insurance, to stock holdings in South Africa, were not functionally related or reasonably germane to one another.[61]

[c] Amendment Versus Revision of the Constitution

The initiative process may be used only to amend, not revise, the state constitution.[62] Again, the courts have been reluctant to invalidate initiatives on this basis, and have done so only on a few occasions. A leading case is *Raven v. Deukmejian*, where the Supreme Court held that a provision of Proposition 115, purporting to limit a criminal defendant's rights to those under the United States Constitution, was an impermissible revision of the California Constitution.[63] The Supreme Court began its analysis by noting that the Court must examine both the quantitative and qualitative effects of the initiative upon the Constitution to make the determination of whether an impermissible revision had occurred. The Supreme Court stated:

> Although the Constitution does not define the terms "amendment" or "revision," the courts have developed some guidelines helpful in resolving the present issue. . . . [o]ur revision/amendment analysis has a dual aspect, requiring us to examine both the quantitative and qualitative effects of the measure on our constitutional scheme. Substantial changes in either respect could amount to a revision.[64]

The Court then ruled that while the quantitative effect of Proposition 115 was minimal (it deleted no sections of the Constitution and added to only one article), the qualitative effect was tremendous (in effect,

---

[60] *Fair Political Practices Commission v. Superior Court*, 25 Cal.3d 33, 157 Cal.Rptr. 855, 599 P.2d 46, 50 (Cal. 1979).

[61] *Chemical Specialties Mfrs. v. Deukmejian*, 227 Cal.App.3d 663, 278 Cal.Rptr. 128, 132 (Cal.App. 1991). See, Note, *Putting the "Single" Back in the Single-Subject Rule: A Proposal for Initiative Reform in California*, 24 *U.C. Davis L.Rev.* 879 (1991).

[62] Cal. Const., art. XVIII, § 1-3.

[63] *Raven v. Deukmejian*, 52 Cal.3d 336, 276 Cal.Rptr. 326, 801 P.2d 1077 (Cal. 1990).

[64] *Id.*

vesting all judicial interpretation of the rights of criminal defendants in the U.S. Supreme Court). Therefore, Proposition 115 was struck down as an impermissible revision of the California Constitution.[65]

[d] Violation of the California or United States Constitution

A *statutory* initiative is subject to the same state and federal constitutional limitations as are statutes enacted by the Legislature. Therefore, any statute or amendment to a statute created through the ballot measure process will be struck down if it violates either the federal or state Constitution.[66] By definition, a successful constitutional amendment measure cannot be held to violate the California Constitution (but could, in theory, violate the Federal Constitution).

In *Mulkey v. Reitman*,[67] a black couple challenged Proposition 14, a 1964 ballot measure that amended the California Constitution. Proposition 14 was a reaction against civil rights legislation passed in California and guaranteed that real property owners could decline to lease or to sell to any person. The *Mulkey* court first stated:

> We note preliminarily that although we are examining a provision which, by its enactment by ballot, has been accorded state constitutional stature, the supremacy clause of the United States Constitution nevertheless compels that [Proposition 14], like any other state law conform to federal constitutional standards before it may be enforced against persons who are entitled to protection under that guarantee.[68]

After finding that Proposition 14 denied the plaintiffs equal protection of the laws under the Fourteenth Amendment, the *Mulkey* court declared the measure to be void.[69]

---

[65] *Id.*

[66] *See Legislature of State of Cal. v. Deukmejian,* 34 Cal.3d 658, 194 Cal.Rptr. 781, 669 P.2d 17 (Cal. 1983) and *Hawn v. County of Ventura,* 73 Cal.App.3d 1009, 141 Cal. Rptr. 111 (Cal. App. 1977).

[67] *Mulkey v. Reitman,* 73 Cal.App.3d 529, 50 Cal.Rptr. 881, 413 P.2d 825 (Cal. 1966).

[68] *Id.*

[69] *Id.*

[e]   Measure May Only Address Legislative, Not Administrative, Matters

The power of the initiative and referendum may only be used for "legislative" acts, not acts which are deemed "administrative."[70] In practice, this distinction is often very hard to grasp. California courts frequently cite the following language from *McKevitt v. City of Sacramento*:

> Acts constituting a declaration of public purpose, and making provision for ways and means of its accomplishment, may be generally classified as calling for the exercise of legislative power. Acts which are to be deemed as acts of administration . . . are those which are necessary to be done to carry out legislative policies and purposes already declared by the legislative body.[71]

In *Simpson v. Hite*, the California Supreme Court blocked a local measure that proposed to intervene in a decision of the Los Angeles County Supervisors' regarding the location of a new courthouse facility. The Supreme Court ruled that the decision on the location of a courthouse was administrative, not legislative, in character and thus not a valid use of the initiative power.[72]

While reported cases on this subject in California have involved challenges to local, not statewide, measures, logically this rule would apply to all initiatives.

[f]   Measure Not a "Statute"

The initiative power is limited to enacting statutes and amending the constitution. If a measure attempts any other action, it is not valid. In *Amer. Fed. of Labor-Congress v. March Fong Eu*,[73] the California Supreme Court heard a challenge to the Balanced Federal Budget Statutory Initiative of 1984. This measure sought to compel the California Legislature to request Congress to call a constitutional convention

---

[70] As the courts often state, the powers are only "legislative" (and reserved to the adoption or rejection of "statutes") because sections 8 and 9 of article II of the California Constitution speak in terms of the electors power to propose or reject "statutes." *See* 17 Cal. Jur. 3d *Initiative and Referendum* secs. 3–5 (1977).

[71] *McKevitt v. City of Sacramento*, 55 Cal.App. 117, 203 P. 132, 136 (Cal. App. 1921).

[72] *Simpson v. Hite*, 36 Cal.2d 125, 222 P.2d 225, 228 (Cal. 1950). *Accord, Mueller v. Brown*, 221 Cal.App.2d 319, 34 Cal. Rptr. 474 (Cal. App. 1963).

[73] *Amer. Fed. of Labor-Congress v. March Fong Eu*, 36 Cal.3d 687, 206 Cal.Rptr. 89, 686 P.2d 609 (Cal. 1984).

for the purpose of drafting a balanced budget amendment to the United States Constitution. The Supreme Court held that such a measure was impermissible:

> We . . . conclude that the measure exceeds the scope of the initiative power under the controlling provisions of the California Constitution (art.II, sec.8 and art.IV, sec.1). The initiative power is the power to adopt "statutes"—to enact laws—but the crucial provisions of the balanced budget initiative do not adopt a *statute* or enact a law. They adopt, and mandate the Legislature to adopt, a *resolution* which does not change California law and constitutes only one step in a process which might eventually amend the federal Constitution. Such a resolution is not an exercise of legislative power reserved to the people under the California Constitution. [74]

[g]   Conflicting Successful Measures

It is not uncommon for two measures to appear on the ballot that address the same subject matter. If both measures pass, the issue arises of which measure shall go into effect. Article II, section 10(b) of the California Constitution specifically addresses this situation: "If provisions of two or more measures approved at the same election conflict, those of the measure receiving the highest affirmative vote shall prevail."

A leading case interpreting this section of the Constitution is *Taxpayers to Limit Campaign Spending v. FPPC*. [75] In this case, the Supreme Court rejected any notion that the courts should attempt to salvage the measure receiving fewer votes by upholding any provisions in that measure that did not conflict directly with the measure receiving the greater number of votes. The Court held:

> [U]nless a contrary intent is apparent in the ballot measures, when two or more measures are competing initiatives, either because they are expressly offered as "all-or-nothing" alternatives or because each creates a comprehensive regulatory scheme related to the same subject, section 10(b) [of the Constitution] mandates that only the provisions of the measure receiving the highest number of affirmative votes be enforced." [76]

---

[74] *Id.*

[75] *Taxpayers to Limit Campaign Spending v. FPPC,* 51 Cal.3d 744, 274 Cal.Rptr. 787, 799 P.2d 1220 (Cal. 1990).

[76] *Id.* This decision overruled a line of cases where the courts attempted to harmonize provisions of successful, competing measures. *See, e.g., Peoples Advocate, Inc. v. Superior Court,* 181 Cal.App.3d 316, 226 Cal.Rptr. 640 (Cal. App. 1986).

§ 5.06 Research Tools

[1] Overview

There are a variety of research tools that must be used for ballot measure research. Each has its strengths, but no one source offers comprehensive guidance. To thoroughly research any particular measure, it is necessary to consult numerous publications.

The law governing ballot measures is found in the California Constitution, the Elections Code, and court decisions. It is important to remember that, in 1994, the California Election Code was repealed and reenacted by Stats. 1994, c. 920 (S.B. 1547). Most of the provisions concerning ballot measures were placed in division 9 of the Elections Code, section 9000, et. seq. Publications produced before 1995 will thus be citing to the now repealed sections of the Elections Code.[77]

[2] Annotated Codes

West's Annotated California Code and *Deering's California Codes Annotated* are obviously essential for research as successful statutes and constitutional amendments find their way into the appropriate titles of the Code. The challenge in using the annotated codes is the fact that the subject indexes to these publications make little provision for the researcher who knows only the proposition number or popular name of a ballot measure. Only the most well-known propositions will have an entry in the indexes or popular name tables of *West's* or *Deering's* codes. Otherwise the researcher must use a subject approach. For example, in 1986 the voters approved Proposition 65, the "California Safe Drinking Water and Toxic Enforcement Act of 1986." Neither *West's* or *Deering's* have a reference to "Proposition 65" in their indexes. *West's* indexes this measure under "Safe Drinking Water and Toxic Enforcement Act of 1986," while *Deering's* indexes it under "Drinking Water." Thus, an understanding of the subject matter of the ballot measure is necessary in order to locate the text using only the indexes to the annotated codes.

[3] Digests

Digests serve as subject access to case reporters. California's two digests, *West's California Digest* and the *California Digest of Official*

---

[77] The researcher may use the disposition tables in either the *West's Annotated California Code* or *Deering's California Codes Annotated* to convert former code section references to the current code sections.

Reports, will aid the researcher in locating state and federal court decisions concerning California ballot measures.

📖 *West's California Digest*

Cases concerning initiatives are generally placed under the digest topic of "Statutes." The "Initiative" is placed under subheading IX, and is covered by keynumbers 301–327. The "Referendum" is covered by keynumbers 341–367.

📖 *California Digest of Official Reports*, Third Series (McKinney's)

Cases concerning initiatives and referendums are placed under the topic of "Initiative and Referendum" (which seems preferable to West's choice to lump this subject under the general heading of "Statutes"). Instead of dividing the topic broadly into "Initiatives" and "Referendums" (the West approach), McKinney's divides the topic into "State Elections" and "Local Elections." This difference may be helpful if you want to limit your research to one of these categories.

[4] Periodicals and Periodical Indexes

[a] Overview

Articles discussing ballot measures appear in a wide variety of publications. The thorough researcher will use not only legal periodical indexes (discussed below) but also more general indexes, such as the *PAIS Bulletin* and *Social Sciences Index*. Periodical indexes are typically available in print, CD-ROM, or online formats. The computer-based formats are generally superior for most uses, but have date limitations which make them less useful when researching ballot measures arising before the 1980s.

[b] *Current Law Index*

The paper version of the *Current Law Index* uses the subject heading of "Referendum" for articles dealing with ballot measures (not an obvious choice, since initiatives are much more common than referendums in California and elsewhere). Unfortunately, as there is no geographic subheading for California, the researcher must scan all entries to be thorough.

🖥 "Legaltrac" is the CD-ROM version of the *Current Law Index*. The computer database frees the researcher from the static subject headings of the print index. Using either the "subject" or "keyword" methods, "Legaltrac" makes it simple to locate articles on specific propositions. The "subject" option uses the subject heading of "California proposition X."[78]

The online version is called the "Legal Resource Index." As with the CD-ROM database, keyword searching makes it simple to locate ballot measures. In Westlaw, this database is identified as LRI. In LexisNexis, this database is found in the "Legal Resource Index" Source (LEXREF; LGLIND).

[c] *Index to Legal Periodicals*

If using a print periodical index, the *Index to Legal Periodicals* is the most efficient because it has a subject subheading for California under the main subject heading of "Initiative and Referendum." Thus, you can quickly find articles relating to California ballot measures. The *Index to Legal Periodicals* also cross-indexes articles. For example, an article on Proposition 187 is indexed not only under "Initiative and Referendum," but also under the California subheading of the subject heading of "Aliens."

"Wilsondisc" is the CD-ROM version of the *Index to Legal Periodicals*. The index is also available on Westlaw in the ILP database and on LexisNexis in the "Index to Legal Periodicals" Source (LEXREF; ILP). As noted above, the computer databases make it relatively easy to find articles concerning specific ballot measures.

[5] **Treatises and Encyclopedias**

  📖 *Witkin's Summary of California Law*, 9th ed.

The most valuable sections of *Witkin's* are found in the "Constitutional Law" topic, under sections 120–126. These sections discuss the constitutional limitations upon initiative and referendum measures.

  📖 *California Jurisprudence*, 3d

Cal. Jur. 3d treats the subject much more thoroughly than does *Witkin's*. See Volume 38, "Initiative and Referendum," secs.

---

[78] Some subject headings used by "Legaltrac" are somewhat obscure, but the researcher will be guided to the cites by cross-referencing. For example, articles concerning Proposition 187 are placed under the subject heading of "California illegal aliens ineligibility for public services." Thankfully, using the search phrase of "Proposition 187" leads the user to this heading.

1–68, for a lengthy discussion of case law related to petition procedure and challenges to ballot measures.

[6] Research Facilities

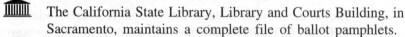 The California State Library, Library and Courts Building, in Sacramento, maintains a complete file of ballot pamphlets.

The Institute of Governmental Studies Library at the University of California, Berkeley, also maintains a complete file of ballot pamphlets and other material related to elections.

§ 5.07 Annotated Bibliography of Selected Titles

📖 Allswang, John M. *California Initiatives and Referendums: 1912–1990.* Los Angeles: Edmund G. "Pat" Brown Institute of Public Affairs (1991). This book is primarily a summary of all measures appearing on the ballot between the years 1912 and 1990. The following information is presented for each measure: (1) a brief summary of the intent of the measure; (2) the outcome of the election; (3) the endorser; and (4) summaries of the arguments for and against the measure. There is an excellent bibliography.

📖 Cain, Bruce E. and Noll, Roger G., Editors. *Constitutional Reform in California: Making State Government More Effective and Responsive.* Berkeley: Institute of Governmental Studies Press, 1995. 514 p. This volume contains over 20 articles by 26 contributors. All articles are about the structure of the constitution, amending the constitution, the separation of powers, general issues of constitutional law. The predominant theme is the search for a better method of constitutional reform than the initiative constitutional amendment. One contributor is Joseph R. Grodin, former Associate Justice of the California Supreme Court.

📖 California Commission on Campaign Financing. *Democracy by Initiative: Shaping California's Fourth Branch of Government.* Los Angeles, Center for Responsive Government, 1992. This work presents the history of the ballot measure in California and sets forth recommendations on reforms to the current system. A very thorough and useful resource.

📖 Christenson, Kara. "Interpreting the Purposes of Initiatives: Proposition 65." 40 *Hastings L.J.* 1031 (1989). This article focuses on what sources California courts have used when interpreting ballot measures.

📖 Council of State Governments. *The Book of the States.* Lexington, Ky. The Council of State Governments, 1998. The chapter on "State Elections, Campaign Finance & Initiatives," has an excellent compilation of tables and statistics on initiatives and referendums in the United States. It also has a good bibliography.

📖 Crouch, Winston W. *The Initiative and Referendum in California.* Los Angeles. Haynes Foundation, 1950. This work should be considered a later edition of the 1939 book bearing the same title, written by Winston W. Crouch and V.O. Key, Jr. (see below). An excellent study of the history and use of initiatives and referendums in California. While now obviously dated, there has been no subsequent work to compare with Mr. Crouch's efforts.

📖 Erler, Edward J. "Californians and their Constitiution: Progressivism, Direct Democracy and the Administrative State." 6 *NEXUS: A Journal of Opinion* 237–253 (Spring 2001). This well-footnoted article addresses the various ways that have been used to update the California Constitution, but concentrates mostly on the initiative process.

📖 Eu, March Fong. *A History of the California Initiative Process.* Sacramento. California Secretary of State, 1989. While there is really very little "history" or other text provided, this work is valuable for its statistical summaries and subject indexing for all ballot measures through 1989.

📖 Eu, March Fong. *A Study of Ballot Measures: 1884–1980.* Sacramento. California Secretary of State, 1981. This study includes a chronology of ballot measures, subject indexing, and election statistics.

📖 Eule, Julian N. "Judicial Review of Direct Democracy." 99 *Yale L.J.* 1503 (1990). Professor Eule considers the role that the judiciary should play in reviewing successful ballot measures. He concludes that courts should be less deferential to law enacted through initiative than that enacted by the Legislature.

📖 Graves, Ernest L. "The Guarantee Clause in California: State Constitutional Limits on Initiatives Changing the California

Constitution." 31 *Loy. L.A. L.Rev.* 1305–1326 (1998). The author argues that the direct democracy of the initiative subverts the founding fathers' goal of having a representative or "republican" government.

📖 Hasen, Richard L. "Judging the Judges of Initiatives: A Comment on Holman and Stern." 31 *Loy. L.A. L.Rev.* 1267–1274 (1998). This is a short rebuttal of the conclusions in the Holman Stern article.

📖 Holman, Craig B. and Stern, Robert. "Judicial Review of Ballot Initiatives: The Changing Role of State and Federal Courts." 31 *Loy. L.A. L.Rev* 1239–1266 (1998). The authors examine the success rate of initiatives in the courts at the various stages where objections might be raised. The article includes a half dozen tables and graphs illustrating court treatment.

📖 Kelso, J. Clark. "California's Constitutional Right to Privacy." 19 *Pepperdine L. Rev.* 327 (1992). Professor Kelso's article contains valuable discussions about how California courts examine the legislative history behind ballot measures. An appendix contains a sample of the type of legislative history that can be found for an initiative.

📖 Key, V.O., Jr. and Crouch, Winston W. *The Initiative and Referendum in California.* Los Angeles. Haynes Foundation, 1939. A classic work on California's experience with the initiative and referendum. This is particularly valuable for its review of the historical origins of the "direct democracy" movement in this state.

📖 Kuehl, Sheila James. "Either Way You Get Sausages: One Legislator's View of the Initiative Process." 31 *Loy. L.A. L.Rev.* 1327–1336 (1998). The author, a California Senator and former Assemblyperson, first reviews the detailed process a bill goes through to become a law. She then follows with the less examined path an initiative takes on its way to becoming a law. The short article has 56 footnotes which provide citations to additional articles and to numerous initiative illustrations.

📖 League of Women Voters. *Initiative and Referendum in California: A Legacy Lost?* Sacramento. League of Women

Voters, 1984. Examines the history of the initiative/
referendum movement in California and specifically addresses
the issue of whether current practice matches expectations of
early proponents of the movement. Includes statistics, state-
by-state summaries, and a good section on proposed changes
to the initiative/referendum process.

Lowenstein, Daniel Hays and Stern, Robert M. "The First
Amendment and Paid Initiative Petition Circulators: A Dissenting View and a Proposal." 17 *Hastings Const. L.Q.* 175
(1989). The authors criticize the increasing role of paid
petition circulators and the role of money in qualifying a
measure.

Manheim, Karl and Howard, Edward P. "A Structural Theory
of the Initiative Power in California." 31 *Loy. L.A. L.Rev.*
1165–1237 (1998). Contains an extensive discussion on the
political origins and philosophy behind California's initiative
process. The article also critically reviews the judicary's
deferential treatment of successful ballot measures.

Salvato, Greg M. "New Limits on the California Initiative:
An Analysis and Critique." *19 Loy. L.A. L.Rev.* 1045 (1986).
This article provides an overview on the judicial limitations
on the use of the initiative. Particular focus is given to the
cases of *Legislature v. Deukmejian* and *AFL-CIO v. Eu*, where
the courts were asked to remove initiatives from the ballot.

Stein, Elizabeth M. "The California Constitution and the
Counter-Initiative Quagmire." 21 *Hastings Const. L.Q.* 143
(1993). Discusses the range of criticisms voiced about the
current state of the ballot measure in California. The recent
trend of using the "counter-initiative," an initiative drafted so
as to compete with another initiative already on the ballot or
in circulation, is explored.

Sutro, Stephen H. "Interpretation of Initiatives by Reference
to Similar Statutes: Canons of Construction do not Adequately
Measure Voter Intent." 34 *Santa Clara L.Rev.* 945 (1994).
This article examines how California courts have interpreted
the meaning of initiatives by reference to existing statutes. The
author argues that such an approach is misguided, and courts
should search for intent only by referencing materials presented to the voters in the ballot pamphlet.

📖 Vitiello, Michael and Glendon, Andrew J. "Article III Judges and the Initiative Process: Are Article III Judges Hopelessly Elitist?" 31 *Loy. L.A. L.Rev.* 1275–1304 (1998). This article addresses the controversey caused when federal judges intervene to block or reject a measure passed by the electorate. The authors conclude that the judicial process produces better results than does the "direct democracy" process.

§ 5.08 Internet Resources

There are several websites that allow the researcher to locate information on both current and historic ballot measures.

💻 The California Secretary of State maintains an excellent website for ballot measure research at: *www.ss.ca.gov.* This site provides the full text of ballot measures, including the ballot pamphlets, from March 1996 to the present date. There is also a current listing of ballot measures that have qualified for the next election, as well as information on measures that are being circulated in an effort to qualify for the ballot.

💻 "A History of California Initiatives," by the Office of the California Secretary of State: *www.ss.ca.gov/elections/init_history.pdf.* This study includes concise summaries of the history of the initiative procedure in California and current procedures for placing an initiative on the ballot. The bulk of this report is dedicated to various statistics related to initiatives appearing on the ballot since 1911.

💻 The California Voter Foundation has ballot measure information for current elections at: *www.calvoter.org.*

💻 Barbara Friedrich, from the Heafey Law Library at Santa Clara University School of Law, has a listing of ballot measures from 1944 to present at: *www.scu.edu/law/library/ballot_propositions.html.* This information enables the researcher to identify the official title of the measure, the summary, whether the measure was successful, and what section of the Code or Constitution would be added or amended by the measure.

💻 The Los Angeles County Law Library has created an excellent site for researching ballot measures at: *lalaw.lib.ca.us/ballot.html.* This site lists every statewide measure from 1884 to the present date and provides the following information:

(1) Official title and ballot number; (2) the summary of the purpose of the measure, as taken from the ballot pamphlet; (3) whether the measure was passed by the voters; and (4) what section of the Code or Constitution would be added or amended by the measure.

The University of California Hastings College of the Law has created a database of searchable information on ballot initiatives from 1911 to present. It contains the full text of the initiatives, along with accompanying material on the filings, the legislative history, and digital images of the documents. See: *holmes.uchastings.edu* (without the www) and choose the California Ballot Initiatives Database.

The law library of the University of California Hastings College of the Law has created the "California Ballot Propositions Database" at: *holmes.uchastings.edu*. This website has a searchable database of ballot propositions from 1911 to the present. As described by the website, "[t]he database contains the full text of the propositions, accompanying material contained in the ballot pamphlets, related legal and legislative history, and digital images of the ballot pamphlets." The website also has a chronological listing of all ballot pamphlets and provides a copy of each pamphlet in pdf format.

Chapter 6

California Case Law[1]

---

[1] This chapter was revised for the 7th edition by Brian Raphael, Assistant Director of the Law Library and Adjunct Assistant Professor of Law, University of Southern California Law School.

(Pub. 64620)

§ 6.01 History of the California Courts

[1] Supreme Court

The Supreme Court was created by article VI, section 1 of the California Constitution of 1849.[2] The first cases were heard by the Supreme Court in the March term of 1850, only a few months after California became a state. There were few written laws prior to that time. Then Justice Nathaniel Bennett stated, "It can scarcely be said that any laws were in existence further than such as were upheld by custom and tradition."[3]

Appeals came to the first session of the Supreme Court directly from trial courts and even from Alcaldes.[4] Case reporting had been mandated by statute almost since the origin of the state.[5] Justice Bennett assumed the task of reporting the cases for the first volume because a fire destroyed the notes of the first reporter, who then resigned. Justice Bennett included a historical preface to volume one and also included in the back of the volume several articles from the Honorable R.A. Wilson, judge of First Instance in the Sacramento district. These articles or essays include "The Alcalde System of California," "The Mexican Appellate Court in California," and "San Francisco and Its Provisional

---

[2] The 1849 Constitution was signed by delegates in Monterey on October 12, and ratified by the people at the November 13, 1849 election.

[3] 1 Cal. Rpts. vi (1851).

[4] *Id.* at p. vii. During Spanish and Mexican rule, an alcalde was a judicial officer with duties similar to that of a mayor or justice of the peace.

[5] 1 Cal. Rpts. viii (1851). This was stated by Justice Nathl. Bennett in his preface to the first volume of reports.

Government." Also included in the back of volume one is a document entitled "Report on Civil and Common Law" written by a committee of the first legislature.[6]

For a flow chart of the California court system, see Chapter 7, Judicial Administration.

[2] Courts of Appeal

District Courts of Appeal were created by Constitutional Amendment in 1904.[7] Three districts, San Francisco, Los Angeles, and Sacramento, were created to relieve the congestion that affected the efficiency of the Supreme Court. The new courts' jurisdiction, which included appeals in cases with an amount in controversy of $300 to $2,000, is described in a reprint of the amendment at the beginning of the first volume of the reporter.[8] By 1918, because of further congestion in the courts in Los Angeles and San Francisco, those two districts were divided, creating divisions of the District Courts of Appeal.[9] The courts were

---

[6] "An Historical Sketch of the Supreme Court of California," by Orrin Kip McMurray, appears at page 22 in *Historical and Contemporary Review of Bench and Bar in California*. San Francisco: Recorder Printing and Publishing, 1926. 132 p. The article gives a history of the court, mentioning each justice from 1850 to the date of publication. The first year of the court has also recently been chronicled. Robert H. Kroninger, The Court's First Year: Colorful and Chaotic, 1 California Supreme Court Historical Society Yearbook 139–(1994).

[7] Constitution, article VI, section 4, adopted November 8, 1904. The spelling of the name of this court, Courts of Appeal, should be distinguished from an appellate court in the federal system, Court of Appeals. Note also that the name was changed in 1966 from the District Courts of Appeal to the Courts of Appeal.

[8] Constitution, article VI, section 4, adopted, November 8, 1904, is reprinted in its entirety at the beginning of the first official volume of appellate reports, 1 Cal.App. (1905). This volume, which was printed in 1906, covers cases back to May 22, 1905. The parallel volume of the Pacific Reporter, v. 83, does not contain the constitutional explanation.

[9] "The District Courts of Appeal" is the title of an article which appears at page 16 or 39 (depending on the printing) of *Historical and Contemporary Review of Bench and Bar in California*. San Francisco: Recorder Printing and Publishing, 1926. 132 p. The short article describes the first few years of the court. Another article, "Some Observations about California Courts of Appeal" by Roy A. Gustafson, a former Court of Appeal judge, traces the early period of the Courts of Appeal. 19 *UCLA L. Rev.* 167 (1971). This article presents a short history of the court and a much longer argument for improvements in its efficiency.

renamed Courts of Appeal in 1966.[10] There are currently six districts of the Courts of Appeal:

- First Appellate District (5 divisions) (includes San Francisco)
- Second Appellate District (8 divisions) (includes Los Angeles and Ventura)
- Third Appellate District (includes Sacramento)
- Fourth Appellate District (3 divisions) (includes San Diego, Riverside, Santa Ana)
- Fifth Appellate District (includes Fresno)
- Sixth Appellate District (includes San Jose)[11]

For a map of the geographic boundaries of the districts, see Chapter 7, Judicial Administration.

[3] Appellate Divisions of the Superior Court

Since 1879, the California Constitution has provided that the superior courts in California have appellate jurisdiction in cases arising from the California inferior courts.[12] In 1929, the Judicial Council of California submitted to the Governor and legislature a report in which it recommended passage of a number of bills, including a pair of bills (S.B. 68 and S.B. 69) designed to increase the civil and criminal jurisdiction of the municipal courts.[13] Because increasing the jurisdiction of the municipal courts would automatically increase the appellate jurisdiction of the superior courts, the Council also recommended passage of S.B. 67, which was designed to create appellate departments in every county in which there were municipal courts.[14] The Council stated in their

---

[10] Grodin, Joseph R., Massey, Calvin R., and Cunningham, Richard B., The California Constitution: A Reference Guide. Westport, CT: Greenwood Press, 1993. 372 p. at 119.

[11] Arnold, Kenneth James, *California Courts and Judges Handbook*, Costa Mesa, CA: James Publishing, Inc., 2004.

[12] Cal. Const., art. VI, § 5, 1880 Cal. Stat. xxxi.

[13] Part Three: Synopsis of Bills Introduced in the Legislature Upon Recommendation of the Judicial Council of California. Second Report of the Judicial Council of California to the Governor and the Legislature, January 1929, pp. 77–78.

[14] Id., at 78. In 1924, the voters of the State of California approved a constitutional amendment that among other things, provided that the legislature could establish appellate departments of the superior court to hear the appellate cases arising in the municipal and other inferior courts. Cal. Const., art. VI, § 5, 1925 Cal. Stat. xxii–xxiii.

report that the series of bills they were recommending were "designed to make our judicial machinery more efficient, to enable the present number of courts and judges to handle a larger volume of business as well as to dispose of the same more expeditiously, and, in a number of important particulars, to simplify our practice and procedure." [15]

Senate Bills 67, 68, and 69 were all enacted by the 1929 legislature, thereby resulting in an increase in the trial jurisdiction of the municipal courts and the creation of the Appellate Departments of the Superior Court [hereinafter Appellate Departments] to help manage the resulting increase in the appellate jurisdiction of the superior courts. [16] S.B. 67, as enacted, specified that the Appellate Departments were to have "appellate jurisdiction on appeal from municipal, justices' and other inferior courts." [17] The statute also designated that each department was to consist of three judges of the superior court, to be chosen by the chairman of the Judicial Council. [18]

The statute governing the Appellate Departments has been amended a number of times since 1929. [19] In 1998, the voters approved amendments to the California Constitution, which among other things, changed the name of the Appellate Departments to "Appellate Divisions of the Superior Court" [hereinafter Appellate Divisions], provided for the unification of the trial courts, and changed the appellate jurisdiction of the Appellate Divisions to reflect the prospective unification. [20] The legislature followed up in the same year with statutory amendments to reflect these constitutional changes. [21] As a result of these amendments, the Appellate Divisions now have appellate jurisdiction in "limited civil cases" [22] and misdemeanor and infraction cases. [23] Limited civil cases consist of civil cases traditionally within municipal court jurisdiction. [24]

---

[15] Part Three: Synopsis of Bills Introduced in the Legislature Upon Recommendation of the Judicial Council of California. Second Report of the Judicial Council of California to the Governor and the Legislature, January 1929, pp. 77–78.

[16] Stat. 1929, ch. 475–477, pp. 836–839.

[17] Stat. 1929, ch. 475, § 2, p. 836.

[18] Stat. 1929, ch. 475, § 1, p. 836.

[19] Cal. Civ. Proc. Code § 77 (West 1982 and Supp. 2004).

[20] Cal. Const., art VI, §§ 4, 11, 23 (West Supp. 2004).

[21] Cal. Civ. Proc. Code § 77 (West Supp. 2004).

[22] Cal. Civ. Proc. Code § 904.2 (West Supp. 2004).

[23] Cal. Penal Code § 1466 (West 2000).

[24] 9 B. E. Witkin, *California Procedure*, Appeal § 28 (4th ed., Witkin Legal Institute, Supp. 2003) (citing Cal. Civ. Proc. Code § 85 et seq.).

§ 6.02　Case Publication

[1]　Overview of Publication Rules[25]

California Reports and *California Appellate Reports* are the official reporters for the state's appellate courts. Publication of these hardbound volumes is delayed until all the opinions have become final, so researchers can be sure that any opinion in either of these bound reporters is final and may be cited.

All Supreme Court opinions are published [Cal. Rules of Ct., Rule 976(a)]. These opinions from the highest court in the jurisdiction serve as precedent for litigants in similar situations with similar legal issues. Courts of Appeal opinions are also authoritative, if they have not been overruled by the California Supreme Court. Only a small number (perhaps 15%) of the opinions of the Courts of Appeal are published. The judges are supposed to choose only the most important cases to be published (Rule 976(b)). This number or percentage will vary from year to year and from district to district. An even smaller number of opinions from the Appellate Departments and Divisions of the Superior Courts have been published.

Under the California Rules of Court, the Court of Appeal or an Appellate Division can decide to certify an opinion for publication based on four criteria laid out in Rule 976(b).[26] Even if an opinion is certified for publication however, the opinion will ultimately not get published if it is superseded by a grant of review (by the California Supreme Court), a rehearing, or some other action.[27] It will also not get published if the Supreme Court orders the opinion not to be published (i.e., depublishes the opinion).[28]

---

[25] There are many articles on depublication/decertification and the relationship between the Courts of Appeal and the Supreme Court; an excellent one explaining this complicated topic is from a Questions & Answers column in a *Law Library Journal* issue: 82 LLJ 641–645 (1990). This short article includes 35 footnote references and a thorough explanation of the entire opinion publication process for California. The column authors, Alice I. Youmans, Joan S. Howland, and Myra K. Saunders, give credit for assisting them to Lindy Carll, Allison Mancini, and Sue Schway.

[26] Cal. Rule of Court 976(c)(1). For the full text of the publication rules discussed in this section, see § 6.02[4].

[27] Cal. Rule of Court 976(d). The exception to this rule is that a superseded opinion will be published if the Supreme Court orders that opinion published (Rule 976(d)).

[28] Cal. Rule of Court 976(c)(2).

On the other hand, opinions that are not certified by an appellate court for publication can still get published if the California Supreme Court orders the opinion published.[29]

As a result of these rules, appellate opinions certified for publication will appear in the official advance pamphlets of the *California Official Reports*, but may be missing in the permanent, bound volumes of the *California Appellate Reports* (if the opinions are later superseded or "depublished"). In these circumstances, they cannot generally be cited by a court or a party in another case.[30]

[2] Partially Published Opinions

In certain circumstances, the Supreme Court, Courts of Appeal, and Appellate Divisions can order only part of an opinion to be published. This partial publication possibility has been in effect since 1983. If an opinion has been published in part, only the published part can be cited.

There are two circumstances in which the Rules provide for the partial publication of opinions. The first circumstance is one in which the Court of Appeal decides to certify an opinion based on one of the four criteria in Rule 976(b), the opinion is then superseded by a grant of review, rehearing, or other action, and the Supreme Court later orders the opinion published in part.[31] The second circumstance is one in which a majority of the Court of Appeal or Appellate Division chooses to certify only the part of the opinion that they feel meets the four criteria in Rule 976(b).[32]

[3] Depublished Opinions

The California Supreme Court has exercised its power to depublish (or decertify) Courts of Appeal opinions since 1971. Depublication is the Supreme Court practice of erasing Courts of Appeal opinions without reviewing the cases as they would if they accepted the cases. Depublication has the same effect as if the Court of Appeal opinion had not been certified for publication from the outset. The Court of Appeal decision stands as to the parties involved, but the opinion is no longer considered to be published and it cannot be cited or serve as precedent. This is not the same thing as the Supreme Court overruling a decision of the

---

[29] Id.

[30] Cal. Rule of Court 977.

[31] Cal. Rule of Court 976(d).

[32] Cal. Rule of Court 976.1.

Court of Appeal, as some writers on the subject might think. Early on, depublication was thought to mean that the Supreme Court disagreed with the Court of Appeal judges' choice to publish the opinion (Rule 976(b)). The opinion was simply not as important as the Court of Appeal judges had thought. A newer interpretation is that depublished opinions are thought to indicate that the Supreme Court agrees with the Court of Appeal decision but disagrees with at least part of the reasoning in the opinion and does not have the time to review the case and draft an opinion.

In *West's California Reporter* (in the Case History Tables), researchers will see two different phrases indicating depublication. "Ordered not officially published" means that a Court of Appeal opinion was certified for publication, that there was no appeal/petition to the Supreme Court, but that the Supreme Court nevertheless depublished the opinion. This could have been because a party involved requested the depublication, but it can also happen when an industry group or association involved in a similar situation wants the precedent removed from the books because of its negative effect on their interests. "Rev. denied and ordered not officially published" means that there was an appeal/petition to the Supreme Court. The Supreme Court both refused to take the case and ordered the Court of Appeal opinion to be depublished. Rev. denied is the same thing as hearing denied or hg. den. in earlier (pre-1985) cases. In the reporters, researchers will also see language such as "deleted on direction of the Supreme Court" indicating depublication.

[4]   Text of the Governing Rules

California Constitution, Article VI, section 14, provides:

> The Legislature shall provide for the prompt publication of such opinions of the Supreme Court and courts of appeal as the Supreme Court deems appropriate, and those opinions shall be available for publication by any person. Decisions of the Supreme Court and courts of appeal that determine causes shall be in writing with reasons stated.

> HISTORY: Adopted November 8, 1966.

Government Code section 68902 provides:

> Such opinions of the Supreme Court, of the courts of appeal, and of the appellate departments of the superior courts as the Supreme Court may deem expedient shall be published in the official reports.

The reports shall be published under the general supervision of the Supreme Court.

HISTORY: Added Stats 1967 ch. 172 § 2. June 2, 2004

California Rules of Court, Rule 976, Publication of Appellate Opinions, provides:

(a). [Supreme Court] All opinions of the Supreme Court shall be published in the Official Reports.

(Subd (a) adopted effective January 1, 1964.)

(b). [Standards for publication of opinions of other courts] No opinion of a Court of Appeal or an appellate department of the superior court may be published in the Official Reports unless the opinion:

(1) establishes a new rule of law, applies an existing rule to a set of facts significantly different from those stated in published opinions, or modifies, or criticizes with reasons given, an existing rule;

(2) resolves or creates an apparent conflict in the law;

(3) involves a legal issue of continuing public interest; or

(4) makes a significant contribution to legal literature by reviewing either the development of a common law rule or the legislative or judicial history of a provision of a constitution, statute, or other written law. (Subd (b) as amended effective January 1, 1983; previously amended effective November 11, 1966, and January 1, 1972; adopted effective January 1, 1964.)

(c). [Publication procedure]

(1). [Courts of Appeal and appellate departments]

An opinion of a Court of Appeal or an appellate department of the superior court shall be published if a majority of the court rendering the opinion certifies, prior to the decision's finality in that court, that it meets one or more of the standards of subdivision (b).

(2). [Supreme Court]

An opinion certified for publication shall not be published, and an opinion not so certified shall be published on an order of the Supreme Court to that effect. (Subd (c) as amended effective January 1, 1983; previously amended effective November 11, 1966, and January 1, 1972; adopted effective January 1, 1964.)

(d). [Superseded opinions]

Unless otherwise ordered by the Supreme Court, no opinion superseded by a grant of review, rehearing, or other action shall be published. After granting review, after decision, or after dismissal of review and remand as improvidently granted, the Supreme Court may order the opinion of the Court of Appeal published in whole or in part. (Subd (d) as amended effective May 6, 1985; previously amended effective January 1, 1983; Subd (e) renumbered subd (d) effective January 1, 1972; adopted effective January 1, 1964.)

(e). [Editing]

Written opinions of the Supreme Court, Courts of Appeal, and appellate departments of the superior courts shall be filed with the clerks of the respective courts. Two copies of each opinion of the Supreme Court, and two copies of each opinion of a Court of Appeal or of an appellate department of a superior court which the court has certified as meeting the standard for publication specified in subdivision (b) shall be furnished by the clerk to the Reporter of Decisions. The Reporter of Decisions shall edit the opinions for publication as directed by the Supreme Court. Proof sheets of each opinion in the type to be used in printing the reports shall be submitted by the Reporter of Decisions to the court which prepared the opinion for examination, correction and final approval. (Subd (f) renumbered subd (e) effective January 1, 1972; previously amended effective November 11, 1966; adopted effective January 1, 1964.)

HISTORY: Rule 976 as amended effective May 6, 1985; previously amended effective November 11, 1966, January 1, 1972, January 1, 1983; adopted by the Supreme Court effective January 1, 1964.

California Rules of Court, Rule 976.1, Partial Publication, provides:

(a). [Partial publication authorized]

A majority of the court rendering an opinion may certify for publication any part of the opinion that meets the standard for publication specified under subdivision (b) of rule 976. The published part shall indicate that part of the opinion is unpublished. All material, factual and legal, that aids in the application or interpretation of the published part shall be in the published part.

(b). [Other rules applicable]

For purposes of rules 976, 977, and 978, the published part of the opinion shall be treated as a published opinion, and the unpublished part as an unpublished opinion.

(c). [Copy to Reporter of Decisions]

One extra copy of both the published and unpublished parts of the opinion shall be furnished by the clerk to the Reporter of Decisions.

HISTORY: Rule 976.1 as amended effective January 1, 1984; adopted effective January 1, 1983.

California Rules of Court, Rule 977. Citation of Unpublished Opinions Prohibited; Exceptions, provides:

(a). [Unpublished opinions] An opinion of a Court of Appeal or an appellate department of the superior court that is not certified for publication or ordered published shall not be cited or relied on by a court or a party in any other action or proceeding except as provided in subdivision (b). (Subd (a) as amended effective January 1, 1983.) (Subd (a) as amended effective January 1, 1997.)

(b). [Exceptions]

Such an opinion may be cited or relied on:

(1) when the opinion is relevant under the doctrines of law of the case, res judicata, or collateral estoppel; or

(2) when the opinion is relevant to a criminal or disciplinary action or proceeding because it states reasons for a decision affecting the same defendant or respondent in another such action or proceeding. (Subd (b) as amended effective January 1, 1983.)

(c). [Citation procedure]

A copy of any opinion citable under subdivision (b) or of a cited opinion of any court that is available only in a computer-based source of decisional law shall be furnished to the court and all parties by attaching it to the document in which it is cited, or, if the citation is to be made orally, within a reasonable time in advance of citation. (Subd (c) as amended effective January 1, 1983.) (Subd (c) as amended effective January 1, 1997.)

(d). [Opinions ordered published by Supreme Court]

An opinion of the Court of Appeal ordered published by the Supreme Court pursuant to rule 976 is citable.[33] (Subd (d) adopted effective May 6, 1985.)

HISTORY: Rule 977 as amended effective May 6, 1985; adopted by the Supreme Court and by the Judicial Council effective January 1, 1974; previously amended effective January 1, 1983.Rule 977 as amended effective January 1, 1997.

California Rules of Court, Rule 978. Requesting Publication of Unpublished Opinions:

---

[33] Any citation to the Court of Appeal opinion shall include reference to the grant of review and any subsequent action by the Supreme Court. (Footnote appears in code.)

(a). [Request procedure; action by court rendering opinion]

A request by any person for publication of an opinion not certified for publication may be made only to the court that rendered the opinion. The request shall be made promptly by a letter stating the nature of the person's interest and stating concisely why the opinion meets one or more of the publication standards. The request shall be accompanied by proof of its service on each party to the action or proceeding in the Court of Appeal. If the court does not, or by reason of the decision's finality as to that court cannot, grant the request, the court shall transmit the request and a copy of the opinion to the Supreme Court with its recommendation for disposition and a brief statement of its reasons. The transmitting court shall also send a copy of its recommendation and reasons to each party and to any person who has requested publication. (Subd (a) as amended effective July 1, 1997; previously amended January 1, 1983, July 1, 1992.)

(b). [Action by Supreme Court]

When a request for publication is received by the Supreme Court pursuant to subdivision (a), the court shall either order the opinion published or deny the request. The court shall send notice of its action to the transmitting court, each party, and any person who has requested publication. (Subd (b) as amended effective January 1, 1983.)

(c). [Effect of Supreme Court order for publication]

An order of the Supreme Court directing publication of an opinion in the Official Reports shall not be deemed an expression of opinion of the Supreme Court of the correctness of the result reached by the decision or of any of the law set forth in the opinion.

HISTORY: Rule 978 as amended effective January 1, 1983; adopted by the Supreme Court and by the Judicial Council effective July 1, 1975.Rule 978 as amended effective July 1, 1997; previously amended effective July 1, 1992.

California Rules of Court, Rule 979, Requesting Depublication Of Published Opinions, provides:

(a). [Request procedure]

A request by any person for the depublication of an opinion certified for publication shall be made by letter to the Supreme Court within 30 days after the decision becomes final as to the Court of Appeal. Any request for depublication shall be accompanied by proof of mailing to the Court of Appeal and proof of service to each party to the action or proceeding. The request shall state the nature of the person's interest and shall state concisely reasons why the opinion should not remain published. The request shall not exceed 10 pages. (Subd (a) as amended effective July 1, 1997.)

(b). [Response]

The Court of Appeal or any person may, within 10 days after receipt by the Supreme Court of a request for depublication, submit a response, either joining in the request or stating concisely reasons why the opinion should remain published. A response submitted by anyone other than the Court of Appeal shall state the nature of the person's interest. Any response shall not exceed 10 pages and shall be accompanied by proof of mailing to the Court of Appeal, and proof of service to each party to the action or proceeding, and person requesting depublication. (Subd (b) as amended effective July 1, 1997.)

(c). [Action by Supreme Court]

When a request for depublication is received by the Supreme Court pursuant to subdivision (a), the court shall either order the opinion depublished or deny the request. The court shall send notice of its action to the Court of Appeal, each party, and any person who has requested depublication.

(d). [Limitation]

Nothing in this rule limits the court's power, on its own motion, to order an opinion depublished.

(e). [Effect of Supreme Court order for depublication]

An order of the Supreme Court directing depublication of an opinion in the Official Reports shall not be deemed an expression of opinion of the Supreme Court of the correctness of the result reached by the decision or of any of the law set forth in the opinion.

HISTORY: Rule 979 as amended effective July 1, 1997; adopted effective July 1, 1990.

§ 6.03 Full Text Opinions

[1] Current Sources

From 1850 until 1859 all Supreme Court opinions were officially published. From 1859 until 1909 opinions were selectively published in the official reports. During this period of selective publication, there was a table of reported cases in the front of the volume and a much shorter table of the unreported cases in either the front or the back of the volume. Since 1909, all Supreme Court opinions have been officially published.[34]

From the first reported cases in 1905 until 1909, cases from the Courts of Appeal were reported selectively. During this period there was a list of reported cases in the front of each volume, immediately followed by a list of cases not reported. From 1909 through 1963 the cases were comprehensively reported. In 1963 Rule 976 was adopted, again reinstating selective publishing of cases, but the earlier practice of listing cases not reported was not reinstated. Only a very small percentage of opinions of the superior court appellate departments/divisions have been reported since these departments were created in 1929.[35]

📖 *California Reports and California Appellate Reports.*

California Supreme Court cases are published officially in *California Reports* and California Court of Appeal and Appellate Division cases are published officially in *California Appellate Reports.*[36] These reports are currently published on a contract basis by LexisNexis; however, until July 2003, they were published by Bancroft-Whitney (which has been a division of West Group since 1996).[37]

📖 *California Reports* (abbreviated Cal. or C.)

    1st series, 1850–1934 (vol. 1–220)

    2d series, 1934–1969 (vol. 1–71)

    3d series, 1969–1991 (vol. 1–54)

    4th series 1991–present (vol. 1–_____)

📖 *California Appellate Reports* (abbreviated Cal. App. or C.A.)

---

[34] Youmans, Alice I., Howland, Joan S., and Saunders, Myra K. Questions & Answers (on depublication), 82 *Law Library Journal* 641, 641 (1990). Regarding the early California Supreme Court cases that were not officially published, there is case law that supports the view that these cases are just as binding on California courts as those California Supreme Court cases that are reported officially. See 9 B.E. Witkin, *California Procedure,* Appeal § 925 (4th ed., Witkin Legal Institute, 1997).

[35] Id., at 641–642.

[36] The Appellate Division cases are placed at the backs of the volumes, separated from the Court of Appeal cases by a divider page. This back section of the volume that contains the Appellate Division cases is referred to as the "California Supplement."

[37] Bancroft Whitney began publishing the official reports in 1898, when an official version was first designated. Volume one (1850) of *California Reports* contains the preface and appendices mentioned in § 6.01[1] above.

1st series, 1905–1934 (vol. 1–140)

2d series, 1934–1969 (vol. 1–276)

3d series, 1969–1991 (vol. 1–235)

4th series 1991–present (vol. 1–____)

📑 *California Official Reports* is the official advance sheet publication for both of these sets of court reports. Like the official bound volumes, these advance sheets are also now being published by LexisNexis. Each advance sheet issue contains a section with gray edging on the outer page edges (formerly light green through 1995) that contains the recent Supreme Court cases followed by a section without gray edging that contains the recent Court of Appeal and Appellate Division cases. Each new issue comes out every nine or twelve days (with the publication days alternating between Tuesdays and Thursdays).[38]

📖 *West's Pacific Reporter.*, Eagan, MN: West Group, 1883–present. (abbreviated P.).[39]

1st series, 1883–1931 (vol. 1–300)

2d series, 1931–2000 (vol. 1–999)

3d series, 2000–present (vol. 1–____)

This set began with the publication of California Supreme Court cases from 1883, officially published in vol. 64 of *California Reports*. In 1904 and 1929, when the Courts of Appeal and the Appellate Departments respectively were established, *West's Pacific Reporter* began carrying these courts' decisions as well. This reporter continued to carry opinions from all of these courts until 1959, when West

---

[38] In addition to new opinions, each issue also currently contains the following items: 1) tables of cases organized by subject, 2) a "Summary of Cases Accepted by the Supreme Court," 3) multivolume cumulative tables of cases, arranged alphabetically by case name, 4) minutes, 5) new court rules, 6) a "Cumulative Subsequent History Table," and 7) tables of review granted cases, depublished opinions, and rehearing granted opinions. Some libraries that save the advance sheets have split the booklets and bound the gray/green edged pages separately from the white sections.

[39] The *Pacific Reporter* is part of West's National Reporter System. It covers California, but it also has cases from Alaska, Arizona, Colorado, Hawaii, Idaho, Kansas, Montana, Nevada, New Mexico, Oklahoma, Oregon, Utah, and Washington since their statehood.

introduced *West's California Reporter* (see below) and went back to only publishing the California Supreme Court cases in *West's Pacific Reporter.*

West's Pacific Reporter not only includes the cases reported officially but also many early California cases that were not released for official publication.

A paperback advance sheet accompanies this reporter set.

📖　*West's California Reporter.* Eagan, MN: West Group, 1959– present (abbreviated Cal. Rptr. or C.R.).[40]

1st series, 1959–1991 (vol. 1–286)

2d series 1991–present (vol. 1–____)

This set contains officially reported opinions (including de-published or superseded opinions) from the California Supreme Court, California Courts of Appeal and the Appellate Departments/Divisions.

A paperback advance sheet also accompanies this reporter set.[41]

▤　Daily Journal Corporation newspapers:

Los Angeles Daily Journal. Los Angeles: Daily Journal Corp.

San Francisco Daily Journal. San Francisco: Daily Journal Corp.

---

[40] Each reported case in *West's Pacific Reporter* and *West's California Reporter* contains a synopsis as well as one or more headnotes that summarize the courts' discussion of the various points of law in that case. The headnotes from all of these cases are then placed topically in a set called a digest, organized by a Topic and Key Number scheme. This scheme is discussed more fully in § 6.05 below.

[41] In addition to the new reported cases, each *West's California Reporter* advance sheet issue also contains a Key Number Digest section, which indexes the headnotes in that issue according to the Topics and Key Numbers under which they are classified. One can thus use these Digest sections in the latest issues to update *West's California Digest,* discussed in § 6.05 below. The other items included in each *West's California Reporter* advance sheet issue are: 1) a brief summary of the cases included in the issue, 2) a "California Newsletter," which includes summaries of notable opinions from California and federal courts, as well as legislative and regulatory highlights, 3) "Summaries of Selected Decisions from Around the Nation," 4) tables of jury instructions, 5) summaries of cases accepted by the California Supreme Court, 6) an alphabetical "Case History Table," 7) a "Cumulative Review, Rehearing, and Hearing Table," 8) parallel citation tables, 9) a cumulative list of cases reported, arranged alphabetically by case name, 10) an ABA Standards for Criminal Justice table, and 11) "Words and Phrases," which provides judicially defined definitions of terms within the cases.

Daily Recorder. Sacramento: Daily Journal Corp.

These three daily legal newspapers carry the Daily Appellate Report (DAR), a report of current California Supreme Court, Court of Appeal, and Appellate Division cases.

The corporation also publishes the *Weekly Directory of Southern (or Northern) California Courts.*

Metropolitan News-Enterprise. Los Angeles, CA: Metropolitan News Company. This daily legal newspaper is accompanied by a Slip Opinion Supplement (S.O.S.), with cases from the California Supreme Court, Courts of Appeal, and Appellate Divisions. A court directory is included in the newspaper issued on the first Monday of each month.

The Recorder. San Francisco: American Lawyer Media, Inc. This legal newspaper carries current reports of the Supreme Court, Courts of Appeal, and Appellate Divisions in its supplement, the *California Daily Opinion Service (CDOS).* Current cases are also posted on the Recorder's web site for 30 days at: *www.callaw.com/.*

California State Cases on LexisNexis CD. Matthew Bender & Company, Inc., a member of the LexisNexis Group. This CD-ROM version covers decisions from the California Supreme Court from 1883, and from the Courts of Appeal and Appellate Divisions from 1944. These cases are from the LexisNexis libraries and include case summaries and Core Concepts.

West's California Reporter, CD-ROM

Contains California cases published in *West's Pacific Reporter* since 1931 and *West's California Reporter* since 1959.

AccessLaw's CalDisc. This CD product contains California Supreme Court and Courts of Appeal opinions from 1932 to present. It is updated by CD quarterly or by their Daily Opinion Service. AccessLaw is the successor to LawDisc, which was produced by National Legal Databases in Tulsa, Oklahoma. AccessLaw uses Folio search software. CD information may be found at: *www.accesslaw.com.*

LexisNexis. Dayton, OH: LexisNexis. Available through *lexis.com®*, this resource contains the following California court sources:

"CA Supreme Court Cases from 1850" (CAL;CAL) (contains all officially reported California Supreme Court cases)

"CA Courts of Appeal Cases from 1905" (CAL;APP) (includes both reported and available unreported appellate cases from the California Courts of Appeal and the Appellate Departments/Divisions)

"CA State Cases Combined" (CAL;CACTS) (from 1850) (includes all of the Supreme Court and lower appellate cases contained in the first two sources)

"CA Published Cases Combined" (CAL;CACTSP) (from 1850) (contains only the California Supreme Court and lower appellate court cases reported in the bound official reports and/or the official advance sheets)

"Published CA Court of Appeal Cases from 1905" (CAL;APP-P) (contains only the lower appellate court cases reported in the bound official reports and/or the official advance sheets)

"Unpublished CA Court of Appeal Cases from 1966" (CAL;APP-U) (contains only available lower appellate court cases *not* reported in the bound official reports (i.e., only reported officially in the advance sheets or not reported at all))

The California cases on LexisNexis contain Lexis case summaries, Core Concepts, and Core Terms. They also contain the summaries and headnotes appearing in the official reports.

LexisOne. Dayton, OH: LexisNexis. Includes decisions from the California Supreme Court and Courts of Appeal from the most recent five years without case summaries or Core Concepts. Data is found found at: *www.lexisone.com.*

Westlaw. Eagan, MN: West Group. Available through westlaw.com, this resource contains the following California state court databases:

"State Cases" (from 1850) (CA-CS) (includes all officially and unofficially reported California cases from the Supreme Court, Courts of Appeal, and Appellate Departments/Divisions as well as unreported cases; contains the West version of each case, if available)

"California Reported Cases" (from 1850) (CA-CSR) (limited to California cases reported officially (in the bound volumes and/or the advance sheets) or unofficially; contains the West version of each case, if available)

"California Reports and California Appellate Reports Cases" (from 1850) (CA-ORCS) (contains only those cases reported in the bound official reports; contains the official version of each case decided before 6/30/03; contains the West version of each case decided thereafter)

🖳 *State of California. Judicial Council.* Located on the internet at *www.courtinfo.ca.gov/opinions*, this site contains the slip opinions of the California Supreme Court, Courts of Appeal, and Appellate Divisions. The opinions are left on the site for 120 days. They are then archived at *www.courtinfo.ca.gov/ opinions/opinarch.htm.* This site also contains a database of searchable California opinions from 1850, powered by Lexis-Nexis. The cases appear as they do on LexisNexis; however, they do not contain the LexisNexis editorial enhancements (i.e., LexisNexis case summaries, Core Concepts, and Core Terms).

🖳 *American LegalNet.* This provider has California Supreme Court and lower appellate court cases from 1934 on its internet site at: *www.americanlegalnet.com.*

🖳 *JuriSearch* has both California Supreme Court and lower appellate court cases from 1934 on the internet at *www.jurisearch.com.*

🖳 *LOIS.* This provider is becoming a major player in the state and federal research game. LoisLaw carries California Supreme Court cases from 1899 and California Court of Appeal cases from 1905 at: *www.loislaw.com.*

🖳 National Law Library. National Law Library carries California Supreme Court and lower appellate court opinions from 1950 at: *www.nationallawlibrary.com.*

🖳 *Netlaw Libraries, Inc..* This provider has California Supreme Court and Court of Appeal decisions from 1932 (through AccessLaw) at: *www.netlawlibraries.com.* The cases are searchable and hyperlinked to codes, rules, and jury instructions.

☐ *VersusLaw*. This provider has California Supreme Court cases back to 1930 and Court of Appeal cases back to 1944 at: *www.versuslaw.com*.

[2] Historical Titles

☐ *San Francisco Law Journal*. Contains all the decisions of the Supreme Court of California, and of the U.S. Circuit Court and U.S. District Courts for the district of California; and important decisions of the U.S. Supreme Court and higher courts of other States. W.T. Baggett, editor. v. 1, September 1, 1877–February 23, 1878. San Francisco, Baggett & Scofield, 1878. Weekly (continued as the *Pacific Coast Law Journal and California Legal Record*).

☐ *California Legal Record*. A weekly journal containing all the decisions of the Supreme Court of California; also important decisions of Oregon and Nevada, and of the United States Circuit and District Courts of California; also of the United State Supreme Court and courts of last resort in other states; also important land decisions of the Department of the Interior. v. 1–2, March 30, 1878–March 29, 1879. San Francisco, F.A. Scofield & Co., 1878–1879. (continuation of *San Francisco Law Journal*). v. 1; v. 2.

☐ *Pacific Coast Law Journal*. Contains all the decisions of the Supreme Court of California, and the important decisions of the U.S. Circuit and U.S. District courts for the district of California, and of the U.S. Supreme Court and higher courts of other states, W.T. Baggett, editor. v. 1–12, March 2, 1878–December 24, 1883. San Francisco, W.T. Baggett & Co., 1878–1884. Weekly. (Superseded by the *West Coast Reporter*.)

☐ *West Coast Reporter*. Contains all the decisions of the following courts: United States Circuit and District Courts of California, Colorado, Nevada, and Oregon, and the Supreme Courts of Arizona, California, Colorado, Idaho, Montana, Nevada, New Mexico, Oregon, Utah, Washington, and Wyoming. Also, legal essays and editorial notes. v. 1–9, v. 10, nos. 1–6., January 3, 1884–May 6, 1886. San Francisco, A.L. Bancroft & Co., 1884–1886. Weekly. (Merged into the *Pacific Reporter*.)

📖 *California Law Journal,* v. 1–2, No.7, October 7, 1862–July 15, 1863. Sacramento CA, 7125 Governors Circle, Mark Larwood Co., 1972. Microfilm, 1 reel, diazo; silver; copyflo.

📖 *Advance California Reports,* 1940–1969 (Supreme Court cases)

Advance California Appellate Reports, 1940–1969 (Court of Appeal and Appellate Department cases)

(predecessor publications of current official advance sheet publication, *California Official Reports,* described above)

📖 *California Decisions,* v. 1 (1890)–v. 100 (1940) (Supreme Court Cases)

California Appellate Decisions, v. 1 (1905)–v. 103 (1940)(Court of Appeal and Appellate Department cases; earliest advance sheet publications for California cases; predecessor publications of *Advance California Reports* and *Advance California Appellate Reports* respectively cited above)

📖 *California Unreported Cases,* v. 1 (1855)–v. 7 (1910). San Francisco, Bender-Moss Co., 1913. (Available from Law Library Microform Consortium in microform.)

📖 *Unwritten Decisions of the Supreme Court of California* (Ragland), v. 1 (1878–1879). San Francisco, California Law Book Exchange, 1923. See also legal periodicals containing reports.

[3] Historical Titles—Trial Courts

There are currently no reported cases at the trial level. However, there are some early reporters that may be found in libraries or purchased in microfilm format from Law Library Microform Consortium (L.L.M.C.).[42]

📖 *Myrick's Probate Reports,* 1873–1879. 1 v. San Francisco, Sumner Whitney, 1880. Dennis.

📖 *Coffey's Reports of Decisions in Probate,* 6 v., 1883–1915. v. 1, 1894; v. 2, 1902, edited by T.J. Lyons and Edmund Tauazky; Syllabus of decisions, 1883–1888; Index to decisions, 1904. San Francisco, Bancroft-Whitney, 1908–1916.

---

[42] *See* list of Publishers/Vendors in Appendix A.

📖 Labatt, Henry J. *Reports of Cases Determined in the District Courts of the State of California.* 2 v. (1857–1858). San Francisco, Whitton, Towne & Co., 1858.

📖 *Superior Court Decisions,* compiled by Rufus Ely Ragland and Charles Edward McGinnis. San Francisco: California Law Book Exchange. (Dennis & Co. reprint.) 2 vols.: v. 1 (1921) and v. 2 (1926). [43] (Also available in microform from the Law Library Microform Consortium.)

§ 6.04 Graphic Images in the Reporters

Graphic images have appeared occasionally in the reporters. These images are usually exhibits that have become part of the record. Examples are the Anaheim stadium parking lot diagram in Golden West Baseball Co. v. City of Anaheim, 25 Cal. App. 4th 11; 31 Cal. Rptr. 2d 378 (May 1994), and two pages from the National Enquirer in Clint Eastwood v. The Superior Court of Los Angeles County, Respondent; National Enquirer, Inc., Real Party in Interest. 149 Cal App. 3d 409; 198 Cal. Rptr. 342 (1983). Images like these appear in the official and West printed reporters, but are not always available in the LexisNexis and Westlaw online services. (However, both of these examples are available on Westlaw's www version.) Both LexisNexis and Westlaw are trying to include more graphics as they move more completely toward the www platform.

§ 6.05 Digests—Research Methods

[1] Description

A digest is an index to case law. The West Group's key number digest is the prototype for case research. West has divided the subject of law into seven broad categories, thirty-two subheadings, and over 400 digest topics. The digest topics are listed in the front of any West digest volume. Each digest topic is divided into points of law, with key numbers assigned to each. New topics and key numbers are created as new areas of law develop. West editors assign a digest topic and key number to each point of law discussed in a case. All cases containing a specific point of law will be given the same topic and key number

---

[43] A microfilm version of these two volumes is available from Trans-Media Publishing Company, Dobbs Ferry, NY 10522.

and will be grouped together in the digest. Both the topic and the key number are necessary for locating the grouped cases.

West has digests prepared for single states, like California, and groups of neighboring states, like the Pacific region, as well as for federal courts. Every West digest has:

1. Table of Cases for use in locating citations and key numbers by case name.

2. Descriptive Word Index for use in locating relevant key numbers by specific descriptive key words.

3. Tables of Contents or topical analyses for use in locating relevant key numbers through a topical outline in which key numbers are arranged in a classified scheme.

In California, there is also a competing digest published by Bancroft-Whitney, now a division of West. This digest is sometimes referred to as the McKinney's Digest or the Digest of Official Reports (see § 6.05[4]). It has the same basic features of the West digests; one notable difference though is that the Digest of Official Reports divides its topics into section numbers instead of "key" numbers.

Digests are not cumulative, meaning that they only cover a specific period of time. So there may be more than one digest series for a single reporter set.

[2] Research Technique in the Use of Digests

1) Follow the fact or topical approach using the descriptive word index or relevant topical outline; look for the party, place, thing, action, issue, defense, and remedy in the index or topical outline.

2) References in the index or topical outline will lead to West topics and key numbers or to Bancroft-Whitney topic and section numbers in the digest bound volume(s) and in any pocket parts or advance paper-bound pamphlets.

3) Examine the "closing" table in the front of the latest digest supplement to determine the reports on which its content is based.

4) Check the subsequent reporter volumes and their advance sheets for later cases using either the West topic and key number section or the Bancroft-Whitney Subject Matter Table.

[3] Instructional Aids for Learning How to Use Digests

West Publishing Company for many years distributed free copies of *West's Law Finder—A Legal Research Guide.* Eagan, MN: West Group, 1994. 76 p. This booklet thoroughly explains the digest system. Another West publication, *West's Sample Pages,*[44] is also a good training book for teaching digest use. The general texts on legal research mentioned in the introduction also cover this topic well.

[4] California Digests

 📖 *McKinney's New California Digest.* San Francisco: Bancroft-Whitney Co., 1930–1973. This set indexes cases in the *California Reports*, 1st and 2d series and the *California Appellate Reports,* 1st and 2d series. Each volume contains a "closing" table of cases in the front to see what span of cases and other cited sources are included in the volume one is using; a table of "titles" (i.e., digest topics); a table of abbreviations; references to text treatment of subject in *California Jurisprudence* 2d, *American Jurisprudence* 2d, and ALR Digests; cross-references to related titles, articles in legal periodicals, and annotations in ALR series. The California official reports are classified in accordance with this digest scheme.

 📖 *California Digest of Official Reports.*, 3d & 4th Series. San Francisco, Bancroft-Whitney, 1974–present. This digest covers California cases from the 3d series to date. It is an extension, not a replacement of McKinney's Digest. As with McKinney's, federal cases pertaining to California are also included. In recent years, Bancroft-Whitney has been part of West Group, so newer volumes of this digest set contain references to the West set of *California Codes, United States Code Annotated,* and the *Supreme Court Reporter* in addition to *Cal. Jur. 3d,* the Witkin Library, *ALR,* and the *Am. Jur.* family of publications.

While many of the features of *McKinney's* have been retained, numerous changes have been made. A Scope of Topic note appears at the beginning of each topic.

To correlate material in this new digest with that in *McKinney's,* tables of parallel references have been placed at the end

---

[44] *Sample Pages: Illustrations of Organization and Research Techniques in West's Key Number Digests.* Third edition. St. Paul: West Group, 1986. 231 p.

of each of the volumes containing case notes. There are two of these tables for each topic of this digest. Table I classifies sections of the original *McKinney's Digest* topic to the corresponding topic(s) and sections of the new digest. Table II classifies sections in the new digest to the corresponding topic(s) and sections in the original *McKinney's Digest.*

This digest is updated by paperbound and pocket part supplements. There are "closing" tables in both the bound volumes and the supplements. The digest is further updated by *California Official Reports,* California's official advance sheet, described in § 6.03[1] *above.*

📖 *West's California Digest.* Eagan, MN: West Group, 1951–present. This is the original West California digest set. It should be used to locate California cases from 1850 to 1950. Users should note that even though West Publishing's reporter coverage did not begin until 1883 (Pacific Reporter), their digest goes back to the earliest reports. Beginning with 1950 researchers should use *West's California Digest* 2d (see below).

Case law headnotes are arranged under the West Key Number system which has national application. Library references are to Corpus Juris Secundum and legal periodicals. Cross references are also provided to related West topics.

📖 *West's California Digest* 2d, Eagan, MN: West Group. Covers cases from 1950 to date. Prior cases will be found by using the original *West's California Digest,* described above.

This digest is updated with pocket part supplements. As a topical area changes over time, the editors at West revise the topical outlines and/or add new West topics. There are library references to *Corpus Juris Secundum,* law reviews, and *Opinions of the Attorney General.* The "closing" table is in the pocket part only.

📖 *West's California Reporter* bound volumes and advance sheets, described in § 6.03[1] *above,* update *West's California Digest* by indexing the latest case law in the Key Number Digest section.

📖 *Pacific Digest.* Eagan, MN: West Group. This is the digest for the first through third series of *West's Pacific Reporter.*

The set contains the same features as *West's California Digest.* Different series of *West's Pacific Digests* exist, each covering a certain range of *West's Pacific Reporter* volumes (which are indicated on the spines of the Digest volumes).

Users should note that, like the *West's California Digest*, the *Pacific Digest* covers cases that predate the *Pacific Reporter.*

§ 6.06 Popular Name Tables—Research Methods

📖 *Shepard's Acts and Cases by Popular Names: Federal and State.* 4th edition. Colorado Springs: Shepard's, 1992. 3 v. plus Cumulative Supplement issued annually. *Shepard's Citations* lists alphabetically federal and state acts and cases which have been cited by popular names.

§ 6.07 Citators for California Case Law

[1] Purpose

If a lawyer is relying upon a case on point, he or she must determine if it has been affirmed, dismissed, modified, or reversed on appeal and whether later decisions have treated it negatively. To determine the present value of a decided case and to locate other authority on point, an attorney uses a citator.

[2] *Shepard's*

Shepard's publications are compilations of citations in the form of references in later cases, statutes or other sources to earlier cases, statutes or other material. The earlier case or statute is known as the "cited" case or statute and the later cases and statutes with references to the earlier case or statute are known as "citing" cases or statutes. *Shepard's* tells the reader if the cited statute or case is still good law. *Shepard's* also is used as a way to find additional sources on the topic of the cited case or statute.

The value of a court decision as authority may be affected either by the subsequent history of that case in appellate proceedings which may affirm, reverse, or modify it or by the subsequent treatment of that case by other courts that may follow, criticize, or even overrule it. In the print *Shepard's* citators, letter abbreviations indicate what a court does with a given case or decision. In addition to citations appearing in cases,

Shepard's includes citations in legal periodicals, ALR annotations, and other services.

A detailed examination of the *Shepard's* citator for California follows. When using any citator it is always advisable to read the preface to determine the scope of content and special features presented.

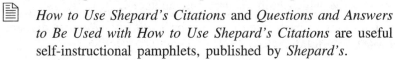 *How to Use Shepard's Citations* and *Questions and Answers to Be Used with How to Use Shepard's Citations* are useful self-instructional pamphlets, published by *Shepard's*.

📖 *Shepard's California Citations—Cases*. Colorado Springs, CO: Shepard's, a member of the LexisNexis Group. Includes Shepard's Signals on treatment of case. Cumulative supplements and paper supplements are used.

Cited Material:
California Supreme Court Reports (all series) (current reports)
California Appellate Reports (all series) (current reports)
California Reporter (all series) (current reports)
Pacific Reporter (California cases) (all series) (current reports)
California Unreported Cases, v. 1–7 (reports not currently published)
Labatt's District Court Reports, v. 1–2 (reports not currently published)
Myrick's Probate Court Reports (reports not currently published)
Coffey's Probate Decisions, v. 1–6 (reports not currently published)
Decisions of the Industrial Accident Commission (administrative agency)
California Compensation Cases (administrative agency)
Opinions and Orders of the Railroad Commission (administrative agency)
Opinions and Orders of the Public Utilities Commission of California (all series) (administrative agency)
Opinions of the Attorney General

Citations to out-of-state cases that cite to California cases in the *Pacific Reporter* and *California Reporter* will be found in *Shepard's Pacific Reporter Citations* or *Shepard's California Reporter Citations*. Thus, *Shepard's California Citations, Case Edition*, when used in combination with *Shepard's Pacific Reporter Citations* and *Shepard's*

California Reporter Citations, provides the complete history and inter-pretation of every California case as passed upon by every state and federal court throughout the United States.

The coverage of the different *Shepard's* divisions will vary from title to title. The user will need to consult the introductory pages of each title to see which citing sources are included.

Citations to each cited case in the *California Reports* division are grouped as follows:

- Citations by the California and federal courts analyzed as to the direct (i.e., appellate) history of the cited case;

- Other citations by the California and federal courts analyzed as to the treatment accorded the cited case;

- Citations in the *Opinions of the Attorney General of California;*

- Citations by state commissions;

- Citations in articles in legal periodicals;

- Citations in annotations of the *United States Supreme Court Reports, Lawyers' Edition,* and annotations of the *American Law Reports;*

- Citations in legal texts.

Syllabi (Superior Numbers). A superior character appearing immedi-ately to the left of the page number of any California or federal court citing reference indicates the particular paragraph of the syllabus or particular headnote of the cited case which states the point of law dealt with in the citing case.

Review/Rehearing Granted. The abbreviation "Gr" shown next to a California court citing reference indicates that a review has been granted. A pound sign (#) shown next to a citing case indicates that the California Supreme Court has granted review in that *citing* case or that the *citing* case was ordered not published and therefore may not have any precedential value. (Note that the # symbol reflects on the citing case, not the cited case that one is Shepardizing.)

Absence from any bound volume or cumulative supplement of a page number for any California case indicates that such case has not been cited within the scope of that volume or cumulative supplement.

The letter "n" to the right of a citing page number indicates a citation in an annotation, such as an ALR annotation. Only the first citation of a case in an annotation or subdivision thereof is shown. A letter "s" to the right of a page number indicates a citation in a supplement to an annotation commencing on that page.

🖥 *Shepard's on LexisNexis.* Dayton, OH: LexisNexis. Available through *lexis.com®*. Includes Shepard's Signals (negative treatment (red stop sign), possible negative treatment (yellow triangle), positive treatment, cited and neutral analysis, cited information available), table of authorities, Focus feature to pinpoint citing references that mention a particular word or phrase, and custom restrictions.

[3] *KeyCite*

KeyCite, released in the summer of 1997, was designed to compete directly with the most current Shepard's online products on LexisNexis. *KeyCite* functions both as an up-to-the-minute citator and case-finder. *KeyCite* traces the history of a case, enabling the researcher to determine if the case is good law. For some cases, within hours after a case is received by Westlaw, the complete appellate history of the case is provided.

KeyCite also provides a listing of citing documents, including published cases, slip opinions, unpublished cases, law review articles, and ALR annotations. *KeyCite* uses depth of treatment stars to indicate how much discussion of the cited case there is in the citing case. Four stars indicate a discussion of more than a printed page. Three stars indicate a discussion of more than a paragraph but not more than a page. Two stars indicate a discussion of a paragraph or less. One star indicates a citation reference.

KeyCite also uses a two flag system. A red flag indicates that at least some aspect of the case is no longer good law. A yellow flag indicates that the case has some negative history, but has not been reversed or overruled.

KeyCite is integrated with West's Key Number System, allowing the lists of citing cases to be restricted to a particular headnote. Citation lists can also be limited by jurisdiction, type of document, date of document, depth of treatment, or keyword (through the Locate feature).

[4] California Citation Guide

📖 *California Citation Guide, Overruled and Disapproved Cases.* San Francisco: Bancroft-Whitney. This guide enables one to tell at a glance if the point of a case in question has been overruled or disapproved by the California Supreme Court, by one of the California Courts of Appeal, or by the United States Supreme Court.

Collected in this volume are all references to overruled or disapproved California Official Reports decisions, with the names, dates, and citations of the overruling or disapproving cases, numbers of the pertinent headnotes, and notes on the points involved.

The work is divided into three major parts: Part One contains a chronological listing of citations of all overruled or disapproved cases. Following the citation is the title, date, and citation of the overruling or disapproving case or cases, the numbers of pertinent headnotes, a concise statement of the points on which the case was overruled or disapproved, and the reasoning involved.

Part Two contains an integrated alphabetical listing, by names of both plaintiff and defendant, of the overruled and disapproved cases, followed by the date and citation of the case.

Part Three is a parallel citation table from unofficial cites to official cites.

Thus, a researcher can easily determine if a particular case has been overruled or disapproved if he or she has the case citation or the name of the parties in that case.

The remaining part of this publication is a "Table of Depublished Cases," which provides information on which cases in the 3d and 4th series of *California Appellate Reports* have been superseded or depublished. The table is arranged alphabetically, though there is also a list of "depublished cases" by citation.

[5] California Subsequent History Table

    📖   *California Subsequent History Table.* St Paul, MN: West Group. The 1999 table was the 15th edition. The table covers all cases in the Supreme Court and the Court of Appeal as reported in the two West reporters, the *Pacific Reporter* and *West's California Reporter* in which there has been a later reported proceeding in California's courts or the U.S. Supreme Court. This is the guide to help the user find if there has been a hearing, rehearing, or review granted or if any subsequent action has been taken on a specific case.

[6] Tracking Status of Recent Depublished or Superseded Opinions

[a] Official Reports

In the most recent *California Official Reports* advance sheets, the user will find the Cumulative Subsequent History Table. The table is in alphabetical order by case name. If a case has been depublished, there will be a statement such as: "reporter of decisions directed not to publish this opinion in the official reports." If review has been granted (the review was formerly called a hearing) or if a rehearing by the same court has been granted, this information is noted under the case name. Note that if an opinion is still subject to Supreme Court review when its scheduled bound volume is being printed, that opinion is reprinted in the Review Granted Opinions Pamphlet (annual and midyear issues). A researcher can still track that opinion in the Cumulative Subsequent History Table.

[b] Unofficial Reports

In the most recent advance sheets for the *California Reporter* see the Case History Table. If a case has been depublished there will be the statement: "ordered not officially published." Other Supreme Court action is also noted. The table is an alphabetical listing of the current published opinions.

§ 6.08 Briefs in California Appellate Courts

[1] Description and Court Rules

"A 'brief' is the vehicle of counsel to convey to the appellate court the essential facts of his client's case, a statement of the questions of law involved, the law he would have applied, and the application he desires made of it by the court." *Bell v. Germain,* 12 Cal.App. 375, 107 P. 630, quoted in *Black's Law Dictionary* (4th ed. rev. 1968).

California Rules of Court, rules 13–18, 29, 29.1, 33, 36, 40, 44, 46, 66 and 80 govern appellate briefs.

Under the direction of the Judicial Council's Appellate Advisory Committee, the Appellate Rules Project Task Force was formed in early 1998 to revise the entire body of rules on appeal. The revision project was undertaken to produce the first general overhaul of the appellate rules since they were originally written in the early 1940's. The first three installments of revised rules on appeal were approved effective January 1, 2002, January 1, 2003, and January 1, 2004 respectively. Most of the rules relating to appellate briefs were revised in these first three installments of revisions. The Appellate Advisory Committee is continuing to work on the fourth and final installment of revisions, which will likely have few substantive changes on the rules relating to appellate briefs.

[2]   Access to Briefs

[a]   Overview

Print briefs are available only in a few large law libraries, which are depositories for the briefs. However, because the briefs distribution system is imperfect, there is no one complete collection of all briefs from the Supreme Court or the Courts of Appeal.

[b]   Brief Depositories

The California State Law Library is one of the libraries that should receive copies of all briefs that have been filed in California appellate court cases. The briefs are sorted, processed, and shelved in docket number order, by court. They are available for use in the State Law Library, which is in the Library-Courts Building in Sacramento. They are also available from the State Law Library through interlibrary loan.

Gary Strong, former State Librarian, has said that "Briefs are a valuable resource to legal researchers since they provide a source those with similar problems can study for the analysis, arguments and authorities cited, with considerable savings of time and money. The form of pleadings can be copied, when the problem is similar, which is particularly valuable when it has withstood attack on appeal." Strong continued, "In addition to their value in legal research, briefs can be a valuable resource to historians, political scientists and writers of trials and scripts."[45]

As a complete depository for California court briefs, the State Law Library has acquired an extensive, historical collection of briefs, beginning with 1850 for those from the Supreme Court and from 1909 for the Courts of Appeal. Near complete collections of California court briefs are also available in the Los Angeles County Law Library and

---

[45] Gary Strong made these remarks in Sacramento on Nov. 16, 1981 as he announced the completion of a large project organizing briefs for public access.

the San Diego County Public Law Library. The Bernard E. Witkin Alameda County Law Library retains its depository status but suspended receiving the hard copy version of briefs in 1996. Finally, the Hastings College of the Law Library has briefs from 1906–1978 (obtained from the San Francisco Law Library).

Most law libraries file their hard copy briefs according to docket number. To locate briefs filed in docket number order, researchers will often need to use an index to provide the docket number. Hastings College of the Law Library has developed indexes for its briefs. Its index for California Supreme Court briefs is availabe on the web at *www.uchastings.edu/library/index.html* (click on "research databses").

[c]   Microfiche Collections

Many law libraries also have microfiche collections of California court briefs. Library Microfilms, a division of BMI Imaging Systems (see the Publishers/Vendors list in Appendix A), has microfiched California Supreme Court and Courts of Appeal briefs from Oct. 1969 (starting with cases published in 1 Cal. 3d and 1 Cal. App. 3d) until 1998. For the period 1969–1996, the microfiche collection is restricted to cases that are officially reported in Cal. and Cal. App., and the briefs are arranged in the order of the citations in the official reports. For the period 1996–1998, the fiche collection is organized by docket number and includes briefs from cases not officially reported. [46]

Briefs from 1996 to the present are also available in a fiche collection made available by Court Record Services (CRS) (now owned by West). CRS obtains its briefs for filming from the San Diego County Law Library.

[d]   Online Access

The following Westlaw databases contain briefs filed in California appellate courts:

---

[46] The differences in coverage for these two time periods stems from the fact that Library Microfilms' source for the 1969–1996 briefs was the Alameda County Law Library, which only kept the briefs in officially reported cases (in citation order), while the source for the more recent 1996–1998 briefs was the Los Angeles County Law Library, which keeps all briefs collected from the depository system (in docket number order).

CA-BRIEF	Contains merit briefs filed with the California Supreme Court. Selective coverage begins with briefs from 1997, and complete coverage begins from 1999. The database only includes briefs in cases where review has been granted.
CA-BRIEF-EXT	Contains selected merit briefs filed with the California Supreme Court *prior* to 1997.
CA-APP-BRIEF	Contains selected briefs filed with the California Courts of Appeal. Coverage begins with briefs from 1997. PDF images are available for the briefs.
CA-PETITION	Contains petitions for review filed with the California Supreme Court (along with the corresponding briefs). Coverage is selective, beginning with petitions from 1993.
CA-RECALL	Contains briefs related to the 2003 California Recall Election.

On LexisNexis, one can access selected California briefs from 1990–2001 in the "Brief Reporter—California Materials" Source (CAL;BRREP). Brief Reporter is a service that publishes legal briefs obtained from leading attorneys throughout the country (along with abstracts of those briefs).

CRS has also created an online database of court briefs (BriefServe.com), which provides researchers with access to court records and briefs in a downloadable PDF electronic format. Currently, BriefServe.com makes available briefs from the U.S. Supreme Court, the U.S. Courts of Appeals, and California courts (with briefs from other states coming soon). While BriefServe is a fee-based service, CRS is making its online database of California briefs available at no charge to the law libraries that are part of the depository system for California court briefs. Free access to this database however can only be obtained in these depository libraries' reading rooms.

§ 6.09   Trial Transcripts

Both LexisNexis and Westlaw have trial transcripts from the O.J. Simpson criminal and civil cases. On Westlaw, the OJTRANS and OJCIVTRANS databases contain the transcripts from the criminal and civil trials respectively. On Lexis, these transcripts can be found respectively in the "Transcripts from People v. Simpson Criminal Trial" Source (CAL;OJTRAN) and the "Simpson Wrongful Death Trial Transcripts" Source (CAL;OJCIV).

Westlaw also contains the transcripts and court documents from the People v. Erik and Lyle Menendez case from the mid-1990s (MENENDEZTRANS).

§ 6.10 Bibliography On Case Reporting

Barnett, Stephen R. "Making Decisions Disappear: Depublication and Stipulated Reversal in the California Supreme Court." 26 *Loy. L.A. L. Rev.* 1033 (1993).

Barnett, Stephen R. "Special Report on California Appellate Justice: Depublication Deflating: The California Supreme Court's Wonderful Law-Making Machine Begins to Self-Destruct." 45 *Hastings L.J.* 520 (March 1994).

Biggs, Julie Hayward. Censoring the Law in California: Decertification revisited. 30 *Hastings L.J.* 1577 (1979).

Brady, Michael J. *Summary of California Appellate Decisions.* Redwood City, Calif., Ropers, Majeski, Kohn, Bentley & Wagner, 1979–present. 1 vol. Looseleaf.

California. Legislature. Senate. Committee on the Judiciary. *Publication of Appellate Court Opinions. Hearing.* Indian Wells, California. November 21, 1975.

California. Supreme Court. Practices and Procedures: Containing Internal Operating Practices and Procedures, As Adopted by the California Supreme Court. San Francisco: Supreme Court of California, 1995. 40 p.

California Supreme Court Survey. Pepperdine Law Review. In each of the quarterly issues the student editors write short summaries of recent decisions by the court. The survey covers all topics except attorney discipline, judicial misconduct, and death penalty appeals. The summaries vary in length from a page up to 10 pages.

Chanin, Leah. "A survey of the writing and publication of opinions in Federal and State Appellate Courts." 67 *L. Libr. J.* 362–379 (1974).

Committee on Legal Publications and Decisions. State Bar of California. "Report, February 21, 1962." Eugene M. Prince, Chairman. Harold R. McKinnon, Homer R. Spence, 37 *J. St. B. Cal.* 371 (1962).

📖　Gerstein, Robert. "Law by Elimination: Depublication in the California Supreme Court." 67 *Judicature* 292 (1984).

📖　Grodin, Joseph R. "The Depublication Practice of the California Supreme Court." 72 *Cal. L. Rev.* 514 (1984).

📖　Gustafson, Roy A. "Some Observations About California Courts of Appeal." 19 *UCLA L. Rev.* 167 (1971).

📖　Jacobstein, J. Myron. "Some reflections on the control of the publication of appellate court opinions." 27 *Stan. L. Rev.* 791–799 (1975).

📖　Kanner, Gideon. "It's a Busy Court: The Effect of Denial of Hearing by the Supreme Court on Court of Appeals Decisions." 47 *Cal. St. B.J.* 188–193 (1972).

📖　Kanner, Gideon. "Unpublished appellate opinion: Friend or foe?" 48 *Cal. St. B.J.* 387 (1973).

📖　Lasky, Moses. "Observing Appellate Opinions From Below the Bench." 49 *Cal. L. Rev.* 831–844 (1961).

📖　Prince, Eugene H. "Law Books, Unlimited." 48 *A.B.A. J.* 134 (1962).

📖　"Publication of Dissenting Opinions." 42 *A.B.A. J.* 161 (1956).

📖　"Selective publication of case law," note by Mark Wood, 39 *S. Cal. L. Rev.* 608 (1966).

📖　Seligson, Robert A. and Warnlof, John S. "Use of Unreported Cases in California." 24 *Hastings L.J.* 37 (1972).

📖　Silverman, Milton J. "The Unwritten law—The Unpublished Opinion in California." 51 *Cal. St. B.J.* 33–40 (1976).

📖　Strauss, J. D. "Historical Study—Written Opinions." 39 *J. St. B. Cal.* 127 (1964).

📖　Thompson, Robert S. Selected Publication. 50 *Cal. St. B. J.* 480 (1975).

📖　Uelmen, Gerald F. "Publication and Depublication of California Court of Appeal Opinions: Is the Eraser Mightier Than the Pencil?" 26 *Loy. L.A. L. Rev.* 1007 (Summer 1993).

Chapter 7

Judicial Administration[1]

[1] This chapter is revised and updated by Jane Evans, Senior Business Systems Analyst, Information Services Division, Administrative Office of the Courts, San Francisco. The author wishes to thank Nanna Frye, Law Librarian, California Courts of Appeal, for her contributions to this chapter.

(Pub. 64620)

§ 7.01　The Court System—Constitutional Background

[1]　Constitutional Authority

The judicial system of California is organized under article VI of the current Constitution.

[2]　Supreme Court

California's courts (Supreme Court and trial courts) were established by the Article VI of the Constitution of 1849. The first Supreme Court had a Chief Justice and two associate justices, all elected by the Legislature, as directed under that Constitution. Today, under the much amended Constitution of 1879, California has a Chief Justice and six associate justices. [2] The Supreme Court is seated in San Francisco, and also hears regular oral arguments in Los Angeles and Sacramento.

[3]　Courts of Appeal

The Courts of Appeal were first established in 1904. [3] At that time only three districts were named: First District located in San Francisco, Second District located in Los Angeles (and now also in Ventura), and Third District located in Sacramento. Today there are three additional districts: Fourth District with Division One in San Diego, Division Two in Riverside and Division Three in Santa Ana, Fifth District located in Fresno, and Sixth District located in San Jose, with the 58 county superior courts divided geographically among the districts (Government Code Section 69100). Under the California Constitution, Article VI, Section 3, the Legislature is responsible for dividing the state into appellate court districts, each with one or more divisions. Each appellate court division consists of a presiding justice and two associate justices (California Constitution Article VI, Section 3). Each division is independent and may decline to follow a prior decision of another district or division (9 Witkin, California Procedure, Section 934). The court is to act as a three-justice court, with concurrence of two justices necessary for a judgment. [4] The Legislature prescribes the number of judges for

---

[2] California Constitution, article VI, section 2 provides that the concurrence of four judges present at the argument is necessary for the judgment.

[3] Cal. Const., art. VI, § 3.

[4] A retired Associate Justice of the Court of Appeal, Roy A. Gustafson, wrote a law review article recommending some improvements in the court. In the article he mentioned some of the history of the court's name and discussed whether it should be capitalized and whether it should be plural or singular. In any case, he felt strongly

each district (California Government Code Sections 69101–69106). Currently, there are 105 Court of Appeal justices. Extensive information about each court and its procedures can be found at: *www.courtinfo.ca.gov/ courts/courtsofappeal.*

[4]   Trial Courts

Article VI, Section 4 of the Constitution provides for a superior court in each of the fifty-eight counties, with the Legislature prescribing the number of judges, officers, and employees of each court. These are courts of general jurisdiction.

Until 1995, California had two types of lower trial courts, justice and municipal. Municipal courts served the larger, more populous counties (over 40,000 people). In a consolidation effort that took effect January 1, 1995 (California Constitution, Article VI, §§ 1, 5, 6, 11, 15), all justice courts were converted into municipal courts.

In 1998, a new court consolidation proposition was passed by the voters. Proposition 220 amended the Constitution[5] to allow municipal and superior courts to merge their operations upon the majority approval of the judges of both courts for that county. The result of a county's adoption of the merger proposal is the abolition of the municipal courts in that county. By February 2001, all counties had approved this merger.

---

that it should not be called an intermediate appellate court, since it did not take appeals from an appellate court below it. Roy A. Gustafson, "Some Observations about California Courts of Appeal," 19 UCLA L. Rev167 (1971).

[5] Cal. Const., art. VI, § 5(c).

California Court System

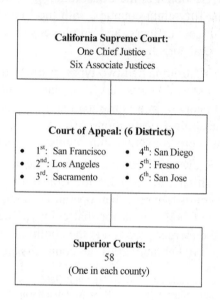

California Supreme Court:
One Chief Justice
Six Associate Justices

Court of Appeal: (6 Districts)

- 1st: San Francisco
- 2nd: Los Angeles
- 3rd: Sacramento
- 4th: San Diego
- 5th: Fresno
- 6th: San Jose

Superior Courts:
58
(One in each county)

Judicial Council:
Makes rules on judicial procedure; surveys and expedites judicial business.

Commission on Judicial Performance:
Recommends censure, removal, or retirement of judges to Supreme Court.

Commission on Judicial Appointments:
Confirms or rejects appellate appointees of Governor.

**DISTRICTS OF
CALIFORNIA COURTS OF APPEAL**

§ 7.02 Court Administration—Constitutional Background

[1] Judicial Council of California

The Judicial Council of California was established by Article VI, Section 6. It is made up of the Chief Justice and one associate justice from the Supreme Court, three justices from courts of appeal, ten judges of superior courts, four members of the State Bar, and one member from each house of the Legislature. The Council's purpose is to improve the administration of justice. It is to survey judicial business and make recommendations to the courts, the Legislature, and the Governor. The Council is also to adopt rules for court administration, practice, and procedure. The Judicial Council may appoint an Administrative Director of the Courts, who performs delegated functions. The Judicial Council's internet page address is: *www.courtinfo.ca.gov/courtadmin/jc.*

The first history of judicial administration in California that explores the evolution of the administration of justice from statehood in 1850 to the beginning of the twenty-first century is Sipes, Larry L. *Committed to Justice: the Rise of Judicial Administration in California.* San Francisco: Administrative Office of the Courts, 2002. 318 p.

The Administrative Office of the Courts came out with a new book on the Judicial Council in 2004: Profile: Judicial Council of California. San Francisco: Administrative Office of the Courts, 2004. 56 p. The book covers the history, structure, and past and present members of the Judicial Council.

[2] Administrative Office of the Courts

California Rules of Court, rule 6.80 establishes the position of Administrative Director of the Court, and the duties of that position. The director serves as the Secretary of the Judicial Council of California.

California Rules of Court, rule 6.81 permits the Administrative Director of the Court to set up the Administrative Office of the Courts, by hiring staff to carry out the assigned duties. The www page for the Administrative Office of the Courts is: *www.courtinfo.ca.gov/courtadmin/aoc.*

[3] The California Center for Judicial Education and Research

The California Center for Judicial Education and Research was formed in 1973 as a joint enterprise of the Judicial Council and the

California Judges Association. As part of the Education Division of the Administrative Office of the Courts since 1994, it conducts orientation programs for new judges, and continuing education programs for veteran judges and judicial attorneys. The center also produces judges' benchbooks and other educational materials, available electronically to judges on the judicial branch extranet, Serranus.

[4]   Commission on Judicial Appointments

The Commission on Judicial Appointments is established by Article VI, Section 7. It is made up of the Chief Justice, the Attorney General, and the presiding justice of the court of appeal of the affected district. The commission reviewsjudicial appointments of the Governor and, after holding a public hearing, votes on whether to confirm the appointment. The internet page for the Commission is: *www.courtinfo.ca.gov/ courtadmin/otheragencies.htm/htm.*

[5]   Commission on Judicial Performance

Article VI, Sections 8 and 18 establish and define the duties of the Commission on Judicial Performance, which deals with judicial misconduct and disability. The commission is made up of three judges appointed by the Supreme Court; two members of the State Bar, appointed by the Bar; two citizens who are not attorneys, appointed by the Governor; and two public members, appointed by the Assembly Speaker and Senate Rules Committee. The www page for the Commission on Judicial Performance is: *www.courtinfo.ca.gov/courtadmin/ otheragencies.htm/htm.*

§ 7.03   Official Publications

[1]   Obtaining

Official publications and other publications such as task force reports, fact sheets, and strategic plans are available at *www.courtinfo.ca.gov/ reference/.* Print copies may be ordered from the Office of Communications at 1/800-900-5980 or *pubinfo@jud.ca.gov.*

[2]   Judicial Council

  📖 *Court Statistics Report.* San Francisco: Judicial Council of California. Annual. This publication is a statistical report of caseload data by individual court.

📖 *Annual Report.* San Francisco: Judicial Council of California. Annual.

📖 *The Supreme Court of California.* San Francisco: Judicial Council of California, 2003.

📖 *Profile: Judicial Council of California.* San Francisco: Judicial Council of California, 2002.

📄 *Court News. San Francisco:* Judicial Council of California. Bi-monthly.

[3] Administrative Office of the Courts

📄 *Journal of the Center for Families, Children & the Courts.* v.1– 1999–. San Francisco: Administrative Office of the Courts. Annual.

📄 *News Release.* San Francisco: Administrative Office of the Courts, Office of Communications. Irregularly published.

§ 7.04 Court Rules

[1] Power to Adopt

The Judicial Council has the power to adopt or amend rules of practice and procedure for the several courts not inconsistent with law.[6] California Rules of Court rules 6.20 through 6.22 address the rule-making process, including provision for public proposals. The council also submits to the Legislature at each session its recommendations with reference to amendments of, and changes in, existing laws relating to practice and procedure. (Cal. Const., art. VI, § 6; Gov. Code, § 68072.)

The various groups of rules are numbered in a single sequence which permits any rule to be cited by its California Rules of Court number without further identification. A Disposition Table from the Rules as originally numbered to the rules as numbered in California Rules of Court enables the user to convert easily from the old rule to the new rule numbers.

The rules are amended on a frequent basis, so the Judicial Council web site should be consulted for the most current version. The Appellate

---

 [6] For background data on the rule-making powers of the Judicial Council see Gibson, Phil S., "For Modern Courts," 32 Journal of the State Bar of California 727 (1959), and Kleps, Ralph N., "The Judicial Council and the Administrative Office of the California Courts," 37 Journal of the State Bar of California 329 (1962). Bernard E. Witkin wrote the original set of California Rules of Court.

Rules Project Task Force has been working since 1998 to produce the first revision of the appellate rules since they were first written in the 1940s. The new rules are posted on the web site as they are approved.

The illustration, *How a Proposal Becomes a Rule*, is reprinted here to explain the rule adoption process. This illustration is available at the Judicial Council web site at: *www.courtinfo.ca.gov/rules/proprule.pdf.*

[2] Finding Court Rules

Rules of court are available in almost all of the locations that codes are available. Court rules, although not legislation, are bound with or shelved with the code volumes in most states, including California. Users may locate the rules within the code volumes by using the same process as locating code sections: by topic, by table, or by index term. California Rules of Court are no longer published in print form in an official edition but are available on the Judicial Council's web site at *www.courtinfo.ca.gov/rules.* Proposed rules inviting public comment and advisory committee responses to the public comments are also available on the web site.

> 📖 *Deering's California Codes: Rules Annotated.* Matthew Bender & Company, Inc., a member of the LexisNexis Group. Annotated Rules of Court, including rule history, drafter's notes, Judicial Council comments, and notes of decision. Cross references and Selected research references to *California Forms of Pleading and Practice,* Matthew Bender & Company, Inc. and *Witkin,* West Group, and *Rutter,* West Group. 4 v. Annual, with mid-year supplement.

> 📖 *Standard California Codes: 6-in-1®.* Matthew Bender & Company, Inc., a member of the LexisNexis Group. Rules of Court, along with Civil, Civil Procedure, Evidence, Family, and Probate Codes. Includes rule history and highlighted changes to rules. Selected research references to *California Forms of Pleading and Practice,* Matthew Bender & Company, Inc. and *Witkin,* West Group, and *Rutter,* West Group. 1 v. Annual, with mid-year supplement.

> 📖 *Standard California Codes: 4-in-1.* Matthew Bender & Company, Inc., a member of the LexisNexis Group. Codes include Civil, Civil Procedure, Evidence, and Rules of Court. 1 v. Includes rule history and highlighted changes to rules. Selected research references to *California Forms of Pleading and*

How a Proposal Becomes a Rule

"To improve the administration of justice the [Judicial Council] shall survey judicial business and make recommendations to the courts, make recommendations annually to the Governor and the Legislature, adopt rules for court administration, practice and procedure, and perform other functions prescribed by statute. The rules adopted shall not be inconsistent with statute." —Cal. Const., art. VI, § 6.

Rule making by the Judicial Council involves several steps. Rules, forms, and standards of judicial administration are circulated for comment twice a year for adoption effective January 1 and July 1. Generally, the council follows the procedure described below. (Cal. Rules of Court, rule 6.20.)

Submitting a Proposal: Any person or organization can submit a request for a new or amended Judicial Council rule, form, or standard of judicial administration. It is helpful if the proposal includes: (1) the text of the proposed rule, standard, form, or amendment; (2) a description of the problem to be addressed; (3) the proposed solution and alternative solutions; (4) any likely implementation problems; (5) any need for urgent consideration; (6) known proponents and opponents; and (7) any known fiscal impact.

Mail, fax, or e-mail proposals to: Judicial Council of California, Attention: General Counsel (Rule/Form Proposal), 455 Golden Gate Avenue, San Francisco, CA 94102-3660, fax: 415-865-7664, legal-services@jud.ca.gov.

Analyzing the Proposal: An advisory committee (on, e.g., civil, criminal, or family law, or court administrators) analyzes the proposal and may take one of the following actions:

- Recommend to the council's Rules and Projects Committee (RUPRO) that the proposal be circulated for public comment, with or without modification, or that it be adopted without being circulated for comment;
- Request further analysis by the proponent; or
- Reject the proposal.

RUPRO Action: RUPRO reviews the advisory committee's recommendation and may take one of the following actions:

- Circulate the proposal for public comment with or without modification;
- Recommend that the council adopt it without circulating it for comment if the proposal presents a nonsubstantial, technical, or noncontroversial change or correction;
- Request further analysis by the advisory committee or the proponent;
- Refer the matter to another council committee, the full council, or the Chief Justice; or
- Reject the proposal if it is contrary to council policy or statute or conflicts with other rules or standards.

Comments and Consideration: After the comment period closes, the advisory committee considers the comments and may:

- Recommend adoption of the original proposal;
- Modify the proposal and recommend adoption as modified;
- Hold the proposal in committee for further study and analysis; or
- Reject the proposal based on the comments received.

February 1999

Final Judicial Council Action: The advisory committee recommendation is reviewed by RUPRO. If the advisory committee recommends adoption of a new or revised rule, form, or standard of judicial administration, the matter is placed on the council's agenda. The council may adopt, modify, or reject the proposed rule, form, or standard. If adopted, it will usually become effective the following January 1 or July 1.

Contact

To find recent rule changes, see the California Courts Web site, www. courtinfo.ca.gov/rules. To comment on proposed changes during a comment period, see www.courtinfo.ca. gov/invitationstocomment/ or contact the Administrative Office of the Courts, 455 Golden Gate Avenue, San Francisco, CA 94102-3660, fax: 415-865-7664.

Practice, Matthew Bender & Company, Inc. and *Witkin,* West Group, and *Rutter,* West Group. 1 v. Annual, with mid-year supplement.

📖 *Matthew Bender's California Desktop Code Sets.* Matthew Bender & Company, Inc., a member of the LexisNexis Group. Rules of court are combined in different sets of selected Codes. Titles with Rules of Court include: *Standard California Penal Code with Evidence Code*; and *Workers' Compensation Laws of California.*

📖 *Deering's California Desktop Code Series.* Matthew Bender & Company, Inc., a member of the LexisNexis Group. Complete or selected rules of court are combined in different Code sets. Titles include: *Civil* Practice; *Family Code*; *Probate Code*; *Penal Code*; *Business and Commercial Code.*

📖 *California Rules of Court:* State [Year] St. Paul, MN: West Group. Semi-annual. Includes: California Rules of Court, Rules regulating admission to practice law in California, Rules of Procedure of the State Bar of California.

📖 *West's Annotated California Codes, Civil and Criminal Rules*, v. 23 pt. 1, v. 23 pt. 2, and v. 23 pt. 2 supplements. Annotations. General information on appellate practice appears in the Appendix and includes time tables, data on form of papers, filing procedures, jurisdictional data, etc.

📖 Daily Journal. *Court Rules.* See entry below in Local Court Rules Section.

📖 Metropolitan News-Enterprise. *California State Rules.* Court Rules Services. See entry below in Local Court Rules Section.

📄 *California Official Reports: Official Advance Sheets.* LexisNexis Matthew Bender. New rules of court, if any, are listed in each issue. Published every ten days.

💿 *Deering's California Codes Annotated on LexisNexis CD.* Matthew Bender & Company, Inc., a member of the LexisNexis Group. Annotated Rules of Court, including rule history, drafter's notes, Judicial Council comments, and notes of decision. Cross references and Selected research references to *California Forms of Pleading and Practice,* Matthew Bender & Company, Inc. and *Witkin,* West Group, and *Rutter,* West Group.

West's Annotated California Codes CD-ROM. Eagan, MN: West Publishing Co.

Deering's California Codes Annotated. Dayton, OH: Lexis-Nexis. Available on *lexis.com®*, Rules of Court are in the "CA—California Court Rules" Source (CAL; CARULE). Annotated Rules of Court, including rule history, drafter's notes, Judicial Council comments, and notes of decision. Cross references and Selected research references to *California Forms of Pleading and Practice,* Matthew Bender & Company, Inc. and *Witkin,* West Group, and *Rutter,* West Group.

Westlaw carries Rules of Court in the CA-RULES database. Judicial amendments to rules are found in CA-ORDERS.

[3] Citators

Shepard's California Citations—Statutes. Colorado Springs, CO: Shepard's, a member of the LexisNexis Group. Rules of Court are located in the Statutes volumes. Citations to history and court opinions.

Shepard's on LexisNexis. Dayton, OH: LexisNexis. Available through *lexis.com®*. Rules of Court may be Shepardized the same as statutes and cases. Includes history or rule. Citations to court opinions and law review articles.

KeyCite—Westlaw. St. Paul, MN: West Group. Citator service available online from Westlaw for Rules of Court.

[4] California Local Court Rules

[a] Authority

Every court of record may make rules for its own administration and the governing of its officers not inconsistent with law or with the rules adopted and prescribed by the Judicial Council [Gov. Code, § 68070; Cal. Rules of Ct., Rule 981].

California Rules of Court rule 981 provides for adopting, filing, distributing, and maintaining local rules of court. This rule was revised in 2002, with an effective date of January 1, 2003, to make better use of computer technology and court web sites to eliminate the paperwork involved in providing public access to local rules. Local rules may be available for examination both remotely and at the courthouse electronically rather than in paper. County law libraries may also be designated to make local rules available on their web sites.

[b] Sources

📖 *California Bay Area Local Court Rules—Superior Courts.* Eagan, MN: West Group. This paperback publication is released semi-annually for the Bay Area counties.

📖 *Central California Local Court Rules—Superior Courts.* Eagan, MN: West Group. This paperback publication is released semi-annually for the Fresno, Inyo, Kern, Madera, Mariposa, Merced, Monterey, San Benito, Santa Cruz, Stanislaus, Tulare, and Tuloumne County.

📖 *Los Angeles County Court Rules—Superior Courts.* Eagan, MN: West Group. This paperback publication is released semi-annually for only Los Angeles County.

📖 *Northern California Local Court Rules—Superior Courts.* Eagan, MN: West Group. This paperback publication is released semi-annually.

📖 *Southern California Local Court Rules—Superior Courts.* Eagan, MN: West Group. This paperback publication is released semi-annually.

📖 *Metropolitan News-Enterprise Court Rules.* Los Angeles: Metropolitan News Company. Court rules are published for all the most populous counties (19 counties available). Volumes for northern counties have gray covers. Volumes for southern counties have black covers. State rules covers are half gray and half black.

📖 *Court Rules: Northern California.* Los Angeles: Daily Journal. 9 v. This set, like the Southern California set, contains complete state rules, federal and appellate rules, Judicial Council forms, and local rules for all counties. The information is updated monthly.

📖 *Court Rules: Southern California.* Los Angeles: Daily Journal. 8 v. This set, like the Northern California set, contains complete state rules, federal and appellate rules, and local rules for all counties. The information is updated monthly.

📖 The Daily Journal Corporation also provides single-volume court rules for several counties. These are:

Alameda/Contra Costa counties
Los Angeles County
Orange County
Riverside County
San Bernardino County
San Diego County
San Francisco County
Santa Clara/San Mateo counties
Ventura/Santa Barbara/San Luis Obispo Counties

📖 Paperbound editions of local court rules may be available from time to time from the county clerks of the various counties.

💿 *California Local Rules of Court on LexisNexis CD.* Matthew Bender & Company, Inc., a member of the LexisNexis Group.

💿 *LexisNexis Automated California County Forms on HotDocs.* Matthew Bender & Company, Inc., a member of the Lexis-Nexis Group. County rules often include local forms, which are compiled on this CD-ROM. Queries prompt for information to fill in forms instead of using a typewriter after printing a blank form. Available in Northern and Southern California versions.

💻 *LexisNexis.* Dayton, OH: LexisNexis. Available on *lexis.com*®, Source, "California Superior Ct. Local Rules" (CAL; CASCLR), includes local court rules for 58 counties. Includes history of rule. Separate sources exist for rules in Los Angeles ("Los Angeles County Superior Ct. Rules" (CAL; LASCRL)).

💻 *Westlaw.* St. Paul, MN: West Group. Carries local court rules in its CA-LOCRULES database.

💻 American LegalNet. On the internet at: *americanlegalnet.com.*

💻 JuriSearch. On the internet at: *www.jurisearch.com.*

[c] County Sites

Superior court web sites post local rules. The main web site for California courts, hosted by the Judicial Council of California at: *www.courtinfo.ca.gov/otherwebsites.htm*, has links to each superior court web site.

§ 7.05 Jury Instructions

In July 2003, the Judicial Council approved 800 new plain English civil jury instructions developed by the Task Force on Jury Instructions.

California Rule of Court rule 855 strongly encourages the use of the official instructions. Links to the complete text, as well as FAQ's, a correlation table, and other supporting documents are available at the Judicial Council web site, *www.courtinfo.ca.gov/jury/civiljuryinstructions.* The rules are cited as CACI, for California Civil Instructions. LexisNexis Matthew Bender is the official publisher of CACI.

California Jury Instructions–Civil (abbreviated as BAJI, for Book of Approved Jury Instructions) is no longer approved by state court rules, and the Los Angeles Superior Court BAJI Committee has disbanded.

📖 *Judicial Council of California Civil Jury Instructions.* Lexis-Nexis Matthew Bender.

📖 *CACI California Jury Instructions: Judicial Council of California Civil Jury Instructions.* Thomson West.

California Jury Instructions-Criminal (abbreviated CALJIC). All editions from the first (1946) through the seventh (2003) have been published by West Group. The set is prepared by the Committee on Standard Jury Instructions, Criminal, of the Superior Court of Los Angeles, California. CALJIC is available from West Group in hard copy, on CD-ROM, and on Westlaw. LexisNexis carries the online version ("California Jury Instructions Criminal (CALJIC)" Source (2NDARY; CALJIC)).

The Judicial Council of California Task Force on Jury Instructions is writing new criminal jury instructions that will be ready for approval in 2005.

Though the Committee adopting CALJIC is not endorsed by the California Legislature or Supreme Court, its instructions have been recommended by the Judicial Council.

Both CACI and CALJIC may be Shepardized in Shepard's California Citations—Statutes volume. Jury Instructions may also be checked online for citing references on LexisNexis or Westlaw by running searches using the citation components as search terms.

Other jury instruction treatises include California Forms of Jury Instructions by Matthew Bender & Company, Inc., a member of the LexisNexis Group. This treatise is available in print or online at *lexis.com®* ("California: Form of Jury Instructions" Source (CAL; CFJURY)). Jury instructions include cross references to statutes and cases.

§ 7.06   Judicial Council Forms

[1]   Major Categories

In addition to adopting rules for the courts, the Judicial Council also adopts forms for use in the courts. The forms are available from several commercial publishers in print as well as electronic format. The official web site, *www.courtinfo.ca.gov/forms*, contains all forms in PDF format, some of which are electronically fillable. There are hundreds of forms available, and they are revised frequently. Forms are mandatory or optional.

[2]   Sources for Forms

In addition to the free version on the Judicial Council web site, there are many commercial publishers that sell the forms in one version or another. The Judicial Council has a listing of over 30 companies at this address: *www.courtinfo.ca.gov/forms/publishers.htm*. Several publishers are listed below.

- *Judicial Council of California. Forms.* American Legal Net. The official publisher of Judicial Council forms publishes only an electronic version. The forms may be obtained at www.uscourtforms.com.

- *California Forms of Pleading and Practice—Judicial Council Forms.* Matthew Bender & Company, Inc., a member of the LexisNexis Group. This 4-volume set contains full-sized forms in a looseleaf format enabling reproduction and return to the set. Forms are separated by topic, and set includes table of contents and list of forms.

- *West's California Judicial Council Forms.* Eagan, MN: West Group. Semiannual. This two-volume set contains full-sized perforated forms designed for easy reproduction. There is a regular index in the back of the book, as well as a spine index.

- *LexisNexis Automated California Judicial Council Forms on HotDocs.* Matthew Bender & Company, Inc., a member of the LexisNexis Group. Queries prompt for information to fill in forms. Data may be saved for transfer to different forms.

- *Legal Solutions Plus Judicial Council Forms.* Eagan, MN: West Group.

- *SmartLaser Judicial Council Forms.* Berkeley, CA: California Continuing Education of the Bar. This is a cd product with online updates that can be downloaded. SmartLaser subscribers have access to complete collection of Judicial Council forms at: *ceb.ucop.edu/catalog/2000smrtl.html.*

 Martin Dean's Essential Forms. San Francisco: Martin Dean's Essential Publishers Inc. CD version.

Chapter 8

California Administrative Law

§ 8.01 Introduction

This chapter covers the executive branch of California government. The material is arranged with the most emphasis on regulations, because that is where there is the most material for research and the most need for research.

In this edition of the *California Law Guide* there are contributions from two knowledgeable persons in the administrative law field. The regulations section was drafted by Mike Ibold.[1] The section on administrative decisions was written by Heather Cline Hoganson.[2]

At the beginning of this chapter is an illustration of the executive branch of government. For another flow chart of the executive branch, including the names of directors and telephone numbers, see *www.cold.ca.gov/Ca_State_Gov_Orgchart.pdf.*

§ 8.02 State Regulatory History

The existing body of California administrative regulations is readily available to the public through *Barclays Official California Code of Regulations* (formerly the *California Administrative Code*) and the *California Regulatory Code Supplement* (formerly the *California Administrative Register*). These publications exist in paper, fiche, CD-ROM, and online formats. State administrative regulations were not always as easy to locate as they are today. Until the 1940s there was no single repository or file for administrative regulations, even within the agencies themselves.[3] Attorneys appearing before state agencies felt that the rules were being made up by the administrators as they went along.[4] Around that time the State Bar became an advocate for change to a more organized system where regulations and administrative decisions were accumulated for publication and made available for study.

The legislation authorizing the publication of regulations is the result of years of effort by many individuals and embodies the work of several sessions of the Legislature. The first provision in California for the central filing of administrative regulations and for their compilation and publication was made by Chapter 628 of the Statutes of 1941. This statute, which took effect on September 13, 1941, required all state agencies to compile their effective regulations and to file them with the Secretary of State on or before March 12, 1942. The statute also created

---

[1] Mike Ibold, law librarian for the Office of Administrative Law from 1987 to 2003.

[2] Heather Cline Hoganson, Staff Counsel, Office of Administrative Hearings.

[3] John G. Clarkson, "The History of the California Administrative Procedure Act," 15 *Hastings L.J.* 237 (Feb. 1964) at 240.

[4] *Id.*

The California Executive Branch

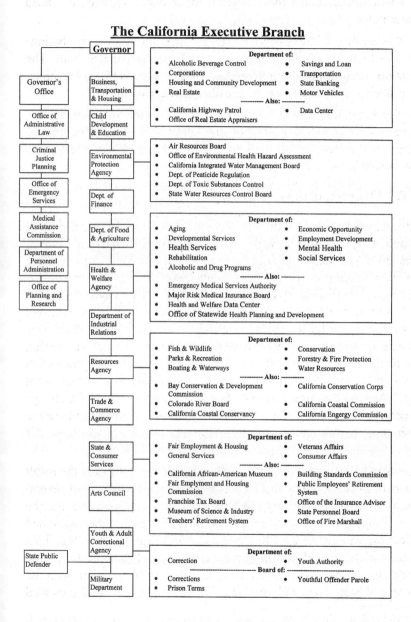

the Codification Board and charged it with the duty of publishing the compiled regulations. The Codification Board published the twenty-three original titles, and Registers 1 through 9.

The functions of the Codification Board were transferred to the Division of Administrative Procedure by Chapter 1425 of the Statutes of 1947, The Administrative Procedure Act. The Division of Administrative Procedure published Register 10, No. 1, and all succeeding registers, and Title 24. It was charged with the continuing duty of compilation, codification, and publication of all regulations required to be filed with the Secretary of State.

By Chapter 2048 of the Statutes of 1961, the Division of Administrative Procedure was designated as Office of Administrative Procedure, in the Department of Finance. By chapter 1786, section 13, Statutes 1963, the office was transferred to the new Department of General Services effective October 1, 1964. Codification continued as one of the functions of the office. Chapter 1303 of Statutes 1971 changed the title of the Office of Administrative Procedure to the Office of Administrative Hearings (OAH) and the title of the executive officer from "presiding officer" to "director." Chapter 142 of the Statutes 1974 expanded the functions of the office by requiring the OAH to print notices of proposed action which are received from state agencies in the California Administrative Register.[5]

The Office of Administrative Law (OAL) was created by the Legislature in 1979 by chapter 567, section 1, Statutes 1979 to review all regulations before adoption. The office was created in reaction to the unprecedented growth in the number of regulations and their unclear and unnecessarily complex language. The OAL's purpose is to ensure that regulations are written in a comprehensible manner, authorized by statute, and consistent with other law.[6]

---

[5] The California Administrative Register was originally entitled the California Administrative Register/Notice Supplement. In 1982 it was changed to the California Administrative Register/Notice Register. In 1988 it was changed to its current title.

[6] Gov. Code, § 11340.

§ 8.03   Administrative Rules and Regulations[7]

[1]   The Official California Code of Regulations (CCR)

State agency regulations were first codified by the old Codification Board and originally published in 1945 as the *California Administrative Code* (CAC) by the Office of the State Publisher. The original regulatory text, in underline/strikeout format, is filed with the Secretary of State (*www.ss.ca.gov*) and permanently preserved at the State Archives. The published *California Code of Regulations* (CCR) is distributed to the law depository libraries under the Library Depository Act[8] and also to the counties pursuant to the Administrative Procedure Act (APA).[9] The Office of Administrative Law (OAL), created in 1980,[10] is now responsible for its publication and updating.[11] In 1988 the California Administrative Code was formally renamed the California Code of Regulations (CCR).[12]

There is a rebuttable presumption that the published CCR is the correct version of the regulations adopted.[13] Certified copies of an original regulatory filing are obtained, for a fee, from the State Archives where they are maintained in alphabetical order by agency name and filing date. The filing dates are obtained from the history notes of the regulations. A sample history note would read: 2. Amendment filed 5-7-92; operative 6-8-92 (Register 92, No. 19).

In 1980, University Microfilms International (*www.umi.com*), now a subsidiary of ProQuest (formerly Bell & Howell Company), made the CCR available in microfiche and produced a comprehensive index. The UMI index was discontinued after 1999 when the CCR went online for the public (ccr.oal.ca.gov), but UMI continues to put the CCR out in fiche.

Every state agency regulation is subject to the Administrative Procedure Act (APA) unless expressly exempted by statute.[14] A handful of

---

[7] This section written by Mike Ibold, law librarian for the Office of Administrative Law from 1987 to 2003.

[8] Gov. Code, § 14900 *et seq.*

[9] Gov. Code, § 11340 *et seq.*

[10] Stats. 1979, ch. 567.

[11] Gov. Code, § 11344.

[12] Stats. 1987, ch. 1375.

[13] Gov. Code, § 11344.6.

[14] Gov. Code, § 11346.

agencies are wholly or partially exempt from the APA such as the Department of Finance,[15] the Public Utilities Commission, and the Workers' Compensation Appeals Board.[16] Another exempt agency is the Lottery Commission.[17] In addition, a few agencies have their own publishing provisions, such as the Department of Social Services (www.dss.cahwnet.gov) Manuals of Policy and Procedure (MPP)[18] and the Building Standards Commission for the California Building Standards Code (Title 24 of the CCR).[19] State agencies often publish inexpensive booklets of their regulations and some have their regulations available on their agency home page such as the Department of Fish and Game, the Integrated Waste Management Board, and the Department of Pesticide Regulation. A state agency's home page can be conveniently located via the California home page's (www.ca.gov) alphabetical listing of state agencies with links to the agency.

The *California Code of Regulations* (CCR), after being printed by the State Printer for forty five years, was suddenly and surprisingly privatized in 1990 without public notice, input, or bidding, raising serious questions about compliance with the Public Contract Code, the State Contract Act, etc.[20] All subscribers had to buy expensive new sets. The CCR database, which had to be converted from incompatible State Printer tapes, had numerous errors and defects. In the privatization process the legal obligation to provide the CCR to the depository law libraries under the Library Depository Act, and to the counties under the Administrative Procedure Act, was overlooked. Most of the depository law libraries and counties had to settle for the CCR in less convenient microfiche. The CCR privatization affair haunts the Office of Administrative Law to this day.

---

[15] Gov. Code, § 11357(b); see Department of General Services (www.dgs.ca.gov), *State Administrative Manual* (SAM).

[16] Gov. Code, § 11351.

[17] Gov. Code, § 8880.26.

[18] Welf. & Inst. Code, § 10554 provides for the Department of Social Services to publish their welfare regulations themselves outside the CCR. But their licensing regulations fall under the Health and Safety Code and are therefore found published in both their MPP and in Title 22 of the CCR.

[19] Health and Safety Code, §§ 18938, 18942.

[20] For more on the privatization of the CCR, see: McFadden, David L. The Privatization of the California Code of Regulations. 22(10) *American Association of Law Libraries Newsletter* 9 (Summer 1991); and Ainsworth, Bill. State Codes Deal May Be Challenged. *The Recorder*. Tuesday, Dec. 31, 1991. pp. 1&9.

In April of 1990, Barclays Law Publishers assumed its publication and changed the print format from the former 6" × 9" to the standard 8.5" × 11". They added a twice yearly Master Index and a Master Table of Contents and a weekly Digest of New Regulations. Barclays also made the CCR available in CD-ROM and fiche but discontinued the fiche in April 2002. In addition, Barclays provided the database to LexisNexis and Westlaw, and the legal community was then able to research the CCR by computer. Barclays is now a part of the West Group *(www.westgroup.com)* which has the current publication contract.

The Office of Administrative Law (OAL) claims a copyright to the California Code of Regulations on behalf of the State of California; therefore, one should contact the Office of Administrative Law about republishing or reprinting it.

Today the CCR is organized into 28 titles contained in 39 full-sized binders:

1. General Provisions

2. Administration

3. Food and Agriculture

4. Business Regulation

5. Education

6. Governor (no regulations filed)[21]

7. Harbors and Navigation

8. Industrial Relations

9. Rehabilitative and Development Services

10. Investment

11. Law

12. Military and Veterans Affairs

13. Motor Vehicles

14. Natural Resources

15. Crime Prevention and Corrections

---

[21] Title 6 was originally reserved for the Governor but has never been used. Current executive orders are available on the Governor's homepage at *www.governor.ca.gov* at the Press Office. All executive orders are kept and preserved at the California State Archives.

16.　Professional and Vocational Regulations

17.　Public Health

18.　Public Revenues

19.　Public Safety

20.　Public Utilities and Energy

21.　Public Works

22.　Social Security

23.　Waters

24.　(Building Standards)[22]

25.　Housing and Community Development

26.　Toxics[23]

27.　Environmental Protection

28.　Managed Health Care

The CCR is updated weekly by the California Regulatory Code Supplement which is identified by Register year and weekly issue number, i.e., Register 89, No. 22. Included with the weekly California Regulatory Code Supplement Barclays has added their Digest of New Regulations which is helpful for tracking new regulatory developments and for regulatory research.

Of the available CCR formats, the print and online are the most current. The public online CCR (*ccr.oal.ca.gov*) is updated the day after mailing the weekly California Regulatory Code Supplement of revisions to the print version. The CCR on fiche and CD-ROM, on the other hand, may be one or more months behind the print and online versions.

---

[22] Title 24 of the CCR is not contained in the main code but is separately published by the Building Standards Commission at: *www.bsc.dgs.ca.gov*. See Health & Safety Code, § 18938. Much of title 24 derives from several copyrighted model building codes. Title 24 is published in its entirety every three years pursuant to Health & Safety Code, § 18942 and is distributed under the Library Depository Act to the law depository libraries.

[23] Title 26 was created to consolidate the various agency regulations on toxics into a second publication. The various toxic regulations still remained in their original generic titles. Most of title 26 has been repealed with history notes referring back to the original title of origin.

[2]　The Online California Code of Regulations (CCR)

All of the available online CCR derive from the Barclays database. The public online version is searchable and available free at ccr.oal.ca.gov and is updated the day after the weekly California Regulatory Code Supplement is mailed out. The regulations are accessed by the alphabetical agency list, the table of contents, which can be expanded (+) or collapsed (−), or by several search methods, including going directly to a specific section. The ability to download and/or print the public online database is limited to a section or page at a time.

The same database is also available on Westlaw (*www.westlaw.com*) at the CA-ADC database for Westlaw subscribers and is current. It is searchable using their natural language search method and also has the further advantage of not limiting the amount of text that can be printed or downloaded. A related database available on Westlaw is CA-REGTRK that contains tracking summaries of California regulations.

The CCR is also available for LexisNexis subscribers (*www.lexis.com*) at their "CA—Barclays Official California Code of Regulations" Source (CAL; CAAOMN), and offers regulatory tracking in their "CA State Regulation Tracking" Source (LEGIS; CARGTR), provided by State Net. It includes a table of contents and has natural language search capability. It also includes the *California Regulatory Law Bulletin*. A combined search of both the CCR and *California Regulatory Law Bulletin* is available in the "CA—California Administrative Code & California Regulatory Law Bulletin" Source (CODES; CAREGS).

[3]　Annotations to the California Code of Regulations (CCR)

Authority and reference citations are found at the end of the text of the regulatory sections.[24] The authority citation provides the legal authority for a state agency to adopt regulations.[25] The authority citation is followed by the important reference citations which are the specific statutes the agency is implementing, interpreting, or making specific.

Finally, a regulation is followed by a history note section. A history note is added whenever a regulation is adopted, amended, repealed, renumbered, or an editorial correction is made. See [8], *below*, for more details about the history notes.

---

[24] As required by Gov. Code, § 11344(d).

[25] It is possible for an agency to have implied authority to adopt regulations.

[4]　Tracking Regulatory Developments

The weekly California Regulatory Notice Register (formerly the California Administrative Register Notice Supplement), often called the notice register, or "Z Register," is published and distributed for the Office of Administrative Law by the Office of the State Publisher (*www.osp.dgs.ca.gov*) and has been published since April of 1974.[26] It is often called the "Z Register" in order to avoid confusion with the registers of the weekly California Regulatory Code Supplement which formerly would have an A, B, C, and even a D section if it was an unusually heavy filing week. The parenthetical citation is (Cal. Reg. Notice Register 98, No. 24-Z). It is the official publication in which the state agencies are required to post notice of their proposed regulatory actions. It includes an "informative digest" of the nature of the proposed rulemaking, where and when the public may submit comments, and the time and place of any public meeting. The effective period of a notice is one year.[27] Also included in the California Regulatory Notice Register are: notices of general public interest, summaries of rulemaking disapproval decisions, rulemaking petition decisions, summaries of regulatory actions filed with the Secretary of State, appeals to the Governor, requests for regulatory determinations, and the full text of the Office of Administrative Law's determinations of the applicability of the Administrative Procedure Act (APA) to certain state agency policies, rules, or standards. An adequate indexing system for the California Regulatory Notice Register remains to be developed, but the Office of Administrative Law maintains on its home page (*www.oal.ca.gov*) the full text of the weekly notice registers for the current and previous year where the table of contents can be viewed.

Barclays California Regulatory Law Bulletin is also offered weekly by the publisher of the CCR as an alternative to the California Regulatory Notice Register and contains much of the same information. While it is not indexed, it is available and searchable online for Lexis subscribers.

The *Digest of New Regulations* accompanies the weekly California Regulatory Code Supplement of updates to the CCR and has been published since the privatization in April of 1990. It is a very helpful research tool that provides a concise informative digest of the rulemaking action in that register, plus the sections affected, the Office of

---

[26] Stats. 1974, ch. 142.

[27] Gov. Code, § 11346.4(b).

Administrative Law file number, the agency contact person and his/her phone number.

The *California Regulatory Law Reporter* is published twice yearly by the Center for Public Interest Law of the University of San Diego School of Law and is available online on Westlaw at their CARLR file *(www.cpil.org)*. Also published twice yearly by the University of San Diego's Children's Advocacy Institute of the Center for Public Interest Law is the Children's Regulatory Law Reporter. Current and back issues are available at CAI's website at: *(www.caichildlaw.org)*.

Online regulatory tracking is available on Westlaw at their CA-REGTRK file and also on LexisNexis at their "CA State Regulation Tracking" Source (LEGIS; CARGTR).

A listing of emergency regulations recently submitted to and recently approved by the Office of Administrative Law can be found on that agency's home page: *www.oal.ca.gov.*

A new development is that agencies that have homepages are now required to post specific information on their regulatory actions online.[28] Also, any person or organization can request a state agency to place them on their mailing list to be notified by the agency of any proposed regulatory actions. In making such a request, it may be necessary to cite the pertinent Administrative Procedure Act (APA) section.[29]

[5]   Office of Administrative Law (OAL) Disapproval Decisions

When an agency's submitted rulemaking file of proposed changes fails to comply with the Administrative Procedure Act (APA), the Office of Administrative Law issues the agency a disapproval decision detailing the specific legal grounds for disapproval.[30] The Office of Administrative Law (OAL) has been inconsistent in publishing its disapproval decisions. Initially OAL published their disapproval decisions in full text in the weekly *California Regulatory Notice Register*. In an effort to trim costs, OAL began to publish just summaries of the disapproval decisions and, starting in June of 1992, the full text was made available in the monthly *California Code of Regulations Decisions* free of charge to interested parties and law libraries. But under the Governor Davis

---

[28] Gov. Code, § 11340.85(c).

[29] Gov. Code, § 11346.4(a)(1).

[30] Gov. Code, § 11349.3(b).

administration (1998–2003), the number of disapproval decisions issued by OAL dropped off by about a drastic and dramatic 75%. In 2001 Government Code §11344.1(a)(3) was amended (Statutes of 2000, Chapter 1060), formally requiring just a summary of the disapproval decisions in the *California Regulatory Notice Register* because the disapproval decisions were readily available. But the *California Code of Regulations Decisions* was discontinued in June of 2002 after ten years, despite the intent of the legislation that electronic versions were not to replace hard print copies as the sole available source. Summaries of the disapproval decisions are published in the weekly *California Regulatory Notice Register*. Recent disapproval decisions are also found on the Office of Administrative Law's home page: *www.oal.ca.gov*.

An agency may appeal a disapproval decision to the Governor, in which case the full result is published in the California Regulatory Notice Register. In recent years appeals to the Governor have been fairly infrequent. The last time an OAL disapproval was appealed and over-ruled by the Governor was in October 1993 on a Postsecondary and Vocational Education file.

[6] Office of Administrative Law (OAL) Determinations and "Underground" Regulations

All state agency regulations are subject to the Administrative Procedure Act (APA) unless expressly exempted by statute.[31] No state agency may issue, utilize, enforce or attempt to enforce any guideline, criterion, bulletin, manual, instruction, order, standard of general application, or other rule which is a regulation under the Administrative Procedure Act unless it has been adopted as a regulation pursuant to the Administrative Procedure Act.[32] A state agency rule that meets the definition of a regulation[33] that should have been adopted pursuant to the Administrative Procedure Act, but was not, is commonly referred to as an "underground regulation." The Office of Administrative Law (OAL) is authorized to issue, upon proper request,[34] an advisory opinion, called a "determination," as to whether a state agency rule is a regulation and, if so, whether it is subject to the Administrative Procedure Act.[35] A

---

[31] Gov. Code, § 11346.

[32] Gov. Code, § 11340.5(a).

[33] Gov. Code, § 11342.600.

[34] See title 1, CCR, section 122, and Form 1013 (Appendix A to Article 3).

[35] Gov. Code, § 11340.5(b).

frequent result is the agency formally adopting the rule in question pursuant to the Administrative Procedure Act or rescinding the agency rule in question. In one notable instance, when OAL issued an adverse determination against the Department of Finance (1990 OAL Determination No. 12) that, plus the CCR privatization misadventure of the same year, resulted in a punitive agency budget cut that caused the devastating loss of half the OAL personnel, a loss from which the agency has never recovered. Later, when requests for determinations fell over seven years behind, Senator Steve Peace called for an investigation that produced a report by the Joint Legislative Task Force on Government Oversight called *The Longest Wait in Government* (May 1998). This led to provisions in the 1998 Budget Act (Statutes 1998, chapter 324, pp 622–623) requiring OAL to meet production goals in reducing the determinations backlog in order to have periodic disbursements of agency funds released. OAL managed to achieve this by borrowing administrative law judges from other agencies.

The determinations are fully published in the weekly California Regulatory Notice Register and can also be ordered from the Office of Administrative Law. A chronological listing of 1986–1999 determinations and an order form are available on the Office of Administrative Law's homepage, as well as recent determinations, at: *www.oal.ca.gov.*

In January of 2003, OAL repealed its determinations regulations in Title 1 of the CCR (§§ 121–128), and discontinued issuing determinations for lack of staffing and resources due to severe statewide budget cuts. But in an interesting development Governor Schwarzenneger, very shortly after taking office, issued Executive Order S-2-03 that, besides imposing a moratorium on state agency regulations and calling for a review of regulatory actions over the last five years, called for a comprehensive review of agency underground regulations.

[7]   California Code of Regulations (CCR) Research Guides

Barclays publishes twice a year a Master Index to the California Code of Regulations along with its companion Table of Statutes to Regulations. The Table of Statutes to Regulations is a practical way to determine whether a regulation has been adopted to implement, interpret, or make specific a certain statute.

Barclays also publishes twice yearly a Master Table of Contents, along with an alphabetical list of State Regulatory Agencies. The Master Table of Contents is a compilation of the Title Table of Contents found at the beginning of each CCR title. It provides the organization down to the article level, but not down to the individual regulation sections. The internal table of contents, found at the beginning of each agency's division of regulations, goes down to the individual regulatory sections, and are updated quarterly if there has been any regulatory action by that agency. The alphabetical list of State Regulatory Agencies, in addition to providing agency names, addresses and phone numbers, is also helpful for locating where an agency's regulations may be found in the CCR as well as the agency's range of regulatory section numbers in a particular title. The list of State Regulatory Agencies is also found on the public online CCR at: *ccr.oal.ca.gov.* [36]

Since 1980, UMI produced an annual *Comprehensive Index/ California Code of Regulations* with periodic pocket supplements as a companion to their CCR on microfiche, located at: *www.umi.com.* The UMI Index included a Subject Index, a Regulations to Statutes Table, a Statutes to Regulations Table, and a History Table. The UMI index to the CCR was discontinued after 1999 when the CCR went online to the public at: *ccr.oal.ca.gov*, but the last History Table of 1999 covers the period from 1975 to 1999 and is helpful to retain for historical research of that time period. The UMI's History Table provides the filing date with the Secretary of State of a regulatory action.

Barclays Digest of New Regulations, published since the privatization of the CCR in April of 1990, accompanies their weekly California Regulatory Code Supplement that provides the updates. They are identified by the Register year and weekly issue number. The weekly *Digest of New Regulations* is very helpful for regulatory research. It provides a concise informative digest of the regulatory action taken as well as identifying the Office of Administrative Law's rulemaking file number, the agency contact person's name and phone number. The agency contact person can be a valuable source for obtaining the agency's regulatory intent.

The CCR, like statutes and cases, can also be cite checked in Shepard's either in print, online via LexisNexis at: *www.lexis.com*, or CD-ROM. The West Group has produced KeyCite as an alternative to Shepard's, and KeyCiting the CCR is now available at: *www.westgroup.com.*

---

[36] Some of the larger state agencies may have their regulations in more than one title of the CCR.

[8] Finding Earlier Regulatory Language

Finding the earlier text of a loose leaf publication can be a daunting task for any researcher and it is for this reason that the CCR has a history note system. Earlier regulatory text, unfortunately, is not available online. The history notes, found at the end of the sections of regulatory text, refer to a Register and a weekly issue number (such as Register 98, No. 11). They simply refer to the weekly *California Regulatory Code Supplement* of regulatory text changes. Complete collections of the CCR Registers are maintained at the Bernie E. Witkin State Law Library in Sacramento and also at the Office of Administrative Law in Sacramento. After Register 30, No. 5 in 1952, the Register numbers jump to Register 53, No. 1, in order that the Register number corresponds with the calendar year. The limitation of the collection of CCR Registers is that it generally does not provide a practical means of reproducing an entire CCR title or an agency's entire body of regulations at an earlier point in time.

The William S. Hein & Co., Inc. of Buffalo, New York, has completed putting the California State Law Library's collection of CCR registers from the original titles of 1945 through 1979 on fiche. In 1980, University Microfilms International (UMI) in Michigan came out with, and continues to put, the CCR out on fiche.

An alternative some law libraries may use for CCR research is to simply save the weekly CCR discards if they have available space. If they subscribe to the CCR in fiche, they will, of course, have less of a storage problem to deal with. The Office of Administrative Law maintains a nearly complete set of CCR discards since it was created in 1980 and also a collection of the CCR in fiche by Barclays since the privatization in April of 1990 until the discontinuation of their fiche in April of 2002.

When the CCR became available on CD-ROM in 1990, libraries have had the additional option of saving their monthly or quarterly CD-ROMs. This provides a major advantage over the weekly register system in that it provides the entire CCR in a searchable format at a given point in time. But the limitation, as any historian or archivist will be sure to point out, is that this CD-ROM system will only be usable so long as the computer hardware and software exists to support it.

If the first history note of a regulation section reads like, 1. New section filed (date); effective (date). . ., you are most likely looking at the full history of that regulation. But in order to prevent the history notes of particularly active regulations from overwhelming the regulatory text, the CCR editors may, from time to time, remove some earlier history notes and write in the first remaining history note such as, For prior history, see Register 64, No. 23.

Another matter is when you find that the first history note of a regulation reads like: "1. Amendment filed (date). . .," you must then search for the "blanket" history note to get the original filing. Blanket history notes cover the adoption of a whole unit of regulations and are nearly always found in the first history note of that unit. The unit can be a division, where an agency's regulations begin, or a chapter, subchapter or article. Blanket history notes were in common usage until the 1980's when it was decided that when a unit of regulations was adopted, each regulation would have its individual history note. An example of a "blanket" history note would read like, "1. New Article 6 (sections 2638–2638.2) filed 7-18-75; effective thirtieth day thereafter (Register 75, No. 29)."

An all but forgotten method of researching through the early Registers is the old cumulative Reference Tables that used to be published periodically. The last Reference Table was published in Register 62, No. 22 and covers the period from the original publication through Register 61, No. 16. These are tables of agency regulations by title and register with the agencies listed in the order in which they appear in the CCR. The table can be used to trace the development of the regulations of the respective agencies from the original publication through Register 61, No. 16. In addition, OAL has saved the old CCR editorial index cards, which provide the same kind of reference tables, but cover the more recent period up to the privatization of the CCR in April of 1990.

For further help, some private regulatory researchers, available for a fee, are: the Legislative Intent Service, Sacramento (800) 666-1917, at: *www.legintent.com*; the Legislative Research Institute, Sacramento (800) 530-7613 at: *www.lrihistory.com*; and Raymond Research (888) 676-1947, *www.naj.net*.

[9] Regulatory Intent

Finding the regulatory intent of an agency's regulation can be a real research challenge, and in cases prior to the 1979 amendment of the Administrative Procedure Act (APA) and the creation of the Office of Administrative Law (OAL) in 1980, may well be impossible. To find the regulatory intent, it is essential to access the particular agency's rulemaking file for that specific regulatory action that the agency submitted to the Office of Administrative Law for APA review. The Office of Administrative Law returns the rulemaking files back to the agencies after its APA review is completed and the agencies have a duty to retain and preserve their rulemaking files as a public record.[37] If an agency does not want to keep their rulemaking files themselves, they have the option of transferring them over to the State Archives.

One resource that can sometimes be very helpful, particularly for recent rulemakings, is the agency contact person listed for that rulemaking. This individual is usually more knowledgeable about the particular rulemaking than anyone else. The agency contact person and phone number can be found on the face sheet of the original filing, the STD 400, and also in *Barclays Digest of New Regulations*.

The agency rulemaking file will contain the Initial Statement of Reasons (ISR), proposed regulatory text, the public comments, data, factual information, studies, reports and the Final Statement of Reasons (FSR).

For emergency regulations, one should look for the statement or finding of emergency within the rulemaking file.[38] Generally, emergency regulations are effective for only 120 days until the agency can submit a Certificate of Compliance, that is, another rulemaking file, after fully complying with APA procedures.[39]

For private regulatory researchers, available for a fee, see [8], *above*.

[10]   The Regulatory Political Scene

The Office of Administrative Law has had a mixed and uneven history since its creation in 1980. The CCR privatization problems, and the troubled and turbulent determination program on underground regulations, with their adverse impact on OAL, have already been previously discussed. But the final point must concern the agency's frequent leadership changes.[40] As an executive agency, OAL has to depend on the support of the Governor who appoints the agency director subject to confirmation by the Senate. Once confirmed by the Senate, the OAL

---

[37] Gov. Code, § 11347.3(e).

[38] Gov. Code, § 11346.1.

[39] Gov. Code, §§ 11346.1(e), 11346.1(h).

[40] OAL agency heads since 1998 include: Char Mathias, David B. Judson, Sheila Mohan, Tal Finney, John Smith, Debra Cornez, Edward Heidig and William Gausewitz.

director is entitled, per Government Code § 11340.2(a), to serve a term coterminous with that of the Governor. The purpose of the coterminous provision, that prevents dismissal of the OAL director, is to provide a stronger agency head with some political independence. But the Senate has had few opportunities in recent years to confirm an OAL director, the last being John Smith in July of 1995, which often left the agency run by acting or interim directors. For a successful regulatory program in California, OAL will need support from the Governor, plus stronger and more stable leadership. Shortly after taking office in November of 2003 in an historic recall, Governor Schwarzenegger issued Executive Order S-2-03, imposing a 180 day moratorium on regulatory activity, a review of agency regulatory actions over the last five years, a statewide review of agency underground regulations, plus the creation of an advisory body.[41] The impact of Executive Order S-2-03 awaits the judgment of political history.

§ 8.04　Administrative Decisions[42]

[1]　Statutory Framework and the Office of Administrative Hearings (OAH)

California has a large number of state agencies that make decisions on a daily basis regarding professional or occupational licenses, entitlement benefits, and personnel actions. Due process requirements (notice and opportunity to be heard) of varying degrees apply to these decisions. Some agencies use mediation or arbitration to resolve disputes, and those decisions would be confidential. Most agencies have some sort of hearing process, either in statute or regulation, and those decisions become public record (minus any redaction for confidential information, such as minor's names). While a few larger agencies (such as State Personnel Board, Worker's Compensation, and Unemployment Insurance) have their own pool of administrative law judges, many agencies rely on the centralized pool of independent judges provided by the Office of Administrative Hearings (OAH).[43] Some agencies (such as the Department of Social Services and the Department of Motor Vehicles) have a mix, with certain types of hearings done in-house, and others

---

[41] For a short commentary on S-2-03 see: Walters, Dan. Obscure office rules over rules. *Fresno Bee*. Monday, December 1, 2003. p. B3.

[42] This section written by Heather Cline Hoganson, Staff Counsel, Office of Administrative Hearings.

[43] The OAH was formerly the Office of Administrative Procedure.

sent to OAH. While an agency may have specific hearing provisions in statute, the default is the Administrative Procedure Act (Government Code §§ 11370–11528).

The Administrative Procedure Act contains provisions for agency adjudication and rulemaking. The Office of Administrative Hearings (OAH) provides adjudicative services (settlement conferences, mediations, arbitrations, informal and formal hearings before an impartial and qualified tribunal) and the Office of Administrative Law (OAL) oversees rulemaking.

The Administrative Procedure Act is divided into Chapters:

- Chapter 3.5 (commencing with section 11340) deals with rulemaking and the Office of Administrative Law;

- Chapter 4 (commencing with section 11370) provides for the Office of Administrative Hearings, a Medical Quality Hearing Panel, and State Agency Reports and Forms Appeals;

- Chapter 4.5 (commencing with section 11400) provides general provisions and procedures of Administrative Adjudication, including alternative dispute resolution, a bill of rights, ex parte communications, language assistance, informal hearings, subpenas, enforcement of orders and sanctions, emergency decisions, declaratory decisions, a code of ethics, and conversion of a proceeding; and

- Chapter 5 (commencing with section 11500) deals with formal hearings.

The Administrative Procedure Act's Adjudication Section (Chapters 4, 4.5, and 5) was revised in 1995 (Chapter 938; SB 523), to be effective July 1, 1997. (See also Stats. 1996, Chapter 390; SB 794 and Stats. 1998, Chapter 95; AB 2164.) The major overhaul was prompted by the California Law Revision Commission, and the new version contains not just formal hearings by OAH, but also informal hearings, authorization for alternative dispute resolution (mediation and/or arbitration), precedential decisions, emergency decisions and declaratory decisions, as well as an "administrative bill of rights." A code of ethics for adjudicators was added in the 1998 legislation. While the Act describes the course of hearings in some detail, procedures for administrative hearings remain more liberal and less restrictive than those for proceedings before courts of law. The Act also provides for judicial review of decisions rendered.

OAH was given the authority to issue regulations under the revised Administrative Procedure Act. Title 1, Cal. Code Regs. 1000 et seq.

covers Formal Hearings, specialized hearings, Alternative Dispute Resolution, Declaratory Decisions, and Public Works Contract Arbitrations.

The "new APA" also provides that any agency "guidelines" for penalties must be adopted as regulations (Gov. Code, § 11425.50(e)). While a few agencies have put their guidelines into the California Code of Regulations as is, most have adopted their guidelines via "incorporation by reference," wherein the agency says their penalties shall be based on a titled and dated guideline package. This package may then be requested from the agency itself (if the agency receptionist to whom you are speaking is unsure about whether or not they have any precedential decisions or guidelines, you might try asking for someone in the agency's enforcement division).

The ability to designate a decision, or part of a decision, as "precedential" is new under the Administrative Procedure Act (Gov. Code, § 11425.60). An agency's index of significant legal and policy determinations made in precedent decisions shall be available to the public by subscription and its availability publicized annually in the California Regulatory Notice Register. As many agencies only have a handful of precedential decisions at this point, there has been no uniform method of printing, digesting, or indexing as is done with court decisions.

The vast majority of decisions by agencies is not precedential and not reported anywhere. Final decisions are, however, available from the agency as a public record (subject to the limitations on public records, of course). While searches based on points of law will not usually be available to a researcher, decisions on cases can be obtained from the agency if the researcher has a name and case number.

[2] Locating Decisions[44]

To see what Agency decisions LexisNexis[45] has in its database, choose States-Legal U.S., California, Agency and Administrative Materials (agencies include Attorney General, Board of Equalization, Department of Corrections, Fair Employment and Housing Commission, Fair Political Practices Commission, Franchise Tax Board, Occupational

---

[44] For a more complete listing of California agency decisions, see Veronica Maclay and Laura Peritore, *California Government Publications and Legal Resources.* [Chicago]: American Association of Law Libraries, 1991. 94 p. at 27.

[45] See the LexisNexis Library Contents list in Appendix F for the File names and for periods of coverage for each file.

Safety and Health Appeals Board, Public Utilities Commission, State Bar Court, and State Water Resources Control Board). To look at the databases in Westlaw,[46] choose U.S. State Materials, California, Administrative & Executive Materials.

Agencies that maintain Precedential Decisions under the Administrative Procedure Act as of April 1, 2004:

- Board of Accountancy
- Chiropractic Board, available via their web page directly at: *www.chiro.ca.gov/.*
- Commission on Teacher Credentialing has precedential waiver decisions available via their web site, directly at *www.ctc.ca.gov/codcor.doc/000021/000021.html.*
- Corporations, available via their web page directly at: *www.corp.ca.gov/notices/pd.htm.*
- Dental Board
- Education Audits Appeal Panel, available via their web page directly at *www.eaap.ca.gov/Precedential.htm.*
- Horse Racing Board, available via their web page at: *www.chrb.ca.gov*, under Administrative Hearing/Precedential Decisions, or directly at: *www.chrb.ca.gov/administrative_ hearings_sorted_by_name.htm.*
- Department of Industrial Relations, Division of Labor Statistics and Research, has Precedential Public Works Decisions, available at their web site, directly at *www.dir.ca.gov/DLSR/ PrecedentialAlpha.htm.*
- Department of Industrial Relations, Independent Medical Counsel, available via their web page directly at *www.dir.ca.gov/IMC/discipline.html.*
- Department of Insurance, via their web page, directly at *www.insurance.ca.gov/docs/FS-Legal.htm.*
- Board of Podiatric Medicine, at their web site, directly at *www.bpm.ca.gov/enforce.*
- CalPERS, the Public Employee's Retirement System, available via their web page directly at: *www.calpers.ca.gov/*

---

[46] See the Westlaw California Database list in Appendix G for database names and for the period of coverage of each database.

index.jsp?bc = /about/leg-reg-statutes/board-decisions/home.
xml.

- Department of Social Services community care licensing administrative actions. Their precedential decision page is accessible via *ccl.dss.cahwnet.gov/DecisionsR_1780.htm* and the decision index can be found directly at: *ccl.dss.cahwnet.gov/IndextoPre_1816.htm.* The actual decisions are available as pdf decisions (need Adobe Acrobat to read) or can be requested from the Department's Community Care Licensing Division by contacting the Department's Public Affairs Office at Department of Social Services, Public Affairs, MS 17-09, 744 P Street, Sacramento CA 95814. A charge of 10 cents per page will be assessed if the request exceeds 100 pages.

- Department of Toxic Substances Control has Mandated Postings, available at their web site, directly at *www.dtsc.ca.gov/Mandated_Postings.html.*

- Unemployment Insurance Appeals Board (Gov. § 409), available directly on their web page at: *www.edd.cahwnet.gov/txprecdt/txpdind.htm.*

- Victim's Compensation and Governmental Claims Unit (formerly known as the Board of Control), available via their web page directly at: *www.boc.cahwnet.gov/PrecDecisions/PrecDecIndex.htm.*

- Workers' Compensation Appeals Board, on their web site, directly at *www.dir.ca.gov/wcab_dars.htm.*

Some other agencies that maintain precedential decisions under their own laws:

- Agricultural Labor Relations Board, directly at *www.alrb.ca.gov/mainpages/information5.html.*

- Alcoholic Beverage Control Appeals Board, directly at *www.abcappealsbd.ca.gov/decisions/index.asp.*

- State Bar Court, on LexisNexis ("CA State Bar Court Decisions" Source (ETHICS; CABAR)).

- State Personnel Board (Gov. Code, § 19582.5), available via their web page at: *www.spb.ca.gov/spblaw/precedrd.cfm*; and also published by CEB as California State Personnel Board Precedential Decisions Service, 1991-present.

- Fair Employment and Housing Commission (Gov. § 12935(h)), published by CEB as Fair Employment & Housing Commission Precedential Decisions Service, 1978–present. Westlaw (CA-FEHC) and LexisNexis (CAFEHC), and via their web site, directly at *www.dfeh.ca.gov/PrecedentialD/Decisions.asp.*

- CalEPA, available via Westlaw, under Administrative Materials. (CAENV-ADMIN), and via their web site, directly at *www.dir.ca.gov/oshab/DAR_Decisions.html.*

- CalOSHA Appeals Board Decisions, on Westlaw (CA-OSHA), and on LexisNexis (CAOSHD), and via their web site, directly at *www.dir.ca.gov/oshab/DAR_Decisions.html.*

- Public Employment Relations Board (PERB), via their web site, directly at *www.perb.ca.gov/html/decisions.htm.* Decisions of the Board are also published, with an index, in the Public Employee Reporter for California (PERC), a publication of the Labor Relations Press. Copies of the PERC are available in many public and university libraries throughout California. The California Public Employee Relations Program at the Institute of Industrial Relations, UC Berkeley, also abstracts PERB decisions in their journal, and copies of Board decisions can be ordered from them, at $0.30 a page, by calling (510) 643-7069.

- Public Utilities Commission on Westlaw (CA-PUR) and on LexisNexis (CAPUC) and via their web site, at *www.cpuc.ca.gov/static/official+docs/index.htm.* In most instances, the California Public Utilities Commission issues a decision in a particular case. In some instances, the Commission provides rules for a category, known as General Orders. Printed copies are also available from the Commission's Document Desk (415) 703-1542.

- Franchise Tax Board, on Westlaw (CATX-ADMIN), and on LexisNexis ("CA Franchise Tax Board Decisions" Source (CAL; CAFTB)), Legal Rulings at their website, directly at: *www.ftb.ca.gov/legal/index.htm#Legal Rulings.*

- State Water Resources Control Board Decisions, Resolutions, and Orders, available on their website, directly at: *www.swrcb.ca.gov/resdec/index.html*; and on LexisNexis (CAENV).

- California Workers' Compensation Appeals Board (Decisions) on LexisNexis (CAWORK) and on Westlaw (CAWC-DEC or CAWC-ADMIN).

Not precedential, but persuasive:

- Determinations from the Office of Administrative Law, available from their web site, directly at *www.oal.ca.gov/ determination.htm.*

- California Department of Corporations (Commissioner's Releases, Opinions and Notices), on LexisNexis (CASEC) or via their web page, directly at *www.corp.ca.gov/commiss/ relcont.htm.*

- Board of Equalization has Franchise and Income Tax Formal Legal Opinions available on their web site, directly at *www.boe.ca.gov/legal/legalopcont.htm.*

- Fair Political Practices Commission (Advisory Letters), published by CEB as California Fair Political Practices Commission: Opinions, Regulations & Notebook Service, 1975-present, available on Westlaw, under Administrative Materials. (CA-ETH), and on LexisNexis ("CA Fair Political Practices Commission" Source (CAL; CAFAIR)). The Fair Political Practices Commission posts summaries of its enforcement decisions, which are decisions under the APA (but not precedential), on its web page, at: *www.fppc.ca.gov.* CEB also publishes California Fair Political Practices Commission: Enforcement Decisions Service, 1976-present.

- Opinions of the Attorney General. These are available in book form, and newer opinions (1997 onward) are on their website, at *caag.state.ca.us/opinions/monthly.htm.* They are also available on LexisNexis ("CA Attorney General Opinions" Source (STATES; CAAG)), and Westlaw (CA-AG).

- Executive Orders of the Gorvernor are available at the Governor's web site, *www.governor.ca.gov,* under "Press Room," then "Executive Orders."

- Industrial Welfare Commission Wage Orders are available on their web site, directly at *ww.dir.ca.gov/Iwc/ WageOrderIndustries.htm.*

- The Division of Labor Standards Enforcement has Opinion letters posted on their web site, directly at *www.dir.ca.gov/ dlse/DLSE_OpinionLetters.htm.*

- For entitlement cases under the Lanterman Act and Early Start Program under the Department of Developmental Services, OAH issues final decisions, which are posted on the OAH web site, at *www.oah.dgs.ca.gov*, under the "DDS Hearings" button.

For updates on new regulations, guidelines, or precedential decisions, see the California Regulatory Law Reporter (published occasionally), available from the Center for Public Interest Law, University of San Diego School of Law, 5998 Alcalá Park, San Diego, CA 92110, phone (619) 260-4806.

For further information concerning the Administrative Procedure Act and its applications, see:

📖 California Administrative Hearing Practice, 2nd edition. CEB.

📖 California Law Revision Commission Recommendation: Administrative Adjudication by State Agencies, 25 Cal.L.Revision Comm'n Reports 55 (1995).

📖 Asimow, Michael, "Toward a New California Administrative Procedure Act: Adjudication Fundamentals." 39 *UCLA L. Rev* 1067 (1992).

📖 Asimow, Michael, "The Adjudication Process." Study of administrative procedure sponsored by California Law Review Commission. Palo Alto (October 1991).

📖 California Law Review Commission, 1991.

📖 Pacific Law Journal (now known as McGeorge Law Review), Review of Selected 1995 California Legislation, Winter 1996 issue, 27 Pac.L.J. 941 (1996).

📖 Jacobs, Michael Douglas, Illuminating a Bureaucratic Shadow World: Precedent Decisions under California's Revised Administrative Procedure Act. This was Mr. Jacobs' thesis for his Master of Judicial Studies from the National Judicial College (NJC), which is on the campus of the University of Nevada, Reno. 21 *J.NAALJ* 247 (Fall 2001).

🖥 The "Laws and Programs" link on the OAH home page provides the user with links to the Administrative Procedure Act, regulations, and other related documents: *www.oah.dgs.ca.gov*.

For historical information on the Administrative Procedure Act, see:

📖   Procedures, 13th Annual Meeting of the State Bar of California (1940).

📖   Summary of California Statutory Provisions Conferring Quasi-Legislative Functions Upon State Agencies, Assembly Interim Committee on Administrative Regulations (1946). A supplement to the report was published in 1947.

📖   Report of the Assembly Interim Committee on Administrative Regulations; House Resolution No. 278, February 3, 1947. Preliminary and Partial Report and Second Preliminary and Partial Report of the Senate Interim Committee on Administrative Regulations (1953).

📖   First Report of the Senate Interim Committee on Administrative Regulations (1955).

📖   First Report of the Senate Interim Committee on Administrative Regulations and Adjudications on the use of Independent Hearing Officers for Administrative Adjudications (1957).

📖   Final Report of the Senate Interim Committee on Administrative Regulations and Adjudications (1959).

📖   First, Second, Third, Fourth, Fifth, Sixth, Seventh, and Eighth Biennial Reports,Division of Administrative Procedure (1947, 1949, 1951, 1953, 1955, 1957, 1959, and 1961) and Ninth Biennial Report, Office of Administrative Procedure (1963), Tenth Report (1968).

§ 8.05   Other Official Administrative Publications

[1]   Governor's Office

The Governor of California is the head of the executive branch of the state. Many of the governor's office publications are mentioned in § 4.02[13] in their relationship to legislative history. Those mentioned there are the Governor's messages published in the Assembly and Senate Journals, the Governor's Chaptered Bill Files, veto messages, proclamations, acts of executive clemency, and press releases. Executive Orders[47] are also important documents which are published by the Governor's office. Documents from the current governor are available on the governor's website at: *www.governor.ca.gov*. These documents include

---

[47] Executive Orders were posted on the www for the first time in 1999. The address is: *www.ca.gov*. The user must link to "Press Room" and then to "Executive Orders."

press releases, public notices, opinion articles, executive orders and proclamations. Documents for former governors must be obtained by contacting that office or the State Archives, where the documents go for permanent storage.[48]

[2] Manuals and Guides

📖 State Administrative Manual (SAM). State Administrative Manual. Sacramento: California Department of Finance. February 1955-present. Looseleaf. This service prints management memoranda and interdepartmental communications relating to the conduct of the governmental business of the State of California. The full text of the manual is on the State Administrative Manual web page at: *sam.dgs.ca.gov*.

📖 Department Operations Manual (DOM). Sacramento: California Department of Corrections.

📖 Benefit Determination Guide (BDG). Sacramento: California Employment Development Department.

📖 Business Taxes Law Guide. Sacramento: California Board of Equalization.

📖 Property Taxes Law Guide. Sacramento: California Board of Equialzation.

📖 Manuals of Policy and Procedure (MPP). Sacramento: California Department of Social Services.

📖 CalTrans Manuals. The Dept. of Transportation has put an entire library of their manuals (Construction, Design, Engineering, Maintenance, Right of Way, etc.) online at: *www.dot.ca.gov*.

[3] Office of Administrative Law (OAL) Web Page

The OAL webpage provides access to the California Code of Regulations, the California Regulatory Notice Register, and the OAL Reference Attorney, as well as much useful information on emergency regulations,

---

[48] See Publishers/Vendors Appendix A for the State Archives listing. Note that some documents from the past administration may still be found on the current governor's page by going to the bottom of the specific page (press releases, proclamations, public notices, or executive orders) to the link for "previous administrations." Both the State Archives and the State Library are working on solutions to the problem of electronic documents and web pages being lost as administrations change.

the rulemaking process, rulemaking training classes, the rulemaking calendar, rulemaking checklists, disapproval decisions, determinations, and forms. All documents are in the PDF format, which can be viewed with Adobe Acrobat at: *www.oal.ca.gov.*

[4]　Individual Agency Web Pages

The agency index, mentioned in the bibliography at the end of this chapter, links the user to all California agencies with a web presence, which is almost all of them. The index can be easily located by going first to the state web page: *www.ca.gov*, then linking to "government," and finally by linking to the Agency Index under California Agencies, Departments, and Commissions. The Agency Index is simply an alphabetical listing of all the state agencies.

[5]　Agency Reports

Every state agency head is required to make written report of the activities of the agency he or she directs at least biennially, a copy of which is filed with the Secretary of State. Not all reports are printed as printing must be approved by the Department of Finance (Gov. Code, § 11091). Reports that are printed may be located by checking the library catalogs of the depository and larger libraries in California. Reports prior to 1944 may be located in the appendixes of the legislative journal. Reorganization Plans are presented by the Governor in the form of separate publications. When effective, the plans are published in the Statutes of California.

For a website that gives users information on recently filed, as well as overdue and anticipated agency reports, see the Legislative Counsel's website at *www.agencyreports.ca.gov.*

The Harvard Law School Library has filmed and made available for purchase many of the older reports of state agencies. The reproduced documents are not of the highest quality (see Appendix A for publishers/ vendors information).

For additional print products:

- 📖 Department of Employment, Research Series Bulletins, 1941–1957

- 📖 Department of Industrial Relations Reports, 1927–1978

- 📖 Employment Development Department Operations Reports, 1936–1978

📖 Fair Employment Practice Commission Reports, 1959–1978

📖 Franchise Tax Board Reports, 1950–1979

📖 Industrial Welfare Commissioners Reports, 1913–1954

📖 Insurance Commissioner Reports, 1868–1978

📖 Pooled Money Investment Board Reports, 1956–1979

📖 Public Utilities Commission Reports, 1876–1979

📖 Savings & Loan Commissioner's Reports, 1891–1979

📖 State Board of Equalization Reports, 1872–1979

📖 State Conciliation Service, Adjustments of Labor-Management Disputes in California, 1948–1969

📖 Superintendent of Banks Reports, 1909–1979

§ 8.06   Bibliography for Administrative Law Research

📖 Boas, Maxwell S. "Expanding Scope of Administrative Law." *Los Angeles Daily Journal* report section, February 23, 1965, pp. 16–19.

📖 Burrow, Inez. "Historical Summary of Regulation Codification." (1967) *Administrative Law Bulletin*. No. 6. pp. 1–4.

📖 *California Administrative Hearing Practice*. Berkeley: California Continuing Education of the Bar, 1984. 466 p. 1994 Supplement.

📖 *California Regulatory Law Reporter*. San Diego: Center for Public Interest Law, University of San Diego. 1980–1995, 1999-present. This journal covers the activities of the major California agencies that regulate business, professions, and trades.

📖 Clarkson, John C. "The History of the California Administrative Procedure Act." 15 *Hastings Law Journal* 237–257 (1964).

📖 Fellmeth, Robert C. and Folsom, Ralph H. *California Regulatory Law and Practice: A Reference Text for Business Lawyers*. Seattle: Butterworth. Looseleaf.

📖 Heckel, John. "The California Administrative Code," 36 *Los Angeles Bar Bulletin* 421 (1961).

     📖   Ogden, Gregory L. *Public Administrative Law*, in volumes 41 and 41A of California Forms of Pleading and Practice Annotated. Matthew Bender, a member of the LexisNexis Group (2002).

     📖   Rose, Carolina. *California Regulatory Research Guide: Reconstructing Regulatory History & Intent:Valuable guideposts for wading through the morass that is California regulatory research.* This guide is on the Legislative Research Inc. internet page at: *www.lrihistory.com/regguide.html.*

§ 8.07   Directories for Locating Agency Offices and Personnel

     📖   *California State Agency Directory.* Sacramento: Capitol Enquiry. Annual.

     📖   *The State of California Telephone Directory.* Sacramento: General Services. Annual.

     📖   *Barclays Official California Code of Regulations Master Table of Contents.* South San Francisco: Barclays Law Publishers. Annual. This volume contains a complete and alphabetical list of all state regulatory agencies in California. It directs users to the title and sections where that agency's regulations are located.

     📖   *Roster. Federal, state, county, city and township officials. Directory of state services of the state of California.* Compiled by Secretary of State. Documents Section. Sacramento: California, Secretary of State. Annual.

     💻   The State of California official web page has a comprehensive agency index of those agencies, boards, and departments with any www presence at all. This is a very helpful directory because it includes links to the individual pages which have a range of information from staff names and addresses to official forms and official regulations with links to state statutory codes. The URL is: *www.ca.gov.*

In addition to the directories listed above, researchers can call the Office of Administrative Law Reference Attorney at (916) 323-6815. This is the office the researcher should call to get additional information about the California regulatory process. The staff will assist callers with questions about California agencies, like the process of adopting regulations, but will not try to interpret regulations or answer other legal questions.

Chapter 9

Local Government[1]

---

[1] This chapter is written by Ellen St. John who is an Adjunct Professor at Pepperdine University School of Law. She edited the book, *Los Angeles: Structure of a City*, for the League of Women Voters in Los Angeles. She is also the author of *Crime and Courts: Cases and Comments for Advanced Criminal Procedure*, 2nd Edition, 1999.

(Pub. 64620)

§ 9.01 Introduction

The state government has its own independent source of power.[2] This power must be exercised with appropriate deference to the federal government.[3] In addition, every state government will delegate some of its powers to the local governments.

In analyzing any issue regarding local government the researcher needs to recognize and acknowledge in his or her analysis the interaction of these three different sovereign powers. To further complicate matters, no two local entities operate in the exact same way. Care must be taken to distinguish these differences in a legal analysis.

§ 9.02 History of California Settlements

California's first residents were tribes of Hupa, Maidu, Miwok, Modoc, Mojave, Pomo, and Quechan natives. Each tribal unit consisted of 130–150 individuals and was headed by a family leader. Each tribe had its own distinct culture and customs. In Pre-Columbian times these natives (later labeled Indians by the Europeans) numbered between 130,000–700,000. While extremely heterogeneous (they spoke over 20 different dialects), California Indians were a prosperous and peaceful people who settled in areas near waterways, valleys, and open canyons.[4]

California was visited by a number of different European explorers. Spanish Explorer Juan Rodriguez Cabrillo sailed up the California Coast in 1542. Twenty-seven years later Sir Francis Drake sailed by California and claimed it for England, naming it New Albion. In 1602 Spanish explorer Sebastian Vizcaino visited California and brought back an enthusiastic review of the "new" land.

To induce settlement in this "New World" the Spanish Crown offered large tracts of land to individuals willing to develop it for Spain. Processing these applications was slow, since everything had to be sent back to Spain. Starting in 1688, the Spanish Crown sent a "Viceroy"

---

[2] U.S. Const., Amend. X.

[3] U.S. Const., Article VI.

[4] An excellent treatment on the early Indians of Southern California can be found in Carey McWilliams, *Southern California: An Island on the Land*. Santa Barbara: Peregrine Smith Edition, 1973. 387 p. See also Elisha Smith Capron. *History of California from its Discovery to the Present Time*. Boston: John P. Jewett & Company, 1854. 356 p.; and Charles Edward Chapman. *A History of California: The Spanish Period*. New York: MacMillan Company, 1921. 527 p.

to "New Spain" to handle such matters. To assist him (and to keep him in check) were regional tribunes called "Audencias" who served as both an "Advisory Council" and as an appellate body in their review of the Viceroy's actions.

The Spanish system of developing California consisted of the construction of forts and missions. The forts were military establishments designed for the protection of Spanish interests. The missions were governed by Franciscan friars and were staffed by soldiers. The centerpiece of the mission was the church. The work of constructing forts and missions was done by Indians.

Soldiers who successfully completed their term of duty were encouraged to settle small parcels of land outside the Mission. These were referred to as pueblos (towns). Wealthy individuals were encouraged to develop large tracts of lands. If the tracts were primarily devoted to raising livestock they were called ranchos (farms). If they were plantation operations they were labeled Haciendas.

Spain had divided California into four military zones: San Francisco, Monterey, Santa Barbara, and San Diego. The head of each district was the Commandant who resided in the Presidio. Every Presidio had a castillo (fort) and a rancho. The former was to protect the Presidio from foreign intruders and irritated Indians, and the latter was to keep the cattle and grain collected as revenue.

The influences of Europe were evident in the history of California. Besides Spain, Russia had taken an interest in the fur trade and had built Fort Ross in 1812. The Monroe Doctrine in 1823 hastened the departure of the Russians to Alaska and allowed American fur trappers to take their place. In 1822 Mexico took over California.

From 1822 to 1848 Mexico controlled California. To manage its affairs Mexico sent a Governor. The local matters were largely left in the hands of an *Alcalde* who acted as a Mayor and Judge.

The Mexican American War (1846–1848) was resolved with the 1848 Treaty of Guadalupe de Hidalgo in which California was turned over to the Americans. In 1849 the Territory Government managed California, and adopted its first Constitution. In the same year gold was discovered at Sutter's Mill and a rush to settle California began. On September 9, 1850 California became the 31st state of the United States. At the time of statehood, there were already many small established cities in California. For instance, the City of Los Angeles was founded in 1781 (as a pueblo) and it was incorporated in the U.S. territory of California in April 1850.

The State of California has an extensive discussion on the history and culture of California. Follow the links at *www.ca.gov.*

§ 9.03   Structure of California Local Government

[1]   Types of Local Government Entities

California has two main types of local government entities. There are the "involuntary" municipal corporations known as counties and the "voluntary" municipal corporations known as cities. In California there are 58 counties. There are approximately 470 cities. A third type of local government entity is the interrelated governmental entity, examples of which are school districts, housing authorities, transit authorities, and water districts. One source reports that there are over 5,000 of these "special districts" in California.[5]

When researching a local entity one needs to know if it is a county or a city and whether or not it has a charter. A charter is much like a constitution for the entity. It sets up the framework of the government. If it is a charter city or a charter county, the researcher should obtain the charter to see the actual details on how the local entity operates. If there is no charter, then it is a general law entity, operated under general state law.

Local governments, like state and federal governments, may also have distinct branches and separations of powers. For instance, in some entities there is a judicial branch, which is folded into the state court system, especially in its system of appeals. (No cases are reported.) In some entities there is an executive branch, with officers like a mayor or a president or board chairman. In all local governments there is a legislative branch, which would be the city councils or the county boards of supervisors or special district boards. This legislative branch produces the legislation or rules that affect the citizens at the grass roots level. These councils or boards pass the ordinances and resolutions that are later included in subject-arranged codes.

---

[5] Levine, Stephen and Newcombe, Barbara T. *Paper Trails: A Guide to Public Records in California.* Second Edition. San Francisco: Center for Investigative Reporting, 1996. 243 p., at p. 12.

[2] Counties

Counties are political subdivisions of the state.[6] They exist for the convenience of the State. A county has certain enumerated powers—for example a county may sue and be sued; it may receive gifts and bequests; hold land, manage land; make contracts; and levy and collect taxes as authorized by law.[7]

Counties can be created and consolidated. Each county has a county seat, listed by statute, where the county conducts its business and has its offices. A county may operate under general law or under a charter.[8] To enact or revise a charter there has to be an ordinance adopted by the majority of the governing body or by a petition signed by qualified electors of the county. The governing body will then hold a special election for the purpose of inquiring whether the electors want a charter and if the answer is in the affirmative, to then vote for membership on a charter commission. If such a commission is selected, their task is to prepare or revise the charter. Such a proposal is then submitted to the electors. A majority vote will either select a charter or revise it.[9] In the absence of a charter, the general law of the state governs the operation of the county.

📖 The State Controller's Office provides news releases, special reports, annual reports and many other useful references on the financial operations of municipal entities. See *www.sco.ca.gov.*

🖥 On the internet the *National Association of Counties* has a website located at: *www.naco.org.* The site has information on news and events as well as an index to information about counties and related legislative affairs. It also will link the researcher to the websites maintained by different California counties.

[3] Cities

Although a city's source of power comes from the state, a city enjoys a degree of autonomy that a county does not have. Cities are "voluntary" creations. They must be "created" by its inhabitants. Conversely a city can be "dissolved" by those same inhabitants.

---

[6] Cal. Const., Art. XI, § 1, subsect. (a); Cal. Gov. Code § 23022.

[7] Gov. Code, § 23004.

[8] Cal. Const., Art. XI, § 3.

[9] Gov. Code, §§ 23701–23708, 23713.

The California Constitution provides for the formation of three types of cities: *general law* cities, *charter* cities and *consolidated city and county*. Approximately 80% of California cities are general law cities. The remaining 20% are charter cities.[10] There is one consolidated city and county—San Francisco.

The difference between the two main classes, *general law*[11] and *charter*,[12] is chiefly with their scope of power. A general law city operates under general law[13] and a charter city[14] has its own adopted charter. The California Constitution confers on charter cities a police power or general welfare clause.[15] This empowers Charter cities with much greater authority to run city affairs than a general law city would possess. Courts have restricted a general law city to "only those powers expressly conferred upon it by the Legislature, together with such powers as are necessarily incident to those expressly granted or essential to declared objects and purposes of a municipal corporation; powers of such a city are strictly construed, so that any fair, reasonable doubt concerning exercise of power is resolved against the corporation."[16]

When a city is created it is a general law city, unless the electors select a charter commission.[17] It is this commission which would propose a charter. The commission's final product is then submitted to the voters for confirmation or rejection. A charter can be revised or amended in a similar fashion. The final charter becomes state law and is treated like a state statute.[18]

📖   For facts and figures on how cities operate see *Cities Annual Report*, published by the California State Controller's Office at: *www.sco.ca.gov*.

🖥   Search the internet for the *League of California Cities*, the organization consisting of all 470 cities in California, at: *www.cacities.org*. It provides information on education programs, legislative advocacy and other useful research tools.

---

[10] Cities Annual Report, State Controller's Office, 1995–1996

[11] Cal. Const., art. XI, §§ 2, 7; Cal. Gov. Code § 34871.

[12] Cal. Const., art. XI, § 5.

[13] Gov. Code, § 34102.

[14] Gov. Code, § 34101.

[15] Cal. Const., art. XI, § 5.

[16] *Martin v. Superior Court*, 234 Cal.App.3d 1765, 286 Cal. Rptr.513 (1991).

[17] Gov. Code, § 34451.

[18] Cal. Const., art. XI, § 3.

🖥   There is a commercial site for cities sponsored by USACI-TYLINK. It connects to a series of city sponsored websites with information varying from tourist information to civic lessons. It can be found at: *www.usacitylink.com/citylink/ca.*

🖥   CEGI (Chris Mays) www page at: *cpsr.org/cpsr/states/california/cegi.html.* This site links to many California cities. The official city/county pages may or may not include links to the charters and ordinances for the jurisdiction.

[4] Interrelated Governmental Entities

There are numerous entities which derive their powers from different governmental sovereignties—Federal, State, County, City. Besides school districts there are also *semi-autonomous agencies* and *special districts.*

Semiautonomous agencies function for the city, but are set up by state law. Examples include *Community Redevelopment Agency, Housing Authority,* and *Los Angeles Memorial Coliseum Commission.*

Special districts are agencies of the state created for the local performance of a governmental or proprietary function within limited boundaries. Special Districts have the same general governmental powers as local governments. Special Districts may perform one function or several services. Examples include *Metropolitan Water District of Southern California, Los Angeles County Metropolitan Transportation Authority,* and *South Coast Air Quality Management District.*

Facts and figures regarding the operation of interrelated governmental entities can be requested from the State Controller's Office, at: *www.sco.ca.gov.* Other reports available from the California State Controller's Office include:

- *Special Districts Annual Report,* at: *www.sco.ca.gov.*

- *Community Redevelopment Agencies Annual Report,* at: *www.sco.ca.gov.*

- *Transportation Planning Agencies Annual Report,* at: *www.sco.ca.gov.*

- *School Districts Annual Report,* at: *www.sco.ca.gov.*

To obtain a copy of just about any California agencies reports, visit the Legislative Counsel's website at: *www.agencyreports.ca.gov.*

A good starting point in researching California government issues is the State Constitution. To obtain a free copy, write to the California

State Senate Rules Committee which publishes a compilation of the Federal and State Constitutions. There is also a website on the internet which contains a copy of the State Constitution of California located at: *www.leginfo.ca.gov/const.html.*

§ 9.04 Organization and Reorganization of Local Government Entities

[1] Counties

A county is defined as "the largest political division of the State having corporate powers."[19] New counties may be formed and created from portions of one or more existing counties.[20] Counties can also be consolidated. "Two or more counties, each contiguous to the other, or to one of the others, may consolidate into one county."[21]

To create a county, a notice of intention needs to be filed with the clerk.[22] Then a petition which describes the boundaries of the proposed county, the population of the proposed county, the area of the county, its proposed name, the names of any affected counties, and a statement that the new boundaries do not pass through, divide or otherwise interfere with the territory of any incorporated city other than the city with a population greater than that of the proposed new county.[23] The petition is then circulated for the required number of signatures. If the petitioners get the appropriate number of signatures, the petition is certified by the clerk and transmitted to the board of supervisors of each affected county.[24] The Board of supervisors of the principal county affected shall then send a copy of the certified petition to the Governor[25] who then creates a County Formation Review Commission (consisting of five persons) to review the proposed county.[26]

It is this Commission which will determine, based on set criteria,[27] the terms and conditions of such a newly created county.[28] Of course,

[19] Gov. Code, § 23000.

[20] Gov. Code, § 23300.

[21] Gov. Code, § 23500.

[22] Gov. Code, §§ 23324–23325.

[23] Gov. Code, § 23320.

[24] Gov. Code, § 23328.

[25] Gov. Code, § 23330.

[26] Gov. Code, § 23331.

[27] Such criteria is delineated in Gov. Code, § 23332.

[28] Gov. Code, § 23342.

such conclusions will have the benefit of the input from the public in the form of public hearings.[29]

Upon receipt of the Commission's determinations, the board of supervisors of each affected county shall order an election.[30] The elections are regulated by a series of statutes.[31] A simple majority is all that is required.[32]

If the voters chose to create a new county, there needs to be an election to select county officers and to select the location of the county seat.[33] In addition there has to be a "transfer" of asset and debts as well as a reallocation of services.[34] The State Court system has to be reallocated.[35]

Counties can also be consolidated. When two or more counties are contiguous to each other they may consolidate into one county.[36] Similar to the creation of a county, there are steps and stages the petitioner must satisfy.[37] Similarly the Governor must appoint a "County Consolidation Review Commission".[38] An election by simple majority[39] determines whether or not there will be consolidation of counties. Upon a successful vote for consolidation there will be a merger of government services, assets, and liabilities.[40] Upon the legal establishment of the consolidated county, all affected counties will transfer title to property held to the consolidated county. If any affected county has a charter, it will then cease to exist.[41]

[2] Cities and/or Special Districts

In California the legislature passed an extensive set of statutes dealing with the "policy of the state to encourage orderly growth and

---

[29] Gov. Code, §§ 23336–23337.
[30] Gov. Code, § 23350.
[31] Gov. Code, §§ 23350 et seq.
[32] Gov. Code, § 23373.
[33] Gov. Code, § 23374.1 et seq.
[34] Gov. Code, § 23375 et seq.
[35] Gov. Code, § 23394 et seq.
[36] Gov. Code, § 23500.
[37] Gov. Code, § 23510 et seq.
[38] Gov. Code, § 23530 et seq.
[39] Gov. Code, § 23567.
[40] Gov. Code, § 23571 et seq.
[41] Gov. Code, § 23571.

development" and the impact this would have on the "logical formation and modification of the boundaries of local agencies."[42] The provisions are commonly known as the *Cortese-Knox Local Government Reorganization Act of 1985.*[43] The entities affected by the act include counties, cities, school districts, special assessment districts, as well as many other specific agencies.[44]

The *Cortese-Knox Act* deals with a change of organization including: city incorporation; district formation; annexation to, or detachment from, a city or district; disincorporation of a city; district dissolution; consolidation of cities or special districts; a merger or establishment of a subsidiary district.[45]

Incorporation refers to the formation or creation of a city with corporate powers.[46] Formation refers to the formation, incorporation, etc. of a district.[47] Annexation means the inclusion, attachment or addition of territory to a city or a district.[48] Detachment refers to the deannexation, exclusion, deletion or removal from a city or district of any portion of that territory.[49] Consolidation means the uniting or joining of two or more cities located in the same county or two or more districts into a single new successor district.[50] A merger is the extinguishment, termination and cessation of the existence of a district of limited powers by the merger of that district with a city.[51]

In California it was determined that a single governmental agency would better be able to address the issue of reorganization.[52] Each county has a "Local Agency Formation Commission". The Legislature determines the qualifications and criteria for establishing such a commission.[53] Each Commission consists of five individuals—two from the

---

[42] Gov. Code, § 56001.

[43] Gov. Code, §§ 56000–57550.

[44] Gov. Code, § 56036.

[45] Gov. Code, § 56021.

[46] Gov. Code, § 56043.

[47] Gov. Code, § 56039.

[48] Gov. Code, § 56017.

[49] Gov. Code, § 56033.

[50] Gov. Code, § 56030.

[51] Gov. Code, § 56056.

[52] Gov. Code, § 56001.

[53] Gov. Code, §§ 56375–56498.

county board of supervisors, two from the cities, and one member of the general public selected by the other four.[54] The Act also provides for some counties to have seven. (For example, Los Angeles County.)[55] The Commission is required to operate pursuant to specific provisions.[56]

A proposal for change or reorganization has some minimal requirements. A petition must satisfy the following: It must state the proposal is made pursuant to the *Act*. It must state the nature of the proposal and lost all proposed changes. It must set forth a description of the boundaries of the affected territories. All proposed terms and conditions must be stated. The reasons for the proposal must be stated. The petition must also state whether it was signed by registered voters or owners of land and it must also designate the chief petitioners.[57]

There is a requirement that the petition be signed by a minimal amount of qualified voters. The numbers vary according to what is being requested.[58] If the required number of signatures is verified then there notices and hearings[59] and if all procedural safeguards are satisfied then the issue is resolved by an election.[60]

    The Assembly Committee on Local Government, Assembly Publications Office, publishes the *Guide to Cortese-Knox Local Government Reorganization Act of 1985.*

§ 9.05   Operation

[1]   Counties

County powers are delineated in the state statutes. Like cities, counties may have a charter, in which case the charter will prevail on how the county operates. In the absence of a charter, the county operates under general law.

The State Constitution requires that every county have an elected county sheriff, an elected district attorney, an elected assessor, and an elected governing body in each county.[61] If the county has adopted a

---

[54] Gov. Code, § 56325.

[55] Gov. Code, § 56326.

[56] Gov. Code, § 56650 et seq.

[57] Gov. Code, § 56700.

[58] Gov. Code, § 56750 et seq.

[59] Gov. Code, § 57000 et seq.

[60] Gov. Code, § 57125, et seq.

[61] Cal. Const., art. XI, § 1(b).

charter, there are requirements that the governing body be of five or more members, all elected. It also will require provisions for the electing (and if necessary, removal) of the sheriff, district attorney, and assessor.

The Constitution also confers on the counties the power to "make and enforce within its limits all local, police, sanitary, and other ordinances and regulations not in conflict with general laws."[62] It is also allowed that counties may perform municipal functions if the cities within their boundaries request they do so.[63]

Similar to cities, county legislative bodies, commonly referred to as the Board of Supervisors, are required to meet regularly and publicly.

[2]　Cities

[a]　Types of Cities

As discussed earlier, there are basically two types of cities—general law and charter. A charter city may select any form of local government so stated in their charter. General law cities are organized as established by state statutes. As a general rule General law cities have a five member city council, a city clerk, city treasurer, police chief, fire chief and another other subordinate officer as required by law.[64] Most general law cities rely on a City Manager, selected by the Council, to run the city on a day to day basis.[65] The citizens also have the choice of electing a Mayor[66] If the Mayor is not an elective office often the Council will chose one of their own to act as Mayor.[67]

[b]　Law Making

The Council acts as the legislative body of the city. The process in which the Council makes law requires appropriate notice to the public, an opportunity for the citizens to be heard on the matter, an open discussion of the issues before the action is voted upon, and a record of how each Council person voted on the issue. There are stringent requirements regarding the appropriate way to handle these meetings.

---

[62] Cal. Const., art. XI, § 7.

[63] Cal. Const., art. XI, § 8.

[64] Gov. Code, § 36501.

[65] Gov. Code, § 34856.

[66] Gov. Code, §§ 34900–34906.

[67] Gov. Code, § 36801.

The *Brown Act*[68] is an elaborate legal treatment on the issues and is required reading for anyone interested in this area of law.

The lawmaking action of the Council takes on two forms—ordinance or resolution. An ordinance is the typical way the Council makes city law. Ordinances are often used to criminalize some sort of conduct, violation of the ordinance being punished as a misdemeanor or an infraction. A resolution is a more informal means of Council action. When a resolution is passed using the same formalities required of an ordinance, it will usually be given the same effect as an ordinance. On the other hand, a resolution passed with less attention to the rules will often be treated as merely being the opinion of the Council. Both resolutions and ordinances may not conflict with federal or state constitutions or laws.[69]

[c]   Employees/Labor Relations

The city may also appoint citizens to assist the Council and Mayor in positions such as Boards and Commissions.[70] The responsibilities of such Boards and Commission vary from city to city. In some locations they practically run a department. In others, they merely serve as advisors.

The city is also required to set up a system of recruitment and hiring. Depending on the city, the system can range from an "at-will" hiring to a protected "civil service." However, any system the city uses must comply with federal and state labor and employment laws such as the Fair Labor Standards Act of 1938, Title VII of the Civil Rights Act of 1964, Fair Employment and Housing Act, the California Unruh Civil Rights Act, to name just a few.

[d]   Financing the Government

Another great responsibility of the local government is in maintaining a budget. Once again, the budget process varies from city to city. Anyone interested in how a city operates should look at its budget, because from this document one can gleam the priorities and purposes of the municipality.

For charter cities and counties, the method for implementing a budget is delineated in the charter. For general law cities and counties there

---

[68] Gov. Code, §§ 54950–54962.

[69] Gov. Code, § 37100.

[70] Gov. Code, § 40605.

is no statutory procedure for a budget. A typical example of a budget is as follows:

The Mayor outlines budget policies in a letter addressed to department heads. The letter requests that all department heads submit a "wish list" of how much money they would like to have and detailing how it would be spent. These requests are evaluated by the Mayor and or Chief Administrative Officer. At this point the government estimates the revenues and expenditures for the fiscal year. A series of hearings is held and a proposed budget is generated. This is submitted to the Council (or similar legislative body) for adoption. The Council holds a series of public hearings in which the budget is discussed, modified, and eventually adopted. This adopted budget is subject to a Mayor's veto.

There are constitutional rules on expenditures and revenues. The voters amended the constitution in 1978 to implement Article XIIIA—Tax Limitations and Article XIIIB—Government Spending Limitations.

[e] Elections and Conduct of Officers and Council

Conduct of elected Council and Officers are largely dictated by the Political Reform Act, Fair Political Practices Commission and California Codes and Regulations. The basics of appropriate conduct include a prohibition of a public official from using their position to unduly influence a government decision in which they have a financial interest; a requirement that public officials must file a conflict of interest statement which reflects their financial holdings; a prohibition from a public official having a financial interest in municipal contracts they are involved with; and a prohibition from holding dual offices which are incompatible with each other, a potential conflict of interest being sufficient.

The ultimate responsibility for the operation of the government belongs to the citizens. They are the ones who not only chose to incorporate/dissolve/annex/consolidate cities, but they are also the ones who chose their elected officials, who determine what laws to pass and what financial decisions to make.

The California Constitution states "[A]ll political power is inherent in the people. Government is instituted for their protection, security, and benefit, and they have the right to alter or reform it when the public good may require."[71]

---

[71] Cal. Const., art. II, § 1.

The right to vote is given to qualified voters. Qualifications are that the person be an eighteen-year old United State citizen and a resident of the State of California.[72] The Legislature defines the standards for residency.[73]

All local government offices—judicial, school, county, and city—are nonpartisan.[74]

The rules regulating the elections—both general and special—are found in the California Election Codes.[75] It should be noted that Charter Cities may adopt these regulations, but they are not mandatory.[76] Charter cities may adopt their own rules and regulations, so delineated in their charters, since adopted charters are given the same force and effects as state legislation.

§ 9.06　Research Sources

[1]　Internet Sources

A good starting place on the internet for information on local and state government can be found at the official California government web page at: *www.ca.gov*. Follow the link to the Local Government page that lists sites to several providers of information on county and city governments. Another good site is the internet page for the California State Association of Counties, at: *csac.counties.org*. The county and city links will then theoretically connect the researcher to the couty supervisors or city council persons. Another page to review is: *usacitylink.com/ ca.html*. This page again provides links to the counties and many cities in the state. There are fifty eight counties in the state of California. Currently fifty-four of them have websites. Another good site to check for California county and city legal materials is Piper Resources' State and Local Government on the Net: *www.statelocalgov.net/state-ca.htm*. This site has links to all the counties with web sites and to over 300 California cities with web sites.

---

[72] Cal. Const., art. II, § 2.

[73] Cal. Const., art. II, § 3.

[74] Cal. Const., art. II, § 6.

[75] Elec. Code, § 12328 et seq.

[76] Cal. Const., art. XI, § 5(b).

[2] Sources for Charters, Codes, and Ordinances

Charters are shorter than the ordinances and are not changed or updated as often. As a practical matter, charters are treated by legal publishers just as they treat constitutions and codes. The two are sometimes, but not always, published together. So the researcher should first look for the codes and ordinances (online or print) and he or she will usually find the charter, if there is one. Researchers may also find charters in the Statutes and Amendments to the Codes by using the index in the back of the California Shepard's Statutes volumes.

Links to ordinances for over 80 California cities and counties may be found at numerous different websites. There is one website maintained by Appellate Counselor WWW Resources located at: *www.appellate-counsellor.com/resource/municode.htm.* There is also a website maintained by Book Publishing Company located at: *www.bpcnet.com/codes.htm#CA.* The site contains ordinances from 171 municipalities. You can find ordinances and zoning laws for California cities at the Municipal Code Corporation website at: *www.municode.com.*

The local public library in the jurisdictional boundaries of the government entity will always carry the local charter, codes, and ordinances.

Original versions of all city and county charters are in the California Statutes and Amendments to the Codes since they must be approved by the California Legislature. Amendments are also published there, but without a cross reference link to the original charters. The difficulty may be surmounted by reference to Deering's California Codes Uncodified Initiative Measures and Statutes Annotated.

To trace municipal or county charters from the original version to the latest amendment one should first consult the index to Deering's Uncodified Initiative Measures and Statutes Annotated. The user should find the entry for the city or county in question, for instance San Francisco. The reference will be to a year and item number (1931-26). In the main part of the volume, the user will locate the year (1931), then the item number (26) and will have references to the original charter and all amendments up to the publication of the volume in 1973. The user should then follow the same procedure in the pocket part to the volume. All of the references then can easily be found in Statutes and Amendments to the Codes.

A copy of a charter can sometimes be obtained by calling or writing to the city or county counsel.

Three large libraries in the state collect charters, codes, and ordinances, which are:

🏛️Institute of Governmental Studies Library (IGS), UC Berkeley

> University of California
> 109 Moses Hall #2370
> Berkeley, CA 94720-2370
> 1-510-642-1472
> 1-510-643-0866 (FAX)
> *www.igs.berkeley.edu*

> The Institute loans codes to and provides code section copying services for Bay Area attorneys. The IGS website also provides direct links to many charters and ordinances of California cities and counties. See: *www.igs.berkeley.edu/library/calcodes.html*.

🏛️California State Law Library

> P.O. Box 2037
> Sacramento, CA 95809
> 1-916-445-8833
> *www.library.ca.gov*

🏛️Maps and Government Information (MGI), UCLA

> Henry J. Bruman Library
> A4510 Young Research Library
> Box 951575
> Los Angeles, CA 90095-1575
> *www.library.ucla.edu/libraries/yrl/referenc/govinfo/stategovs.htm*

[3]   Citators for Ordinances

Shepard's California Citations, Statutes Edition covers ordinances of California cities. The publication lists court decisions, administrative law decisions, and law review articles that cite to any California city or county ordinances. The publication also provides an index to municipal charters, giving the Statutes of California citations relating to each one.

Shepard's Ordinance Law Annotations is a multi-volume set listing American cases that have interpreted ordinances in U.S. cities.

[4]   Local Law Publishers

Traditional law publishers are not in the charter and code publishing business. Some cities and counties publish their own charters and codes, but many times they will contract out the work to an outside company like the two listed below:

> Book Publishing Co.
> 201 Westlake Ave. North
> Seattle, WA 98109
> 1-206-343-5700
> 1-800-837-7881

This company has had the contract to publish San Francisco's codes up until late 1999.

> Brackett Publishing
> 120 N. Santa Fe Ave.
> Los Angeles, CA 90012
> 1-213-625-8345
> 1-213-625-5779 (FAX)

This company has the contract to publish the city and county codes of Los Angeles.

[5] Bibliography on Local Government

📕 California City Hall Telephone Book. *Sacramento: League of California Cities.* (alphabetical listing w/phone & fax numbers) Item 988 $24. 1400 K street, 4th floor Sacramento, CA 95814. 916-444-8671; fax 916-444-5219. In addition there is a SoCal office in Monrovia: 818-305-1315. Their website is at: *www.cacities.org.* In addition to the Publications catalog (need Adobe Acrobat to view) there is a searchable Cities Online database The database of online cities can be sorted by city name, county, or League division.

📕 California [year] Local Government Directory. *Sacramento: Statenet & California Journal.* Annual. This thick directory lists all the counties and major cities in the state. Under each county or city are listed the web page, government site, and the names, addresses, and phone numbers of all officers.

📕 *The California Municipal Law Handbook.* Sacramento: League of California Cities, 1998, looseleaf. A great practical guide designed for city attorneys, city officers, and municipal law practitioners.

📕 *California's Municipal & County Charters, Codes and Ordinances: A Directory of Availability, 2nd Edition.* (s.l.: Northern California Association of Law Libraries, 1989) 110 p. (city section) 16 p. (county section). Although this book is 10 years old, it still has value. It lists documents available for either purchase or just for inspection. It also lists addresses and phone numbers for the city and county clerks, who control access to those documents.

📖 City Attorneys Telephone Book. *Sacramento: League of California Cities*, Publications Office. (About $50.)1400 K street, 4th floor Sacramento, CA 95814. 916-444-8671; fax 916-444-5219. In addition there is a SoCal office in Monrovia: 818-305-1315. Their website is at: *www.cacities.org* In addition to the Publications catalog (need Adobe Acrobat to view) there is a searchable Cities Online database. The database of online cities can be sorted by city name, county, or League division.

📖 Detwiler, Peter M. *Creatures of Statute . . . Children of Trade: The Legal Origins of California Cities.* Background paper published in California Constitution Revision Commission History and Perspective, 1996. 9 p. This article is also available on the www at: *www.library.ca.gov/CCRC/reports/ html/h_cities.html.*

📖 Levin, Marc A. *How to Find Local Law: A California Paradigm.* 14 Legal Reference Services Quarterly 79-96 (1994). This article is one of the best overviews of city and county government law in California. Special districts are not included. Mr. Levin is Head of Public Services at the Institute of Governmental Studies, Berkeley, which is mentioned above. The article is dated in that it came out in 1994, just before the www explosion took place, so he was not able to cover the those sources.

📖 Levine, Stephen and Newcombe, Barbara T. *Paper Trails: A Guide to Public Records in California. Second Edition.* San Francisco: Center for Investigative Reporting, 1996. 243 p. This is a valuable research guide in that it shows researchers how to find many types of smaller, more detailed legal and non-legal records kept by local government bodies.

📖 McCarthy, David J., Jr. *Local Government Law in a Nutshell. Third Edition.* St. Paul: West, 1990. 435 p.

📖 McQuillin, Eugene. *The Law of Municipal Corporations. Third Edition* by Clark Asahel Nichols and others. Willmette,

IL: Callaghan. 20 v., kept up to date with supplements. A definitive guide to the legal principles of municipal corporations.

Meeker, Amanda. *Local Government: An Overview of the History of Constitutional Provisions Dealing with Local Government.* Background paper published in California Constitution Revision Commission History and Perspective. 8 p. This article is also available on the internet at: *www.library.ca.gov/CCRC/reports/html/h_local_government.html.*

Reynolds, Osborne M., Jr. *Local Government Law.* St. Paul: Westgroup, 1982. 860 p. This West hornbook provides a good background on the subject.

Sato, Sho. *"Municipal Affairs"* in *California.* 60(4) California Law Review 1055-1115 (June 1972).

Tailor-Made Government: A Citizen's Guide to California's Charter Cities and Counties. (Sacramento: California Senate Committee on Local Government, 1998). 23 p. This is one of the best explanations of charter cities and counties. It provides a list of the 13 counties with charters (Los Angeles, San Bernadino, Butte, Tehama, Alameda, San Francisco, Fresno, Sacramento, San Diego, San Mateo, Santa Clara, Placer, and El Dorado) and a list of the counties where charter proposals failed at the polls. There is also a list of the 94 charter cities in California.

Western City: The Monthly Magazine of the League of California Cities. Sacramento: League of California Cities.

Your Government at a Glance: The City of Los Angeles. Los Angeles: City of Los Angeles, 1989. 36 p.

California Local Planning Documents Database. On the internet at:: *www.igs.berkeley.edu:8880/library/calplans.html.* University of California, Berkeley, The Institute of Governmental Studies Library accumulates planning documents from the 500-plus cities and counties and makes the documents available at this website.

[6] Sample Government and/or Charter/Code Web Pages

Alameda	*www.co.alameda.ca.us*
Alpine	*www.co.alpine.ca.us*
Amador	*www.co.amador.ca.us*

Butte	*www.buttecounty.net*
Calaveras	*www.co.calaveras.ca.us*
Colusa	*www.colusacountyclerk.com*
Contra Costa	*www.co.contra-costa.ca.us*
Del Norte	*www.co.del-norte.ca.us*
El Dorado	*www.co.el-dorado.ca.us*
Fresno	*www.fresno.ca.gov*
Glenn	*www.countyofglenn.net*
Humboldt	*www.co.humboldt.ca.us*
Imperial	*www.co.imperial.ca.us*
Inyo	*www.countyofinyo.org*
Kern	*www.co.kern.ca.us*
Kings	*www.countyofkings.com*
Lake	*www.co.lake.ca.us*
Lassen	*www.co.lassen.ca.us*
Los Angeles city	*cityfolio.ci.la.ca.us*
Los Angeles county	*www.co.la.ca.us*
Madera	*www.madera-county.com*
Marin	*www.co.marin.ca.us*
Mariposa	*www.mariposacounty.org*
Mendocino	*www.co.mendocino.ca.us*
Merced	*www.co.merced.ca.us*
Monterey	*www.co.monterey.ca.us*
Napa	*www.co.napa.ca.us*
Nevada	*www.co.nevada.ca.us*
Orange	*www.oc.ca.gov*
Placer	*www.placer.ca.gov*
Plumas	*www.countyofplumes.com*
Riverside	*www.co.riverside.ca.us*
Sacramento	*www.saccounty.net*
San Benito	*www.san-benito.ca.us*
San Bernardino	*www.co.san-bernardino.ca.us*
San Diego city	*clerkdoc.sannet.gov/Website/mc/mc.html*
San Diego county	*www.co.san-diego.ca.us*
San Francisco	*www.ci.sf.ca.us*
San Joaquin	*www.co.san-joaquin.ca.us*
San Luis Obispo	*www.co.slo.ca.us*
San Mateo	*www.co.sanmateo.ca.us*
Santa Barbara	*www.countyofsb.org*
Santa Clara	*www.santaclaracounty.org*
Santa Cruz	*www.co.santa-cruz.ca.us*

Shasta	*www.co.shasta.ca.us*
Sierra	*www.sierracounty.ws*
Siskiyou	*www.co.siskiyou.ca.us*
Solano	*www.co.solano.ca.us*
Sonoma	*www.sonoma-county.org*
Stanislaus	*www.co.stanislaus.ca.us*
Sutter	*www.co.sutter.ca.us*
Trinity	*www.trinitycounty.org*
Tulare	*www.co.tulare.ca.us*
Ventura	*www.ventura.org/vencty.htm*
Yolo	*www.yolocounty.org*
Yuba	*www.co.yuba.ca.us*

[7] Key Organizations in Local Government Issues

Association of Bay Area Governments
Joseph P. Bort MetroCenter
101 8th Street (8th & Oak Streets)
Oakland, CA 94607
1-510-464-7900
1-510-464-7970 (FAX)
www.abag.ca.gov/home.html

California State Association of Counties
1100 K Street, Suite 101
Sacramento, CA 95814
Tel.: (916) 327-7500
Fax: (916) 441-5507
www.csac.counties.org

League of California Cities
1400 K Street, Suite 400
Sacramento, CA 95814
Main Telephone: 916-658-8200
Main Fax: 916-658-8240
www.cacities.org

Chapter 10

Secondary Legal Sources[1]

§ 10.01 Introduction

Secondary sources, as discussed in Chapter 1, are not the law itself, but information about the law. Authors of secondary sources critique, interpret, explain, summarize, restate, or predict the law. These sources may be in the hard copy format of treatises, practice guides, encyclopedias, journals, or individual journal articles. They may also be in the form of documents on CD-ROM and/or in an electronic database.

---

[1] Jennifer Lentz, Reference Librarian, Hugh & Hazel Darling Law Library, UCLA School of Law, contributed to the revising of this chapter.

(Pub. 64620)

§ 10.02   Treatises and Practice Guides

[1]   Overview

A treatise is a book written to help clarify and explain a particular area of law. Treatises consist of one or more volumes and are used by judges, lawyers and law students. They often contain citations to primary materials, such as cases, statutes, and regulations, which make them a popular starting point for many legal research problems. Treatises are often complete reviews of particular areas of law and generally do not include practice materials; however, some treatises will include forms.

From the drafting of complaints to the filing of appeals, practice guides provide crucial information for attorneys practicing law. Practice guides include, among other things, pleading and transaction forms, step-by-step procedures for drafting memoranda, advice on court procedure, and help interpreting the law.

[2]   Treatises

Some of the most widely used treatises in California were originally authored by Bernard E. Witkin. Considered the grandfather of California law, Witkin was responsible for compiling and organizing the vast body of state legal jurisprudence into a series of treatises that bear his name. Witkin began his career in 1930 as a bar review course instructor and his course outlines later became the foundation for the *Summary of California Law*.[2] For nearly 70 years, Witkin was a prolific author and continuing legal education lecturer, serving as an advisor to two California Supreme Court Justices and as an advisory member of the California Judicial Council.[3] Today, Witkin's treatises are published by the Witkin Legal Institute.[4] They continue to be widely used by practitioners in the state. Witkin treatises include:

---

[2] Remarks of the Hon. Justice Chin, *Memoriam of Bernard E. Witkin*, Dec. 3, 1996. 13 Cal. 4th 1267, 1270. A memorial to Bernard E. Witkin (1904–1995) was published in v. 13 of the California Official Reports, 4th Series, and reprinted as a separate pamphlet by the Witkin Legal Institute. The memorial includes comments of several California Supreme Court Justices.

[3] *Remarks of Justice Chin*, at 1270–71.

[4] The Witkin Legal Institute, founded in 1996, is located in Alameda, CA. This site gives the reader much information about legal research, the Witkin treatises in the various formats, the philosophy behind the publication, and biographical information on the board and staff. For more information, visit the Witkin Legal Institute at *www.witkin.com*.

California Criminal Law, 3rd ed. 6 vols. 2000–. Pocket parts and supplements.

California Evidence, 4th ed. 3 vols. 2000–. Pocket parts.

California Procedure, 4th ed. 10 vols. 1996–. Pocket parts.

Summary of California Law, 9th ed. 13 vols. 1987–. Pocket parts and supplements.

All of the Witkin treatises are available on both LexisNexis and Westlaw.[5]

For over 30 years Matthew Bender & Company has produced a 56 volume set entitled *California Forms of Pleading and Practice.* This set is both treatise and practice guide, providing complete coverage of civil procedure and encyclopedic coverage of all civil practice areas, including torts, business and commercial, real estate, public administrative law, and family law. Attorney ethics and other practice issues are included. Includes research guide, checklists, and forms of pleading for topics analyzed. Updated five times a year. See Appendix S for a list of selected Matthew Bender products.

[3] Practice Guides

Major publishers of legal practice guides in California include Matthew Bender, the California Continuing Education of the Bar (CEB), the Rutter Group, and West Group.

Matthew Bender has been publishing analytical practice materials for over 100 years, and is now a member of the LexisNexis Group. Matthew Bender produces practice materials on a complete range of topics of California law. Matthew Bender products also include titles from Parker Publishing, Michie, and Mealey Publications. The largest California product is the 56 volume set of *California Forms of Pleading and Practice,* discussed in [2], above. Other extensive sets include the 36 volume set of *California Legal Forms: Transaction Guide* (a step-by-step guide through all non-litigation business and personal transactions that are likely to arise in day-to-day practice, with guidance on drafting and filing requisite forms), and the 24 volume set of *California Points and Authorities* (a compilation of pre-drafted points and authorities with accompanying analysis for civil practice). See Appendix S for a selected list of Matthew Bender titles arranged by topic.

---

[5] Lexis: CAL; WITKIN (all titles), CAL; WITCRM, CAL; WITEVD, CAL; WITPRO, CAL; WITSUM. Westlaw: WITKIN (all titles), WITSUM, WITEVID, WITCRIM, WITPROC.

The CEB, founded in 1947, is jointly sponsored by the State Bar and the University of California, and provides continuing education seminars for attorneys in the state. The CEB also publishes over eighty titles aimed at the practitioner, as well as brief "how to" guides for attorneys called Action Guides.[6] Over 50 CEB publications are available on LexisNexis in the CEB Library. See Appendix S for a selected list of CEB titles by topic.

The Rutter Group was founded in 1979 with the purpose of producing a series of authoritative guides written in the bar review, or outline, format.[7] It is now the publisher of the Practice Guide Series, a collection of over fifteen looseleaf guides written by judges and practitioners. In 1994, the Encino-based Rutter Group became affiliated with West Group. Most of the Rutter practice guides are available on Westlaw.[8] See Appendix S for a selected list of Rutter products by topic.

West Group, formerly known as West, has been publishing analytical practice materials for over 120 years. West Group provides an extensive range of practice materials in California. In addition to the Witkin and Rutter titles, West Group also produces titles under the Bancroft-Whitney brand. Extensive practice guide sets include the 33 volume *California Civil Practice Guide Series*, and the 17 volume set, *California Forms, Legal and Business*. See Appendix S for a selected list of West Group products by topic.

§ 10.03 Encyclopedias

Legal encyclopedias offer a broad overview of the law in a particular area. California has one legal encyclopedia, *California Jurisprudence, 3d*, published by West Group. *Cal Jur 3d*, as it is popularly known, began publication in 1972. Consisting of over 70 volumes, it contains a general subject index, a table of cases and table of statutes. It is updated with supplemental volumes and pocket parts. The full-text version of *Cal Jur 3d* is available on Westlaw in the CAJUR database. *Cal Jur 3d* was preceded by *California Jurisprudence* (Bancroft-Whitney, 1921–1959) and *California Jurisprudence, 2nd ed.* (Bancroft-Whitney, 1952–1980).

---

[6] For a complete list of titles published by the CEB, *see* ceb.ucop.edu.

[7] Paul D. Freeman. *CEB v. Rutter: The Competition Heats Up*, 8 Cal. Lawyer 48 July 1988, p. 51.

[8] For more information on the Rutter Group Practice Guide series, *see* www.rutter.com. Many Rutter Group guides are also available on CD-ROM.

§ 10.04 Periodicals

[1] Overview

Legal periodical literature may be generally classified into four types of publications: law reviews, bar association journals, legal newspapers, and newsletters. There are some publications, however, that may cross over the lines and appear to be hybrids of two or more types.

[2] Law Reviews

In California, as in rest of the United States, a law review or journal (the terms are used interchangeably) is sponsored by a law school and edited by a student board, usually composed of students with high scholastic standing.

The content of such publications typically includes (1) leading articles by professors, practitioners, or judges, (2) student-written "notes" analyzing recent cases or legislation, (3) student-written "comments" on timely topics of law, and (4) book reviews. The notes and comments sections are sometimes combined.

Some law reviews survey the law of a particular court or jurisdiction.[9] Others concentrate on a particular subject area. In recent years it has become the trend for law schools to sponsor two or more legal publications, one of a more general nature, and others in special subject areas such as international law, legislation, or civil rights. Users should contact the editorial office of the specific journal for available back issues in hard copy or microform. Some journal issues are posted on the Internet.

For a list of law reviews currently published in California, see *Appendix P.* For a comprehensive list of legal journal websites, consult the USC Law Library's *Legal Journals on the Web.*[10] California law reviews are available on LexisNexis ("California Law Reviews, Combined" Source [LAWREV; CALRV]) and on Westlaw in the JLR database.

[3] Bar Association Journals

Bar association journals are publications aimed at practicing attorneys. They help keep bar members informed of the organization's events and

---

[9] For example, the *Pacific Law Journal,* from the McGeorge School of Law, devotes part of one issue each year to a review of selected California legislation.

[10] Legal Journals on the Web. *lawweb.usc.edu/library/resources/journals.html.*

provide updates on member activities. Many of the articles are written by practicing attorneys and discuss timely legal issues. The William S. Hein Company carries a microform version of the back issues of several California bar journals.

   📖 *California Bar Journal,* 1994–. Monthly. Published in a newspaper format, the *California Bar Journal* replaces the State Bar Report, previously an insert of the *California Lawyer.* It serves as a current awareness tool for California attorneys. Attorney discipline records are also included.

   📖 *California Lawyer,* 1981–. Daily Journal Corporation. Monthly. Previously published as the *Journal of the State Bar of California* (1942–1971), and the *California State Bar Journal* (1972–1981), *California Lawyer* is a magazine providing articles and analysis of current legal events relevant to California attorneys.

Other local bar publications include the *Los Angeles Lawyer* 1978– (Los Angeles Bar Journal 1925–1977) *San Francisco Attorney* 1982–, *San Diego Lawyer* 1997–, (*Dicta* 1951–1997) and *Orange County Lawyer* 1988–.

California bar association journals may be found on LexisNexis (States Legal–U.S.>California>Law Reviews & Journals folder) and Westlaw in the TP-ALL database.

[4] Legal Newspapers

Legal newspapers contain information pertinent to a region's legal community. Published either daily or weekly, they reprint or summarize important cases, provide profiles of attorneys and judges, and give legal notices and law firm news.

   📄 *Los Angeles Daily Journal,* 1888–. Daily Journal Corporation. Includes the Daily Appellate Report (DAR), which reprints appellate and Supreme Court opinions. The paper is accompanied by two weekly supplements: Verdicts and Settlements and California Law Business. Online access is provided to subscribers at: *www.dailyjournal.com.* The LA Daily Journal is indexed by both *Legal Resource Index* and *Legaltrac.* A microfiche backfile is available from Library Microfilm, Inc. beginning in 1888.

   📄 *Metropolitan News-Enterprise (Met-News),* 1987–. Metropolitan News Company. Daily. This is another Los Angeles area newspaper. It competes directly with the *Los Angeles Daily Journal.* Includes the daily insert Slip Opinion Supplement (SOS), which reprints decisions from the California Supreme Court and Courts of Appeal. Selected articles from the previous six months appear on the paper's website at: *www.metnews.com.*

 The Recorder (San Francisco), 1877–. American Lawyer Media. Daily. The Recorder is the Bay Area's oldest legal newspaper. Library Microfilms, Inc. carries a microfilm backfile beginning with 1906. *The Recorder* is available on Lexis-Nexis in the CAL Library, RECRDER file, from January 1991, and on Westlaw in the RECORDER-SF database. Select portions of *The Recorder* are also available online through the subscription-based web news service Cal Law: *www.law.com/jsp/ca/index.jsp.*

 San Francisco Daily Journal, 1893–. Daily Journal Corporation. Includes the Daily Appellate Report (DAR), Verdicts and Settlements (weekly) and California Law Business (weekly). Online access available to subscribers at: *www.dailyjournal.com.*

 Cal Law at: *www.law.com/jsp/ca/index.jsp.* Cal Law is a subscription-based California news service providing legal news, court opinions, judicial profiles and links to a variety of services for lawyers. Subscribers to the print version of the Recorder are offered a discount on the online subscription.

Other legal newspapers include the *Daily Recorder*[11] (Sacramento) 1911–, and the *Orange County Reporter* 1921–, both published by the Daily Journal Corporation.

[5]   Newsletters

Law firms and specialized bar organizations publish newsletters with information for the specialist. Firms sometimes use these publications to let people know they concentrate in particular fields of law. Specialized bar organizations use the publications to keep members up-to-date on latest developments in the field. These publications are usually published monthly or quarterly and most do not carry outside advertising.

---

[11] The *Daily Recorder* has the same supplements and features as the *Los Angeles Daily Journal.* Library Microfilms, Inc. carries a microfilm version beginning in 1911.

Examples of newsletters are *New Matter: Offical Publication of the State Bar of California Intellectual Property Section; California International Law Section Newsletter; Business Law News: Official Publication of the Business Law Section—State Bar of California; CYLS Quarterly: California Young Lawyers Association; The California Business Law Reporter* (CEB); and the *California Tort Reporter* (West Group).

§ 10.05 Indexes to Legal Periodicals

[1] Overview

Although there are no current legal periodicals indexes specific to California, California law reviews, bar journals and legal newspapers are included in several national legal indexes. All of the indexes listed in [2] and [3], *below*, provide bibliographic (citation) information for articles as opposed to full text.

[2] Current Indexes

   Current Index to Legal Periodicals, 1968–. Weekly.

      Published by the University of Washington, this index serves as current awareness tool for academic law reviews. Issued on a weekly basis, it is not cumulative.

   Current Law Index, 1980–. Monthly.

      Published by The Gale Group, the CLI indexes over 875 law reviews, bar journals, legal newspapers and specialty legal publications. It appears monthly, with cumulative quarterly volumes which are bound in two print volumes per year. Subject, author, and title indexes are provided, along with tables of cases and statutes.

   Legal Resource Index, 1980–. LRI is the online version of the CLI. In addition to containing all the material indexed on CLI, it also includes more articles in legal newspapers. It is available on LexisNexis ("Legal Resource Index" source [LEXREF; LGLIND]), Westlaw (LRI), and on Dialog.

   Legaltrac, 1980–. *Legaltrac* is the name given to both the CD-ROM and web-based version of the LRI.

   Index to Legal Periodicals and Books, 1908–. Monthly.

      Published by the H.W. Wilson Company, ILP indexes over 800 law reviews, bar journals, and legal books. ILP was published in annual volumes from 1908–1925. Since 1981, it has been issued monthly and quarterly, and is bound annually. Since 1940 it has had a separate book review index. Since 1993, legal books have been included.

The ILP is also available in several electronic formats, including CD-ROM (WilsonDisc), on the Internet at *www.hwwilson.com* (WilsonWeb), on LexisNexis (LAWREV library; ILP file) and on Westlaw in the ILP database. The online version of ILP covers materials dating back to 1981 and indexes over five hundred legal periodicals and other printed documents. An Index to Legal Periodicals Retrospective, covering the years between 1918 and 1981, is scheduled to debut in the summer of 2004 and will be available at *www.hwwilson.com*.

Index to Periodical Articles Related to Law, 1958–.

This index includes articles about law in social science journals not covered in *Index to Legal Periodicals* or the *Current Law Index*. Volumes 1–4 cover 1958–1988. A fifth volume covers 1989–1993. Since 1993, it has been published quarterly and cumulated annually.

[3] Historical Indexes

All Cal Index to Law Reviews and Periodicals, 1963–1974. A subject index to California legal periodicals.

Index to California Legal Periodicals and Documents, 1964–1976.

Produced by the State Library in Sacramento, this index provides citations to articles in California law reviews, journals and other documents. A subject, author, case and statute index are provided.

Index to Legal Periodical Literature, 1887–1937. 6 vols. Compiled by L.A. Jones and F.E. Chapman, this index includes the early volumes of California bar journals and law reviews. Volume 1 includes legal citations prior to 1887. Both subject and author indexes are provided.

§ 10.06   Full-Text Legal Periodical Database

Full-text legal periodicals are available through the following databases:

HeinOnline. William S. Hein & Co., Inc. *www.heinonline.org.* HeinOnline is a web-based subscription service database offering full-text coverage of selected law reviews, some dating back to the early part of the twentieth century. The database offers both full-text and field-restricted searching. The articles appear in pdf format, providing an exact replica of the original journal.

Index to Legal Periodicals Full Text. H.W Wilson Company. *www.hwwilson.com.* Provides the full text of over two hundred legal periodicals dating back to the early 1990s.

LexisNexis (LAWREV library, ALLREV file), and Westlaw (JLR or CA-JLR database) also provide the full text of legal journals back to the early 1980s.

§ 10.07 Citators

Citators serve two major purposes. The first is to determine if a judicial decision is still good law, that is, to see whether a subsequent case has overruled a prior one. Citators are also used to find other legal materials, including both primary and secondary sources, which have cited a particular case or statute. For a review of citators in print, CD, and online, see § 6.08.

§ 10.08 Self Help Manuals

One of the most prolific publishers of law books for the lay person is California's Nolo Press. Nolo Press puts out a series of easy to read books on a variety of legal topics, including landlord-tenant law, estate planning, neighbor law, and employee rights. For a complete list of Nolo Press titles, see their website at: *www.nolo.com.*

§ 10.09 Reference Sources

> *California Style Manual: A Handbook of Legal Style for Courts and Lawyers,* 4th ed. 2000. West Group. Now in its fourth edition, the Style Manual governs the citation of legal documents in California appellate courts.

Chapter 11

Attorney General[1]

§ 11.01   Organization and History

The Attorney General is the chief law officer of the state and the head of the California Department of Justice. Some of the powers and duties of the office are listed in the California Constitution, article V, section 13. Among those duties are to see that the laws are uniformly and adequately enforced, to supervise district attorneys and sheriffs, to prosecute violations of the law, and to assist district attorneys in the discharge of their duties, when required by public interest or directed by the Governor. Other powers and duties are listed in Government Code section 12510 and following. "The California Department of Justice carries out the constitutional responsibilities of the Office of Attorney General . . . through 10 main divisions."[2] In addition to the legal work performed by the Civil, Criminal and Public Rights Divisions, the

---

[1] This chapter is revised and updated by Fay Henexson, Supervising Librarian I, California Attorney General's Office, San Diego.

[2] "About the Department of Justice," can be found at: *http://caag.state.ca.us/ag/aboutdoj.htm.*

Department carries out a number of law enforcement duties and tracks criminal statistics.

Edward J.C. Kewen became the first California Attorney General in 1849, just twelve days after arriving in the state. It was perhaps fitting that the young state chose an equally young candidate to become its first Attorney General: he was just 24 years old. [3] To date, 29 men (and no women) have served as Attorney General. Over its 150-year history, the Department has evolved to meet the changing needs of California's citizens. "Gradually, through the protection of state lands and resources, through monitoring corporate practices, by asserting the rights of the people against discrimination, and by assuming leadership as the state's central law enforcement authority, the Attorney General has grown to play a critical and, like the Constitution, an enduring role in the life of California." [4]

§ 11.02   Publications

[1]   Reports

Biennial reports to the Governor are required by Government Code section 12522. The title of the report has varied slightly over the years. From the 1850's through 1940's it was *Report of the Attorney General of the State of California*. The current title is *Biennial report*. Publication has been somewhat irregular: during some years, most recently 1993/94–1997/98, no report was issued.

📖 California. Attorney General's Office. *Biennial report*. Sacramento. [The Department]

💻 California. Attorney General's Office. *Report of the Attorney General of the State of California*. Trans-Media Publishing has 35mm microfilm copies of Reports as part of their multi-reel set of A.G. opinions and reports. Their coverage is from 1852 to 1958.

[2]   Opinions

[a]   Statutory Authority and Treatment

Government Code section 12519 covers the responsibility to write opinions. That section states:

---

[3] California. Dept. of Justice. *A History of the California Attorney General's Office.* [Sacramento, 1988?], p.13.

[4] "History of Attorney General," *caag.state.ca.us/ag/history.htm*.

The Attorney General shall give his or her opinion in writing to any Member of the Legislature, the Governor, Lieutenant Governor, Secretary of State, Controller, Treasurer, State Lands Commission, Superintendent of Public Instruction, Insurance Commissioner, any state agency, and any county counsel, district attorney, or sheriff when requested, upon any question of law relating to their respective offices.

The Attorney General shall give his or her opinion in writing to a city prosecuting attorney when requested, upon any question of law relating to criminal matters.

This code section was added by Stats 1945, ch 111, section 3., and amended by Stats 1980, ch 258, section 1, and by Stats.2001, c. 76 (S.B.99), section 1.

Opinions of the Attorney General are not primary authority since they are of an advisory nature only. However, they may be persuasive in the absence of primary authority, and are entitled to great respect and great weight.[5] In California the opinions of the Attorney General which have stood for some time have credence because the Legislature is presumed to know of the opinions, could have changed the law, but did not do so.[6]

Opinions are numbered as they are assigned to be drafted, with a five or six digit number indicating the year and month assigned, and the order in which the opinion was assigned. For example, opinion number 93-208 stands for the 8th opinion assigned in February of 1993. Once published, opinions are also given a citation consisting simply of volume and page number.

[b] Print Sources

📖 *Opinions of the Attorney General of California.* v.1– _____. Jan./June 1943–present. Various publishers over time. Currently published by Matthew Bender & Company, Inc., a member of the LexisNexis Group. The current subscription may be for either bound volumes only or bound volumes with

---

[5] *Phyle v. Duffy,* 334 U.S. 431 (1948); *Moore v. Panish,* 32 Cal.3d 535, 652 P.2d 32 (Cal. 1982); *Smith v. Municipal Court of Glendale Judicial Dist., Los Angeles County,* 167 Cal.App.2d 534, 334 P.2d 931 (Ct.App. 1959); *People v. Berry,* 147 Cal.App.2d 33, 304 P.2d 818 (Ct.App. 1956); *People v. Shearer,* 30 Cal. 645 (Cal. 1866).

[6] *Napa Valley Educators' Assn. v. Napa Valley Unified School Dist.* (1987) 194 Cal.App.3d 243, 251, 239 Cal.Rptr. 395; *Meyer v. Board of Trustees* (1961) 195 Cal.App.2d 420, 431–432, 15 Cal.Rptr. 717.

monthly advance sheets. Prior to 1943, the opinions were not published. Opinions were sent to the person requesting the information and a few copies were made for internal use. These unpublished, mimeographed opinions, if not confidential in character, might sometimes be obtained from the Attorney General's Library. This system proved to be unworkable, and the department adopted the system of publishing the opinions that exists today.

Each bound volume contains a roster of the office, including the Attorney General, Assistant Attorneys General, and Deputy Attorneys General. Also included are a table of contents; the text of the opinions; a numerical table of published opinions for the year; a table of opinions cited; a table of statutes; and an index for the year. Each monthly advance sheet includes a list of opinions currently pending.

The bound opinion set also includes several index volumes: a Thirty Year Index and Tables covering 1943–1972, a ten-year index covering 1973–1982, and another ten-year index which is printed in the back of v. 75 (1992). The index volumes include a subject index, and tables of codes and laws cited. Since 1993 the subject index is cumulative in each successive volume.

📖 *Opinions of the Attorney General of California.* Numerical set antedating the published set described above. Consists of typewritten opinions bound by the Attorney General's Library.

[c] CD-ROM and Online Sources

💿 *Opinions of the Attorney General of California.* Matthew Bender & Company, Inc., a member of the LexisNexis Group. This product contains opinions from 1991 through the present. Also available as part of Bender's "California Library" CD-ROM product.

💿 *Opinions of the Attorney General of California.* In West CD-ROM Libraries. West California Reporter CD set. Disc 3: AG Opinions 1977 date. This three CD set includes West's California Reporter (including earlier cases from the Pacific Reporter) and Attorney General Opinions. They are accessible by using Premise search software.

💻 *Opinions of the Attorney General of California.* LexisNexis. Available through *lexis.com®*, the "CA Attorney General

Opinions" Source (STATES; CAAG) contains Attorney General Opinions from 1977. The coverage is current and includes all new documents as they are released by the state.

Opinions of the Attorney General of California. Westlaw. Opinions of the Attorney General are in the CA-AG database beginning in 1977. The coverage is current and includes all new documents as they are released by the state. Researchers should use the Scope command to get instructions and tips for the use of the database.

Opinions of the Attorney General of California. Opinions from 1986–present are posted on the AG's web page at: *http://caag.state.ca.us/opinions/index.htm.* These opinions are accessible by keyword search or citation. For 1997 through the present, opinions may also be located by browsing the annual summaries. This portion of the website also provides access to the monthly report, which includes the current month's opinions and opinion requests, and a list of pending opinions.

[d] Microforms

Opinions of the Attorney General of California. Buffalo, NY: William S. Hein. Fiche set offered in conjunction with Trans-Media's film. William S. Hein & Company has a 24x microfiche copy of the Opinions from 1943 through the latest bound volume. They can also supply the Trans-Media microfilm version noted below.

Opinions of the Attorney General of California. Trans-Media Publishing Company publishes a 35mm microfilm copy of the unpublished opinions from 1899 through 1943, when volume one of the current series began.

Opinions of the Attorney General of California. Chronological microfilm edition, reels 1-42, January 1899–January 27, 1943. New York, Recordak, 1955. Some libraries may still have this Recordak set of the unpublished opinions. It is difficult to use because it is not numerically arranged.

[e] Opinion Summaries

The best source for summaries of recent opinions is the AG's website at: *http://caag.state.ca.us/opinions/index.htm.* At the "Attorney General

Legal Opinions" page, click "Monthly Opinion Report" to see a summary of the past month's opinions with links to full text. The "Yearly Index" will link not to an index but to a year-by-year summary of opinions from 1997 to present.

[f] Opinion Citators

Citations to Attorney General Opinions can be found using *Shepard's California Citations. Cases.* The cases volumes, the CD-ROM version, and *Shepard's* on LexisNexis all include Opinions of the Attorney General of California. Features on *lexis.com*® include Shepard's Signals (negative treatment, possible negative treatment, positive treatment, cited and neutral analysis, cited information available), table of authorities, and custom restrictions. Links to point pages of cited cases.

Westlaw's *KeyCite* does not include AG opinions in its citator services. However, researchers can use the opinion numbers or citations as search terms in any database to find out if the opinion has been cited. The numbers may also be used in the AG database to see if the opinion has been altered in some way or overruled by a subsequent opinion.

[3] Other Publications

The Department of Justice publishes a variety of special reports on criminal statistics, crime prevention, civil rights, open meeting laws and consumer protection. Most of the current publications are available on the website—*http://caag.state.ca.us/publications/index.htm.* This site also has a list of other publications that aren't available on line but may be obtained upon request.

§ 11.03 Website

The California Attorney General's website is *http://caag.state.ca.us/.* The site includes:

- Information about the office of the AG, including history, mission statement and description of the ten divisions within the Department of Justice

- Information about programs and services: Consumer protection; Crime and violence prevention; Criminal justice; Crime statistics; Firearms; Government; Legal (AG) opinions; Online registration service (for charities, sellers of travel, and others who must register with the state); and Social justice

- Publications (links to online documents, and information about ordering hard copy materials)
- News releases and special alerts
- Contact and employment information
- Links to other California agency websites
- Site search

§ 11.04 Bibliography

📖 Ashby, Alan. "Evolution of A.G.'s Office Marked by Speedier Opinions." *Los Angeles Daily Journal.* January 28, 1981. p. 1.

📖 California. Dept. of Justice. *A history of the California Attorney General's office.* [Sacramento; 1988?]

📖 Kerr, Jennifer. "Ask the attorney general: they aren't binding, but AG opinions generally carry a lot of weight." *California Lawyer.* (January 1986, p. 47)

📖 Mosk, Stanley. "Extemporaneous reflections of a working Attorney General." 1 *Santa Clara Lawyer* 8. (Spring 1961)

📖 O Brien, Charles A. "The Role of the Attorney General As a Public Lawyer." 44 *Los Angeles Bar Bulletin* 495 (September 1969)

Chapter 12

State Bar of California[1]

§ 12.01   Constitutional Authority

California Constitution, Article 6, section 9 establishes the California State Bar as a public corporation. The State Bar both regulates California attorneys and represents their interests.[2]

---

[1] This chapter is written by Laura A. Cadra, Reference Librarian, Hugh & Hazel Darling Law Library, UCLA School of Law and Erin Murphy, Reference Librarian, Law Library, UC Davis School of Law. The authors wish to thank Myra Saunders, Associate Dean and Law Librarian, UCLA School of Law, for reviewing a draft of this chapter and offering helpful suggestions.

[2] See Harriet Katz, *What is the State Bar–A Platypus?* 52 *California State Bar Journal* 432 (September/October 1977).

§ 12.02 History of the California State Bar[3]

The first California State Bar Association was organized in July 1889 in San Francisco. At the first annual meeting in January 1890, membership of over 250 lawyers was reported. Enthusiasm seems to have waned, however, as there is no record that the second annual meeting was ever held. A second California State Bar Association was organized in 1901. Due to the inactivity of this second California State Bar Association, a San Francisco lawyer established the Lawyers' Club of California in 1904. Permanent committees were established and branch clubs were organized in forty-eight counties. In 1905, these two organizations merged under the California State Bar Association name. Unfortunately, the 1906 San Francisco earthquake and subsequent fire caused the Association to cease operations.

On November 10, 1909, the precursor to the present California State Bar Association was organized, again in San Francisco. Sixty-eight delegates from twenty-seven counties were present at the organizing meeting. A constitution and bylaws were adopted and it was reported that the assets and charter of the 1901 California State Bar Association would be tendered to the new Association. Annual conventions were held beginning in 1910.

The self-governing bar movement[4] was first discussed in California at the 1917 Annual Convention held in Santa Barbara when Jeremiah Sullivan, President of the Bar Association of San Francisco, asked Frank H. Short, President of the California Bar Association, to "devise some scheme that will establish a legal status for the California Bar Association."[5] Fred Lindley, reporter for the Committee on Constituent Associations, approved of the goal of "getting legislatures to recognize the State Bar Association . . . and compel all attorneys in the State to become

---

[3] This summary is taken from the following two sources which offer very detailed descriptions of the development of the State Bar: Andrew Younger Wood, State Bar Organization in California, published in *Historical and Contemporary Review of the Bench and Bar in California* (San Francisco: Recorder Printing and Publishing Co., 1926) pages 41–69 and Introduction, 1 *State Bar of California Proceedings* xiii (1928).

[4] For information on the self-governing bar movement, see Joseph J. Webb, "The Self Governing Bar Movement in America, published in *Historical and Contemporary Review of the Bench and Bar in California, supra* at pages 82–85.

[5] California Bar Association, *Proceedings of the 8th Annual Convention* (San Francisco: The Recorder, 1917) at 205.

members"[6] but felt the goal would only come true with "a lot of work and several years of long, tedious labor."[7] He was right.

In 1921, the San Francisco Bar Association prepared an integrated bar bill based on a Model Bar Incorporation Act published in the *Journal of the American Judicature*.[8] The bill[9] was introduced in the 1921 Legislature by Assemblyman Albert A. Rosenshine, but died in the Judiciary Committee.[10] The California State Bar appointed special committees to investigate the need for an inclusive bar with disciplinary powers and in 1923 a report calling for the creation of an integrated bar was passed unanimously at the State Bar Convention. Legislation to create a public corporation known as the State Bar of California was passed in 1925 but Governor Friend Wm. Richardson failed to sign it.

A bill creating a State Bar was introduced again in the 1927 legislative session.[11] This bill passed the Legislature on March 16, 1927 and was signed by Governor C.C. Young on March 31, 1927.[12] The State Bar Act became effective on July 29, 1927, and a full Board of Governors was elected at the first organizational meeting of the new State Bar on November 18, 1927.[13] As of that date, 9,602 members of the bar had registered with the new Bar Association.[14]

Though not the first state to establish an integrated Bar, California was the first large state to do so.[15] The State Bar Act is now codified in the Business & Professions Code.[16]

---

[6] *Id.* at 205–206.

[7] *Id.* at 206.

[8] Bar Organization Act. 4 *Journal of the American Judicature Society* 111 (1920).

[9] Assembly Bill No. 894.

[10] Introduction, 1 State Bar of California Proceedings, supra, at xv.

[11] Senate Bill No. 9.

[12] Stats. 1927, ch. 34.

[13] See, California Has Integrated Bar, 12 *Journal of the American Judicature Society* 13 (June 1928).

[14] Introduction, 1 State Bar of California Proceedings, supra, at xviii.

[15] Dayton David McKean, *The Integrated Bar* (Boston: Houghton Mifflin, 1963) at 46.

[16] Bus. & Prof. Code, § 6000 et seq.

§ 12.03   Organization

[1]   Governance

A twenty-three member Board of Governors including a President elected by the Board governs the State Bar.[17] There are sixteen attorney members and six public members. Fifteen of the attorney members are elected for three-year terms by active members of the Bar in good standing.[18] Any active member of the State Bar who maintains his or her principal office for the practice of law within the State Bar district in which there is a vacancy is eligible to run for a seat on the board. The remaining attorney member is appointed by the Board of Directors of the California Young Lawyers Association and serves a one-year term. The six non-attorney members of the Board represent the general public and serve three-year terms. Four of these members are appointed by the Governor of the State of California subject to the confirmation of the Senate. The Senate Committee on Rules and the Speaker of the Assembly each appoint one member. The Board of Governors meets approximately eight times a year to debate organizational, policy and professional issues.

[2]   Sections

Sections are voluntary organizations comprised of attorneys who share a particular interest. Some sections allow non-attorneys and students to join them. There are currently sixteen sections of the Bar.[19] Supported by annual fees, typical section activities may include publishing a newsletter, conducting educational programs, and advising the Board of Governors on pending legislation. The Sections also participate in the Annual Meeting and host the Section Education Institute.

The current State Bar sections are:

Antitrust and Unfair Competition Law
Business Law

---

[17] Bus. & Prof. Code, § 6010 et seq.

[18] Rules and Regulations of the State Bar of California, Art. IIB § 5. For election purposes, the 58 counties in California are divided into nine districts with each district represented by at least 1 Board member. District 7, Los Angeles County, has five members. District 3, which includes Contra Costa, Alameda, Santa Clara, and San Mateo counties, has two as does District 4 which combines San Francisco and Marin counties. These districts are adjusted every ten years in order to maintain an equitable distribution of attorney members to governors.

[19] Information on the sections may be found at: *www.calbar.ca.gov.*

Criminal Law
Environmental Law
Family Law
Intellectual Property Law
International Law
Labor and Employment Law
Law Practice Management and Technology
Litigation
Public Law
Real Property Law
Solo and Small Firm
Taxation
Trusts and Estates
Workers' Compensation Law

[3] Offices and Website

The main office of the State Bar is located in San Francisco with an additional office in Los Angeles. The addresses and phone numbers are:

Sacramento
1201 K Street
Suite 720
Sacramento, CA 95814
916-442-8018

San Francisco
180 Howard Street
San Francisco, CA 94105-1639
415-538-2000

Los Angeles
1149 South Hill Street
Los Angeles, CA 90015-2299
213-765-1000

The State Bar's website provides a wealth of information including member records and information on how to file a complaint against an attorney. The url address is: *www.calbar.ca.gov*.

[4] Funding Crisis in Late 1990s

The State Bar experienced a debilitating blow in 1997 when California Governor Pete Wilson vetoed legislation that was necessary to maintain the Bar's authority to collect membership fees.[20] This reduced the annual fee from $478 to $77. As a result of Governor Wilson's action, the Bar laid off most of its employees, closed the toll-free complaint hotline, and no longer investigated written complaints filed against attorneys. The California Supreme Court, prompted by a request to intervene from the Bar and concerned about the breakdown in the discipline process, issued an order in December 1998 authorizing a $175 increase in dues.[21] This increase was to be allocated strictly to support the discipline system of the Bar. The Bar reopened on March 1, 1999 at approximately 65% of the pre-layoff levels. Later that year, the Legislature passed and Governor Gray Davis signed legislation which raised the annual dues to $395.[22] Members have the option of reducing this amount by $5 if they do not want to fund lobbying and legislative activities of the Bar. Members also have the additional choice to reduce the fee by $5 if they do not want to fund programs the Bar conducts to reduce bias. Reduced fee scaling is available based on individual annual earned income.

§ 12.04 Functions and Activities of the California State Bar

[1] Admission to Practice of Law

California has an integrated (unified) Bar Association.[23] In order to practice law in California, attorneys must be active members of the California State Bar.[24]

Admission to the practice of law in California is authorized by the California Supreme Court[25] which has delegated the responsibility for establishing and administering qualifications for admission to the State Bar Examining Committee.[26] The general requirements for admission to the practice of law in California are found in Business & Professions

---

[20] S.B. 1145 (Ca. 1997).

[21] *In re Attorney Discipline System*, 19 Cal.4th 582, 79 Cal. Rptr.2d 836, 967 P.2d 49 (1998).

[22] Stats. 1999, ch. 342.

[23] Some states do not require that attorneys be members of the state bar association. For instance, in Indiana, four out of five attorneys belong to the Indiana State Bar Association (*www.inbar.org*).

[24] Bus. & Prof. Code, § 6125.

[25] Bus. & Prof. Code, § 6064.

[26] Bus. & Prof. Code, § 6046 et seq.

Code section 6060 (for general applicants) and in Business & Professions Code section 6062 (for applicants who are licensed to practice law in other states). These requirements are summarized on the State Bar website as follows:[27]

- Complete the necessary general education;
- Register with the Committee of Bar Examiners as a law student or attorney applicant;
- Complete the requisite legal education;
- File an application to take the First-Year Law Students' Examination and pass, or establish exemption from the examination;
- File an application for a moral character determination and receive a positive moral character determination from the Committee of Bar Examiners;
- File an application to take the bar examination and after eligibility has been confirmed, take and pass the examination;
- File an application, take and pass the Multistate Professional Responsibility Examination with a scaled score of 79.00 or greater, which examination is administered and graded by the National Conference of Bar Examiners;
- Be in compliance with California court ordered child or family support obligations.

The three-day California Bar Examination is administered twice a year, in February and July. The Bar Examination is composed of three parts: six essay questions, two performance test questions, and the Multistate Bar Examination.[28] The application to take the Bar Examination can be found on the State Bar website.[29] The California State Bar publishes old examination questions as *Essay Questions and Selected Answers from the California Bar Examination*. Study aids are also available at the State Bar website.

---

[27] *See* About the Bar at: *www.calbar.ca.gov.*

[28] The essay questions are designed to measure the ability to analyze legal issues arising from fact situations. The performance test questions are designed to test the ability to apply legal authorities to fact situations. The Multistate Bar Examination (MBE) is developed by the National Conference of Bar Examiners and consists of 200 questions in six subjects: constitutional law, contracts, criminal law, evidence, real property, and torts. For information, see About the Bar at: *www.calbar.ca.gov.*

[29] *www.calbar.ca.gov.*

Bar Examination pass lists are printed by the California legal newspapers upon release by the State Bar. The pass list from the most recent Bar Examination is available at the State Bar website. Statistics for Bar Examinations from February 1997 forward are also available at the website.

Attorneys who are licensed to practice in other states may elect to take the two-day Attorneys' exam if they have been of active status in good standing for the previous four years.[30] Attorneys who are admitted to practice law in jurisdictions outside of the United States must take the three-day Bar Examination.

Recognizing that the practice of law has changed and that the practice of many attorneys crosses geographic boundaries, the California Supreme Court formed the Multijurisdictional Practice Implementation Committee. On April 8, 2004, the Court announced that it had adopted the Committee's recommendations:

> For in-house and legal services counsel, the court adopted the Committee's recommendation that a registration system be established that will permit attorneys in these two categories, once registered, to practice in California to the extent specified in each rule. For litigation attorneys in California in contemplation of litigation, and non-litigation attorneys temporarily in California, the court adopted the Committee's recommendations to create "safe harbors" defining when and to what extent attorneys in these categories who are not licensed to practice in California may provide legal services in California without engaging in the unauthorized practice of law.[31]

The new rules, 964 through 967, become effective November 15, 2004.[32] In early 2005, the court will appoint a committee to monitor the effect of the rules and any other developments in multijurisdictional practice nationwide.

[2] Membership

Members of the California State Bar are divided into two classes: active members and inactive members.[33] Only active members are entitled to practice law.

---

[30] For exam information, see Attorney Applicants under "About the Bar" at www.calbar.ca.gov

[31] *www.courtinfo.ca.gov/presscenter/newsreleases/NR19-04.HTM.*

[32] For text of the rules and the Implementation Committee's Final Report, see *www.courtinfo.ca.gov/reference/documents/mjpfinalrept.pdf.*

[33] Bus. & Prof. Code, § 6003 et seq.

The California Constitution, Article 6, section 9, exempts judges from membership in the State Bar.

California has one of the largest state bars in the United States. As of March 2004, there are over 145,000 active members and over 195,000 total members. Membership statistics (total membership, active members, inactive members, and judges) are published each month on Page 3 of the *California Bar Journal* as well as on the State Bar's website.

[3]   Legal Specialization[34]

California attorneys may become "certified" specialists in the following eight areas:

> Appellate Law
> Immigration and Nationality Law
> Criminal Law
> Personal and Small Business Bankruptcy Law
> Estate Planning, Trust, and Probate Law
> Taxation Law
> Family Law
> Workers' Compensation Law

Attorneys are certified either by the State Bar Board of Legal Specialization or by an organization whose certification program has been accredited by the State Bar. Certification requires a written examination in the specialty field, a demonstrated high level of experience in the specialty field, ongoing education requirements, and favorable evaluation by attorneys and judges.

The written examination is given every other year in odd-numbered years. Registration forms and past exams as well as specific requirements for each specialty can be accessed at the Board of Legal Specialization website.

The State Bar Board of Legal Specialization maintains an online directory of certified specialists at www.californiaspecialist.org/. Members of the public can search for a certified specialist by specialty or by location. The State Bar member records online database also indicates whether an individual attorney has been certified as a specialist.

---

[34] See the State Bar of California Board of Legal Specialization website at: *www.californiaspecialist.org/index.htm.*

[4] Attorney Discipline

In order to protect California consumers and maintain high professional standards, the California State Bar maintains an attorney discipline system.[35] The discipline system investigates complaints against attorneys and assists consumers in dealing with attorney-client problems which do not rise to the level of complaint such as fee arbitration. In addition, the State Bar Ethics Hotline responds to State Bar member inquiries. See Chapter 13, Legal Ethics and Attorney Discipline.

[5] Legal Education and Professional Competence

Active members of the California State Bar are required to engage in continuing legal education.[36] The State Bar certifies continuing education providers, monitors attorney compliance with education requirements, and directly offers legal education programs. See Chapter 16, Legal Education.

[6] Consumer Services

The State Bar publishes a number of consumer pamphlets and makes them available on their website.[37] The State Bar website also provides a list of certified lawyer referral services.

§ 12.05 Publications

[1] Website

The State Bar's website, *www.calbar.ca.gov*, includes links to full-text publications including the *California Bar Journal*, ethics opinions, and Publication 250, a compilation of selected legal provisions relating to the practice of law in California. The website also includes a number of pamphlets written for consumers of legal services such as "Seniors & the Law" and "Kids & the Law."

[2] Bar Journal

This publication has undergone several title changes since it began publication in 1926.

---

[35] California Business & Professions Code § 6075 et seq.

[36] Bus. & Prof. Code, § 6070 et seq.

[37] See the website at: *www.calbar.ca.gov*.

1926–Feb. 1942:	*The State Bar Journal of the State Bar of California.* San Francisco: State Bar of California.
March/April 1942–1971:	*Journal of the State Bar of California.* San Francisco: The Bar.
1972–Aug. 1981:	*California State Bar Journal.* Los Angeles: State Bar of California.
Sept. 1981–Sept. 1988:	*California Lawyer.* Published by the State Bar until 1988 when the Daily Journal Corporation took it over completely (following a short period when the Bar and Daily Journal issued the magazine cooperatively). During this entire period it was the official State Bar publication.
Oct. 1988–1993:	No official bar publication but the *California Lawyer* included a regular section or "Report" on the Bar's activities. From 1994 to the present, the publication still includes a disciplinary report in each monthly issue.
1994–Present:	*California Bar Journal.* San Francisco: State Bar of California.

[3]   Section Publications

Each section publishes one or more publications for its members. For many of these, a table of contents may appear on the section's web page but the full text is available to members only either in print by subscription or through a password-protected area on the web page.

[4]   Member Directories

Information on a particular attorney may be found in the Attorney Search portion of the State Bar website, *www.calbar.ca.gov.* Members are designated active, inactive, not entitled to practice, resigned or disbarred. Basic data available on this site includes address, telephone number, e-mail address, date admitted to practice, and the law school and undergraduate institutions the member attended. There are several private companies who publish annual directories of attorneys.[38]

---

[38] Two of the better known are *California Lawyers,* published semi-annually by The Daily Journal Corporation, and *Parker Directory of California Attorneys,* published

[5] Reports

The annual "Discipline Report" is an overview of all of the activities of the Bar during a particular year. In addition to information on the number of discipline actions, there is also a listing of legislative developments, an in-depth look at the economic status of the Bar, and a brief discussion of the educational programs conducted by the Bar. The Bar frequently produces specialty reports in response to requests from the California legislature. Most of these reports are available for free on the website.

§ 12.06 Local, Specialty, and Minority Bar Associations

California has a number of local, specialty and minority bar associations. Membership in these associations is voluntary. Benefits include group insurance rates, information on local judges, local bar publications, and networking with local attorneys.

The California State Bar Association has a complete listing of local, specialty, and minority bar associations at their website under Public Services.[39]

---

annually with a mid-year revision by Parker & Son Publications. See also Appendix L, which includes legal directories.

[39] Historical accounts of local California bar associations include:

Graves, Jackson A. *Reminiscences of the Early Bar of Los Angeles.* Los Angeles: 1909.

Hallan-Gibson, Pamela. *The Bench and the Bar: A Centennial View of Orange County's Legal History.* Chatsworth, CA: Windsor Publications, 1989.

Hickson, Alonzo L. *A Short History of the Pomona Valley Bar.* Pomona, CA: 1955.

Johnson, Kenneth M. *The Bar Association of San Francisco: The First Years, 1872–1972.* San Francisco: Bar Association of San Francisco, 1972.

A Pictorial Directory of Attorneys Whose Principal Offices are in San Bernardino County, California and of the Judges of the County: Together with a History of the Bench and Bar of the County. San Bernardino: San Bernardino County Bar Association, 1975.

Robinson, William W. *Lawyers of Los Angeles: A History of the Los Angeles Bar Association and the of the Bar of Los Angeles County.* Los Angeles: Los Angeles Bar Association, 1959.

Stanford, Leland Ghent. *San Diego's LL.B.: Legal Lore & the Bar: A History of Law and Justice in San Diego County.* San Diego: San Diego County Bar Association, 1968.

Taylor, Charles W. *Bench and Bar of Alameda County.* Angwin, CA: Pacific Union College Press, 1953.

Chapter 13

Legal Ethics and Discipline[1]

§ 13.01   Attorney Ethics

[1]   California Rules of Professional Conduct

[a]   History

The Board of Governors of the Bar were given the power to "formulate and enforce rules of professional conduct" in 1927.[2] Rules can come

---

[1] This chapter is written by Erin Murphy, Reference Librarian, Law Library, UC Davis School of Law and Laura A. Cadra, Reference Librarian, Hugh & Hazel Darling Law Library, UCLA School of Law.

[2] Stats. 1927, ch. 34, § 1.

either from the Board itself or from members through an initiative process.[3] The California Supreme Court must approve any rules before they are binding.[4] The first rules were adopted in 1928 with major revisions effective in 1975 and again in 1989. Draft rule amendments can be found at the State Bar's website.

[b] Rules[5]

The Rules of Professional Conduct of the State Bar of California cover five general areas:

Rules 1-100–1-710: Professional Integrity in General
Rules 2-100–2-400: Relationship Among Members
Rules 3-110–3-700: Professional Relationship With Clients
Rules 4-100–4-400: Financial Relationship With Clients
Rules 5-100–5-320: Advocacy and Representation

Rule 1-100(A) outlines their purpose:

> The following rules are intended to regulate professional conduct of members of the State Bar through discipline. . . . These rules are not intended to create new civil causes of action. Nothing in these rules shall be deemed to create, augment, diminish, or eliminate any substantive legal duty of lawyers or the non-disciplinary consequences of violating such a duty.

[2] Additional Sources of Professional Standards Governing Lawyers

The State Bar Act,[6] under which authority the Board of Governors promulgates the Rules of Professional Conduct, is the main source for legislative standards governing members of the Bar. However, sprinkled throughout the California codes are various practice area-specific sections outlining additional duties and responsibilities.[7]

The Ethics Information area of the State Bar website includes the full-text of most of the rules and regulations governing the conduct of attorneys.

---

[3] Bus. & Prof. Code, § 6076.5.

[4] Bus. & Prof. Code, § 6077.

[5] Available in the California Court Rules found in *Deering's California Codes Annotated* and *West's Annotated California Codes*, on the California State Bar website at: *www.calbar.ca.gov.*, and *California Compendium on Professional Responsibility*.

[6] Bus. & Prof. Code, § 6000 et seq.

[7] The State Bar of California, *Publication 250: California Rules of Professional Conduct*.

[3] American Bar Association Model Rules of Professional Conduct

The ABA first adopted "Canons of Professional Ethics" in 1908.[8] Throughout the years, these standards went through several major revisions, producing the Model Rules of Professional Conduct in 1983. While the majority of the states have chosen to adopt the Rules in some form, California has only used them in an advisory capacity. They are included in *California Compendium on Professional Responsibility* as well as separately published in various ABA sources.[9]

[4] Ethics Opinions

Opinions are issued in response to specific requests from practicing attorneys. Although not binding, these opinions "should be consulted by members for guidance on proper professional conduct."[10] The State Bar of California has issued Formal Opinions since 1965. As the Bar's website explains, "These advisory opinions regarding the ethical propriety of hypothetical attorney conduct, although not binding, are often cited in the decisions of the Supreme Court, the State Bar Court Review Department, and the Court of Appeal."[11] All of the opinions can be found on the State Bar's website[12] as well as in the Bar-produced *California Compendium of Professional Responsibility*. Several of the larger county bar associations also issue opinions. The full-text of those from Los Angeles, San Diego, San Francisco, and Orange counties can be found in the *California Compendium of Professional Responsibility*. The Compendium also provides a detailed subject index which includes references to cases from the United States Supreme Court, Ninth Circuit Court of Appeals, District Courts within California, and all California appellate courts.

The ABA has issued opinions on ethical issues since 1922 when it authorized the Committee on Professional Ethics and Grievances to "express its opinions . . . concerning proper professional conduct with various modifications."[13] Per the Rules of Procedure of the Standing

---

[8] American Bar Association, House of Delegates. *Model Rules of Professional Conduct*, 2001, Preface.

[9] Id and *ABA/BNA Lawyers' Manual on Professional Conduct*.

[10] California Rules of Professional Conduct, Rule 1-100(A).

[11] Website located at: *www.calbar.ca.gov*.

[12] *Id.*

[13] American Bar Association, Committee on Professional Ethics and Grievances, *Opinions of the Committee on Professional Ethics and Grievances*, 3 (1931).

Committee on Ethics and Professional Responsibility, *formal* opinions are those that are of general interest to members of the bar while all other opinions are *informal.*[14] The American Bar Association Journal has always reprinted the formal opinions in full text while summarizing the informal ones. Many informal opinions were published in digest form first in 1952 with the researcher needing to contact the Committee for the full text.[15] Since 1967, the Committee on Professional Ethics and its successors have published the complete text of published opinions in various sources.

Opinions of the Committee on Professional Ethics, 1967:	Formal: 1924–1965
Informal Ethics Opinions, vols. I and II, 1975:	Informal: 1961–1973
Formal & Informal Ethics Opinions, 1985:	Informal: 1974–1982
	Formal: 1967–1982
Formal & Informal Ethics Opinions, 2000:	Informal: 1983–1989
	Formal: 1983–1998
Recent Ethics Opinions, 1999–:	Formal & Informal: 1999–

From 1980 to the present, a private publisher, Bureau of National Affairs, has included the ABA Formal opinions as well as summaries of opinions issued by State Bar Associations in their multi-volume set *ABA/BNA Lawyers' Manual on Professional Conduct.* Since 1982, University Publications has published the *National Reporter on Legal Ethics and Professional Responsibility* which includes ABA Formal and Informal opinions as well as the full text of State Bar Associations' Informal and Formal opinions, federal and state court cases on attorney ethics, and a literature survey.

[5] State Bar Services for Attorneys

Since 1983, the California State Bar has offered an Ethics Hotline to California attorneys. This confidential research service helps California attorneys analyze their professional responsibilities by referring them to statutes, Rules of Professional Conduct, and ethics opinions. The Hotline can be reached at (800) 2-ETHICS or (415) 538-2150 on weekdays from 9:00 a.m. to 5:00 p.m. and is available to California lawyers only.

---

[14] Standing Committee on Ethics and Professional Responsibility, Rules of Procedure, reprinted in Center for Professional Responsibility, American Bar Association, *ABA Compendium of Professional Responsibility Rules and Standards* 498 (1999).

[15] American Bar Foundation, *Opinions of the Committee on Professional Ethics* 6, 1967.

The staff of the Ethics Hotline also publishes the *Ethics Hotliner*. Begun in 1992 as a bi-annual newsletter, the State Bar funding crisis forced a cessation after only four issues.[16] The *Ethics Hotliner* is now available on the State Bar website in the Ethics area. Although the case area is not kept current, articles on topics such as client relations as well as proposed changes to the Rules of Professional Conduct and survey data compiled from the Ethics Hotline are available.

The larger bar association within the state may also offer some guidance to attorneys with ethical questions. For example, the Los Angeles County Bar Association's Professional Responsibility and Ethics Committee provides help to members of that organization. Written questions are submitted to the committee, which responds either by private letter or by posting a formal question on the Committee's website: *www.lacba.org/opinions*.

The Ira Sherman Center for Ethical Awareness was originally founded as a joint project between the Los Angeles Daily Journal and the Pepperdine University School of Law. Today the service to attorneys is provided by Pepperdine Professor Gregory Ogden, who may be contacted at 310-506-4671.

§ 13.02   Attorney Discipline

[1]   Complaints Against Attorneys[17]

Consumers who believe their attorney has engaged in unethical conduct should make a complaint to the State Bar Office of Chief Trial Counsel's Intake Unit. Complaints may be registered via telephone[18] or letter but the complainant is usually asked to file a complaint form.[19] An inquiry is opened for every written complaint received. A State Bar attorney reviews each complaint and determines how the complaint will proceed. Many complaints do not rise to the level where investigation

---

[16] Volume 1, Number 1 was published in the Winter of 1992–1993. Volume 2, Number 2, published in the Spring of 1995, was the final printed edition. The State Bar has made some of the feature articles from the original four issues available full-text on their website at: *www.calbar.ca.gov*. Back issues are available for purchase from the State Bar.

[17] The State Bar website contains complete information on registering complaints against attorneys at: *www.calbar.ca.gov*.

[18] (800) 843-9053 (in California); (213) 765-1200 (outside California).

[19] Complaint forms are available on the State Bar's website under Public Services at: *www.calbar.ca.gov*.

or prosecution is warranted.[20] If the complaint indicates that an attorney's conduct only borders on a violation or was a minor breach, a warning letter or an admonition might be issued or an agreement in lieu of discipline may be reached. If the attorney is a repeat offender or has committed a violation likely to result in discipline, an investigator and a prosecutor from the Bar's Enforcement Unit will take over the investigation. The attorney has an opportunity to respond to the complaint and witnesses are contacted. At the end of the investigation, the complaint may be dismissed, an informal resolution might be imposed, or disciplinary charges might be filed.

[2] State Bar Court

For most of its history, the State Bar's disciplinary system operated through the use of volunteer referees who made recommendations to the Bar's Board of Governors.[21] The Board then made recommendations regarding the disciplinary action to be taken to the California Supreme Court. In 1988, the Legislature directed the establishment of the State Bar Court.[22] The State Bar Court acts as the arm of the California Supreme Court, which adjudicates all cases involving disciplinary proceedings brought against California attorneys.

Once the State Bar Enforcement Unit's investigation reveals that disciplinary charges should be filed, a Notice of Disciplinary Charges is filed in the State Bar Court. The attorney must file an answer to the charges. If a settlement is not reached, the case goes to trial.

The State Bar Court has two departments: a Hearing Department and a Review Department.[23] The Hearing Department is the trial level of the State Bar Court and has five hearing judges. At the hearing level, the attorney complained against has the right to counsel, to examine witnesses, and to introduce evidence on his or her own behalf.[24] The attorney can also exert the Constitutional right against self-incrimination.[25] The Review Department is the appellate department

---

[20] American Bar Association. *California: Report on the Lawyer Regulation System* (June 2001) at 13. California Business & Professions Code § 6043.5 makes it a misdemeanor to file a false or malicious complaint against an attorney.

[21] *In re Rose.* 22 Cal.4th 430, 93 Cal. Rptr.2d 298 (2000).

[22] Bus. & Prof. Code, § 6086.5.

[23] Bus. & Prof. Code, §§ 6079.1, 6086.65.

[24] Bus. & Prof. Code, § 6085.

[25] *Id.*

of the State Bar Court. It consists of the Presiding Judge of the State Bar Court and two Review Department judges, all of whom are appointed by the California Supreme Court. The Review Department conducts an independent review of the record of the Hearing Department and may make findings different than those of the hearing judge.[26] Appeal from the Review Department can be taken to the California Supreme Court. The California Supreme Court must approve a State Bar Court recommendation to disbar or suspend an attorney.[27]

The *State Bar Court Reporter* is the official publication for the opinions of the Review Department. It contains the full-text of the opinions, case summaries, and an index. The decisions of the State Bar Court can also be found on LexisNexis and Westlaw in the California cases databases/folders.

[3] Criminal Activities

An attorney who is convicted of a felony or a misdemeanor involving moral turpitude is subject to suspension or disbarment.[28] To ensure that the Bar will be notified, the convicted attorney, the district attorney, and the court are all required to notify the Bar. The attorney is placed on interim suspension during the pendency of the disciplinary proceedings in the State Bar Court.

[4] Disciplinary Statistics

The annual *Report on the State Bar of California Discipline System* includes statistics on many aspects of the disciplinary system including the number of complaints and their disposition, the speed of complaint handling, and the number of backlogged cases.[29]

[5] Client Security Fund

The Client Security Fund was established in 1972 to reimburse clients who have lost money or property by dishonest acts of a California attorney acting in a professional capacity.[30] This fund is supported through annual Bar dues.

---

[26] California Rule of Court 951.5.

[27] Bus. & Prof. Code, § 6100.

[28] Bus. & Prof. Code, § 6101.

[29] Bus. & Prof. Code, § 6086.15.

[30] Bus. & Prof. Code, § 6140.5.

[6] Information on Disciplined Attorneys

State Bar investigations and inquiries are confidential until formal disciplinary charges are filed.[31]

Lists of disciplined attorneys appear each month in the *California Bar Journal* and in *California Lawyer*. Attorneys are identified by name, location, and Bar number. Listings of disbarred and suspended attorneys include a description of the wrongful conduct involved.

The State Bar Member Records Online database[32] includes a statement as to whether an attorney has a public record of discipline. No details as to why an attorney was disciplined are provided although information on obtaining the attorney's public record of discipline is given. The *California Bar Journal* is available full-text on the Bar's website, however, and industrious researchers can search by attorney name to find information on the disciplinary action.

Martin Dean's *Essential Attorneys* CD contains disciplinary information on every member of the California bar. This information is more detailed and comprehensive than that on the bar web page. It is updated twice a year in April and October and contains records going back to 1989.

§ 13.03 Judicial Ethics and Discipline

[1] History[33]

The first formal standards for judicial conduct in California were adopted by the Conference of California Judges[34] in 1949. These standards were a modified version of the original American Bar Association Canons of Judicial Ethics. In 1972, the ABA adopted a new Code of Judicial Conduct and in 1975, the California Judges Association[35]

---

[31] Bus. & Prof. Code, § 6086.1.

[32] *www.calbar.ca.gov.*

[33] For a detailed history of the development of California Judicial Ethics, see the Preface to the current *California Code of Judicial Ethics*.

[34] Now the California Judges Association. For a history of the California Judges Association, see Cameron Estelle Anderson, *The Story of the California Judges Association: The First Sixty Years*. San Francisco: California Judges Association, 1992.

[35] The California Judges Association is a voluntary professional organization for state court judges. It conducts educational workshops and reviews and sponsors legislation regarding the court system. Their offices are in Oakland, California.

again adopted a modified version of the new ABA Code. California amended this Code in 1986 to reflect gender-neutral language. A revised California Code of Judicial Conduct was adopted by the California Judges Association in 1992. Proposition 190[36] created a new Constitutional provision directing the Supreme Court to make rules for the conduct of judges both on and off the bench.[37] The Code of Judicial Ethics was formally adopted by the Supreme Court and became effective on January 15, 1996. The Code is amended periodically, most recently in June 2003.

[2] California Code of Judicial Ethics[38]

Recognizing that judges are central to American concepts of justice and the rule of law, the Code of Judicial Ethics establishes standards for the ethical conduct of judges both on and off the bench and for candidates for judicial office.[39] These standards are binding.

The Code consists of broad declarations called Canons and Commentary prepared by the Supreme Court Advisory Committee on Judicial Ethics. The six Canons are:

> Canon 1: A judge shall uphold the integrity and independence of the judiciary.
>
> Canon 2: A judge shall avoid impropriety and the appearance of impropriety in all of the judge's activities.
>
> Canon 3: A judge shall perform the duties of judicial office impartially and diligently.
>
> Canon 4: A judge shall so conduct the judge's quasi-judicial and extrajudicial activities as to minimize the risk of conflict with judicial obligations.
>
> Canon 5: A judge or judicial candidate shall refrain from inappropriate political activity.
>
> Canon 6: Compliance with the Code of Judicial Ethics.

---

36 Approved by the voters on November 8, 1994 and operative March 1, 1995.

37 Cal. Const. art. 6, § 18(m).

38 Available in the Appendix to the California Court Rules (West Annotated California Codes), on the California Commission on Judicial Performance website at: *cjp.ca.gov* and on the California Judicial Council's website at: *www.courtinfo.ca.gov*.

39 While judges are prohibited from practicing law, candidates are not. California Constitution, Art. 6, § 17.

[3]　Commission on Judicial Performance

The California Commission on Judicial Performance[40] was created as an independent state agency by voter referendum in the November 1960 election as part of a judicial administrative reform package. The Commission is charged with responsibility for investigating complaints against California judicial officers for judicial misconduct or wrongdoing and has the authority to discipline judges. The Commission is composed of eleven members: one justice of a court of appeal, two trial court judges, two members of the California State Bar, and six citizens who are not judges, retired judges, or members of the State Bar.[41]

The Commission is authorized to conduct proceedings against any active California judge and has some authority to discipline former judges and court commissioners and referees. The Commission investigates all complaints received for evidence of willful misconduct in office, failure or inability to perform the duties of office, habitual intemperance, conduct prejudicial to the administration of justice, or a permanent disability which seriously interferes with the performance of duties. The Commission is authorized to remove, retire, or censure a judge.[42]

Complaints to the Commission must be in writing but are not required to be on a particular form. All complaints are confidential. Information as to how to file a complaint is available on the Commission's website.

Names of judges who have been publicly disciplined along with the action taken are available on the Commission's website from 1960 to the present.[43] For recent years, the website includes detailed information about the behavior involved, the Canon violated, and actions taken.

The Commission also publishes an Annual Report which includes statistics on complaints received and investigated, case summaries, and information on the Commission staff and budget. The Annual Report is not currently available on the Commission's website but ordering information is available there.

The California Judges Association publishes the *California Judicial Conduct Handbook*, currently in its second edition. This handbook includes the California Code of Judicial Ethics and the Ethics Opinions

---

[40] *cjp.ca.gov.*

[41] Cal. Const. art. 6, § 8.

[42] *Id.*

[43] *cjp.ca.gov/pubdisc.htm.*

of the California Judges Association as well as advice on issues facing judges.

Chapter 14

Law Libraries[1]

§ 14.01   History and Development

Law libraries include academic law libraries, private law libraries (law firms and corporate), and government law libraries (state, county, and city). Many academic and government libraries are open to the public, especially if the library is a federal or state government document depository. California has a large number of all types of law libraries with excellent collections, staffs, and services. In fact, the Los Angeles County Law Library is one of the "seven largest law libraries in the United States."[2]

Rosamond Parma, in a presentation given at the Annual Meeting of the American Association of Law Libraries in 1925, noted that "the importance of law libraries was recognized at an early date by the [California] legislature.[3] In 1870, the legislature passed, "An act to provide for increasing the law library of the corporation known as the San Francisco Law Library, and to secure the use of the same to the

---

[1] This chapter is revised and updated by Jennifer Hill, Librarian, Keller Rohrback L.L.P., Seattle, WA.

[2] Gail H. Fruchtman, *The History of the Los Angeles County Law Library*, 84 Law. Lib. J. 687 (1992).

[3] Rosamond Parma, *Law Libraries in California, in Historical and Contemporary Review of Bench and Bar in California*, 86 (The Recorder Printing and Publishing Co. 1926).

(Pub. 64620)

Courts held at San Francisco, the Bar, the City and County Government, and the people of the City and County of San Francisco."[4] The preamble of this act stated:

> Whereas, In the great and rapidly increasing City of San Francisco, a large and more complete law library, which shall be conveniently located, and at all appropriate times be readily accessible to the various Courts, the bar, the municipal officers, and litigants, is essential to the orderly, speedy and correct administration of the city and county government, and more especially to the administration of justice therein; and whereas, in view of such want it is deemed important for the complete and perfect accomplishment of the public purposes for which the municipal government of the City and County of San Francisco is organized and maintained that a complete public law library should be established, and its use secured to the various Courts, the bar, the municipal authorities, and the citizens of San Francisco.[5]

Parma pointed out that even though "long before this there had been libraries established and legislation on the subject of libraries . . . this particular statute . . . perhaps shows the intent and purposes of the Legislature in the matter of the establishment of law libraries and their view as to their importance better than the earlier statutes."[6]

Today, the importance of law libraries in California is quite evident just by looking at the number of law libraries located in the state. Each of the state's fifty-eight counties has its own law library, thanks to a legislative act in 1891 that allowed for the establishment of county law libraries.[7] There are also over twenty-five law school libraries and numerous law firm and corporate law libraries.

§ 14.02 Resources for Law Library History

The history of California's government law libraries is well-documented in books, articles, and individual library websites. Some information about Southern California law schools is also available. It's difficult to find published information about California's private libraries. Below are some resources for California law library history:

---

[4] Stats. 1869–1870, ch. 173, at 235.

[5] *Id.* at 235–236.

[6] Parma, *supra* note 2.

[7] Stats. 1891, ch., at 430.

📖   Fruchtman, Gail. "The History of the Los Angeles County Law Library." 84(4) *Law Libr. J.* 687–705 (Fall 1992).

📖   Linneman, Mark A. "The California State (Law) Library at 150." *San Francisco Daily Journal*, May 18, 2000 at p. 18; June 15, 2000 at p. 18; and July 20, 2000 at p. 18. Also available at *nocall.org/dj000518.htm.*

📖   Parma, Rosamond. "Law Libraries in California." This is an article at page 86 in the book, *Historical and Contemporary Review of Bench and Bar in California.* San Franciso: The Recorder Pinting and Publishing Co., 1926. 132 p.

📖   Robinson, William W. *Lawyers of Los Angeles: A History of the Los Angeles Bar Association and of the Bar of Los Angeles County.* Los Angeles: Los Angeles Bar Association, 1959. Chapter 14, "Developing the Profession," covers the development of law libraries and law schools in Los Angeles. Pages 263–269 are devoted to the history of the Los Angeles County Law Library.

📖   Watson, Benjamin. "Origins of California's County Law Library System," 81(2) *Law. Libr. J.* 241–251 (Spring 1989).

💻   Bernard E. Witkin Alameda County Law Library. *History of the Alameda County Law Library* at: *www.co.alameda.ca.us/law/history.htm.*

💻   San Francisco Law Library. *History of the San Francisco County Law Library* at: *www.sfgov.org/site/sfll_page.asp?id=6493.*

💻   Victor Miceli Law Library. *History of the Riverside County Law Library* at: *www.co.riverside.ca.us/depts/lawlib/AboutUs.html#anchor140432.*

§ 14.03   Law Librarians

Law librarians are well-educated and highly trained professionals who provide valuable assistance with legal research. Most law librarians have masters degrees in library science and many, especially academic law librarians, also have law degrees. They are committed to service and continually update their skills by attending conferences and workshops and by reading professional literature. They also communicate with each other by telephone and through e-mail and listservs. Law librarians work together nationally and regionally so that they remain aware and up to date on national, state and local information. In California, there are three regional chapters of the American Association of Law Libraries:

- Northern California Association of Law Libraries (NOCALL) at: *www.nocall.org.*

- San Diego Area Law Libraries (SANDALL) at: *www.aallnet.org/chapter/sandall/.*

- Southern California Association of Law Libraries (SCALL) at: *www.aallnet.org/chapter/scall/.*

As more information becomes available electronically, law librarians strive to keep informed about the latest commercial legal databases and legal information on the web. They are excellent online searchers as they are experienced in determining the right search terms to use so that they perform economical and efficient research. They are also expert web searchers. They know the best search engines and the right search terms and, most importantly, know how to judge the authority and accuracy of web page content.

§ 14.04   Directories of Law Libraries and Law Librarians

    📖   *AALL Directory and Handbook.* Chicago: Published for the American Association of Law Libraries (AALL) by Commerce Clearing House, Inc. Annual. The American Association of Law Libraries is a national, professional organization for law libraries and law librarians. The 41st edition (2001–2002) is arranged so that the user may search for librarians alphabetically by last name. Libraries can be found geographically by state and then by city. There is also a locator section which allows the user to search for a library by its name to find the city in which it is located. The book also includes information about AALL, including its bylaws, procedures, and lists of committees and special interest sections. It also has a directory of minority law librarians. The Directory is available on the association's website. However, it is available to AALL members only at: *www.allnet.org.*

    📖   *NOCALL.* San Francisco: Northern California Association of Law Libraries (NOCALL). Annual. The Northern California Association of Law Libraries is a professional law library organization that focuses on law librarianship and law libraries in or north of Kern, San Bernardino, and San Luis Obispo counties in California. The directory has an alphabetical listing for individual members and an institutional/individual listing that is arranged by city. The organization's constitution and bylaws are also included.

Membership Directory. Southern California Association of Law Libraries. Los Angeles: Southern California Association of Law Libraries (SCALL). Annual. The Southern California Association of Law Libraries focuses on law libraries and law librarianship in Southern California from San Luis Obispo County to the Mexican border and to the east as far as the California, Arizona, and Nevada boundaries. The directory includes alphabetical listings of members by name and also by affiliation. The directory is also available online at the chapter's website at: *www.aallnet.org/chapter/scall.*

FindLaw California Law Libraries. This website includes California law school libraries, library associations, internet mailing lists, and public law libraries. Many of the law school library links also include links to the libraries' online catalogs. The list of mailing lists includes directions on how to subscribe to each list. The website is located at: *california.lp.findlaw.com/ ca05_law_libraries.*

SANDALL Membership Directory. San Diego: San Diego Area Law Libraries (SANDALL). Annual. The San Diego Area Law Libraries association is the newest regional chapter of AALL in California. The organization is open to anyone interested in law libraries or law librarianship. The directory is available online at the chapter's website at: *www.aallnet.org/ chapter/sandall/directory.html.*

§ 14.05   California Depository Libraries

[1]   State Depository Libraries

State depository libraries carry copies of many of the documents, including legal materials, published by the state printing office and various state agencies. According to the State Library:

> In 1945 the California Legislature, in order to make all state publications freely available, passed the Library Distribution Act (Government Code sections 14900–14912), and thereby established a system of complete and selective depository libraries. Each

depository has contracted with the Department of General Services to receive, record, shelve, and preserve state publications and to give free service to patrons wishing to use them.[8]

The State Library coordinates California's system of depository libraries and the State Library works with the State Printer to be sure that the proper government documents are supplied free of charge, under the contract, to each depository library. For more information on depository status, users should contact the Government Publications Section, California State Library, P.O. Box 942837, Sacramento, California, 94237-0001.

The California State Library publishes a monthly listing of many state publications in, *California State Publications: A Monthly Listing of Official California State Documents Received by the Government Publications Section California State Library*. Sacramento: Government Publications Section, California State Library. Monthly, with cumulative annual issue. Many of the publications listed are also available electronically and the website addresses are included within the publication listings. The State Library also makes state publications available online at: *www.library.ca.gov/CSP/index.cfm*. This web page includes publications from January 2001 to the present.

[2] Complete Depositories

Complete depository libraries are to be sent one copy of every state publication. Even so, it can sometimes be difficult to find state documents and so researchers may need to contact the State Library or look at the Library's website. Researchers may also need to contact a particular issuing agency. All of California's state agencies can be found on the state website, www.ca.gov. A list of California's complete depository libraries, which is included in Appendix B, is available from the California State Library.

The California State Library probably has the most complete collection of state publications. Researchers may need to check for them in the government publications section and also in the law library of the State Library. They are both housed in the same building at 914 Capitol Mall, Sacramento. The University of California at Berkeley and the Los Angeles Public Library also have extensive collections of state publications.

---

[8] Government Publications Section. California State Library. 55 *California State Publications* iv (2001).

[3] Selective Depositories

Selective depository libraries receive a single copy of publications from the State Printer and other publications on request from issuing agencies. A list of California's selective depository libraries, which is included in Appendix C, is available from the California State Library.

[4] Law Library Depositories

Libraries classified as law library depositories have retention requirements that differ from the other two categories. According to the State Library:

> Law library depositories must retain publications in accordance with Government Code section 14909 as administered by the State Library. Section 14909 stipulates that maintenance of basic general documents shall not be required of law library depositories but basic legal documents shall be maintained by them. Such basic legal documents shall include legislative bills, legislative committee hearings and reports, legislative journals, statutes, administrative reports, California Code of Regulations, annual reports of state agencies and other legal materials published by the state.[9]

A list of California's law library depositories, which is included in Appendix D, is available from the California State Library.

---

[9] *Id.* At viii.

Chapter 15

Electronic Legal Databases[1]

§ 15.01 Introduction

Much of the legal information that in the past could only be found in books can now also be found by using electronic legal databases. Electronic legal databases are available online and on CD-ROM. These databases can contain the equivalent of thousands of book volumes and sometimes a researcher can complete all of his or her research without ever opening a book.

§ 15.02 Early History

Today's electronic legal databases probably owe their existence to a project headed by Professor John Horty at the University of Pittsburgh in the 1960s.[2] Horty and a group of employees converted public health statutes of all the fifty states into digital format creating an electronic database.[3] Using this database, a researcher could enter search terms and a computer would scan the statutes and identify those that included

---

[1] This chapter was written by Jennifer Hill, Librarian, Keller Rohrback L.L.P., Seattle, WA.

[2] William G. Harrington, *A Brief History of Computer-Assisted Legal Research*, 77 Law Libr. J. 543, 544 (1984–1985).

[3] *Id.*

(Pub. 64620)

the search terms.[4] Eventually, United States Supreme court cases and Pennsylvania statutes were also added to show how the database could deal with larger files.[5] Horty eventually left the university and set up his own electronic legal research business called Aspen Systems.[6] Some other companies involved in the early years of electronic legal research included Data Retrieval Corporation with their SIRS (Statutory Information Retrieval System) program, IBM with their STAIRS (Storage and Information Retrieval System) program, FLITE (Federal Legal Information Through Electronics), JURIS (Justice Retrieval and Inquiry System), and a system called LEXIS.[7]

In 1966, a group of Ohio State Bar Association attorneys set out to define exactly what it was they wanted from a computerized legal research system that would eventually be developed.[8] The group "defined what it wanted as a nonindexed, full-text, online, interactive, computer-assisted legal research service."[9] They also decided that they wanted something that would search the full text of documents and not just the headnotes.[10] The group ended up meeting with the Data Corporation which wanted to show the group its (Data) Central database which was a "nonindexed, full-text, online, interactive system that had been developed . . . for the Air Force, to search huge files of procurement contracts."[11] The system met the group's needs and the two entities set out to create a computerized legal research system.

The system was produced and first marketed to Ohio law firms. A number of firms signed on as the first subscribers and the feedback was both positive and negative.[12] More work needed to be done to improve the system's performance, but money was becoming a problem.[13] Luckily, in 1969, the Mead Corporation acquired the Data Corporation and Mead committed to producing a better version of this system.[14]

---

[4] *Id.*

[5] *Id.*

[6] National Association of Attorneys General, Committee on the Office of Attorney General, *Computerized Research in the Law* 13 (The Association 1976).

[7] *Id.* at 13-22.

[8] Harrington, at 545.

[9] *Id.*

[10] *Id.* at 546.

[11] *Id.* at 547.

[12] *Id.* at 549.

[13] *Id.* at 550.

[14] *Id.*

Mead formed a new subsidiary called Mead Data Central (MDC) to work on the legal database.[15] In 1973, LEXIS was released and "introduced to the world."[16] The original database included Ohio law, some federal law, some cases, and some other state laws. In 1980, news and business information were included with the addition of NEXIS.[17]

In 1975, West Publishing Company introduced WESTLAW.[18] It started out with only West headnotes available for searching. In 1976 the company decided to create a more comprehensive database that would include the headnotes as well as judicial opinions and other West editorial content.[19] Soon after its introduction, West installed WESTLAW terminals in a few public law libraries around the country to see if the system would be suitable for use in public law libraries.[20] One of the law libraries that received one of these terminals was the Los Angeles County Law Library.[21] The terminals were available for public use at a charge of twenty-five dollars for one half hour and then one dollar per minute for additional usage.[22]

§ 15.03 LexisNexis and Westlaw

LexisNexis and Westlaw are the two major online legal information providers and have come a long way since their beginnings. Both of the databases are part of the core legal research curriculum in most American law schools and are continually increasing the amount of information they have available. They are also committed to creating more user-friendly interfaces which are much easier to use than in their early days. They are both also more accessible to the general public as they have added credit card access for users who do not subscribe, but who want to get a document or two. Both companies publish database directories in print and also on their websites. They also offer tutorials on using the features of the services through their special law school websites (these may require subscriber passwords).

---

[15] *Id.*

[16] *Id.* at 553.

[17] *Id.*

[18] *Id.*

[19] *Id.* at 553–554.

[20] In the early days, Westlaw had stand-alone terminals through which users could conduct only Westlaw searching.

[21] William T. Ford and Frank G. Houdek, *Automated Legal Research at the Los Angeles County Law Library*, 53 Los Angeles Bar Journal 46 (1977).

[22] *Id.* at 50.

- **LexisNexis**

LexisNexis is available on the web at: *www.lexisnexis.com.*

- *LexisNexis by Credit Card*—users can pay for a single document or subscribe for just a day, a few days, or a few weeks at: *web.lexis.com/xchange/ccsubs/cc_prods.asp.*

- *LexisNexis Directory of Online Services.* Dayton, OH: LexisNexis.

- *LexisNexis Searchable Directory of Online Sources*: *web.nexis.com/sources/*

- *LexisNexis Tutorials* (on LexisNexis for Law Schools): *www.lexisnexis.com/lawschool/resource/tutorials* (requires LexisNexis ID)

- **Westlaw**

Westlaw is available on the web at: *www.westlaw.com.*

- *Westlaw by Credit Card*—credit card access to Westlaw documents at: *creditcard.westlaw.com.*

- *Westlaw Database Directory.* Eagan, MN: West Group.

- *Westlaw Database Directory*—online at: *directory.westlaw.com/.*

- *West Instructional Aids Series* on *lawschool.westlaw.com* at:
  lawschool.westlaw.com/research/InstructionalAids.asp (these aids are geared to be used as teaching tools, but are also useful for independent learning).

§ 15.04   Internet Research

[1]   State Materials

In 1993, the California Legislature recognized that the Internet was a useful and cost effective tool that could be used to distribute legislative information. Assembly Bill 1624 states:

> The Legislature finds and declares that it is now possible and feasible in this electronic age to more widely distribute legislative information by way of electronic communication in order to better inform the public of the matters pending before the Legislature and its proceedings. The Legislature further finds that it is desirable to make information regarding these matters and proceedings available to the

citizens of this state, irrespective of where they reside, in a timely manner and for the least possible cost.[23]

Up until this point, legislative information had always been in print form requiring users to visit a library and then hope the items were on the shelves. Now users with Internet access can find this information without leaving their homes. In October 1993, the bill was chaptered into law and codified as Government Code section 10248.

(a) The Legislative Counsel shall, with the advice of the Assembly Committee on Rules and the Senate Committee on Rules, make all of the following information available to the public in electronic form:

(1) The legislative calendar, the schedule of legislative committee hearings, a list of matters pending on the floors of both houses of the Legislature, and a list of the committees of the Legislature and their members.

(2) The text of each bill introduced in each current legislative session, including each amended, enrolled, and chaptered form of each bill.

(3) The bill history of each bill introduced and amended in each current legislative session.

(4) The bill status of each bill introduced and amended in each current legislative session.

(5) All bill analyses prepared by legislative committees in connection with each bill in each current legislative session.

(6) All vote information concerning each bill in each current legislative session.

(7) Any veto message concerning a bill in each current legislative session.

(8) The California Codes.

(9) The California Constitution.

(10) All statutes enacted on or after January 1, 1993.

(b) The information identified in subdivision (a) shall be made available to the public by means of access by way of the largest nonproprietary, nonprofit cooperative public computer network. The information shall be made available in one or more formats and by one or more means in order to provide the greatest feasible access to the general public in this state. Any person who accesses the

---

[23] Stats. 1993, ch. 1235, § 1 (A.B. 1624).

information may access all or any part of the information. The information may also be made available by any other means of access that would facilitate public access to the information. The information that is maintained in the legislative information system that is operated and maintained by the Legislative Counsel shall be made available in the shortest feasible time after the information is available in the information system. The information that is not maintained in the information system shall be made available in the shortest feasible time after it is available to the Legislative Counsel.

(c) Any documentation that describes the electronic digital formats of the information identified in subdivision (a) and is available to the public shall be made available by means of access by way of the computer network specified in subdivision (b).

(d) Personal information concerning a person who accesses the information may be maintained only for the purpose of providing service to the person.

(e) No fee or other charge may be imposed by the Legislative Counsel as a condition of accessing the information that is accessible by way of the computer network specified in subdivision (b).

(f) The electronic public access provided by way of the computer network specified in subdivision (b) shall be in addition to other electronic or print distribution of the information.

(g) No action taken pursuant to this section shall be deemed to alter or relinquish any copyright or other proprietary interest or entitlement of the State of California relating to any of the information made available pursuant to this section.

History: Added Stats 1993 ch 1235 § 2 (AB 1624).

The state of California's website is designed to be used as a portal to other websites containing legal and non-legal information. The front page includes general links such as *Business*, *Government*, and *Travel and Transportation*. Behind those links are other links to resources such as California's agencies, legislative information, courts, and laws. It's also possible to use the website to make DMV appointments, check on the status of state tax refunds, make state park camping reservations, and much more. The site is even designed so that a user can personalize the page to include the user's favorite and most used links. The State of California website can be found at: *www.ca.gov*.

[2] Legal Portals

Internet portals are websites that have selected links which are organized in a way that will provide users with a "one stop shopping" way of searching the Internet. Legal portals are Internet portals that provide organized links to legal websites.

- **American Law Sources On-Line (ALSO!)**: *www.lawsource.com.*

  Includes local law sources and California law reviews online. ALSO!'s California page: *www.lawsource.com/also/usa.cgi?ca.*

- **FindLaw**: *www.findlaw.com.*

  Includes California cases and codes, legal forms, links to California legal associations, as well as many other links. FindLaw's California page: *california.lp.findlaw.com/.*

- **HierosGamos**: *www.hg.org.*

  Includes links to California cases, codes, and courts, including links to cases and codes through LexisNexis (LexisNexis ID required). Access California sources through: *www.hg.org/usstates.html.*

- **Legal Information Institute (LII)**: *www.law.cornell.edu.*

  From Cornell Law School. Includes California Supreme Court and Appeals Courts decisions, Administrative Code, and links to other California sources. LII's California page: *www.law.cornell.edu/states/california.html.*

- **Law Library Resource Xchange (LLRX.com)**: *www.llrx.com.*

  News and information about Internet legal research and technology. Includes reviews of legal research websites.

- **lexisONE**: *www.lexisone.com.*

  Site aimed at small law firms or solo practices. Some free content and some fee-based. California page has links to free web resources related to California law and government at: *www.lexisone.com/legalresearch/legalguide/states/california.htm.* Also includes legal encyclopedia, "Zimmerman's Research Guide." Zimmerman's Research Guide for California: *www.lexisone.com/zimmermanguide/C/California.html.*

- **WashLaw**: *washlaw.edu.*

  Huge list of legal resources arranged alphabetically. California sources are categorized by topic (Legislative Information, Courts, etc.). Washlaw's California page: *www.washlaw.edu/uslaw/uslal_co.html#California.*

[3] Subscription Databases

Many online legal databases are available to users by subscription, only. Users must sign up and pay to use these databases. The fees differ by resource.

- **AccessLaw**: *www.accesslaw.com.**

  California cases and codes and also a Daily Opinion Service which provides access to slip opinions and advance sheets. Also available on CD-ROM as CalDisk.

- **American LegalNet**: *www.americanlegalnet.com.**

  California cases, codes, forms, attorney directory, and court directory.

- **JuriSearch**: *www.jurisearch.com.**

  Includes California cases, codes, and forms.

- **law.com**: *www.law.com.*

  Includes California court daily opinions. Some information, like legal news articles, are free. Law.com's California page: *www.law.com/ca.*

- **LexisNexis**: *www.lexisnexis.com.*

- **Loislaw**: *www.loislaw.com.*

  Cases, statutes, administrative law as well as some treatises.

- **Matthew Bender Online**: through *bender.lexisnexis.com.*

  Access to Matthew Bender practice materials including California Law and Practice.

- **National Law Library**: *www.itislaw.com.*

  Includes California cases and statutes.

- **Netlaw Libraries**: *www.netlawlibraries.com.**

  California cases, codes, court rules.

- **VersusLaw**: *www.versuslaw.com.*

  Includes state and federal cases.

- **Westlaw**: *www.westlaw.com.*

* Emphasis on California information.

[4] Subscription-Based Journal and Book Indexes

- **HeinOnline**: *www.heinonline.org.*

Access to legal periodicals, including some dating back to the early 1900s. Articles are full text and image-based so users can see the pages exactly as they appear in print.

- **H.W. Wilson's Index to Legal Periodicals & Books**: through *www.hwwilson.com.*

  Article citations from legal periodicals and journals from 1981; full text from 1994. Also available as a CD-ROM subscription.

- **IndexMaster**: *www.indexmaster.com.*

  Searchable and viewable database of indexes and/or tables of content for thousands of legal book titles.

- **Legaltrac**: through *www.galegroup.com.*

  Indexes major law reviews, legal newspapers, bar journals and also legal articles from business and general interest titles. Also available as a CD-ROM subscription.

[5]   Library Catalogs

Many law library catalogs are available on the web and are excellent sources for finding legal information.

- **California Digital Library**: *www.cdlib.org.*

  Includes the Melvyl® catalog which includes the collections of all of the University of California law school libraries and the California State Library.

- **California State Library**: *www.lib.state.ca.us.*

  Includes the California State Law Library collection.

  Many other law libraries, especially law school libraries, have their catalogs available online.

§ 15.05   CD-ROM Databases

A CD-ROM disk can hold more than 600 MB of data. That can equal thousands of pages and many volumes of information. Some legal products are on multiple CDs and require specialized equipment, such as a CD tower, to provide efficient access. The CD-ROM format offers the user the full-text searching advantages of the online services, without the charges that come with online access, such as a phone line, cable, etc., as well as transaction or charges for time used. Many of the major vendors produce CD-ROMs for California legal research, including LexisNexis, West Group, Matthew Bender, and others. For a list of CD-ROM titles for a particular primary or secondary source (e.g., codes, cases, treatises, etc.), see the chapter discussing that topic.

Chapter 16

Legal Education[1]

§ 16.01   California Law Schools

There are three categories of law schools in California: ABA accredited, State Accredited, and unaccredited. Schools in all three categories must register with the Committee of Bar Examiners ("Committee") and fulfill annual reporting requirements.[2]

1. If a school is already accredited by the American Bar Association, the institution is automatically deemed to be accredited by the Committee. ABA approved schools are listed in Appendix M.

2. Alternatively, a school can be accredited only by the Committee. The Committee of Bar Examiners has accredited all law schools that are ABA approved, plus a number of additional schools. California-approved schools are listed in Appendix N.

---

[1] This chapter is written by Erin Murphy, Reference Librarian, Law Library, UC Davis School of Law.

[2] Rules Regulating Accreditation of Law Schools in California, San Francisco: State Bar of California; available at: *www.calbar.ca.gov*. Rules also may be purchased from the State Bar.

(Pub. 64620)

3. Besides the state accredited schools, California also has unaccredited law schools—schools that have not applied for accreditation or have applied but do not meet California accreditation standards. Law students attending unaccredited schools must pass the First Year Law Students Examination (commonly called the "baby bar") at the end of their first year in order to receive credit for further law school education and to be eligible to take the general bar examination upon graduation. These schools are listed on the State Bar web page at: *www.calbar.ca.gov.*

§ 16.02   Alternatives to Law School

California is the only state that permits students to complete correspondence school courses as bar preparation.

California is one of seven states that still permit bar candidates to apprentice in a law office as bar preparation.[3] The supervising attorney/judge must file semi-annual reports with the Committee.[4]

§ 16.03   Accrediting Agencies

[1]   California

The State Bar of California is the accrediting agency for California law schools. Listed here are two state offices of the same organization:

Office of Admissions
The State Bar of California
1149 S. Hill Street
Los Angeles, CA 90015-2299
(213) 765-1500

Office of Admissions
The State Bar of California
180 Howard Street
San Francisco, CA 94105-1639
(415) 538-2303

---

[3] Permitted Means of Legal Study, *Comprehensive Guide to Bar Admission Requirements*, 2004 ed., *www.abanet.org/legaled* (site last visited March 17, 2004).

[4] Rule VII, § 3 Educational Requirements, Rules Regulating Admission to Practice Law in California.

[2] National

[a] Association of American Law Schools

The Association of American Law Schools (AALS) is a membership organization that concentrates on maintaining and improving the quality of legal education generally, but it does not work with state bar examining committees around the country. AALS accreditation of a school is not necessary for graduates of the school to be able to take the state bar exam.

The AALS sometimes works with the ABA to form combined site inspection teams to inspect law schools. The AALS does not concentrate on the minimum standards that a school must meet. It is not in the business of protecting the public or the consumer. The AALS leaves that for the ABA to do because the ABA is acting for the state bar or the supreme court of a state.

The AALS contact information and publications are:

Association of American Law Schools
1201 Connecticut Avenue, NW, Suite 800
Washington, DC 20036-2065
202-296-8851
202-296-8869 (FAX)
www.aals.org

> 📖 *The AALS Directory of Law Teachers.* (Washington, D.C.: AALS. (annual)) carries a list of approved schools.

[b] American Bar Association

The ABA coordinates efforts with the California Bar in accrediting certain California law schools. As it is noted above, ABA accreditation of a school is not necessary for graduates of the school to be able to take the California bar exam, but it is necessary for application to take the bar exam in most states. The contact information for the ABA is:

Office of the Consultant on Legal Education/Section of
 Legal Education and Admissions to the Bar
American Bar Association
750 N. Lake Shore Drive, 7th Floor
Chicago, IL 60611
312-988-6738
312-988-5681 (FAX)
www.abanet.org

Publications from the ABA that are related to law school inspections include:

📖   American Bar Association. Office of the Consultant on Legal Education. *Annual Report.* Chicago: ABA, Office of the Consultant on Legal Education. Annual. This report includes statistics on legal education, accreditation activities of the year, and any standards changes proposed.

📖   American Bar Association. Office of the Consultant on Legal Education. *American Bar Association Standards for Approval of Law Schools.* Chicago: ABA, Office of the Consultant on Legal Education. Annual. This publication is published each October and contains all the accrediting standards in effect.

§ 16.04   Minimum Continuing Legal Education (MCLE)

[1]   History

Since 1991 (with a short break in the late 1990s)[5] all lawyers in the state have had to attend seminars, take courses, teach classes, write articles, or study independently to comply with the Minimum Continuing Legal Education (MCLE) requirements described in California Business and Professions Code section 6070 and California Rules of Court, rule 958. The State Bar published a booklet to help attorneys understand the rules for compliance:

Detailed information on the compliance requirements can be found at the Bar's web site *www.calbar.ca.gov.*

[2]   Controlling Law of MCLE

MCLE statutory authority is found in Business and Professions Code section 6070, which provides:

     a.   The State Bar shall request the California Supreme Court to adopt a rule of court authorizing the State Bar to establish and administer

---

[5] On March 13, 1997, in *Warden v. The State of California,* 53 Cal.App.4th 510, 62 Cal.Rptr.2d 32 (Cal.App. 1997) the First Appellate District, Division Five, held that the MCLE statute was unconstitutional on equal protection grounds because the various exemptions contained in the statute did not pass the rational basis test. MCLE was not enforced during the appeal period. However, the case on appeal was reversed by the California Supreme Court, reinstating MCLE for most attorneys, and retaining the exempted categories. See *Warden v. The State Bar of California,* 21 Cal. 4th 628, 982 P.2d 154, 88 Cal. Rptr. 2d 283 (1997).

a mandatory continuing legal education program. The rule that the State Bar requests the Supreme Court to adopt shall require that, within designated 36-month periods, all active members of the State Bar shall complete at least 25 hours of legal education activities approved by the State Bar or offered by a State bar approved provider, with four of those hours in legal ethics. A member of the State Bar who fails to satisfy the mandatory continuing legal education requirements of the program authorized by the Supreme Court rule shall be enrolled as an inactive member pursuant to rules adopted by the Board of Governors of the State Bar.

b.   For purposes of this section, statewide associations of public agencies and incorporated, nonprofit professional associations of attorneys, shall be certified as State Bar approved providers upon completion of an appropriate application process to be established by the State Bar. The certification may be revoked only by majority vote of the board, after notice and hearing, and for good cause shown. Programs provided by the California District Attorneys Association or the California Public Defenders Association, or both, including, but not limited to, programs provided pursuant to Title 1.5 (commencing with Section 11500) of Part 4 of the Penal Code, are deemed to be legal education activities approved by the State Bar or offered by a State Bar approved provider.

c.   Notwithstanding the provisions of subdivision (a), officers and elected officials of the State of California, and full-time professors at law schools accredited by the State Bar of California, the American Bar Association, or both, shall be exempt from the provisions of this section. Full-time employees of the State of California, acting within the scope of their employment, shall be exempt from the provisions of this section. Nothing in this section shall prohibit the State of California, or any political subdivision thereof, from establishing or maintaining its own continuing education requirements for its employees.

d.   The State Bar shall provide and encourage the development of low-cost programs and materials by which members may satisfy their continuing education requirements. Special emphasis shall be placed upon the use of internet capabilities and computer technology in the development and provision of no-cost and low-cost programs and materials. Towards this purpose, the State Bar shall ensure that by July 1, 2000, any member possessing or having access to the internet or specified generally available computer technology shall be capable of satisfying the full self-study portion of his or her MCLE requirement at a cost of fifteen dollars ($15) per hour or less. (Added by Stats. 1989, ch. 1425. Amended by Stats. 1999, ch. 342)

HISTORY: Added Stats 1989 ch 1425. Amended Stat 1999 ch 342.

California Rules of Court, Rule 958 also controls MCLE, providing:

(a). [Statutory Authorization] This rule is adopted under section 6070 of the Business and Professions Code.

(b). [State Bar Minimum Continuing Legal Education Program] The State Bar shall establish and administer a minimum continuing legal education program, beginning on or after January 1, 1991, under rules adopted by the Board of Governors of the State Bar. These rules may provide for carry forward of excess credit hours, staggering of the education requirement for implementation purposes, and retroactive credit for legal education.

(c). [Minimum Continuing Legal Education Requirements]

Each active member of the State Bar (1) not exempt under Business and Profession Code section 6070, (2) not a full-time employee of the United States Government, its departments, agencies, and public corporations, acting within the scope of his or her employment, and (3) not otherwise exempt under rules adopted by the Board of Governors of the State Bar, shall, within 36-month periods designated by the State Bar, complete at least 25 hours of legal education approved by the State Bar or offered by a State Bar-approved provider. Four of those hours shall address legal ethics. Members may be required to complete legal education in other specified areas within the 25-hour requirement under rules adopted by the State Bar. Each active member shall report his or her compliance to the State Bar under rules adopted by the Board of Governors of the State Bar.

(d). [Failure to Comply with Program]

A member of the State Bar who fails to satisfy the requirements of the State Bar's minimum continuing legal education program shall be enrolled as an inactive member of the State Bar under rules adopted by the Board of Governors of the State Bar.

(e). [Fee]

The State Bar shall have the authority to set and collect appropriate fees and penalties.

HISTORY: Rule 958 adopted by the Supreme Court December 6, 1990. Amended effective December 25, 1992, October 27, 2000.

[3]   MCLE Providers

New courses, conferences, workshops, etc. must be approved by the State Bar. The Bar's website at *www.calbar.ca.gov* outlines several types of activities that qualify as "continuing legal education."

"Live" education

"Electronic" education: courses offered via the web, CD, or audio/videotape

Self-assessment tests

Attending and teaching law school classes

Writing published legal materials

Approval of an education activity is required in order for credit to be granted although an attorney may attend an unapproved course and then file a "Member Credit Request" to seek approval. The Bar's website includes a database of providers that is searchable by legal specialization, city, or name. The Bar itself provides more than 500 hours of online programming.

Appendices

(Pub. 64620)

Appendix A

Publishers/Vendors of California Legal Information

This appendix provides the names, addresses, phone numbers, and a short company description for most California legal information suppliers. The individual products are more fully described in the body of the text or in other appendices. For an up-to-date listing of law publishers see *A Legal Publishers List: Corporate Affiliations of Legal Publishers*, 2d ed., which is maintained at the American Association of Law Libraries web site: *www.aallnet.org/committee/criv/resources/tools/list/*.

AccessLaw, Inc.
711 East Bronco Dr.
Spring Creek, NV 89815-7313
1-775-753-4780
1-775-753-5420 (FAX)
Email: info@accesslaw.com
www.accesslaw.com

AccessLaw produces both online and CD products. The online product is one of the upstart legal databases that is aimed at the lower end of the LexisNexis and Westlaw markets. The CD-ROM product, called CalDisc, contains all California appellate cases, California codes, and court rules. It is the next generation of the floppy disk product issued first about 10 years ago by National Legal Databases of Tulsa, Oklahoma. The product is competitively priced and uses Folio access software.

American LegalNet
16133 Ventura Boulevard, Suite 265
Encino, California 91436
1-800-293-2771
1-818-817-9225
1-818-817-9239 (FAX)
Email: info@americanlegalnet.com
www.americanlegalnet.com

(Pub. 64620)

This company provides access to California codes, bills, court rules, cases (Cal. Since 1934), public records, jury instructions, a court directory, an attorney directory, a court reporter directory, and a legal yellow pages. Live Publish is used as the search engine for all of the databases. The company also provides services including www page development, customized chat rooms, and sales of legal industry products and services.

Bancroft-Whitney
50 California Street, 19th Floor
San Francisco, CA 94111-4624

Bancroft-Whitney
P.O. Box 7005
San Francisco, CA 94120-7005
1-800-848-4000
www.westgroup.com

Bancroft-Whitney is a part of West Group, which is a subsidiary of Thomson Professional Publishing. Bancroft-Whitney is the oldest continuous supplier of publications for the California legal market. The original company, H.H. Bancroft & Co., was founded in 1856, and merged with a company owned by business rival Sumner Whitney in 1870. Today the historic Bancroft-Whitney name is being phased out by West and Thomson. The Witkin sets, which were published by Bancroft-Whitney for decades, are now being published by the Witkin Legal Institute, a subsidiary of West and Thomson. California Jurisprudence, also formerly published by Bancroft-Whitney, is now published by West. The publisher for California Reports and California Appellate Reports was changed from Bancroft-Whitney to West in 1997 and then to LexisNexis in 2003.

Barclays Law Publishers
400 Oyster Point Boulevard
P.O. Box 3066
South San Francisco, CA 94083-3066
1-415-244-6611
1-800-888-3600
1-415-244-0408 (FAX)
www.westgroup.com

Barclays, purchased in 1995 by Bancroft-Whitney and now a part of West Group, is the official publisher of the California Code of Regulations. This product is available on line, on CD-ROM, and in hard copy.

BMI Imaging Systems (formerly Bay Microfilm, Inc.)
1115 E. Arques Avenue
Sunnyvale, CA 94086
1-408-736-7444
1-800-359-3456
1-408-736-4397 (FAX)

BMI Imaging Systems
749 W. Stadium Ln.
Sacramento, CA 95834
1-916-924-6666
1-916-928-0277 (FAX)
www.bmiimaging.com

This company supplies briefs from the Supreme Court and Courts of Appeal, legislative bills, Assembly File Analysis, Senate and Assembly Daily Journals, and various legal newspapers (including *The Daily Recorder* (Sacramento), *The Recorder* (San Francisco), and the *Los Angeles Daily Journal*). They also have voter arguments for all propositions (Constitutional amendments and statutes). The company has done archival microfilming for the State Library and has microfilm copies of many of the State Archives' legal materials available for sale.

Butterworth Legal Publishers
See Matthew Bender & Company, Inc.

California Historical Society
Administrative Headquarters and North Baker Research Library
678 Mission St.
San Francisco, CA 94105
1-415-357-1848

California Historical Society
Editorial Offices: History Department
Loyola Marymount University
One LMU Drive
Los Angeles, CA 90045
1-310-338-2324

This organization publishes the journal *California History*, which sometimes includes fine articles on the history of California law and legal institutions.

California Journal
2101 K Street

Sacramento, CA
1-916-444-2840
www.statenet.com

California Journal publishes a magazine, a newsletter, an almanac, directories, a legislative roster, and several books on California government. The legislative roster is also available on diskette. The parent company, Information for Public Affairs, also produces State Net.

California Supreme Court Historical Society
22130 Clarendon Street
Woodland Hills, CA 91367
1-818-348-6054
1-818-883-5569 (FAX)
director@cschs.org

This organization produces an annual Yearbook and a journal, presently called the *California Supreme Court Historical Society Journal*, but soon to be renamed *California Legal History*.

Capital Research
7582 Community Drive 100
Citrus Heights, CA 95610
1-916-955-4488

This company was organized in about 2002. It is probably the smallest of the four commercial California legislative history research services listed in Chapter 4. Capital Research did not have a web page as of May 2004.

Capitol Enquiry, Inc.
1228 N Street, Suite 10
Sacramento, CA 95814-5610
1-916-442-1434
916-442-1260(FAX)
www.capenq.com

Capitol Enquiry annually publishes the California State Agency Directory and the Pocket Directory of the California Legislature. The company also issues a weekly e-mail newsletter, the Capitol Action Weekly.

CEB Continuing Education of the Bar—California
University of California
300 Frank H. Ogawa Plaza, Suite 410
Oakland, CA 94612-2001
1-800-232-3444

1-510-302-2000 (Outside CA)
www.ceb.com

CEB has been providing continuing education materials in California since its founding in 1947. This joint effort of the State Bar and the University of California offers over 600 publications, audio tapes, video tapes, software packages, and CD-ROM products to California attorneys.

CIS Congressional Information Service, Inc.
4520 East-West Highway, Suite 800
Bethesda, MD 20814-3389
1-301-654-1550
1-800-638-8380
www.lexisnexis.com/academic/3cis/cisMnu.asp

CIS, which is a subsidiary of LexisNexis, which is a subsidiary of Reed Elsevier, publishes a microfiche version of California's constitutional convention documents. CIS also publishes a printed guide to the fiche collection.

Daily Journal Corporation
Los Angeles Daily Journal
915 East First Street
Los Angeles, CA 90012-4042
1-213-229-5300
1-213-680-3682 (FAX)
www.dailyjournal.com

Daily Journal Corporation
San Francisco Daily Journal
1390 Market Street, #1210
San Francisco, CA 94102-5306
1-415-252-0500

Daily Journal Corporation (Sacramento Office)
Daily Recorder
1115 H Street
Sacramento, CA 95814
1-916-444-2355

Daily Journal Corporation (San Diego Office)
1-619-232-3486

This corporation is a major publisher of legal newspapers in the state. The papers carry the Daily Appellate Report (DAR) as a supplement and feature daily Judicial Profiles. The Daily Journal Corporation also publishes court rules, a magazine (California Lawyer), and a semiannual directory (California Lawyers: Directory of Attorneys). There is an online subscription-only database, which is not accessible through any other legal vendors.

Gould Publications
J. & B. Gould
1333 North U.S. Highway 17-92
Longwood, FL 32750
1-800-847-6502
Email: info@gouldlaw.com
www.gouldlaw.com

Gould publishes selected California codes.

Governor's Office
State of California
State Capitol
First Floor
Sacramento, CA 95814
1-916-445-2841
1-916-445-4633 (FAX)
www.governor.ca.gov

The Governor's Office is the source for press releases and executive orders.

Harvard Law School
Library Preservation Department
Langdell Hall
Cambridge, MA 02138
1-617-495-4815 or 1-617-496-2086

Harvard Law Library's Preservation Officer is in charge of their fiche duplication and sales efforts. They have many reports from several California state agencies up until the late 1970s. Their publications are listed in the Law Library Microform Consortium catalogs as a courtesy.

Hein Company
See William S. Hein & Company

Information for Public Affairs
See California Journal and State Net

JuriSearch
801 S. Grand Avenue, 22nd Floor
Los Angeles, CA 90017

1-800-576-4800
1-213-996-1919
1-213-622-2241 (FAX)
E-mail: jurisearch@instanet.com
www.jurisearch.com

JuriSearch is another company that offers low cost access to California cases, codes, local court rules, Judicial Counsel forms, and recent legislation. The system uses the Folio search engine.

Law Library Microform Consortium (LLMC)
P.O. Box 1599
Kaneohe, HI 96744
1-800-235-4446
1-808-235-1755 (FAX)
www.llmc.com

LLMC produces a microfiche version of the Martindale-Hubbell legal directory covering the years from 1868 to 1980. The California volumes are available for purchase separately.

League of California Cities
Publications Unit
1400 K Street, 4th Floor
Sacramento, CA 95814
1-916-658-8253
1-916-658-8240 (FAX)
www.cacities.org

This organization, profiled in the local government chapter, publishes a newsletter, a magazine, a quarterly, and several books on local government.

Legislative History & Legislative Intent
218 Guaymas Place
Davis, CA 95616
1-888-676-1947
1-530-750-0190 (FAX)
E-mail: jray@lhclearinghouse.com
www.lhclearinghouse.com

This is a newer company that provides research services in legislative history. The www page has background information on the value of legislative intent.

Legislative Intent Service
712 Main Street

Woodland, CA 95695
1-800-666-1917
1-530-668-5866 (FAX)
www.legintent.com

This company, the oldest and largest of its type in California, prepares full legislative histories on any California law. They have access to materials not held elsewhere. They have a current inventory of over 30,000 histories.

Legislative Research Incorporated
926 J Street, Suite 1100
Sacramento, CA 94814
1-916-442-7660
1-916-442-1529 (FAX)
www.lrihistory.com

Legislative Research Incorporated (LRI) has been in the business of preparing California legislative histories since 1983. LRI has compiled a collection of over 10,000 histories in their files. The company's www page is informative, and it goes far beyond advertising the company's services. It contains two lengthy articles, one on researching legislative history and a second one on researching regulatory history. In addition there is a "morgue" list containing cases that invalidate agency regulations.

LEXIS Publishing
See Matthew Bender & Company, Inc.

LexisNexis
9393 Springboro Pike-DM
P.O. Box 933
Dayton, OH 45401
1-800-543-6862 (Customer Service)
www.lexisnexis.com
www.lexis.com

LexisNexis
611 West 6th Street, Suite 1900
Los Angeles, CA 90017
1-800-554-8986

LexisNexis
201 Mission Street, 26th Floor
San Francisco, CA 94102
1-800-523-8168

LexisNexis is a subsidiary of Reed Elsevier plc. The Lexis® service, the first commercial, full-text legal information service, began in 1973 to help legal practitioners research the law more efficiently. The companion Nexis® news and business information service launched in 1979 to richen research with recent and archival news and financial information. Since that time, the service has grown to become the largest news and business online information service, including comprehensive company, country, financial, demographic, market research and industry reports. Services and products provided by LexisNexis include Lexis-Nexis at *lexis.com®*, Academic & Library Solutions from LexisNexis, CourtLink eAccess, LexisNexis Person Locators, Time Matters, Martin-dale-Hubbell, and SmartLinx. LexisNexis at *lexis.com®* is a site for legal research that includes primary and secondary law resources, including Cutomized eSolutions, lexisOne, Matthew Bender, and Mealeys. The LexisNexis at *lexis.com®* libraries and files contain California codes, reports, administrative regulations, legislative history information, law reviews, newspapers, specialized practice materials, and general/business information. See Appendix F for a listing of LexisNexis sources pertaining to California law.

LOIS, Inc.
105 North 28th Street
Van Buren, AR 72956
1-800-364-2512
1-501-471-5635 (FAX)
www.loislaw.com

LOIS, or Law Office Information Systems, is becoming a major player in the CD-ROM and www research fields. It has a strong presence in federal research and has primary and secondary resources for many states, including California.

Martin Dean's Essential Publishers, Inc.
401 Francisco Street
San Francisco, CA 94133
1-415-986-3700
1-800-286-0111
1-415-986-2110 (FAX)

This company publishes Judicial Council forms, county forms, local rules, court directories, and attorney directories in Essential Forms, Essential Courts, and Essential Attorneys.

Martindale-Hubbell
121 Chanlon Road

New Providence, NJ 07974
1-800-526-4902
1-908-464-6800
www.martindale.com

Martindale-Hubbell is a subsidiary of Reed Elsevier. The Law Directory covers California, along with the other forty-nine states. The California directory (2 volumes) is available separately to customers who have purchased the full set. An online version is on LexisNexis. Note that Law Library Microfilm Consortium (LLMC) has produced a microfiche version of editions from 1868 to 1980. There is a more detailed description of these directories in Appendix L.

Matthew Bender & Company, Inc.
744 Broad Street
Newark, NJ 07102
1-800-252-9257
1-800-543-6862 (Customer Service)
www.bender.com

Matthew Bender is a member of the LexisNexis group. It produces primary sources such as *Deering's California Codes Annotated* and secondary titles on a complete range of California and national topics such as *California Forms of Pleading and Practice, California Legal Forms: Transaction Guide, and California Points and Authorities.* Titles are available in print, on CD-ROM, and online at *lexis.com®*. Matthew Bender products also include titles from Parker Publishing, Michie, and Mealey Publications, and former titles of LEXIS Publishing, LEXIS Law Publishing, Butterworth, and Michie Butterworth.

Mealey Publications
P.O. Box 62090
King of Prussia, PA 19406-0230
1-610-768-7800
1-800-MEALEYS
www.mealeys.com/

Mealey Publications is a member of the LexisNexis group and offers publications that provide targeted legal news reports and conferences to plaintiff, defense, insurance, and in-house counsel. Mealey's Online provides immediate access to a searchable editorial archive of stories, as well as online access to current documents. Pre-March 2000 documents are also cited and may be ordered through Mealey's Document

Service. Mealey's Online is updated daily and is available by subscription or on a pay-per-view basis. Mealey's Conference Department provides high-level educational programs to supplement the editorial coverage provided in Mealey's reports.

Metropolitan News-Enterprise
210 South Spring St.
Los Angeles, CA 90012
1-213-628-4384 (main number)
1-213-346-0039
1-213-346-0033
1-213-687-6509 (FAX)
1-213-687-3886 (FAX)
metnews.com
lawzone.com
mnc.net

Metropolitan News Company
P.O. Box 60859
Los Angeles, CA 90060-0859

This publisher provides a daily legal newspaper for Los Angeles, with a daily Slip Opinion Supplement (SOS). On the first Monday of each month the paper carries a court directory supplement. The Met-News also publishes court rules for the state and for the most populous counties.

Meyer Boswell Books
Rare and Scholarly Books on the Law
2141 Mission St.
San Francisco, CA 94110
1-415-255-6400
1-415-255-6499 (FAX)
Email: rarelaw@meyerbos.com
www.meyerbos.com

This is one of the best sources in the country for used books.

Michie Butterworth
See Matthew Bender & Company, Inc.

Netlaw Libraries, Inc.
Tobiasson Road
Poway, CA 92064-3647
1-619-486-3329/874-0544

1-619-486-9079 (FAX)
www.netlawlibraries.com

NetLaw Libraries is one of the new vendors offering appellate court decisions 2nd, 3rd, and 4th series. It also provides links to free state services such as codes, court rules, etc.

Nolo Press
950 Parker Street
Berkeley, CA 94710
1-510-548-5902
www.nolo.com

Nolo publishes a complete line of books about law for the nonlawyer. Many subjects in California Law are covered.

Northern California Association of Law Libraries (NOCALL)
1800 Market Street
Box 109
San Francisco, CA 94102
www.nocall.org

This organization of law libraries and law librarians issues a newsletter and a directory. It also sponsors educational programs and hosts a www site.

OCLC Online Computer Library Center, Inc.
6565 Frantz Road
Dublin, OH 43017-3395
1-800-848-5878
1-614-764-6096 (FAX)
www.oclc.org

OCLC Pacific
9227 Haven Ave.
Suite 260
Rancho Cucamonga, CA 91730-5451
1-800-854-5753
1-909-948-9803 (FAX)

OCLC is one of the two large databases (the other is RLIN) of bibliographic records. These databases are important for locating books on any subject, including legal subjects, in libraries around the world.

Parker Publications
See Matthew Bender & Company, Inc.

Proquest Information and Learning
300 North Zeeb Road
P.O. Box 1346
Ann Arbor, MI 48106-1346
1-734-761-4700
1-800-521-0600
www.proquest.com

Proquest, formerly Bell and Howell Information and Learning (formerly UMI) produces a fiche version of the California Code of Regulations.

Recorder
625 Polk Street
San Francisco, CA 94102
1-415-749-5406
www.callaw.com
www.law.com

This is another of California's oldest publishers. It began publishing a San Francisco legal newspaper in 1877. The Recorder has been acquired by a national legal newspaper chain, American Lawyer Media. The newspaper is a daily and is supplemented by the California Daily Opinion Service (CDOS).

Reed Elsevier
www.reed-elsevier.com
See LexisNexis, CIS, Martindale-Hubbell, Shepard's, Matthew Bender, and Mealeys

Research Libraries Information Network (RLIN)
1200 Villa Street
Mountain View, CA 94041-1100
1-800-537-7546
www.rlg.org/rlin.html

RLIN is one of the two large databases (the other is OCLC) of bibliographic records. These databases are important for locating books on any subject, including legal subjects, in libraries around the world.

The Rutter Group
15760 Ventura Blvd. Suite 630
Encino, CA 91436
1-818-990-3260
1-800-747-3161
www.ruttergroup.com

This publisher, a subsidiary of the West Group, is well known for continuing education seminars and practice guides. They have CD-ROM and online versions of some of their more popular works.

San Diego Association of Law Libraries (SANDALL)
www.aallnet.org/chapter/sandall

This is the newest of the California library organizations. Its monthly newsletter is SANDALL News.

Shepard's
555 Middle Creek Parkway
Colorado Springs, CO 80921
1-719-488-3000
1-800-743-7393
www.shepards.com

Shepard's, a subsidiary of Reed Elsevier, publishes the main, print-version citator for the state. They also furnish a CD-ROM version and offer an online version through LexisNexis at *lexis.com®*.

Southern California Association of Law Libraries (SCALL)
8391 Beverly Blvd., Suite 300
Los Angeles, CA 90048
www.aallnet.org/chapter/scall

This organization issues a membership directory and newsletters. The members hold educational programs throughout the year and host a www site.

State Bar of California (Main Office)
180 Howard Street
San Francisco, CA 94105-1639
Main Number: 415-538-2000
www.calbar.ca.gov

State Bar of California (Discipline Section Only)
1149 South Hill Street
Los Angeles, CA 90015-2299
1-213-765-1000

State Bar of California (Sacramento Office)
915 L Street, Suite 1260
Sacramento, CA 95814-2762
1-916-444-2762

The State Bar is the publisher of the *California Bar Journal*, which became the official publication of the State Bar in January, 1994. Prior to that, the *California Lawyer*, published by Daily Journal Corporation, carried official Bar information. The State Bar also publishes other periodicals, pamphlets, and brochures aimed at both the practicing bar and the public. Other functions of the bar are described in the Chapter on the State Bar of California.

State Net
2101 K Street
Sacramento, CA 95816
1-916-444-0840
1-916-446-5369 (FAX)
www.statenet.com

State Net is a provider of current online legislative information, including bill text, bill status, etc. The company is part of Information for Public Affairs, Inc., which also produces the California Journal and its related publications. Its data is accessible through LexisNexis and Westlaw.

State of California
Department of General Services
Office of Procurement
Publications Section
P.O. Box 1015
North Highlands, CA 95660
1-916-574-2200
www.dgs.ca.gov

This office sends out publications catalogs listing government documents for sale to the public.

State of California
Legislative Information System
Legislative Data Center
Legislative Cousel Bureau
1100 J Street, Suite 200
Sacramento, CA 95814
1-916-445-4965
1-916-327-3392 (FAX)
www.leginfo.ca.gov

This office is in charge of maintaining all of the information databases for the state legislature. In response to 1993 AB 1624, the Legislative Counsel has made all of the required information available to the public through its www site.

State of California
Legislative Publication Services
Legislative Bill Room
State Capitol Rm. B32
Sacramento, CA 95814-4997
1-916-445-2323
www.osp.dgs.ca.gov/services/legbill.asp

This office provides printed legislative publications to the public. Bills can be mailed or picked up in the Bill Room. There is no charge to individuals for the first 100 bills requested.

State of California
Secretary of State
State Archives
1020 "O" Street
Sacramento, CA 95814
1-916-653-7715 Information
1-916-653-2246 Reference
1-916-653-7363 (FAX)
1-916-653-7134 Administration
www.ss.ca.gov/archives/archives.htm

The State Archives, operating under the Secretary of State, provides photocopies of materials in their care. They can also arrange to have rolls of their microfilm duplicated for a fee. Users should call them in advance for current prices and turn-around times. In 1998, the Archives opened the Golden State Museum on the first and second floors of the building.

Thomson Corporation
See West Group, Barclays, Bancroft-Whitney, Rutter Group, and Westlaw
www.thomcorp.com

Trans-Media Publishing Co.
(Parent Company: Hudson House)
60 Main St.
Dobbs Ferry, NY 10522
1-914-693-1100
pfclegal@aol.com

Trans-Media publishes a 35mm microfilm version of Attorney General Reports and early, unpublished California Attorney General Opinions.

University of California
Institute of Governmental Studies (IGS)
102 Moses Hall
Berkeley, CA 94720-2370
1-510-642-6723
www.igs.berkeley.edu

This is an institute within UC Berkeley. Its library is a great source of California legal history. It is also a publisher of books, including titles on California government.

VersusLaw, Inc.
2613 151st Place NE
Redmond, WA 98052
1-425-250-0142
1-425-250-0157 (FAX)
www.versuslaw.com

VersusLaw is one of the important newcomers into the www legal research field. The company has a national presence and has developed products for the California market. Currently the site carries California appellate cases (back to 1930) and codes.

West Group
620 Opperman Drive
Eagan, MN 55123
1-800-328-9352
www.westgroup.com

West, purchased by Thomson in 1996, is a publisher of codes, reports, a legislative service, forms, practice books, and treatises on California subjects. West Group is also the umbrella company over smaller companies such as Bancroft-Whitney, Barclays, Rutter Group, and Westlaw.

Westlaw
Customer Service Number 1-800-Westlaw
Reference Attorneys 1-800-REF-ATTY
www.westlaw.com

Westlaw, a subsidiary of West Group, contains many databases of California legal and law-related materials. Among the primary materials they carry are the code, the Constitution, reports, and administrative regulations. They also provide bills, bill tracking, and bill analysis. Westlaw supplies much nonlegal information through DIALOG and

Dow Jones News/Retrieval, which contain thousands of general and business resources. Appendix G provides a listing of Westlaw's California databases.

William S. Hein & Co., Inc.
1285 Main Street
Buffalo, NY 14209-1987
1-800-828-7571
1-716-883-8100 (FAX)
www.wshein.com

The Hein company provides session laws, superseded codes, attorney general opinions, selected bar journals, selected law reviews, administrative regulations, and bar exams on microfiche. The HeinOnline product (*www.heinonline.org*) contains pdf images of many of the California law journals, back to the first issue published.

Appendix B

California State
Complete Depository Libraries
(See also Chapter 14, Law Libraries)

California State Archives
1020 O Street
Sacramento, CA 95814

California State Library
Government Publications
 Section
Library and Courts Building
914 Capitol Mall
Sacramento, CA 94237-0001
(LMS: 914 Capitol Mall, E-29)

California State University,
 Chico
Merriam Library
Government Publications Dept.
Chico, CA 95929-0295

California State University,
 Long Beach
Library Government
 Documents
1250 Bellflower Blvd.
Long Beach, CA 90840-1901

Fresno County Free Library
Government Publications
2420 Mariposa St.
Fresno, CA 93721-2285

Los Angeles Public Library
Serials Division
630 W. 5th St.
Los Angeles, CA 90071-2002

San Diego Public Library
Science and Industry
 Department
820 E. St.
San Diego, CA 92101-6478

San Diego State University
Malcolm A. Love Library
Government Publications &
 Maps Div.
5500 Campanile Dr.
San Diego, CA 92182-8050

San Francisco Public Library
Government Information
 Center
100 Larkin St.
San Francisco, CA 94102

Stanford University
Government Document
 Receiving
Green Library
Stanford, CA 94305-6004

University of California,
 Berkeley
Library
Acq. Dept. Rec/Docs
Berkeley, CA 94720-6000

University of California, Davis
Shields Library

(Pub. 64620)

Government Information and
  Maps Dept.
Davis, CA 95616-5224

University of California, Los
  Angeles
Bruman Library
Maps and Government
  Information
A4510 URL
P.O. Box 95175
Los Angeles, CA 90095-1575

University of California, San
  Diego
Ser Acq Dept., Lib 0175A
9500 Gilman Drive
La Jolla, CA 92093-0175

University of California, Santa
  Barbara
Library
Serials Receiving
Santa Barbara, CA 93106-9010

Appendix C

California State
Selective Depository Libraries
(See also Chapter 14, Law Libraries)

A.K. Smiley Public Library
125 West Vine St.
Redlands, CA 92373

Alameda Free Library
Reference Dept.
2200 A Central Ave.
Alameda, CA 94501

Alhambra Public Library
410 West Main Street
Alhambra, CA 91801-3432

Anaheim Public Library
Documents Section
500 West Broadway
Anaheim, CA 92805

Auburn-Placer County Library
350 Nevada Street
Auburn, CA 95603

Berkeley Public Library
2090 Kittredge Street
Berkeley, CA 94704

Butte County Library
1820 Mitchell Avenue
Oroville, CA 95966-5387

California Institute of
  Technology
Documents Library (1-32)
Pasadena, CA 91125

California Polytechnic State
  University
Robert Kennedy Library
Government Documents
  Section
San Luis Obispo, CA 93407

California State Polytechnic
  University, Pomona
Library-Serials Unit
3801 W. Temple Ave.
Pomona, CA 91768

California State University,
  Bakersfield
Walter Stiern Library
Library-Documents Section
9001 Stockdale Highway
Bakersfield, CA 93311-1099

California State University,
  Dominguez Hills
Library-Government
  Documents
800 E. Victoria St.
Carson, CA 90747

California State University,
  Fresno
Henry Madden Library
Government Documents Dept.
5200 N. Barton, M/S ML34
Fresno, CA 93740-8014

(Pub. 64620)

California State University,
Fullerton
Library-Documents State
P.O. Box 4150
Fullerton, CA 92834-4150

California State University,
Hayward
Library-Acquisition/Documents
Dept.
Hayward, CA 94542

California State University,
Los Angeles
John F. Kennedy Memorial
Library
Government Information
Services
5151 State University Dr.
Los Angeles, CA 90032-8300

California State University,
Northridge
Oviatt Library
18111 Nordhoff St.
Northridge, CA 91330-8327

California State University,
Sacramento
Library-Documents
2000 State University Dr., East
Sacramento, CA 95819-6039

California State University,
San Bernardino
Library
5500 University Parkway
San Bernardino, CA 92407

California State University,
San Marcos
Library Services, State
Documents
333 S. Twin Oaks Valley
Road

San Marcos, CA 92096-0001

California State University,
Stanislaus
Library, Document Dept.
801 West Monte Vista Ave.
Turlock, CA 95382

California State University
Board of Trustees
Office of Governmental Affairs
915 L Street, Suite 1160
Sacramento, CA 95814

Chula Vista Public Library
365 F Street
Chula Vista, CA 91910

Contra Costa County Library
Documents Section
1750 Oak Park Blvd.
Pleasant Hill, CA 94523-4497

Corona Public Library
650 S. Main St.
Corona, CA 91720-3417

El Centro Public Library
539 State Street
El Centro, CA 92243

El Dorado County Library
345 Fair Lane
Placerville, CA 95667

Escondido Public Library
239 South Kalmia
Escondido, CA 92025

Fremont Main Library
2400 Stevenson Blvd.
Fremont, CA 94538-2326

Fullerton Public Library
353 West Commonwealth
Avenue

Fullerton, CA 92632

Garden Grove Regional Branch
Orange County Public Library
11200 Stanford Avenue
Garden Grove, CA 92840

Glendale Public Library
222 East Harvard Street
Glendale, CA 91205-1075

Hayward Public Library
835 "C" St.
Hayward, CA 94541

Honnold/Mudd Library
Government Publications Dept.
Claremont Colleges
800 N. Dartmouth Ave.
Claremont, CA 91711-3907

Humboldt County Library
1313 Third Street
Eureka, CA 95501-0533

Humboldt State University
Library-Documents Department
Arcata, CA 95521

Inglewood Public Library
101 West Manchester Blvd.
Inglewood, CA 90301-1771

John F. Kennedy Library
Solano County Library System
Depository Program
505 Santa Clara Street
Vallejo, CA 94590

Kern County Library
California Documents Dept.
701 Truxtun Avenue
Bakersfield, CA 93301-4517

Long Beach Public Library
101 Pacific Avenue

Long Beach, CA 90822-1097

County of Los Angeles Public
Library
Angelo M. Iacoboni Library
4990 Clark Ave.
Lakewood, CA 90712

County of Los Angeles Public
Library
Carson Regional Library
151 East Carson Street
Carson, CA 90745-2703

County of Los Angeles Public
Library
Culver City Library
4975 Overland Avenue
Culver City, CA 90230

Los Angeles County Public
Library
Lancaster Library
601 W. Lancaster Blvd.
Lancaster, CA 93534

County of Los Angeles Public
Library
Montebello Library
1550 West Beverly Blvd.
Montebello, CA 90640

County of Los Angeles Public
Library
Norwalk Library
12350 Imperial Highway
Norwalk, CA 90650

County of Los Angeles Public
Library
Rosemead Library
8800 Valley Blvd.
Rosemead, CA 91770

County of Los Angeles Public
Library
Valencia Library
23743 West Valencia Blvd.
Valencia, CA 91355

Los Angeles County Public
Library
West Covina Library
1601 West Covina Parkway
West Covina, CA 91790

Mills College Library
5000 MacArthur Blvd.
Oakland, CA 94613-1301

Monterey County Library
26 Central Avenue
Salinas, CA 93901

Napa City-County Library
580 Coombs Stree
Napa, CA 94559-3340

Oakland Public Library
125 Fourteenth St.
Oakland, CA 94612

Oceanside Public Library
330 North Coast Highway
Oceanside, CA 92054

Ontario City Library
Government Documents
 Section
215 East C Street
Ontario, CA 91764-4198

Pasadena Public Library
285 East Walnut Street
Pasadena, CA 91101-1556

Plumas County Library
445 Jackson Street
Quincy, CA 95971

Redwood City Public Library
Documents
1044 Middlefield Road
Redwood City, CA 94063-
 1868

Richmond Public Library
Government Documents Dept.
325 Civic Center Plaza
Richmond, CA 94804

Riverside Public Library
3581 Mission Inn Avenue
Riverside, CA 92501

Sacramento Public Library
Central Library-Reference
 Department
828 I Street
Sacramento, CA 95814-2508

San Bernardino County Library
Government Documents
104 West Fourth Street
San Bernardino, CA 92415-
 0035

San Bernardino Public Library
Documents
555 W. Sixth St.
San Bernardino, CA 92410

San Bernardino Valley College
 Library
701 South Mt. Vernon Avenue
San Bernardino, CA 92410

San Diego County Library
 Vista Branch Library
Documents Librarian
700 Eucalyptus Ave.
Vista, CA 92084-6245

San Francisco State University
Government Publications Dept.

1630 Holloway Avenue
San Francisco, CA 94132-4030

San Jose Public Library
Dr. Martin Luther King, Jr.
 Main Library, Reference
 Dept.
180 West San Carlos Street
San Jose, CA 95113

San Jose State University
Clark Library-Government
 Publications
One Washington Square
San Jose, CA 95192-0028

San Luis Obispo City-County
 Library
P.O. Box 8107
San Luis Obispo, CA 93403

San Mateo Public Library
55 West Third Avenue
San Mateo, CA 94402-1592

Santa Ana Public Library
Reference Section
26 Civic Center Plaza
Santa Ana, CA 92701

Santa Barbara Public Library
P.O. Box 1019
Santa Barbara, CA 93102-1019

Santa Clara University
Michel Orradre Library
Documents Department
500 El Camino Real
Santa Clara, CA 95053-0500

Santa Cruz Public Library
Documents Section
224 Church Street
Santa Cruz, CA 95060

Santa Maria Public Library
Reference Dept.
420 South Broadway
Santa Maria, CA 93454

Santa Monica Public Library
1343 6th St.
Santa Monica, CA 90401

Shasta County Library
1855 Shasta Street
Redding, CA 96001

Sonoma County Library
Third and E Streets
Santa Rosa, CA 95404

Sonoma State University
Library-Documents Dept.
1801 East Cotati Ave.
Rohnert Park, CA 94928

Stanislaus County Free Library
1500 I Street
Modesto, CA 95354-1166

Stockton-San Joaquin County
 Public Library
605 North El Dorado Street
Stockton, CA 95202

Thousand Oaks Library
Attn. Serials
2331 Borchard Rd.
Newbury Park, CA 91320

Torrance Public Library
3301 Torrance Blvd.
Torrance, CA 90503

Tulare County Free Library
Documents Section
200 West Oak
Visalia, CA 93291

University of California, Irvine
Libraries
Government Information
Department
P.O. Box 19557
California Government
Document Librarian
Irvine, CA 92623-9557

University of California,
Riverside
Rivera Library, Government
Publications
P.O. Box 5900
Riverside, CA 92517-5900

University of California, Santa
Cruz
University Library
Government Publications
1156 High Street

Santa Cruz, CA 95064

Government Documents Dept.
University of Southern
California
Doheny Memorial Library
Los Angeles, CA 90089-0182

University of the Pacific
Library
3601 Pacific Avenue
Stockton, CA 95211-0197

Whittier College
The Wardman Library
7031 Founders Hill Road
Whittier, CA 90608

Whittier Public Library
7344 Washington Avenue
Whittier, CA 90602-1778

Appendix D

California State
Selective Depository Libraries: Law Libraries
(See also Chapter 14, Law Libraries)

Bernard E. Witkin Alameda
County Law Library
125 -12 St.
Oakland, CA 94607-4912

California Judicial Center
Library
455 Golden Gate Avenue
Room 4617
San Francisco, CA 94102

California Western School of
Law Library
225 Cedar St.
San Diego, CA 92101-3090

Continuing Education of the
Bar
Library
300 Frank H. Ogawa Plaza,
Suite 410
Oakland, CA 94612

Court of Appeal Library
Second Appellate District
300 S. Spring St.
Los Angeles, CA 90013

Golden Gate University Law
Library
536 Mission St.
San Francisco, CA94105

Hastings College of the Law
Library
200 McAllister St.
San Francisco, CA 94102

Kern County Law Library
1415 Truxtun, Room 301
Bakersfield, CA 93301

Los Angeles County Law
Library
301 W. First St.
Los Angeles, CA 90012-3100

Loyola Law School
William M. Raines Library
Special Collections
1440 W. Ninth St.
Los Angeles, CA 90015

McGeorge School of Law
Library, Documents Dept.
3282 Fifth Ave.
Sacramento, CA 95817

Orange County Law Library
515 N. Flower
Santa Ana, CA 92703-2354

Riverside County Law Library
3989 Lemon St.
Riverside, CA 92501-4203

Sacramento County Public
Law Library

(Pub. 64620)

813 Sixth Street, Room No. 1
Sacramento, CA 95814-2403

San Bernardino County Law
  Library
P.O. Box 213
San Bernardino, CA 92402-
0213

San Diego County Public Law
  Library
1105 Front St.
San Diego, CA 92101-3999

San Joaquin County Law
  Library
Room 300, Court House
222 E. Weber Ave.
Stockton, CA 95202-2787

San Luis Obispo County Law
  Library
1050 Monterey St., Room 125
San Luis Obispo, CA 93408

San Mateo County Law
  Library
710 Hamilton St.
Redwood City, CA 94063

Santa Barbara County Law
  Library
Courthouse
1100 Anacapa Street, 2nd
  Floor
Santa Barbara, CA 93101

Santa Clara County Law
  Library
360 N. First St.
San Jose, CA 95113-1004

Santa Cruz County Law
  Library

701 Ocean St., Rm. 070
Santa Cruz, CA 95060

Sonoma County Law Library
Hall of Justice
600 Administration Dr., Room
  213 J
Santa Rosa, CA 95403

Southwestern University
  School of Law Library
Government Documents
675 South Westmoreland Ave.
Los Angeles, CA 90005-3992

Stanford University
Law Library
Stanford, CA 94305-8612
University of California,
  Berkeley
Law Library
Boalt Hall
Berkeley, CA 94720-7210

University of California
Law Library
Documents Dept.
400 Mrak Hall Drive
Davis, CA 95616-5203

University of California, Los
  Angeles
Law Library
1106 Law Building.
405 Hilgard Ave.
Los Angeles, CA 90095-1458

University of La Verne
College of Law Library
320 East D St.
Ontario, CA 91764

University of San Diego
School of Law Library
5998 Alcala Park
San Diego, CA 92110-2492

University of San Francisco
Zies Law Library
Kendrick Hall
2130 Fulton St.
San Francisco, CA 94117

University of Southern
 California
Law Library
699 Exposition Blvd.
Los Angeles, CA 90089-0072

Ventura County Law Library
Courthouse
800 S. Victoria Ave.
Ventura, CA 93009-2020

Whittier College School of
 Law
Library
3333 Harbor Blvd.
Costa Mesa, CA 92626

Appendix E

California Government Texts

Below is a sampling of California government texts, written over the last several decades. They all give good overviews of the state government and each gives the political/economic/social perspective of the particular time period of the writing.

Bell, Charles G. and Price, Charles M. *California Government Today: Politics of Reform?* 4th ed. Pacific Grove, CA: Brooks/Cole Pub. Co., 1992. 319 p. The authors cover the branches of government, history, politics, local government, and the economy. The book is well illustrated with photographs, cartoons, charts, and graphs.

Boyum, Keith O. and Gianos, Phillip L., editors. *California Government in National Perspective.* Dubuque: Kendall/Hunt, 1984. 148 p. This text covers subjects related to California politics and government, putting California's positions into a national context.

Cain, Gerald C. and Cain, Bruce, E., editors. *Governing California: Politics, Government, Public Policy in the Golden State.* Berkeley, CA: Institute of Governmental Press, 1997. 373 p.

Crouch, Winston W., Bollens, John C., Scott, Stanley, and McHenry, Dean E. *California Government and Politics,* Fourth Edition. Englewood Cliffs, NJ: Prentice-Hall, 1967. 318 p. This college text covers its topic well, provides many additional references, and is sprinkled with political cartoons.

Gerston, Larry N. and Christensen, Terry. *California Politics & Government: A Practical Approach.* Pacific Grove, CA: Brooks/Cole, 1991. 116 p. This short book, intended to be a college text, adequately covers the three branches of government, state finances, local government, and political parties. It also has a helpful glossary.

Guide to California Government. 14th ed. Sacramento: League of Women Voters, 1992. 186 p. The original version of this title was published in 1940. Today's small, paperback text is illustrated with charts, graphs, and maps. It contains a short history, followed by indepth

(Pub. 64620)

373

descriptions of the three branches of government. There is also coverage of county, city, and special district governance.

Hyink, Bernard L.; Brown, Seyom; and Provost, David. *Politics and Government in California.* New York: Harper & Row, 1989. 294 p.

Leary, Mary Ellen. *Phantom Politics: Campaigning in California.* Washington: Public Affairs Press, 1977. 191 p.

Lee, Eugene, editor. *The California Governmental Process: Problems and Issues.* Boston: Little, Brown, 1966. 301 p. This book has dozens of readings on government and politics, including short articles by Stanley Mosk, Roger J. Traynor, and Earl Warren.

Lubenow, Gerald C. and Cain, Bruce E., eds. *Governing California: Politics, Government, and Public Policy in the Golden State.* Institute of Governmental Studies: Berkeley, 1997. 372 p. This book is intended to become a government or civics textbook. Contributing authors include John Jacobs (Sacramento Bee), Eugene Lee (former IGS director), and several Berkeley professors.

Muir, William K. Jr. *Legislature: California's School for Politics.* Chicago: University of Chicago Press, 1982. 219 p.

Owens, John Robert. *California Politics and Parties.* New York: Macmillan, 1970. 338 p.

Sohner, Charles P. and Field, Mona. *California Government and Politics Today.* Fifth Edition. Glenview, IL: Scott, Foresman/Little Brown, 1990. 120 p. This short text is intended for college students. It is very up-to-date in its statistics and charts.

Walker, Robert A. and Cave, Floyd A. *How California Is Governed.* New York: Dryden Press, 1953. 251 p. This text covers the three branches of government, the economy, local government, the Constitution, and the people of the state.

Appendix F

LexisNexis Sources[1]

Below is a list of California sources available on LexisNexis. The sources are a mixture of primary sources, secondary sources, and law-related sources that are helpful in California research. The list is published with the permission of the publisher. More specific information on individual sources is available in the Source Description entry for each source. The LexisNexis internet address is *www.lexisnexis.com.*

In this list, the left column provides the "short name" of each source and the right column provides the more descriptive "long name." Either the short or long name can be used to access a source using the "Find a Source" feature.

§ I. Courts and Litigation

[A] General Case Law

CAL;CACASE	CA Cases, Administrative Decisions & Attorney General Opinions, Combined
CAL;CACTS	CA State Cases, Combined
CAL;CACTSP	CA Published Cases, Combined
CAL;CAL	CA Supreme Court Cases from 1850
CAL;APP	CA Courts of Appeal Cases from 1905
CAL;APP-P	Published CA Court of Appeal Cases from 1905
CAL;APP-U	Unpublished CA Court of Appeal Cases from 1966
MEGA;9MEGA	9th Circuit—Federal & State Cases, Combined
MEGA;CAMEGA	CA Federal & State Cases, Combined

[B] Case Law by Area of Practice

CAL;ADMIN	CA Administrative Agency Cases
BANKING;CACTS	CA Banking Cases
CAL;CIVPRO	CA Civil Procedure Cases

---

[1] This appendix was revised for the 7th edition by Brian Raphael, Assistant Director of the Law Library and Adjunct Assistant Professor of Law, University of Southern California Law School.

(Pub. 64620)

TELCOM;CACTS	CA Communications Cases
CAL;CONLAW	CA Constitutional Cases
CAL;CONSTR	CA Construction Cases
CAL;K-LAW	CA Contract Cases
CAL;CORP	CA Corporate Cases
CAL;CRIME	CA Criminal Cases
CAL;CYBRLW	CA Cyberlaw Cases
CAL;ELDER	CA Elder Cases
CAL;ENERGY	CA Energy & Utility Cases
CAL;ENVIRN	CA Environmental Cases
CAL;ESTATE	CA Estate Cases
CAL;ETHICS	CA Ethics Cases
CAL;EVIDNC	CA Evidence Cases
CAL;FAMILY	CA Family Cases
CAL;HEALTH	CA Health Cases
CAL;INSURE	CA Insurance Cases
CAL;LABOR	CA Labor & Employment Cases
CAL;M&A	CA Merger & Acquisition Cases
CAL;PUBHW	CA Public Benefits & Social Security Cases
CAL;REALTY	CA Real Estate Cases
CAL;STSEC	CA Securities Cases
CAL;STTAX	CA Tax Cases
CAL;TORTS	CA Torts Cases
CAL;TRADE	CA Trade Cases
CAL;TRDMRK	CA Trademark Cases
CAL;UCC	CA Uniform Commercial Code Cases
CAL;WCSSD	CA Workers' Comp. & Disability Cases

[C] Litigation

DOCKET;CACIVL	CA Combined Civil Court Filings From Superior and Municipal Courts
DOCKET;CACRIM	CA Criminal Case Filings
INSOLV;CABKT	CA Bankruptcy Filings
MATBEN;CJCJUR	Judicial Council of California Civil Jury Instructions (CACI)
2NDARY;BAJI	California Jury Instructions Civil (BAJI)
2NDARY;CALJIC	California Jury Instructions Criminal (CALJIC)
VERDCT;CAJURY	VerdictSearch California Reporter
VERDCT;CAEXPT	Legal Expert Pages
LEXREF;LAEXPT	expert4law—The Legal Marketplace, LA County Bar Association Expert Witness Dir
LEGNEW;CASCSV	California Supreme Court Service (from 1/98)
CAL;BRREP	Brief Reporter—California Materials
CAL;OJTRAN	Transcripts from People v. Simpson Criminal Trial

CAL;OJCIV   Simpson Wrongful Death Trial Transcripts

§ II. Public Records

ASSETS;CAOWN   CA Deed Transfers, Tax Assessor Records and
                          Mortgage Records—Selected Counties
ASSETS;CAPROP   Combined CA Tax Assessor Records—All
                          Counties
ASSETS;CASALE   CA Deed Transfers—Selected Counties
ASSETS;CAMORT   CA Mortgage Records
DOCKET;CAJGT   CA Judgment and Lien Filings
INCORP;CABIZ   CA Business and Corporation Information
INCORP;CASOS   Secretary of State Corporation, LP and LLC
                          Information
INCORP;CAINC   Secretary of State Corporation Information
INCORP;CALTP   Secretary of State Limited Partnership
                          Information
INCORP;CACON   CA Contractors State License Board Information
INCORP;CALBUS   CA Business Locator
INCORP;CADBA   Business Leads and Fictitious Business Name
                          Information
INCORP;CALIC   CA Professional Licenses
INCORP;CACON   CA Contractors State License Board Information
LICNSE;CALIQ   CA Liquor Licenses
LICNSE;CAREAL   California Real Estate Licenses
LIENS;CATXLN   CA Tax Liens, Federal and State
LIENS;CAUCC   CA Uniform Commercial Code Lien Filings
LIENS;CAFDLN   CA Federal Tax Liens

§ III. Legislative Materials

CAL;CACODE   CA—Deering's California Codes Annotated,
                          Constitution, Court Rules & ALS, Combined
CAL;CODE   CA—Deering's California Codes Annotated
                          (current)
CAL;CAARCH   CA—Deering's California Codes Annotated
                          Archive from 1991
CAL;CA19xx   CA—Deering's California Codes Annotated, 19xx
CAL;CA20xx   CA—Deering's California Codes Annotated, 20xx
CAL;CACNST   CA—California Constitution
CAL;CAALS   CA—California Advance Legislative Service
CAL;CABILL   CA Bill Tracking & Full-Text Bills, Combined
CAL;CATRCK   CA Bill Tracking Reports
CAL;CATEXT   CA Full-Text Bills
CAL;CACOMM   CA Legislative Committee Analysis of Pending
                          Bills

LEGIS;CAJRNL	California Journal (10/89-present)
CAL;CARULE	CA—California Court Rules
CAL;LASCRL	Los Angeles County Superior Court Rules

§ IV. Administrative Materials

[A] General

CODES;CAREGS	CA—California Administrative Code & California Regulatory Law Bulletin
CAL;CAADMN	CA—Barclays Official California Code of Regulations
LEGIS;CARGTR	CA State Regulation Tracking
CAL;RGALRT	RegAlert—California Documents

[B] By Agency or Subject Area

CAL;CAALRB	CA Agricultural Labor Relations Board (from 1990)
STATES;CAAG	CA Attorney General Opinions (from 1/77)
CAL;CASBE	CA Board of Equalization Decisions (from 1/30)
CAL;CATAX	CA Board of Equalization and Franchise Tax Board Decisions
INSURE;CABLTN	CA—California Bulletins and Notices (from 10/91)
CAL;CAWORK	CA—California Compensation Cases (from 1/36)
CAL;CASEC	CA Department of Corporations Decisions (from 1/69)
CAL;CAFEHC	CA Fair Employment and Housing Commission (from 1985)
CAL;CAFAIR	CA Fair Political Practices Commission (opinions from 1975; advice letters from 1990)
CAL;CAFTB	CA Franchise Tax Board Decisions (from 12/53)
CAL;CAETOP	National Reporter on Legal Ethics and Prof. Responsibility—CA Opinions (from 1991)
LABOR;CAOSHD	CA Occupational Safety & Health Appeals Board (from 2/93)
LABOR;CAPER	California Public Employee Reporter (from 1981)
ENERGY;CAPUC	CA Public Utilities Commission Decisions (from 2/69)
ETHICS;CABAR	CA State Bar Court Decisions (from 3/90)
ENVIRN;CAENV	CA Water Resources (from 3/23) and Toxic Substances Control (from 12/99)

§ V. Matthew Bender Publications

| CAL;CAMBGR | CA Matthew Bender Publications, Combined |

CAL;CACOLW	Ballantine and Sterling California Corporation Laws
CAL;CAPRAC	California Civil Actions
MATBEN;CACAPP	California Class Actions Practice and Procedure
CAL;CACPRO	California Community Property With Tax Analysis
2NDARY;CACEVD	California Courtroom Evidence
MATBEN;CRMDEF	California Criminal Defense Practice
MATBEN;CCDPRE	California Criminal Defense Practice Reporter
2NDARY;CACRMD	California Criminal Discovery
CAL;CALDDP	California Deposition and Discovery Practice
CAL;CAEMGU	California Employer's Guide to Emp. Handbk & Personnel Policy Manuals
CAL;CAEMLW	California Employment Law
CAL;CAEMLR	California Employment Law Reporter (from 1/98)
CAL;CAELLP	California Environmental Law & Land Use Practice
MATBEN;CENLRE	California Environmental Law Reporter
CAL;CAFML	California Family Law Monthly (from 1/01)
CAL;CAFLAP	California Family Law Practice and Procedure
MATBEN;CAFLTG	California Family Law Trial Guide
MATBEN;CAFTXP	California Family Tax Planning
CAL;CFJURY	California Forms of Jury Instruction
CAL;CAFPAP	California Forms Of Pleading and Practice
2NDARY;CAELDL	California Guide to Tax, Estate & Financial Planning for the Elderly
CAL;CAINSL	California Insurance Law & Practice
CAL;CAIPHB	California Intellectual Property Handbook
MATBEN;CAJCPP	California Juvenile Courts Practice and Procedure
CAL;CALEIC	Hanna, California Law of Employee Injuries and Workers Compensation
CAL;CALFTG	California Legal Forms Transaction Guide
MATBEN;CAMECH	California Mechanic's Lien Law and Construction Industry Practice
CAL;CAP&A	California Points and Authorities
MATBEN;CAPROB	California Probate Practice
2NDARY;CAPPRO	California Probate Procedure
CAL;CAPRLA	California Products Liability Actions
MATBEN;CAPSLR	California Public Sector Labor Relations
MATBEN;CAREGU	California Real Estate Guide: Litigation and Transactions
CAL;CARELP	California Real Estate Law and Practice
CAL;CALRER	California Real Estate Reporter (from 1/01)
CAL;CACTAX	California Small Business Guide: Formation, Operation, and Taxation

CAL;CATORT	California Torts
CAL;CATRYL	California Trial Guide
MATBEN;CATRHB	California Trial Handbook
MATBEN;CATRPR	California Trust Practice
MATBEN;CAUIML	California Uninsured Motorist Law
2NDARY;CAWCCC	California White Collar Crime—Civil Remedies and Criminal Sanctions
MATBEN;CAWILL	California Wills and Trusts: Text
2NDARY;CALCOM	Herlick, California Workers' Compensation Law (6th Edition—treatise)
MATBEN;MCCIVL	Deskbook on the Management of Complex Civil Litigation
2NDARY;CAEMP	Labor & Employment in California: Guide to Employment Laws, Regulations, and Practices
MATBEN;TAXTEC	Major Tax Planning-USC Annual Institute on Federal Taxation
MATBEN;CAPG	Matthew Bender® Practice Guide: California
MATBEN;CALTDS	Matthew Bender® Practice Guide: California Civil Discovery
MATBEN;CALTLT	Matthew Bender® Practice Guide: California Landlord-Tenant Litigation
MATBEN;CALTCP	Matthew Bender® Practice Guide: California Pretrial Civil Procedure
CAL;CACORP	Practice Under the California Corporate Securities Laws

§ VI. Continuing Education of the Bar (CEB) Publications

CEB;ALLCEB	CEB Combined All CEB Publications
CEB;CEBBUS	CEB Combined Business & Corporation Law Publications
CEB;CEBEST	CEB Combined Estate Planning Publications
CEB;CEBLIT	CEB Combined Litigation Publications
CEB;CEBPRO	CEB Combined Property Publications

§ VII. Miscellaneous Secondary Sources

CAL;CADIG	CA—Martindale-Hubbell® Law Digest
MARHUB;CADIR	CA Listings—Martindale-Hubbell® Law Directory
2NDARY;CAEVCM	California Evidence Courtroom Manual
CLE;CAEVOB	California Evidence Code with Objections
CAL;CAREST	CA Restatement Annotated Case Citations
CAL;WITKIN	Witkin Treatises
CAL;WITSUM	Witkin Summary of California Law (Ninth Edition)

CAL;WITPRO	Witkin California Procedure (Fourth Edition)
CAL;WITEVD	Witkin California Evidence (Fourth Edition)
CAL;WITCRM	Witkin and Epstein California Criminal Law (Third Edition)

§ VIII. News Sources

CAL;CANEWS	California News Publications
NEWS;ALMTS	Alameda Times-Star (Alameda, CA) (from 11/01)
NEWS;ARGUS	The Argus (Fremont, CA) (from 11/01)
NEWS;BPRESS	The Business Press / California (from 1/95)
LEGNEW;CAOSHA	Cal-OSHA Reporter (from 8/96)
LEGNEW;MSCAEN	California Environment Law Monitor (from 10/95)
NEWS;CALIFN	The Californian (Salinas, CA) (from 6/02)
NEWS;LAD	The Daily News of Los Angeles (from 1/97)
NEWS;DLYREV	The Daily Review (Hayward, CA) (from 11/01)
NEWS;DESSUN	The Desert Sun (Palm Springs, CA) (from 4/02)
NEWS;EBEXP	East Bay Express (California) (from 7/01)
NEWS;FRESNO	The Fresno Bee (from 1/94)
NEWS;IVDB	Inland Valley Daily Bulletin (Ontario, CA) (from 4/02)
NEWS;KIPPUB	Kiplinger Publications—California Stories
NEWS;KRTBUS	Knight Ridder/Tribune Business News—California Stories (from 1/97)
NEWS;LBEACH	Long Beach Press-Telegram (Long Beach, CA) (from 11/01)
NEWS;LAT	Los Angeles Times (from 1/85)
NEWS;MARIN	Marin Independent Journal (Marin, CA) (from 8/02)
NEWS;METNWS	Metropolitan News Enterprise (from 7/95)
NEWS;MODBEE	Modesto Bee (from 1/01)
NEWS;LANEWT	New Times Los Angeles (California) (from 8/96 until 10/02)
NEWS;OAKTRB	The Oakland Tribune (Oakland, CA) (from 11/01)
NEWS;PASDNA	Pasadena Star-News (Pasadena, CA) (from 11/01)
NEWS;PRSENT	The Press Enterprise (Riverside, CA) (from 1/95)
LEGNEW;RECRDR	The Recorder (from 1/91)
NEWS;SBSUN	San Bernadino Sun (San Bernadino, CA) (from 11/01)
NEWS;SDUT	The San Diego Union-Tribune (from 12/83)
NEWS;SFCHRN	The San Francisco Chronicle (from 10/89)
NEWS;SFEXAM	San Francisco Examiner (from 8/93)
NEWS;SVGT	San Gabriel Valley Tribune (San Gabriel Valley, CA) (from 11/01)

NEWS;SMCT	San Mateo County Times (San Mateo, CA) (from 11/01)
NEWS;SFWKLY	SF Weekly (California) (from 4/96)
NEWS;TVHLD	Tri-Valley, Herald (Pleasanton, CA) (from 11/01)
NEWS;TULARE	Tulare Advance-Register (Tulare, CA) (from 8/02)
NEWS;VENCST	Ventura County Star (Ventura County, CA) (from 7/97)
NEWS;VISTIM	Visalia Times-Delta (Visalia, CA) (from 8/02)
LEGNEW;WCOMEX	Workers' Comp Executive (from 9/91)

§ IX. Law Reviews and Bar Journals

LAWREV;CALRV	California Law Reviews, Combined
LAWREV;ASICL	Annual Survey of International & Comparative Law (from 1997)
LAWREV;ASIAN	Asian Law Journal (from 1995)
LAWREV;BJELL	Berkeley Journal of Employment and Labor Law (from 2001)
LAWREV;BJILAW	Berkeley Journal of International Law (from 1996)
LAWREV;BRKTLJ	Berkeley Technology Law Journal (from 1998)
LAWREV;BRKWOM	Berkeley Women's Law Journal (from 1998)
LAWREV;CALLR	California Law Review (from 7/82)
LAWREV;CAWILJ	California Western International Law Journal (from Fall 1994)
LAWREV;CAWEST	California Western Law Review (from Fall 1993)
LAWREV;CHALRV	Chapman Law Review (from Spring 1998)
LAWREV;CHILAT	Chicano-Latino Law Review (from Fall 1995)
LAWREV;ENVRON	ENVIRONS Environmental Law and Policy Journal (from Spring 2000)
LAWREV;GGLR	Golden Gate University (from 1993)
LAWREV;HCELJ	Hastings Communications and Entertainment Law Journal (from Summer 1998)
LAWREV;HCLQ	Hastings Constitutional Law Quarterly (from Spring 1998)
LAWREV;HICLR	Hastings International and Comparative Law Review (from Summer 1998)
LAWREV;HASTLJ	Hastings Law Journal (from 9/82)
LAWREV;HWNJEP	Hastings West-Northwest Journal of Environmental Law and Policy (from 2/00)
LAWREV;HWLJ	Hastings Women's Law Journal (from 12/98)
LAWREV;JCCC	Journal of the Center for Children & the Courts (from 1999)
LAWREV;JCLGLI	Journal of Contemporary Legal Issues (from Spring 1998)

LAWREV;JJUVLW	Journal of Juvenile Law (from 1996)
LAWREV;JLSC	Journal of Law & Social Challenges (from Fall 1997 through Spring 1999)
LAWREV;JLADVP	Journal of Legal Advocacy & Practice (from 2/00)
LAWREV;LARAZA	La Raza Law Journal (from Spring 1998)
LAWREV;LOSAL	Los Angeles Lawyer (from 10/96)
LAWREV;LLAELJ	Loyola of Los Angeles Entertainment Law Review (from 1995)
LAWREV;LICLR	Loyola of Los Angeles International & Comparative Law Review (from Fall 1993)
LAWREV;LLALR	Loyola of Los Angeles Law Review (from 6/93)
LAWREV;MCGLR	McGeorge Law Review (from Spring 1995)
LAWREV;NEXUS	Nexus, A Journal of Opinion (from Spring 1996)
LAWREV;OCLAW	Orange County Lawyer (from 1/96)
LAWREV;PEPPDR	Pepperdine Dispute Resolution Law Journal (from 2000)
LAWREV;PEPPLR	Pepperdine Law Review (from 1993)
LAWREV;SDINTL	San Diego International Law Journal (from 2000)
LAWREV;SDLREV	San Diego Law Review (from Spring 1993)
CAL;SFATTY	San Francisco Attorney (from Feb./Mar. 2000)
LAWREV;SJALR	San Joaquin Agricultural Law Review (from 1996)
LAWREV;CHTLJ	Santa Clara Computer and High Technology Law Journal (from 1994)
LAWREV;SCLREV	Santa Clara Law Review (from 1994)
LAWREV;SCILJ	Southern California Interdisciplinary Law Journal (from Fall 1993)
LAWREV;SOCALR	Southern California Law Review (from 9/82)
LAWREV;SCRLWS	Southern California Review of Law and Women's Studies (from Spring 1994)
LAWREV;STRADE	Southwestern Journal of Law and Trade in the Americas (from 1994)
LAWREV;SOULR	Southwestern University Law Review (from 1994)
LAWREV;SELJ	Stanford Environmental Law Journal (from 1993)
LAWREV;STJIL	Stanford Journal of International Law (from 1993)
LAWREV;SJLBF	Stanford Journal of Law, Business and Finance (from Spring 1995)
LAWREV;SLPR	Stanford Law and Policy Review (from Spring 1994)
LAWREV;STANLR	Stanford Law Review (from 11/82)
LAWREV;STTLR	Stanford Technology Law Review (from 1997)

LAWREV;TJLR	Thomas Jefferson Law Review (from Summer 1993)
LAWREV;TRANSL	The Transnational Lawyer (from Spring 1995)
LAWREV;UCDAVI	U.C. Davis Journal of International Law & Policy (from Winter 1995)
LAWREV;UCDJLP	UC Davis Journal of Juvenile Law & Policy (from Summer 2001)
LAWREV;UCDAV	U.C. Davis Law Review (from 1993)
LAWREV;UCLAAP	UCLA Asian Pacific American Law Journal (from Fall 1995)
LAWREV;UENTLR	UCLA Entertainment Law Review (from Fall 1997)
LAWREV;UCJELP	UCLA Journal of Environmental Law & Policy (from 1995/96)
LAWREV;UCLAFA	UCLA Journal of International Law and Foreign Affairs (from Spring 1996)
LAWREV;JINEL	UCLA Journal of Islamic and Near Eastern Law (from Fall 2001/Winter 2002)
LAWREV;UCLALT	UCLA Journal of Law and Technology (from 2000)
LAWREV;UCLALR	UCLA Law Review (from 10/82)
LAWREV;UCLAPB	UCLA Pacific Basin Law Journal (from 1993)
LAWREV;UCLAWJ	UCLA Women's Law Journal (from 1991)
LAWREV;USFLR	University of San Francisco Law Review (from Spring 1994)
LAWREV;UWLALR	UWLA Law Review (from 1998)
CAL;WSULR	Western State University Law Review (from Spring 1991)
LAWREV;WHITLR	Whittier Law Review (from 1993)

Appendix G

Westlaw Databases[1]

Below is a list of California databases available on Westlaw. This information is used with the publisher's permission. The databases include primary and secondary sources as well as law-related sources that are helpful in California research. More specific information on individual databases is available in the Scope note for each database. The Westlaw internet address is *www.westlaw.com*.

In this list, the left hand column provides the database names, the middle column provides the database identifiers, and the right hand column provides the dates of coverage.

§ I. Courts and Litigation

[A] General Case Law

Ninth Circuit Federal and State Cases	CTA9-ALL	Varies by court
California State and Federal Cases	CA-CS-ALL	Varies by court
California Cases	CA-CS	
Supreme Court		1850–
Courts of Appeal		1905–
Appellate Departments/ Divisions of the Superior Court		1929–
Review Dept. of the State Bar Court		1990–
California Official Reports	CA-ORCS	
Supreme Court		1850–
Courts of Appeal		1905–
Appellate Departments/ Divisions of the Superior Court		1929–

---

[1] This appendix was revised for the 7th edition by Brian Raphael, Assistant Director of the Law Library and Adjunct Assistant Professor of Law, University of Southern California Law School.

(Pub. 64620)

California Reported Cases	CA-CSR	
Supreme Court		1850–
Courts of Appeal		1905–
Appellate Departments/ Divisions of the Superior Court		1929–
California Unreported Cases	CA-CSU	
Supreme Court		1992–
Courts of Appeal		1970–
Appellate Departments/ Divisions of the Superior Court		1970–
Review Dept. of the State Bar Court		1990–

[B]   Case Law by Area of Practice

Business Organizations Law Cases	CABUS-CS	1850–
Civil Rights Cases	CACIV-CS	1850–
Commercial Law & Contracts Cases	CACML-CS	1850–
Criminal Justice Cases	CACJ-CS	1850–
Education Cases	CAED-CS	1850–
Energy Cases	CAEN-CS	1850–
Environmental Law Cases	CAENV-CS	1850–
Estate Planning & Probate Cases	CAEPP-CS	1850–
Family Law Cases	CAFL-CS	1850–
Finance & Banking Cases	CAFIN-CS	1850–
Government Benefits Cases	CAGB-CS	1850–
Government Contracts Cases	CAGC-CS	1850–
Health Law Cases	CAHTH-CS	1850–
Insurance Cases	CAIN-CS	1850–
Labor & Employment Cases	CALB-CS	1850–
Legal Ethics & Professional Responsibility Cases	CAETH-CS	1850–
Pension & Retirement Benefits Cases	CAPEN-CS	1850–
Products Liability Cases	CAPL-CS	1850–
Professional Malpractice Cases	CAMAL-CS	1850–
Public Employee Reporter	CA-PER	1982–
Public Utilities Reports	CA-PUR	1850–
Real Property Cases	CARP-CS	1850–
Securities & Blue Sky Law Cases	CASEC-CS	1850–

Taxation Cases	CATX-CS	1850–
Tort Law Cases	CATRT-CS	1850–
Workers' Compensation Cases	CAWC-CS	1850–

[C] Litigation

California Court Rules	CA-RULES	Current data
California State Trial Court Rules	CA-TRIALRULES	Current data
California Court Orders	CA-ORDERS	Current data
Lawsuit Filings—California	LS-CA	Varies by court
Criminal Records—California	CRIM-CA	Varies by county
Bankruptcy Filings—California	BKR-CA	Varies by county
California Litigation Preparation	LITPREP-CA	Current data
California Jury Instructions	CA-JI	Current data
Judicial Council of California Civil Jury Instructions	CACI	Current data
California Civil Jury Instructions	CA-BAJI	Current data
California Jury Instructions—Criminal	CA-CALJIC	Current data
California Jury Verdicts Combined	CA-JV-ALL	1983– (varies by source)
ALM VerdictSearch California Jury Verdicts and Settlements	ALMVS-CA-JV	1998–
Legal Expert Pages	CA-LEP	1999 ed.
West's Legal Directory—California	WLD-CA	Current data
California Briefs Multibase	CA-BRIEF-ALL	1997–
California Supreme Court Briefs	CA-BRIEF	1997–
California Supreme Court Briefs	CA-BRIEF-EXT	1980–1996 (archival)
California Court of Appeal Briefs	CA-APP-BRIEF	1997–
California Recall Election Briefs	CA-RECALL	2003
California Supreme Court Petitions	CA-PETITION	1993–
O.J. Simpson Civil Trial Transcripts and Documents	OJCIV-TRANS	1994–1997
O.J. Simpson Trial Transcripts and Documents (criminal)	OJ-TRANS	1994–1995
Menendez Trial Transcripts and Documents		1994–1996

§ II. Legislative Materials

[A] General Sources

California Statutes—Annotated	CA-ST-ANN	Current data
California Statutes—Unannotated	CA-ST	Current data
California Statutes—Annotated (historical)	CA-STANNYY (use last two digits of a year for YY)	1987–2003
California Statutes—General Index	CA-ST-IDX	Current data
California Legislative Service	CA-LEGIS	Current data
California Historical Legislative Service	CA-LEGIS-OLD	1987–2003
California Committee Analyses	CCA	1999–
California Committee Analyses—Archive	CCA-OLD	1991–1998
California Bill Tracking	CA-BILLTRK	Current data
California Bill Tracking—Full Text	CA-BILLTXT	Current data
California Bill Tracking—Summaries & Full Text Combined	CA-BILLS	Current data

[B] Statutes by Topic Area

Blue Sky Statutes Annotated	CASEC-ST	Current data
Criminal Justice Statutes Annotated	CACJ-ST	Current data
Environmental, Health, and Safety Statutes Annotated	CAENV-ST	Current data
Human Resources Statutes Annotated	CAHR-ST	Current data
Insurance Statutes Annotated	CAIN-ST	Current data
Taxation Statutes Annotated	CATX-ST	Current data
Workers' Compensation Statutes Annotated	CAWC-ST	Current data

§ III. Administrative Law Materials

[A] General

California Code of Regulations	CA-ADC	Current data
California Regulation Tracking	CA-REGTRK	Current data
California Regulation Tracking—Full Text	CA-REGTXT	Current data

California Regulation Tracking & Text Combined	CA-SNREGS	Current data

[B] By Agency or Subject Area

California Attorney General Opinions	CA-AG	1977–
California Environmental, Health, and Safety Regulations	ENFLEX-CA	Current data
California Environmental Law Administrative Decisions	CAENV-ADMIN	
Water Resources Control Board		1957–
Dept. of Energy Resources Conservation and Development Commission		1982–
California Fair Employment and Housing Commission Decisions	CA-FEHC	1978–
California Fair Political Practices Commission Opinions and Letters	CA-ETH	1975– (opinions) 1985– (advice letters)
California Human Resources Regulations	CAHR-REG	Current data
California Insurance Regulations	CAIN-ADC	Current data
California Insurance Bulletins	CAIN-BUL	1939–
California Legal Ethics and Professional Responsibility—Ethics Opinions	CAETH-EO	1977–
California Occupational Safety and Health Appeals Board Decisions	CA-OSHA	1974–
California Public Employee Reporter	CA-PER	1982–
California Public Utilities Reports (Public Utilities Commission Decisions)	CA-PUR	1953–
California Securities Administrative Decisions	CASEC-ADMIN	1969–
California State Personnel Board Decisions	CASPB	1992–
California Tax Regulations	CATX-ADC	Current data
California Taxation Administrative Decisions	CATX-ADMIN	1930–
California Workers' Compensation Regulations	CAWC-ADC	Current data

California Workers' Compensation Administrative Decisions	CAWC-ADMIN	May 1981–

§ IV. Public Records

California Business Finder Records	BUSFIND-CA	Current data
Business Locator Abstract Records—California	BUSLOC-CA	Current data
California Fictitious Business Name Records	FBN-CA	Current data
Professional License—California	LICENSE-CA	Current data
Real Property Tax Assessor Records	RPA-CA	Varies by county
Real Property Transaction Records—California	RPT-CA	Varies by county
California Corporate Records & Business Registrations	CORP-CA	Current data
UCC, Lien & Civil Judgment Records—California	ULJ-CA	Varies by source
Uniform Commercial Code Records—California	UCC-CA	Current data
California Environmental Records	EDR-CA	Current data

§ V. California Treatises, Forms, and Practice Materials

[A] Combined databases (containing materials from a variety of texts)

California Texts, Periodicals, and Legal Forms	CA-TPLF	Current data
California Business Law	CA-BUSLAW	Current data
California Civil Litigation	CA-CIVLIT	Current data
California Estate Planning and Probate	CA-EPP	Current data
California Insurance	CA-INS	Current data
California Miller and Starr Plus (Real Estate)	CA-MILREPLUS	Current data
California Tort/Personal Injury Law	CA-PITORT	Current data
California Workers' Compensation	CA-WC	Current data

[B] The Rutter Group—California Practice Guides

Multibase (combined database of all The Rutter Group Guides)	TRG-CA	Current data
Alternative Dispute Resolution	TRG-CAADR	Current data
Business and Professions Code § 17200 Practice	TRG-BUSPROF	Current data
Civil Appeals and Writs	TRG-CACIVAPP	Current data
Civil Procedure Before Trial	TRG-CACIVP	Current data
Civil Trials and Evidence	TRG-CACIVEV	Current data
Corporations	TRG-CACORP	Current data
Employment Litigation	TRG-CAEMPL	Current data
Enforcing Judgments and Debts	TRG-CADEBT	Current data
Family Law	TRG-CAFAMILY	Current data
Federal Civil Procedure Before Trial	TRG-CAFEDCIVP	Current data
Federal Civil Trials and Evidence	TRG-FEDCIVEV	Current data
Insurance Litigation	TRG-CAINSL	Current data
Landlord-Tenant	TRG-CALANDTEN	Current data
Ninth Circuit Civil Appellate Practice	TRG-CA9CIR	Current data
Personal Injury	TRG-CAPI	Current data
Probate	TRG-CAPROBTE	Current data
Professional Responsibility	TRG-CAPROFR	Current data
Real Property Transactions	TRG-CAPROP	Current data

[C] Witkin Treatises

Witkin's California Treatises (combined)	WITKIN	Current data
California Criminal Law	WITCRIM	Current data
California Evidence	WITEVID	Current data
California Procedure	WITPROC	Current data
Summary of California Law	WITSUM	Current data

[D] Other Individual Texts and Treatises

BNA's California Corporation: Legal Aspects of Organization and Operation	BNACPS-CA	Current data
California Affirmative Defenses, 2d	CAAFDEF	Current data
California Common Interest Developments: Law and Practice	CACID	Current data

California Community Property Law	CACPL	Current data
California Construction Law Manual	CACLM	Current data
California Foreclosure Law and Practice	CAFCLP	Current data
California Insurance Law Dictionary and Desk Reference	CAINLAWDDR	Current data
California Insurance Law Handbook	CAINLAWH	Current data
California ISO State Filing Handbook	CA-ISOSFH	Current data
California Jurisprudence	CAJUR	Current data
California Medical Malpractice: Law and Practice	CMMLP	Current data
California Premises Liability: Law and Practice	CAPREMLIAB	Current data
California Style Manual	CASTYLE	Current data
CJER Mandatory Criminal Jury Instructions Handbook	CJER-MCJIH	Current data
Cohelan on California Class Actions	CACLASSACT	Current data
Dunne on Depositions in California	CADEPOS	Current data
Miller and Starr California Real Estate Multibase	MILCALRE-ALL	Current data
Miller and Starr California Real Estate	MILCALRE	Current data
Miller and Starr California Real Estate Digest, 3d	CALREDG	Current data
Overly on Electronic Evidence in California	CAELECEVID	Current data
Residential Mortgage Lending: State Regulation Manual—West	RML-SRW	Current data
RIA State and Local Taxes—California	RIA-CA	Current data
RIA State and Local Taxes—California Explanations	RIA-CAEXP	Current data
Simons on California Evidence	SIMCAEVID	Current data
Taxing California Property	TAXCAPROP	Current data
Younger on California Motions	CAMOTIONS	Current data

[E] Form Books

California Civil Practice—Combined (comprehensive form set)	CCP-ALL	Current data
California Civil Practice—Business Litigation	CCP-BUS	Current data
California Civil Practice—Civil Rights Litigation	CCP-CIVRGT	Current data
California Civil Practice—Employment Litigation	CCP-EMP	Current data
California Civil Practice—Environmental Litigation	CCP-ENV	Current data
California Civil Practice—Family Law Litigation	CCP-FAM	Current data
California Civil Practice—Probate and Trust Proceedings	CCP-PROB	Current data
California Civil Practice—Procedure	CCP-PROC	Current data
California Civil Practice—Real Property Litigation	CCP-REPROP	Current data
California Civil Practice—Torts	CCP-TORTS	Current data
California Civil Practice—Workers' Compensation	CCP-WCOMP	Current data
California Criminal Forms and Instructions	CACFI	Current data
California Environmental, Health, and Safety Forms	ENFLEX-FRM-CA	Current data
California Real Estate Forms (Miller and Starr)	MILCALRE-FRM	Current data
California Transactions Forms—Combined	CTF-ALL	Current data
California Transactions Forms—Business Entities	CTF-BE	Current data
California Transactions Forms—Business Transactions	CTF-BT	Current data
California Transactions Forms—Estate Planning	CTF-EP	Current data
California Transactions Forms—Family Law	CTF-FAM	Current data
West's California Code Forms with Practice Commentaries	CACF	Current data

(Pub. 64620)

West's California Judicial Council Forms	CAJCF	Current data

§ VI.   California Legal News and Current Awareness

Cal-OSHA Reporter	CA-COR	Aug 1974–
Cal-OSHA Reporter (newsletter portions)	CA-CORNL	Jan 1994–
Cal-OSHA Reporter Decision Summaries	CA-CORSUM	Aug 1974–
California Employment Law Letter	SMCAEMPLL	Jan 1997–
California Environmental Insider	SMCAENVIN	Jan 1997–
California Health Law Monitor	SMCAHTHLM	Jan 1997–
California Insurance Law and Regulation Reporter	CAILRR	Jan 1996–
California Tort Reporter	CATRTR	Jan 2000–
California Workers' Comp Newsletter Multibase	CAWC-NL-ALL	Varies by publication
California Workers' Comp Advisor	CAWC-ADV	Dec 1995–
California Workers' Compensation Appeals Board Reporter	CAWC-ABR	1999–
California Workers' Compensation Appeals Board Reporter (newsletter portions)	CAWC-ABRNL	1999–
California Workers' Compensation Appeals Board Reporter Case Summaries	CAWC-ABRSUM	1999–
California Workplace Monitor	SMCAWKPLM	Jan 1997–
Miller and Starr Real Estate Newsalert	MILCALRE-NA	Jan 2003–
O.J. Simpson Case Commentaries	OJ-COMMENT	1994–1997
Recorder	RECORDER-SF	Jan 1998–
Westlaw State Bulletins—California	WSB-CA	Current data
Workers' Comp Executive	WC-EXE	Sep 1991–

§ VII.   California News and Business

California News	CANEWS	Varies by source
Newspapers Full Text—California	PAPERSCA	Varies by source
California Papers	CANP	Varies by source

Antelope Valley Press (Palmdale, CA)	BSX-AVPRS	Dec 1991–Jul 1997
Argus Courier (Petaluma, CA)	BSX-ARGCOR	Dec 1992–Apr 1997
Bakersfield Californian	BKRSFLDCA	Jan 1994–Nov 1998
Business Journal	BUSJNL	Jan 1994–Sep 2000
Business Journal-Sacramento	BUSJSACR	Jun 1999–Sep 2000
Business News-San Diego	BNSANDIEGO	Apr 1985–Mar 1986
Business Press	BSPS	Sep 1995–
California Business	CALBUS	Mar–Sep 1994
California Construction Link	CACONSTLINK	Feb 1998–
California Executive	CAEXEC	Oct–Nov 1987
California Journal	CALJ	Jan 1997–
California Management Review	CAMGTR	Jan 1994–Jul 2001
California Public Finance	CAPUBFIN	Jul 1993–Aug 1998
California Voice	ENWCALV	Sep 1994–Feb 1998
Californian (Salinas, CA)	CALIFORNIAN	Jun 2002–
Contra Costa Times (Walnut Creek, CA)	CCTIMES	Jun 2001–
Contra Costa Papers	CONTRA-PPRS	Jun 1995–
Daily Midway Driller (Taft, CA)	BSX-DMD	Mar 1993–Jul 1997
Daily News of Los Angeles	DNLA	Jan 1989–
Daily Press (Victorville, CA)	BSX-DLYPRS	Dec 1991–Aug 1997
Desert Sun	DESERTSUN	Jan 2002–
Diablo Business (Walnut Creek, CA)	DIABLOBUS	May 1990–Dec 1994
Federal Reserve Bank of San Francisco Economic Review	FEDRESSF	Jan 1997–
Government Contracting Opportunities	GOVCONTRACT	Mar 2001–
Hanford Daily Sentinel	BSXHDS	Jan 1993–Jul 1997
Independent Journal (Novato, CA)	BSX-INDJ	Dec 1992–Aug 1997
Jewish Bulletin of Northern California	ENWJBNC	Oct 1994–Oct 1998
Kiplinger California Letter	KIPCL	Jan 2001–

(Pub. 64620)

Long Beach Press-Telegram	LONGB-PTEL	Jan 1992–
Los Angeles Business Journal	LABUSJ	Jan 1994–
Los Angeles Daily News	LADLYNWS	Jan 1989–
Los Angeles Magazine	LAMAG	May 1988–Dec 1999
Los Angeles Times	LAT	Jan 1985–
Napa Valley Register	BSX-NVREG	Jan 1993–Jul 1997
News Chronicle (Thousand Oaks, CA)	BSX-NWSCHR	Dec 1991–Aug 1997
Oakland Tribune	OKLDTR	May 2003–
Orange County Business Journal	ORGCTYBUSJ	Jan 1985–
Orange County Metropolitan (Newport Beach, CA)	OCMET	Jul 1994–
Orange County Register	OCREG	
Selected coverage		Jul 1986–Dec 1986
Full coverage		Jan 1987–
Press Democrat (Santa Rosa, CA)	PDEMSR	Aug 1994–
Press-Enterprise (Riverside, CA)	PRES-ENT	
Selected coverage		Dec 1991–Aug 1992
Full coverage		Sep 1992–
Public Record (Palm Desert, CA)	PUBREC	Dec 1993–
Record-Gazette (Banning, CA)	BSX-RECGAZ	Feb 1993–Jul 1997
Sales Prospector California, Arizona, Nevada and Hawaii	SALESPW	Oct 1991–Jan 1993
San Bernardino County Sun	BSX-SBSUN	Dec 1991–Jul 1997
San Diego Business Journal	SDGOBUSJ	Apr 1985–
San Diego Daily Transcript	SDGOTRANS	Jan 1991–Aug 1998
San Diego Union-Tribune	SDUT	Jan 2000–
San Francisco Business Magazine	SFBUSMAG	Jun 1985–Jun 1994
San Francisco Business Times	SFBUSTIMES	Jun 1998–Sep 2000
San Francisco Chronicle	SFCHR	Jan 1985–
San Francisco Examiner	SFEXAMINER	Jun 1990–
San Jose Mercury News	SJMERCURY	Jun 1985–
San Luis Obispo Tribune	SLOTRIBUNE	Apr 2001–
Santa Clara County Business	SCLARABUS	Jan 1985–Dec 1986

Santa Cruz County Business	SCRUZBUS	Feb 1985–Mar 1986
Santa Cruz Sentinel	BSX-CRUZ	Jan 1992–Aug 1997
Santa Maria Times	BSX-SMARIA	Dec 1992–Aug 1997
Signal and Saugas Enterprise (Valencia, CA)	BSX-SSE	Jan 1992–Jun 1997
Silicon Valley	SVALLEY	Jan 1985–Aug 1986
Southern California Business	SCABUS	Feb 1985–Jan 1998
Sun Reporter	ENWSUNR	Oct 1994–Oct 1998
Times (San Mateo, CA)	BSX-TIMES	Dec 1991–Aug 1997
Visalia Times-Delta	BSX-VTD	Dec 1992–Jun 2002
Western Folklore	WTRNFOLK	Jan 1997–
Yuba-Sutter Appeal Democrat (Marysville, CA)	BSX-YUBA	Dec 1991–Aug 1997

§ VIII. California Journals and Law Reviews

California Journals and Law Reviews (combined)	CA-JLR	Varies by publication
African-American Law and Policy Report	AALPR	
Full coverage		1994 (vol.1)–
American Journal of Comparative Law	AMJCL	
Full coverage		1994 (vol.42)–
Annual Survey of International and Comparative Law	ANNSICL	
Full coverage		1995 (vol.2)–
Asian Law Journal	ASLJ	
Full coverage		1994 (vol.1)–
Asian Pacific American Law Journal	ASPAMLJ	
Full coverage		1993 (vol.1)–
Berkeley Journal of Employment and Labor Law	BERKJELL	
Selected coverage		1984 (vol.6)–1993 (vol.14)
Full coverage		1994 (vol.15)–

Berkeley Journal of International Law	BERKJIL	
Selected coverage		1983 (vol.1)–1992 (vol.10)
Full coverage		1993 (vol.11)–
Berkeley La Raza Law Journal	BERKLARLJ	
Selected coverage		1992 (vol.5)–1993 (vol.6)
Full coverage		1994 (vol.7)–
Berkeley Technology Law Journal	BERKTLJ	
Selected coverage		1986 (vol.1)–1992 (vol.7)
Full coverage		1993 (vol.8)–
Berkeley Women's Law Journal	BERKWLJ	
Selected coverage		1990 (vol.5)–1993 (vol.8)
Full coverage		1994 (vol.9)–
Beverly Hills Bar Association Journal	BEVHBAJ	
Selected coverage		1991 (vol.25)–
California Bankruptcy Journal	CABKRJ	
Selected coverage		1991 (vol.19)–
California Law Review	CALR	
Full coverage		1982 (vol.70)–
California Regulatory Law Reporter	CARLR	
Full coverage		1994 (vol.14)–
California Western International Law Journal	CAWILJ	
Selected coverage		1987 (vol.18)–1993 (vol.23)
Full coverage		1993 (vol.24)–
California Western Law Review	CAWLR	
Selected coverage		1987 (vol.24)–1993 (vol.29)
Full coverage		1993 (vol.30)–
Chapman Law Review	CHAPLR	
Full coverage		1998 (vol.1)–
Chicano-Latino Law Review	CHLLR	
Selected coverage		1990 (vol.10)–1992 (vol.12)

Full coverage		1993 (vol.13)–
Ecology Law Quarterly	ECGLQ	
Selected coverage		1984 (vol.11)–1993 (vol.20, no.2)
Full coverage		1993 (vol.20, no.3)–
Environs Environmental Law and Policy Journal	ENVIRONS	
Full coverage		1996 (vol.20)–
Family Court Review	FAMCR	
Full coverage		1998 (vol.36, no.2)–
Golden Gate University Law Review	GGULR	
Selected coverage		1983 (vol.13)–1993 (vol.23)
Full coverage		1994 (vol.24)–
Hastings Communications and Entertainment Law Journal (COMM/ENT)	COMENT	
Selected coverage		1982 (vol.5)–1993 (vol.15)
Full coverage		1993 (vol.16)–
Hastings Constitutional Law Quarterly	HSTCLQ	
Selected coverage		1983 (vol.10)–1993 (vol.20, no.2)
Full coverage		1993 (vol.20, no.3)–
Hastings International and Comparative Law Review	HSTICLR	
Selected coverage		1983 (vol.6)–1993 (vol.17, no.1)
Full coverage		1994 (vol.17, no.2)–
Hastings Law Journal	HSTLJ	
Full coverage		1982 (vol.33, no.3)–
Hastings West-Northwest Journal of Environmental Law and Policy	HSTWJELP	

Selected coverage		1994 (vol.1)–
Hastings Women's Law Journal	HSTWLJ	
Selected coverage		1992 (vol.3, no.2)–1993 (vol.4, no.1)
Full coverage		1993 (vol.4, no.2)–
Intellectual Property Law Bulletin	IPLB	
Full coverage		2000 (vol.5)–
International Dimensions	INTDI	
Full coverage		1996 (vol.1)–
Journal of the Center for Families, Children, and the Courts	JCFAMCC	
Full coverage		1999 (vol.1)–
Journal of Contemporary Legal Issues	JCLI	
Full coverage		1994 (vol.1994)–
Journal of Juvenile Law	JJUVL	
Full coverage		1996 (vol.17)–
Journal of Legal Advocacy and Practice	JLEGAP	
Full coverage		1999 (vol.1)–
Law and Literature	LAWLIT	
Full coverage		1994 (vol.6)–
Los Angeles Lawyer	LALAW	
Full coverage		2000 (vol.22-JAN)–
Loyola of Los Angeles Entertainment Law Review	LYLAELR	
Selected coverage		1989 (vol.9)–
Loyola of Los Angeles International and Comparative Law Review	LYLAICLR	
Selected coverage		1990 (vol.13)–1993 (vol.16, no.1)
Full coverage		1994 (vol.16, no.2)–
Loyola of Los Angeles Law Review	LYLALR	
Selected coverage		1983 (vol.16)–1993 (vol.26)

Full coverage		1993 (vol.27)–
McGeorge Law Review	MCGLR	
Selected coverage		1983 (vol.14)–1993 (vol.25, no.1)
Full coverage		1994 (vol.25, no.2)–
National Black Law Journal	NBLJ	
Selected coverage		1993 (vol.12, no.3)–1993 (vol.13, no.2)
Full coverage		1994 (vol.13, no.3)–
NEXUS: A Journal of Opinion	NEXJOP	
Full coverage		1996 (vol.1)–
Orange County Lawyer	OCLAW	
Full coverage		1998 (vol.40)–
Pepperdine Dispute Resolution Law Journal	PEPDRLJ	
Full Coverage		2000 (vol.1)–
Pepperdine Law Review	PEPLR	
Selected coverage		1982 (vol.10)–1993 (vol.20, no.3)
Full coverage		1993 (vol.20, no. 4)–
San Diego International Law Journal	SANDILJ	
Full coverage		2000 (vol.1)–
San Diego Law Review	SANDLR	
Selected coverage		1983 (vol.21)–1992 (vol.29)
Full coverage		1993 (vol.30)–
San Joaquin Agricultural Law Review	SANJALR	
Selected coverage		1991(vol.1)–
Santa Clara Computer and High Technology Law Journal	SCCHITLJ	
Selected coverage		1988 (vol.4)–
Santa Clara Law Review	SANCLR	
Selected coverage		1982 (vol.22)–
Southern California Interdisciplinary Law Journal	SCAIDLJ	

Selected coverage		1992 (vol.1)–
Southern California Law Review	SCALR	
Selected coverage		1981 (vol.55)–1987 (vol.60, no.5)
Full coverage		1987 (vol.60, no.6)–
Southern California Review of Law and Women's Studies	SCARLWS	
Full coverage		1992 (vol.1)–
Southwestern Journal of Law and Trade in the Americas	SWJLTA	
Full coverage		1994 (vol.1)–
Southwestern University Law Review	SWULR	
Selected coverage		1983 (vol.13)–1993 (vol.23, no.1)
Full coverage		1994 (vol.23, no.2)–
Stanford Environmental Law Journal	STENVLJ	
Selected coverage		1986 (vol.6)–1993 (vol.12)
Full coverage		1994 (vol.13)–
Stanford Journal of International Law	STJIL	
Selected coverage		1982 (vol.18)–1993 (vol.29)
Full coverage		1994 (vol.30)–
Stanford Journal of Law, Business, and Finance	STNJLBF	
Full coverage		1994 (vol.1)–
Stanford Law and Policy Review	STNLPR	
Selected coverage		1989 (vol.1)–
Stanford Law Review	STNLR	
Selected coverage		1982 (vol.35)–1984 (vol.36, no.4)
Full coverage		1984 (vol.36, no.5)–
Stanford Technology Law Review	STNTLR	

Full coverage		1997 (vol.1997)–
Thomas Jefferson Law Review	TJLR	
Full coverage		1996 (vol.18)–
Transnational Lawyer	TRNATLAW	
Selected coverage		1988 (vol.1)–1993 (vol.6)
Full coverage		1994 (vol.7)–
U.C. Davis Journal of International Law and Policy	UCDJILP	
Full coverage		1995 (vol.1)–
U.C. Davis Law Review	UCDLR	
Selected coverage		1983 (vol.16)–1993 (vol.26)
Full coverage		1993 (vol.27)–
UCLA Entertainment Law Review	UCLAELR	
Full coverage		1994 (vol.1)–
UCLA Journal of Environmental Law and Policy	UCLAJELP	
Selected coverage		1990 (vol.9)–1992 (vol.10)
Full coverage		1992 (vol.11)–
UCLA Journal of International Law and Foreign Affairs	UCLAJILFA	
Full coverage		1996 (vol.1)–
UCLA Journal of Islamic and Near Eastern Law	UCLAJINEL	
Selected coverage		2001 (vol.1)–
UCLA Journal of Law and Technology	UCLAJLT	
Full coverage		1996 (vol.1997)–
UCLA Law Review	UCLALR	
Full coverage		1982 (vol.30)–
UCLA Pacific Basin Law Journal	UCLAPBLJ	
Selected coverage		1991 (vol.9)–1992 (vol.10)
Full coverage		1992 (vol.11)–
UCLA Women's Law Journal	UCLAWLJ	
Selected coverage		1991 (vol.1)–1993 (vol.4, no.1)
Full coverage		1994 (vol.4, no.2)–
University of San Francisco Law Review	USFLR	

Selected coverage		1983 (vol.17)–1993 (vol.27)
Full coverage		1993 (vol.28)–
University of San Francisco Maritime Law Journal	USFMLJ	
Selected coverage		1989 (vol.1)–1991 (vol.3)
Full coverage		1992 (vol.4)–
UWLA Law Review	UWLALR	
Full coverage		1999 (vol.30)–
Western State University Law Review	WSULR	
Full coverage		1998 (vol.25, no.2)–
Whittier Journal of Child and Family Advocacy	WTJCFA	
Full coverage		2003 (vol.2)–
Whittier Law Review	WTLR	
Selected coverage		1983 (vol.5)–1993 (vol.14, no.3)
Full coverage		1993 (vol.14, no.4)–

Appendix H

Governors of the State of California

The governor of California website lists all of the governors from 1849 to the present, with short biographical links to each one. See: *http://www.governor.ca.gov/govsite/govsgallery/h/biography/index.html.*

Name:	Term:
Peter H. Burnett	1849–1851
John McDougal	1851–1852
John Bigler	1852–1856
J. Neeley Johnson	1856–1858
John B. Weller	1858–1860
Milton S. Latham	1860–1860
John G. Downey	1860–1862
Leland Stanford	1862–1863
Frederick F. Low	1863–1867
Henry H. Haight	1867–1871
Newton Booth	1871–1875
Romualdo Pachecco	1875–1875
William Irwin	1875–1880
George C. Perkins	1880–1883
George Stoneman	1883–1887
Washington Bartlett	1887–1887
Robert W. Waterman	1887–1891
Henry H. Markham	1891–1895
James H. Budd	1895–1899
Henry T. Gage	1899–1903
George C. Pardee	1903–1907
James N. Gillett	1907–1911
Hiram W. Johnson	1911–1917
William D. Stephens	1917–1923
Friend W. Richardson	1923–1927
Clement C. Young	1927–1931
James Rolph, Jr.	1931–1934
Frank F. Merriam	1934–1939
Culbert L. Olson	1939–1943
Earl Warren	1943–1953
Goodwin J. Knight	1953–1959

(Pub. 64620)

Edmund G. "Pat" Brown, Sr.	1959–1967
Ronald Reagan	1967–1975
Edmund G. "Jerry" Brown, Jr.	1975–1983
George Deukmejian	1983–1991
Pete Wilson	1991–1999
Gray Davis	1999–2003
Arnold Schwarzenegger	2003–present

Appendix I

Attorneys General of the State of California[1]

Name:	Date Assumed Office:
Edward J.C. Kewen	Dec. 22, 1849
James A. McDougall	Oct. 8, 1850
Serranus Clinton Hastings	Jan. 5, 1852[2]
John Randolph McConnell	Jan. 2, 1854
William M. Stewart	June 7, 1854[3]
William T. Wallace	Jan. 7, 1856[4]
Thomas H. Williams	Jan. 4, 1858
Frank M. Pixley	Jan. 6, 1862
John C. McCullough	Dec. 7, 1863
Jo Hamilton	Dec. 2, 1867
John L. Love	Dec. 4, 1871
Jo Hamilton	Dec. 6, 1875
Augustus L. Hart	Jan. 5, 1880
Edward C. Marshall	Jan. 8, 1883
George A. Johnson	Jan. 3, 1887
William H.H. Hart	Jan. 5, 1891
William F. Fitzgerald	Jan. 7, 1895[5]
Tirey L. Ford	Jan. 2, 1899
Ulysses S. Webb	Sept.15, 1902
Earl Warren	Jan. 2, 1939[6]
Robert W. Kenny	Jan. 4, 1943
Frederick N. Howser	Jan. 6, 1947
Edmund G. Brown	Jan. 8, 1951[7]
Stanley Mosk	Jan. 5, 1959[8]

[1] This appendix has been revised and updated by Fay Henexson, Supervising Librarian I, California Attorney General's Office, San Diego.

[2] California Supreme Court Chief Justice 1850—1852

[3] Appointed by Governor to fill the office during a temporary absence of John R. McConnell.

[4] California Supreme Court Justice 1869–1872; Chief Justice 1872-1879

[5] California Supreme Court Justice 1893-1895

[6] California Governor 1943-1953; U.S. Supreme Court Chief Justice 1953–1969

[7] California Governor 1959-1967

[8] California Supreme Court Justice 1964-2001

(Pub. 64620)

Thomas C. Lynch	Aug. 31, 1964
Evelle J. Younger	Jan. 4, 1971
George Deukmejian	Jan. 8, 1979[9]
John K. Van De Kamp	Jan. 3, 1983
Daniel E. Lungren	Jan. 7, 1991
Bill Lockyer	Jan. 4, 1999

---

[9] California Governor 1983-1991

Appendix J

History of California Law

Bates, J.C., Editor. *History of the Bench and Bar of California.* San Francisco: Bench and Bar Publishing Co., 1912. 572 p. Well over half of this volume is a biographical directory of the California bar. Photographs are included with many entries. The historical portion is brief and mostly anecdotal. However, that section includes a good report on the development of the first four codes.

Belz, Herman. *Popular Sovereignty, the Right of Revolution, and California Statehood.* 6 NEXUS: A Journal of Opinion 3–20 (Spring 2001). The author covers the national considerations of statehood for California during a period when the Mexican war and slavery were major issues. The military government of the 1840s is covered, as is the Constitutional Convention of 1849.

Browne, J. Ross. *Muleback to the Convention: Letters of J. Ross Browne, Reporter to the Constitutional Convention,* Monterey, September–October, 1849. San Francisco: The Book Club of California, 1950. 42 p. Only 400 copies were printed. Some libraries have microfilm copies.

Burns, John F. and Orsi, Richard J., editors. *Taming the Elephant: Politics, Government, and Law in Pioneer California.* Berkeley: Published for the California Historical Society by the University of California Press, 2003. 288 p. This publication is both a serial and a monograph. It was issued as v. 81, no. 3/4 of California History (2003). It was also promoted as a stand-alone book on the history of California. The chapters include: "Taming the Elephant: An Introduction to California's Statehood and Constitutional Era", by John F. Burns. pp. 1–26; "A Violent Birth: Disorder, Crime, and Law Enforcement, 1849–1890," by Roger D. McGrath. pp. 27–73; "The Courts, the Legal Profession, and the Development of Law in Early California," by Gordon Morris Bakken. pp. 74–95 " 'We Feel the Want of Protection': The Politics of Law and Race in California, 1848–1878," by Shirley Ann Wilson Moore. pp. 96–125; "Capturing California," by Joshua Paddison. pp.

(Pub. 64620)

126–136; " 'Officialdom': California State Government, 1849–1879," by Judson A. Grenier. pp. 137–168; " 'None Could Deny the Eloquence of This Lady': Women, Law, and Government in California, 1850–1890," by Donna C. Schuele. pp. 169–198; "The Beginnings of Anglo-American Local Government in California," by Edward Leo Lyman. pp. 199–223; "An Uncertain Influence: and The Role of the Federal Government in California," by Robert J. Chandler. pp. 224–271.

California Supreme Court Historical Society. *Yearbook*. San Francisco: Published for the Society by the Institute of Governmental Studies Press, University of California, Berkeley, 1994– v. 1–

Field, Stephen J. *California Alcalde*. Oakland, CA: Biobooks, 1950. 174 p. This is a finely printed limited edition of the Personal Reminiscences of Early Days in California, which was published in 1893.

Field, Stephen J. *Personal Reminiscences of Early Days in California: To which is added the story of his attempted assassination by a former associate on the supreme bench of the state*, by George C. Gorham. New York: Da Capo Press, 1968. 406 p. Reprint of 1893 edition. This is Field's biography of his years in California, beginning with the gold rush days and proceeding to his appointment to the U.S. Supreme Court. The second part of the book is about former California Supreme Court Justice David Terry's attempt to assassinate Justice Field.

Goodwin, Cardinal Leonidas. *The Establishment of State Government in California: 1846–1850*. New York: MacMillan, 1914. 359 p. This book was written as a Ph.D. thesis at U.C. in 1916.

Hansen, Woodrow James. *The Search for Authority in California.* Oakland: Biobooks, 1960. 192 p.

Henry E. Huntington Library and Art Gallery. *California Legal History Manuscripts in the Huntington Library: A Guide*, By the Committee on History of Law in California of the State Bar of California. San Marino, CA: The Library, 1989. 233 p.

Historical and Contemporary Review of Bench and Bar in California. San Francisco: The Recorder Printing and Publishing Co., 1926. 132 p. This thin volume contains a series of articles on different facets in California's legal history. The articles include: Legal Journalism in San Francisco, by Andrew Younger Wood; An Historical Sketch of the Supreme Court of California, by Orrin Kip McMurray (this article includes photographs of all justices); The District Courts of Appeal; State Bar Organization in California, by Andrew Younger Wood (including photographs of California Bar Association Presidents); Legal Aid Work in California; The Proposed Judicial Council; Superior Courts of California Under the Constitution of 1879, by Jeremiah F. Sullivan; The Self-Governing Bar Movement in America, by Joseph J. Webb; Law Libraries in California, by Rosamond Parma; In Memoriam— Maurice T. Dooling; Legal Education in California, by Maurice E. Harrison; Our Criminal Procedure—A Query, by William T. Aggeler; Legal Bibliography—The Citation Phase; Bench and Bar of San Francisco and California, which is a biographical section, including photographs of bar members.

Johnson, J. Edward. *History of the Supreme Court Justices of California, 1850–1900,* v. 1. San Francisco: Bender-Moss, 1963. 219 p. 1900–1950, v. 2. San Francisco: Bancroft-Whitney, 1966. 219 p. This oversized two volume set presents biographical sketches of the individual justices. Photographs or drawings of all justices are included. There is a chart listing the justices and chief justices in the order in which they took their positions.

Jones, Herbert C. *'The First Legislature of California': Address by Senator Herbert C. Jones before California Historical Society, San Jose, December 10, 1949.* Sacramento: Senate, 1949 (1983 reprint). 18 p. This speech transcript gives details of the early days in the legislature. These details include the different capital locations, the inferior housing of legislators, the early legislative issues, the small state budget, and anecdotes about the people involved.

Kens, Paul. *Justice Stephen Field: Shaping Liberty from the Gold Rush to the Guilded Age.* Lawrence: University of Kansas Press, 1997. 376 p. This is a recent biography of one of the most colorful figures in California legal history. It follows Mr. Field from his arrival in California through his term on the U.S. Supreme Court.

Kleps, Ralph N. The Revision and Codification of California Statutes 1849–1953. 42 *California Law Review* 766–802 (1954).

Langum, David J. "The Legal System of Spanish California: A Preliminary Study." 7(1) *Western Legal History* 1–23 (Winter/Spring 1994). This article covers the period of Spanish rule, from 1769 to 1822.

Lee, Bartholomew. "The Civil Law and Field's Civil Code in Common-Law California—A Note on What Might Have Been." 5(1) *Western Legal History* 13–36 (Winter-Spring, 1992).

Lloyd, Gordon. "Nature and Convention in the Creation of the 1849 California Constitution," 6 *NEXUS: A Journal of Opinion* 23–42 (Spring

2001). The author, now a professor in the School of Public Policy of Pepperdine University, covers the delegates to the Monterey constitutional convention in 1849, along with their backgrounds, the events taking place in Europe and elsewhere, and the individual topics addressed in the final document.

Mason, Paul. "Constitutional History of California," in *California—Legislature Assembly, Constitution of the State of California and of the United States and Other Documents.* Sacramento: California Printing Office, 1951. 418 p. pp. 67–97. This short historical summary appears in many editions of this widely-circulated state government document issued from the 1930s into the 1970s. Copies available from either the Senate or the Assembly are identical except for the title pages and introductions. The title varies. It is sometimes titled "Constitution of the United States and of the State of California and Other Documents."

Morrow, William W. "Introduction" [To *California Jurisprudence Second*]. San Francisco: Bancroft-Whitney, 1952. This article, which appears on pp. xix–lvii of the first volume of *Cal Jur 2d* is a reprint of an article written in 1920 and published in the first volume of the first edition of *Cal Jur.* The article presents a good picture of events leading up to statehood and the activities surrounding the first constitutional convention, held in Monterey. The article also covers the early history of the state, the adoption of codes, the second constitution, a biographical sketch of Stephen J. Field, and a history of the state law schools.

Nunis, Doyce B., Jr. "Legal History in Southern California: A Review Essay." (Review of California Legal History Manuscripts in the Huntington Library: A Guide.) 3(1) *Western Legal History* 67–77 (Winter-Spring, 1990).

Ohnimus, Arthur A. The Legislature of California, in *California—Legislature Assembly, Constitution of the State of California and of the United States and Other Documents.* Sacramento: California Printing Office, 1951. 418 p. pp. 111–198. This essay is both a history of the Legislature and a guide to the Legislature's procedures and purposes. It is found in several editions of this Constitution volume from the 1940s into the 1950s. Copies available from either the Senate or the Assembly are identical except for the title pages and introductions. The title varies. It is sometimes titled "Constitution of the United States and of the State of California and Other Documents."

Palmer, William J. and Selvin, Paul P. *The Development of Law in California.* St. Paul, MN: West Publishing Co., 1983. 64 p. This soft-bound book is reprinted from the first volume of the 1954 West's Annotated California Codes Constitution volumes. The 1983 replacement volume did not include the article, which was published separately by West. The author covers the history of California law, lawyers, the constitutions, the courts, and especially the codes. The author concentrates almost one half of the work on the development of the codes and their subsequent revisions.

Robinson, William W. *Lawyers of Los Angeles: A History of the Los Angeles Bar Association and the Bar of Los Angeles County.* Los Angeles: Los Angeles Bar Association, 1959. 370 p. This is an excellently written account of the beginning and growth of the legal community in the Los Angeles area from the early 1800s. The author covers bar associations well, but also covers libraries, law schools, businesses, buildings, and social movements. The book is well illustrated with photographs, maps, and drawings. The appendices cover Los Angeles Bar Association officers, county judges, Superior Court judges, county clerks, Municipal Court judges, District Court of Appeal justices, United States District Court judges, Ninth Circuit judges, and California Supreme Court justices. Hugh W. Darling was president of the Los Angeles Bar Association in 1959 and wrote the foreword to this text.

Rodman, Willoughby. *History of the Bench and Bar of Southern California.* Los Angeles: William J. Porter, Publisher, 1909. 267 p. More than one-half of this book is made up of biographical sketches of bar members. Photographs are included with many of the entries. The author also covers lawyers, courts, trends in the law, and the history of laws as illustrated by certain subjects.

Saunders, Myra K. "California Legal History: A Review of Spanish and Mexican Legal Institutions." 87:3 *Law Library Journal* 487–514 (Summer 1995). This article reviews some of the roots of California's present system of laws. The author also covers the language and availability of records and legal materials. An annotated list of bibliographic aids, primary sources, and secondary sources is attached.

Saunders, Myra K. "California Legal History: The California Constitution of 1849." 90:3 *Law Library Journal* 447–480 (Summer 1998). This article, the third in the series written for Law Library Journal, examines the differences between the Anglo-American and the Spanish-Mexican legal traditions and the influence these differences had on the state's first Constitution. A lengthy annotated bibliography is included.

Saunders, Myra K. "California Legal History: The Legal System Under the United States Military Government, 1846–1849." 88:4 *Law*

Library Journal 488–522 (Fall 1996). The author covers the short, four-year-period just prior to California's statehood. A bibliography of sources such as reports, records, memoirs, codes, newspapers, books, and journal articles is included.

Skaife, Alfred Charles. *Early California Law Books* (1850–1851). 1937.

Swisher, Carl Brent, and Stephen J. Field: *Craftsman of the Law.* Washington: Brookings Institution, 1930. 473 p. This biography follows the subject from his birth in 1816 to his death in 1899. It covers his family life and relationships, but also examines his days as a legislator and justice in California and his 34 years on the bench of the U.S. Supreme Court.

Women's Legal History Biography Project. Robert Crown Law Library at Stanford Law School. This is an internet site developed by Stanford Professor Barbara Allen Babcock and her students located at: *www.stanford.edu/group/WLHP/.* It includes several student papers in addition to articles by Professor Babcock on Clara Shortridge Foltz, a powerful political and legal figure in California in the late 1800s and early 1900s.

Appendix K

California Legal Research Guides and Bibliographies

Below are in-print and out-of-print publications addressing California legal research.

Adan, Adrienne, and Cadra, Laura. *California Legal Research on the Internet.* Chapter 5 in the CEB book, Internet Guide for California Lawyers, Third Edition. Oakland: CEB, 2001.

Berring, Robert C. *California Research.* [Los Angeles]: Legal Resource Communications, Inc., 1992. 1 audio cassette with accompanying 17 page guide. This tape and guide are a good introduction to research in California. They are part of a series of Tapes on Legal Research and therefore presume some basic research skills (e.g., familiarity with federal materials) either from previous training or from listening to the other tapes. Professor Berring, an excellent lecturer, entertains as he instructs.

Bricker, Ralph O. Research Manual of Legal Bibliography and Use of Law Books. Los Angeles: R.O. Bricker, 1936.

Dabagh, Thomas S. *Legal Research Guide for California Practice.* San Francisco: The Canterbury Press, 1936. 66 p. (A 1985 reprint was produced by William S. Hein.) The author was the librarian at Boalt Hall at the University of California at Berkeley and later the librarian at the Los Angeles County Law Library. His research guide covers California case law and statutory law. It also touches lightly on federal and foreign law. Administrative law is not addressed. About one third of the book is appendices, some of which seem unnecessary, or even humorous, today (e.g., rule of legal writing: "Unless thoroughly familiar with the material, do not dictate important papers. Dictation makes for verbosity and inaccuracy.").

Dershem, Larry. *California Legal Research Handbook.* Littleton, CO: Rothman, 1997. Looseleaf (unpaged, but over 500 pages). The author uses this broadly focused book to teach not only California legal research, but beginning research, federal law research, and legal citation.

(Pub. 64620)

Donnelly, Terrence M. *California Legal Resources: A Manual of Selected Materials and Organizations for Advocates and Attorneys.* Terrence M. Donnelly and Patricia L. McGinnis, Editors. Sacramento: National Paralegal Institute, [1976, 1978 printing]. 54 p. Prepared for the California Department of Aging. This title, which is very out-of-date now, was never intended to be a general research guide. It is merely a bibliography on such subjects as age discrimination, ADC, food stamps, Medicare, veterans' benefits, and wills. Materials covered are a mixture of federal and state.

Fink, Myron. *Research in California Law, Second Edition.* Buffalo, NY: Dennis & Co., 1964. 132 p. This is the best model of all of the early books available on the subject. However, it is very short and very out-of-date. It concentrates on California legal research without straying into federal research or other subjects. It has a very professional appearance. It has two good directories in the back: California state depository libraries and major California law libraries.

Frantz, Benjamin D. *Legal Research in California, Third Edition.* [s.l.: s.n.] 1983. 402 p. This text is reproduced from the original typescript and sample pages from various publishers. It is longer and more thorough than some of the other guides. However, a large portion of the book is dedicated to U.S. federal legal research.

Granberg, Ronald. *California Legal Research.* Monterey, CA: R.S. Publications, [1979]. This 85 page book is reproduced from a typescript. It is actually the second edition of a 1977 work. It attempts to cover both federal and California materials. It has very informally prepared illustrations.

Hanft, John K. *Legal Research in California.* San Francisco: Water-melon Books, 1993. 255 p. This text is intended as a tool for teaching basic research skills. It therefore presumes no earlier instruction in the basics from one of the commonly used texts, such as How To Find the Law, Fundamentals of Legal Research, or The Process of Legal Research. The author does not totally focus on California, but covers federal materials as well.

Hanft, John K. *Legal Research in California.* San Francisco: Bancroft-Whitney, 1996. 351 p. The text comes with an accompanying CD-ROM version. The author is an attorney, a legal editor, and a director of the Witkin Legal Institute. He provides a thorough overview of legal research, putting much emphasis on practice materials. A 70 page sample research problem on gender discrimination is included.

Hanft, John K. *Legal Research in California,* Third Edition. [s.1]: West Group, 1999. 434 p. As in the 1996 edition, the author covers some non-California materials. A CD-ROM version is included.

Hanft, John K. *Legal Research in California,* Fourth Edition. [s.1]: West Group, 2001. 532 p.

Locating the Law: A Handbook for Non-Law Librarians, With an Emphasis on California Law. 3rd Edition, Fay Henexson, editor. [San Diego] Southern California Association of Law Libraries, 1995. 67 p. This is a brief guide for librarians working in nonlaw libraries. It was prepared by the Southern California Association of Law Libraries (SCALL) Committee on Public Access to Legal Information and is reproduced from a typescript. The handbook begins with the basics of legal research because it presumes no previous law training. It is simple and straightforward throughout. It covers both U.S. and California legal research.

Maclay, Veronica and Peritore, Laura. *California Government Publications and Legal Resources.* [Chicago]: American Association of Law Libraries, 1991. 94 p. This work was compiled for the Government Documents Special Interest Section as an Annual State Documents Bibliography. This is a very good bibliography, listing hundreds of California's legal and governmental sources. It is devoted exclusively to California materials. It is divided into sections which cover legislative materials, executive branch materials, judicial materials, legal organizations/publishers, and general guides. It also has helpful appendices, which list depository libraries, law reviews, and instructions for compiling a legislative history.

Ochal, Bethany J. California Current State Practice Materials: An Annotated Bibliography. 74 *Law Library Journal* 281–297 (1981).

Ranharter, Kathryn. *The State of California: An Introduction to Its Government Publications and Related Information.* 1979. 35 p. This paper was prepared for the 1979 American Association of Law Libraries (AALL) meeting in San Francisco. It is part of the AALL Government Documents Special Interest Section (SIS) series.

Zimmerman, Andrew. *Zimmerman's Research Guide: California.* This internet research guide, formerly hosted on the LLRX web page, is now part of LexisOne. The well-organized list includes links to all types of web sites and print materials containing California legal information.

http://www.lexisone.com/zimmermanguide/C/California.html.

Appendix L

Legal/Governmental Directories and Almanacs

In addition to all of the print and www-based directories listed below, internet users may easily go to some of the most useful sites without using a directory. Most organizations, including universities, corporations, and law firms, try to buy the domain name closest to the name of the entity. For many researchers, looking for the logical name is the first research step on the net. It is necessary to observe the internet protocol of using the suffixes .com for companies, .edu for schools,.gov for governmental bodies, and.org for organizations. Here are a few California examples:

Amgen: *www.amgen.com*
Cooley Godward: *www.cooley.com*
Irell & Manella: *www.irell.com*
Loeb & Loeb: *www.loeb.com*
Luce Forward Hamilton & Scripps: *www.luce.com*
Manatt, Phelps & Phillips: *www.manatt.com*
O'Melveny & Myers: *www.omm.com* (the firm also has a link from *www.omelveny.com*)
Orrick, Herrington & Sutcliffe: *www.orrick.com*
Pepperdine University: *www.pepperdine.edu*
Sun Microsystems, Inc.: *www.sun.com*
UCLA: *www.ucla.edu*
USC: *www.usc.edu*

American LegalNet. This company is an internet-based vendor with database access and other services for attorneys. It carries two directories: California Court Directory and California Attorney Directory (with over 120,000 listings) located at: *www.americanlegalnet.com.*

California Blue Book. [Sacramento: State of California.] The Blue Book is required to be published every four years, according to statutory mandate (Gov. Code, § 14885, formerly § 13606). However, it has not been published in many years. The copies that are available are of very high quality and provide photographs and detailed biographies of state officials and legislators. There are also good descriptions of all administrative agencies, departments, committees, and boards.

California Cities, Towns, & Counties: Basic Data Profiles for All Municipalities & Counties. Edith R. Hornor, ed. Palo Alto: Information Publications, 1994. 587 p. This directory includes listings for municipal officials and employees.

California Court Directory. Los Angeles: Daily Journal Corp. Weekly supplement to the Los Angeles Daily Journal, the San Francisco Daily Journal, and the Daily Recorder (Sacramento). This newsprint directory gives an up-to-date listing of all courts and their officers in the state. Addresses and phone numbers are given for court houses, judges, clerks, sheriffs, and court administrators.

California Courts and Judges Handbook. 1999 edition, by Helen Y. Chang. Costa Mesa: James Publishing Co., 1999. 742 p. This title has been published since 1967. It gives biographical information on all judges of all courts in the state. Biographies of the constitutional officers are also included. Part One covers the government of California, the separation of powers, the organization of the courts, and the legislative and constitutional powers and limitations on the courts. Part Two is the directory of courts. Part Three is the biographical directory. Part Four is the appendix, which contains lists of past federal and state officials, judicial districts, the Code of Judicial Conduct, and general facts about the state. This one of the best reference sources available.

California Courts Directory and Fee Schedule. Sacramento: Association of Municipal Court Clerks. Annual. This publication provides names, addresses, and telephone numbers for all courts, clerks, sheriffs, marshals, recorders, and district attorneys in California. It also lists fees for all California courts.

The California Handbook. Seventh Edition. Edited by Thaddeus C. Trzyna. Sacramento: California Institute of Public Affairs, 1994. 272 p. This handbook provides facts about California and references to hundreds of other sources for facts. The book is arranged into seven broad categories, with numerous subcategories under each one. It is part directory, part bibliography, and part almanac. It has chapters on government and politics, the state legislature, the executive branch, local and regional government, city governments, law and justice, politics, elections, and how to obtain information from the California government. This is a valuable reference source.

California Lawyers: Directory of Attorneys. Los Angeles: Daily Journal Corp. Semiannual. Spine title: Directory of California Lawyers. This paperback directory is published in January and July as a supplement to the Los Angeles Daily Journal, the San Francisco Daily Journal, and the Daily Recorder (Sacramento). The table of contents is on the cover. It provides listings for the attorneys of the state, divided into north and south halves. Also covered are bar associations, state and federal courts and judges, state legislators, state offices, state officers, law libraries, law schools, county governments, large law firms, private judges, mediators, and arbitrators. Most of the book is printed on newsprint.

California Legal Directory. Dallas, TX: Legal Directories Publishing Co., Inc. Annual. The California volume also contains listings for Arizona, Hawaii, and Nevada. The directory is divided into sections of attorney biographies, fields of practice, state government, courts, county officials, and a city and county list.

California Legal Filing Directory. By Patricia A. Britton. [s.l.]: West Group, 1999. 412 p. This directory contains listings of cities, towns, courts, court houses, filing rules, and fees.

California Legislature at Sacramento. Biographies and Photographs of Senate and Assembly Members, Officers, Attaches, Committees, and Rules of the Two Houses, and Standards of Conduct of the Senate, Together With a List of the Members of Congress, State officers, Etc. [Sacramento: State Printer] Annual. Spine Title: Handbook [year]. This pocket-size book is very useful for following any legislative activity. It is available from the Legislative Bill Room (see the Publisher/Vendor appendix).

The California Local Government Directory [year]. Compiled and edited by State Net and California Journal. Sacramento: California Journal Press.

California Political Almanac 1997-98. Fifth Edition. Edited by A.G. Block & Claudia Buck. Sacramento: StateNet/California Journal Press, 1997. 566 p. This series appears to be the successor to the Almanac of California Government & Politics [year], published biennially by the California Journal Press from 1975-1987. After publishing the first edition of the new title in 1989 and the second in 1991, the publisher's obvious intention is to publish this almanac at the beginning of each biennial legislature. The publication is a comprehensive and critical look at California's government. The writers provide biographical sketches,

(Pub. 64620)

as well as photographs, of all constitutional officers, Supreme Court justices, and legislators. County governments are also covered. In the back of the book are descriptive listings of county governments and political/ governmental news providers. This is one of the best sources of information on political figures and government in California.

California Public Sector: A Directory of Official Personnel in State, Local, and Federal Governments within the State of California. Stockton: Public Sector Publications. Annual. This directory of over 1,000 pages covers the state executive offices, the legislature, the judicial branch, and all of the state agencies. It also covers the governments of cities and counties throughout California, as well as California's representative in Washington, D.C.

California State Agency Directory [year]. Sacramento: Capitol Enquiry. Annual. This is an extremely useful directory for navigating the administrative agency maze in Sacramento and around the state. It is arranged alphabetically by agency and department, with many cross references. The directory provides names, addresses, and phone numbers of all state officials.

California State Government Directory. Compiled and edited by State Net and California Journal. Sacramento: California Journal Press. Looseleaf or bound volume. Updated quarterly with inserts.

California's Legislature 1994. by E. Dotson Wilson. [Sacramento: California Assembly.] Biennial. This title has been published irregularly since 1942. The most recent edition had been published in 1986. The book provides a brief California history, a discussion of the Constitution, and chapters on voting, the executive branch, and the judiciary. The bulk of the work is on the Legislature, its history, its accomplishments, and its various publications. The appendices contain historical listings of state officials, legislative sessions, and explanations or descriptions of historical facts and symbols.

California's The Green Book. Sacramento: Dutra Communications. Quarterly. This work is a directory of California's officials.

Directory of California Corporate Counsel [year]. San Francisco: Corporate Law Departments Committee of the Business Law Section of the State Bar of California. Annual.

Directory of Legal Services Programs in California. San Francisco: State Bar of California. The directory lists over 250 nonprofit legal services programs that provide legal assistance to low-income citizens.

Directory of San Francisco Attorneys. San Francisco: Bar Association of San Francisco. Appeared up to 1973 as part of The Brief Case.

[year] *Directory of The Los Angeles County Bar Association.* Los Angeles: Los Angeles Bar Association. Annual. Cover title: LACBA Directory [year]. A supplement to the Los Angeles Lawyer Magazine.

Essential Courts Premium. San Francisco: Martin Dean's Essential Publishers. This current service supplies a cd database of all California attorneys and their disciplinary records. It provides more searchable information than is posted on the State Bar website. For example a user may search for undergraduate school, law school, or email address in addition to the other personal data that is searchable in both systems. The database contains complete records for over 225,000 past and present California attorneys. (The State Bar website lists only partial records for deceased attorneys.) The cd also contains a judges' directory, a court directory, local rules for 58 California counties, a filing fees list, and other data. Another product, *Essential Attorneys*, covers only the State Bar records.

Judicial Profiles. Los Angeles: Daily Journal Corp. Looseleaf, multi-volume set. These judicial biographies are reprinted from the Daily Journal newspapers front page daily profiles. The biographies are arranged by court and county.

List of Constitutional Officers, Congressional Representatives, Members of the California State Legislature and Members of the Supreme Court, 1849-1985. Published by James D. Driscoll, Chief Clerk of the Assembly, and Darryl R. White, Secretary of the Senate, California Legislature. [Sacramento]: J.D. Driscoll and D.R. White, 1985. 149 p. "Originally published in the California Blue Book, the material contained has been expanded and updated."

Los Angeles County Almanac: Government, Politics, Civics. Los Angeles: Los Angeles County Almanac/Republican Central Committee of Los Angeles County. Annual. This almanac provides information for all offices and elected officials that govern Los Angeles, from the federal government down to the city government. It contains maps, organizational charts, photographs, drawings, charts,

Martindale-Hubbell Law Directory. New Providence, NJ: Martindale-Hubbell. In 1868, Martindale published its first legal directory, Martindale's United States Law Directory. The name was later changed to Martindale's American Law Directory. Martindale purchased the rights to Hubbell's Legal Directory in 1930, and since then the name has been the Martindale-Hubbell Law Directory. The directory covers all the states in the United States. The California section currently covers two volumes, and is divided into blue, white, and yellow paged sections. The blue section is an alphabetical list of attorneys by city or town. The white section is the professional biographies section, with firms arranged alphabetically within each city or town. The yellow section is a listing of services, suppliers, and consultants. The listings are arranged by type of service within each city or town. The directory is well known for its attorney rating system, which has been in place for over 100 years. Martindale-Hubbell is currently owned by Reed Elsevier Inc. Microfiche copies of the directory covering the years from 1868-1980 are available from Law Library Microform Consortium (LLMC).

Martindale-Hubbell Law Directory. Online on LexisNexis. The directory is the equivalent of the paper volumes. The proper source is "CA Listings -Martindale-Hubbell(R) Law Directory" [MARHUB;CADIR]. For background information and search tips, the user should search for marhub in the CAL library and the GUIDE file.

Martindale-Hubbell Law Directory. CD-ROM version. This product is similar to the online version offered on LexisNexis. The advantage is that there is no charge for connect time or communications.

Martindale-Hubbell Law Directory. WWW version. The www address for the directory is *www.lawyers.com/.* The simple search permits a user to find an attorney who practices a particular type of law in a certain jurisdiction. The advanced search lets a user find a particular attorney by name.

Members of the California Legislature and Other Public Officials. Sacramento. The Sacramento Newsletter. 1961–date. [Sacramento].

Metropolitan News-Enterprise Directories. [Los Angeles: Metropolitan News Company] Monthly supplement to the daily Los Angeles area newspaper. The newsprint directory includes detailed listings for all courts in Los Angeles County and less detailed information for other counties. There are photographs of the Supreme Court justices, Second District Court of Appeal judges, and Los Angeles County Superior Court officers.

[year] *Parker Directory of California Attorneys.* New Providence, NJ: Reed Elsevier. Annual (in December). 2v. with six-month update supplement to Volume One. Volume One is the guide to attorneys and firms. Volume Two gives information on court information, bar associations, government agencies, court reporters, expert witnesses, etc. This

publication is available in hard copy (two volumes), or on high-density floppy disks, or on CD-ROM.

Pocket Directory of the California Legislature. Sacramento: Capitol Enquiry. Annual. This publication contains legislators' photographs and office information, such as addresses, phone numbers, committee memberships, and staff information.

Pocket Roster. Sacramento: State Net and California Journal. Annual. This pocket-sized book contains photographs and biographies of all California senators and assembly persons along with district descriptions, legislative offices, committee lists, and staff listings.

Roster & Government Guide. Sacramento. State Net and California Journal. Annual. This directory lists all constitutional officers, heads of agencies, representatives in Washington, and state senators and assembly persons. There are also lists of standing committees, charts on the legislative process, the courts, and the executive branch.

Roster: California State, County, City and Township Officials: State Officials of the United States: Directory of State Services of the State of California. Sacramento: California Secretary of State's Office. Annual. Cover title: California Roster. The title of this work describes its coverage. It is probably the best source of local California government information. The directory gives names and addresses for all government officials at the state level and adds the phone numbers for officials at local levels in California.

The State Bar of California has an online directory of over 195,000 living licensed attorneys. The site address is: *www.calbar.ca.gov.* One may use name or bar number for the basic search. Under the advanced search on my look for first, middle, or last names, firm names, or any part of the address. The search software for either the basic or advanced search permits searching for "sounds like," "begins," "contains," or "is exactly." The search will pull up complete bar records for living attorneys. These records include undergraduate school, law school, email address, and a list of bar disciplinary problems. The records of deceased attorneys include only the bar number, city, and admission date.

State of California Telephone Directory [year]. Sacramento: [Department of General Services], Documents Section. Annual. This may be the best directory for locating state agencies and their employees.

West's Legal Directory—California. This directory is in the WLD-CA database in Westlaw and on the internet at: *www.findlaw.com.* For background information and search tips, the user should use the Scope (SC) command within the database.

Who's Who in the California Legislature. Sacramento: Capitol Enquiry. Biennial. This directory lists legislators, lobbyists, trade associations, and government officials. The legislative section provides a photograph and a lengthy biographical sketch for each legislator.

Appendix M

Law Schools Approved by
the American Bar Association[1]

The following schools have been approved by the American Bar Association, as well as the Committee of Bar Examiners of the State Bar of California. The most current information on ABA approved schools is available from the ABA office in Chicago or the ABA Consultant's office in Indianapolis. All schools listed are also members of the Association of American Law Schools (AALS). Also see the State Bar of California for an up-to-date list: *www.calbar.ca.gov.*

California Western School of
Law
225 Cedar Street
San Diego, CA 92101
1-619-239-0391
1-619-696-9999 (FAX)
www.cwsl.edu

Chapman University School of
Law
370 North Glassell Street
Orange, CA 92866
(888) 242-1913
(714) 628-2500
www.chapman.edu/law

Golden Gate University
School of Law
536 Mission Street
San Francisco, CA 94105
1-415-442-6600
1-415-442-6609 (FAX)
www.ggu.edu/Schools/Law

Loyola Law School
919 S. Albany Street
Los Angeles, CA 90015
1-213-736-1000
1-213-380-3769 (FAX)
www.lls.edu

McGeorge School of Law
University of the Pacific
3200 Fifth Avenue
Sacramento, CA 95817
1-916-739-7191
1-916-739-7111 (FAX)
www.mcgeorge.edu

Pepperdine University
School of Law
24255 Pacific Coast Highway
Malibu, CA 90265
1-310-506-4611
1-310-506-4266 (FAX)
www.law.pepperdine.edu

---

[1] This appendix was updated by Erin Murphy, Reference Librarian, Law Library, UC Davis School of Law.

(Pub. 64620)

Santa Clara University
School of Law
Santa Clara, CA 95053
1-408-554-4361
1-408-554-4426 (FAX)
www.scu.edu/law

Southwestern University
School of Law
675 South Westmoreland Ave.
Los Angeles, CA 90005
1-213-738-6700
1-213-383-1688 (FAX)
www.swlaw.edu

Stanford Law School
559 Nathan Abbott Way
Stanford, CA 94305-8610
1-650-723-2465
1-659-725-0253 (FAX)
lawschool.stanford.edu

Thomas Jefferson School of
Law
2121 San Diego Avenue
San Diego, California 92110
1-619-297-9700
1-619-294-4713 (FAX)
www.tjsl.edu

University of California at
Berkeley
School of Law
Boalt Hall
Berkeley, CA 94720
1-510-642-1742
1-510-643-6171 (FAX)
www.law.berkeley.edu

University of California at
Davis
School of Law
King Hall
400 Mrak Hall Drive
Davis, CA 95616-5201
1-916-752-0243

1-916-752-4704 (FAX)
www.law.ucdavis.edu

University of California at Los
Angeles
School of Law
P.O. Box 951476
Los Angeles, CA 90024-1476
1-310-825-4841
1-310-206-7010 (FAX)
www.law.ucla.edu

University of California
Hastings College of the Law
200 McAllister Street
San Francisco, CA 94102
(FAX)
1-415-565-4600
1-415-565-4865 (FAX)
www.uchastings.edu

University of San Diego
School of Law
Alcala Park
San Diego, CA 92110
1-619-260-4527
1-619-260-4616 (FAX)
www.acusd.edu/usdlaw

University of San Francisco
School of Law
Kendrick Hall
2130 Fulton St.
San Francisco, CA 94117-1080
1-415-422-6586
1-415-422-6433 (FAX)
www.usfca.edu/law

University of Southern
California Law Center
University Park
Los Angeles, CA 90089-0071
1-213-740-7331
1-213-740-5502 (FAX)
www.usc.edu/dept/law

Western State University
College of Law
1111 N. State College Blvd.
Fullerton, CA 92831-3014
1-714-738-1000
www.wsulaw.edu

Whittier Law School
3333 Harbor Blvd.
Costa Mesa, CA 92626
(714)444-4141
www.law.whittier.edu

Appendix N

Law Schools Approved by the State Bar of California But Not by the American Bar Association[1]

The most current information on these schools is available from the Office of Admissions of the Committee of Bar Examiners of the State Bar of California. Published information is also available in certain legal directories, such as the Parker Directory of California Attorneys or California Lawyers: Directory of Attorneys (from the Daily Journal Corporation). See the State Bar of California for the most up-to-date list: *www.calbar.ca.gov.*

Cal Northern School of Law
1395 Ridgewood Drive
Chico, CA 95973
1-530-891-6900
www.calnorthern.edu

California Pacific School of
Law
1600 Truxtun Avenue, Suite
100
Bakersfield, CA 93301
1-805-322-5297

Empire College
School of Law
3038 Cleveland Ave.,
Suite 102
Santa Rosa, CA 95403
1-707-546-4000
www.empcol.com

Glendale University
College of Law

220 North Glendale Avenue
Glendale, CA 91206
1-818-247-0770
www.glendalelaw.edu

Humphreys College of Law
6650 Inglewood Avenue
Stockton, CA 95207
1-209-478-0800
www.humphreys.edu/law

John F. Kennedy University
School of Law
547 Ygnacio Valley Road
Walnut Creek, CA 94596
1-925-930-6040
www.jfku.edu/law

Lincoln Law School of
Sacramento
3140 "J" Street
Sacramento, CA 95816
1-916-446-1275

---

[1] This appendix was updated by Erin Murphy, Reference Librarian, Law Library, UC Davis School of Law.

(Pub. 64620)

www.lincolnlaw.edu

Lincoln Law School of San
  Jose
2160 Lundy Avenue
San Jose, CA 95131-1852
1-408-434-0727
www.lincolnlawsj.edu

Monterey College of Law
404 West Franklin Street
Monterey, CA 93940
1-408-373-3301
www.montereylaw.edu

New College of California
School of Law
50 Fell Street
San Francisco, CA 94102
1-415-863-4111
www.newcollege.edu/law

San Francisco Law School
20 Haight Street
San Francisco, CA 94102
1-415-626-5550
www.sfls.edu

San Joaquin College of Law
901 5th Street
Clovis, CA 93612-1312
1-209-323-2100
1-800-522-0994 (California
  only)
www.sjcl.edu

Santa Barbara College of Law
20 E. Victoria Street
Santa Barbara, CA 93101
1-805-966-0010
www.santabarbaralaw.edu

Southern California Institute of
  Law
Santa Barbara Campus
1525 State Street, #202

Santa Barbara, CA 93101
1-805-963-4654
www.lawdegree.com

Southern California Institute of
  Law
Ventura Campus
877 South Victoria Ave., #111
Ventura, CA 93003
1-805-644-2327
www.lawdegree.com

Trinity Law School
2200 North Grand Avenue
Santa Ana,
CA 92705 (714)836-7500
www.tiu.edu/law

University of La Verne
College of Law
320 East "D" Street
Ontario, CA 91764-4128
(909) 460-2000
(909) 460-2081 FAX
law.ulv.edu

University of West Los
  Angeles
School of Law
1155 West Arbor Vitae Street
Inglewood, CA 90301-2902
1-310-215-3339
www.uwla.edu/law

University of West Los
  Angeles
School of Law
San Fernando Valley College
  of Law Campus
21300 Oxnard Street
Woodland Hills, CA 91367
1-818-883-0529
*http://www.uwla.edu/campus/
  san-fernando.html*

(Pub. 64620)

Ventura College of Law   1-805-658-0511
4475 Market Street   *www.venturalaw.edu*
Ventura, CA 93001

Appendix O

County Law Libraries[1]

Each of California's 58 counties has a county law library. These vary in size from just a few thousand volumes to Los Angeles County's collection of over 700,000 volumes. Listings of the county law libraries may be found in various directories such as the *Parker Directory of California Attorneys* and the *California Lawyers: Directory of Attorneys* (from the Daily Journal Corporation). Many of the libraries will also be listed in the *AALL Directory and Handbook* (American Association of Law Libraries), or the *NOCALL Membership Directory-Handbook* (Northern California Association of Law Libraries), or the *Southern California Association of Law Libraries Annual Directory*. One can also find a list of the county law libraries with website links on the Council of California County Law Librarians website at: *www.cccll.org*.

Refer to Chapter 7 for a map of California counties and their Court of Appeal districts.

1. Bernard E. Witkin Alameda
   County Law Library
   125 - 12th Street
   Oakland, CA 94607-4912
   510-208-4800
   510-208-4836 (FAX)
   Email: lawlib@acgov.org
   www.co.alameda.ca.us/law/index.htm

   Alameda County Law Library
   South County Branch
   224 West Winton Ave., Room 162
   Hayward, CA 94544
   510-670-5230
   510-670-5292 (FAX)
   Email: lawlib@acgov.org

---

[1] This appendix has been revised and updated by Jennifer Hill, Librarian, Keller Rohrback L.L.P.

2. Alpine County Law Library
   99 Water Street
   Markleeville, CA 96120
   530-694-2113

3. Amador County Law Library
   Superior Court
   108 Court Street
   Jackson, CA 95642
   209-223-2144

4. Butte County Law Library
   One Court Street
   Oroville, CA 95965
   530-538-7122
   530-538-4350 (FAX)
   E-mail: buttelaw@cncnet.com
   www.quiknet.com/~buttelaw

5. Calaveras County Law Library
   Government Ctr.
   891 Mountain Ranch Rd.
   San Andreas, CA 95249
   209-754-6314

6. Colusa County Law Library
   Courthouse
   547 Market Street
   Colusa, CA 95932
   530-458-0640
   530-458-4242 (FAX)

7. Contra Costa County Law Library
   1020 Ward Street, 1st Floor
   Martinez, CA 94553-1276
   925-646-2783
   925-646-2438 (FAX)
   www.cccpllib.org

Contra Costa County Public Law Library
Richmond Branch
100 - 37th Street, Room 237
Richmond, CA 94805
510-374-3019
510-374-3607 (FAX)
www.cccpllib.org

8. Del Norte County Law Library
    Courthouse
    450 H Street
    Crescent City, CA 95531
    707-464-7217

9. El Dorado County Law Library
    550 Main Street, Suite A
    Placerville, CA 95667-5699
    530-621-6423
    www.co.el-dorado.ca.us/lawlibrary.html

    El Dorado County Law Library
    South Lake Tahoe Branch
    1000 Rufus Allen Blvd.
    South Lake Tahoe, CA 96150
    530-621-6423
    www.co.el-dorado.ca.us/lawlibrary.html

10. Fresno County
    Frank J. Creede, Jr. Public Law Library
    1100 Van Ness Ave., Room 600
    Fresno, CA 93721
    559-237-2227
    559-442-4960 (FAX)
    www.co.fresno.ca.us/9899/index.htm

11. Glenn County Law Library
    526 W. Sycamore Street
    Willows, CA 95988
    530-934-6415

12. **Humboldt** County Law Library
Courthouse
825 - 5th Street, Room 812
Eureka, CA 95501
707-269-1270

13. **Imperial** County Law Library
Courthouse
939 W. Main Street
El Centro, CA 92243
619-339-4374

14. **Inyo** County Law Library
Courthouse
168 N. Edwards Street
P.O. Drawer K
Independence, CA 93526
760-878-0270

15. **Kern** County Law Library
1415 Truxtun Ave., Room 301
Bakersfield, CA 93301
661-868-5320
661-868-5368 (FAX)
E-mail: librarian@kclawlib.org
www.kerncountylawlibrary.org

16. **Kings** County Law Library
Government Ctr.
1400 W. Lacey Blvd.
Hanford, CA 93230
559-582-3211, Ext. 4430

17. **Lake** County Law Library
255 N. Forbes Street
Lakeport, CA 95453
707-263-2205

18. Lassen County Law Library
    Courthouse
    220 S. Lassen Street, Suite 6
    Susanville, CA 96130
    530-251-8203

19. Los Angeles County Law Library
    301 W. 1st Street
    Los Angeles, CA 90012
    213-629-3531
    213-613-1329 (FAX)
    lalaw.lib.ca.us

    Los Angeles County Law Library
    Beverly Hills Branch
    Beverly Hills Municipal Court Building
    9355 Burton Way, Room 405
    Beverly Hills, CA 90210
    310-859-2902

    Los Angeles County Law Library
    Compton Branch
    County Courts Building
    200 W. Compton Blvd., Room 201
    Compton, CA 90220
    310-983-7088

    Los Angeles County Law Library
    Long Beach Branch
    County Building
    415 W. Ocean Blvd., Room 505
    Long Beach, CA 90802
    562-491-5970

    Los Angeles County Law Library
    Norwalk Branch
    Southeast Superior Court Building
    12720 Norwalk Blvd., Room 714
    Norwalk, CA 90650
    562-807-7310

Los Angeles County Law Library
Pasadena Branch
County Building
300 E. Walnut Ave., Room 300
Pasadena, CA 91101
626-356-5253

Los Angeles County Law Library
Pomona Branch
East District Superior Court Building
400 Civic Ctr. Plz., Room 102
Pomona, CA 91766
909-620-6353

Los Angeles County Law Library
Santa Monica Branch
County Building
1725 Main Street
2nd Floor, Room 219
Santa Monica, CA 90401
310-260-3644

Los Angeles County Law Library
Torrance Branch
South Bay County Building
825 Maple Ave., Room 110
Torrance, CA 90503
310-222-8816

Los Angeles County Law Library
Van Nuys Branch
Van Nuys Courts Building
6230 Sylmar Ave., Room 350
Van Nuys, CA 91401
818-374-2499

20. Madera County Law Library
209 W. Yosemite Ave.
Madera, CA 93637
559-673-0378

21. Marin County Law Library
    20 N. San Pedro Rd., Suite 2015
    San Rafael, CA 94903
    415-499-6355

22. Mariposa County Law Library
    Courthouse
    5088 Bullion Street
    P.O. Box 189
    Mariposa, CA 95338-0189
    209-966-3222

23. Mendocino County Law Library
    Courthouse
    100 N. State Street, Room 307
    Ukiah, CA 95482
    1-707-463-4201
    E-mail: lawlib@pacific.net
    www.pacificsites.com/~lawlib

24. Merced County Law Library
    670 W. 22nd Street
    Merced, CA 95340
    209-385-7332
    www.co.merced.ca.us/lawlibrary/

25. Modoc County Law Library
    Courthouse
    205 S. East Street
    Alturas, CA 96101
    530-233-6515

26. Mono County Law Library
    Mono County Free Library
    Mammoth Lakes Branch
    960 Forest Trail
    (P.O. Box 1120)
    Mammoth Lakes, CA 93546
    760-934-4777

27. Monterey County Law Library
    Courthouse
    1200 Aguajito Rd., Room 202
    Monterey, CA 93940
    831-647-7746
    831-372-6036 (FAX)
    E-mail: mcolawlib@redshift.com
    fp.redshift.com/mcolawlib

    Monterey County Law Library
    Salinas Branch
    Federal Office Bldg.
    100 W. Alisal Street, Suite 144
    Salinas, CA 93901
    831-755-5046
    831-422-9593 (FAX)
    E-mail: mcolawlib@redshift.com

28. Napa County Law Library
    Old Courthouse
    825 Brown Street, Room 132
    Napa, CA 94559
    707-299-1201

29. Nevada County Law Library
    201 Church Street
    Nevada City, CA 95959
    530-265-2918
    E-mail: Law.library@nevadacountycourts.com
    new.mynevadacounty.com/lawlibrary

30. Orange County Public Law Library
    515 N. Flower Street
    Santa Ana, CA 92703
    714-834-3397
    714-834-4375 (FAX)
    www.oc.ca.gov/lawlib

31. Placer County Law Library
    1523 Lincoln Way
    Auburn, CA 95603
    530-823-2573

32. Plumas County Law Library
    w/ Plumas County Library
    445 Jackson
    Quincy, CA 95971
    530-283-6310
    www.psln.com/PCLibQ

33. Riverside County
    Vicor Miceli Law Library
    3989 Lemon Street
    Riverside, CA 92501-4203
    909-955-6390
    909-955-6394 (FAX)
    E-mail: lib-r@co.riverside.ca.us
    www.co.riverside.ca.us/depts/lawlib

    Riverside County Law Library
    Desert Branch
    Larson Justice Center
    46-200 Oasis Street
    Indio, CA 92201
    760-863-8316
    760-342-2581 (FAX)
    E-mail: lib-i@co.riverside.ca.us

34. Sacramento County Public Law Library
    813 - 6th Street, 1st Floor
    Sacramento, CA 95814
    916-874-6012
    916-874-5691 (FAX)
    www.saclaw.lib.ca.us

    Sacramento County Public Law Library Branch
    The William R. Ridgeway Family Relations Courthouse
    3341 Power Inn Rd., Room 112
    Sacramento, CA 95826
    916-875-3490
    916-874-3493 (FAX)

35. San Benito County Law Library
Courthouse
440 - 5th Street
Hollister, CA 95023
831-637-0071

36. San Bernardino County Law Library
402 N. D Street
San Bernardino, CA 92415-0015
909-885-3020
909-885-1869 (FAX)
www.sbcba.org/courts/sbdlawlib.html

San Bernardino County Law Library
West End Branch
8303 Haven Ave.
Rancho Cucamonga, CA 91730
909-944-5106

San Bernardino County Law Library
High Desert Branch
15455 Seneca Rd.
Victorville, CA 92392
760-243-2044

37. San Diego County Public Law Library
Main Library
1105 Front Street
San Diego, CA 92101-3904
619-531-3900
619-238-7716 (FAX)
www.sdcpll.org

San Diego County Public Law Library
East County Branch
250 E. Main Street
El Cajon, CA 92020-3941
619-441-4451
619-441-0235 (FAX)

San Diego County Public Law Library
South Bay Branch
500 3rd Ave.
Chula Vista, CA 91910-5617
619-691-4929
619-427-7521 (FAX)

San Diego County Public Law Library
North County Branch
325 S. Melrose Dr., Suite 300
Vista, CA 92081-6697
760-940-4386
760-724-7694 (FAX)

38. San Francisco Law Library
Veterans War Memorial Building
401 Van Ness Ave., Room 400
San Francisco, CA 94102
415-554-6821
415-554-6820 (FAX)
www.sfgov.org/site/sfll_index.asp

San Francisco Law Library
Courthouse Reference Room
Courthouse
400 McAllister Street, Room 512
San Francisco, CA 94102
415-551-3647
415-551-3787 (FAX)

San Francisco Law Library
Financial District Branch
Monadnock Building
685 Market Street, Suite 420
San Francisco, CA 94105
415-882-9310
415-882-9594 (FAX)

39. San Joaquin County Law Library
    Courthouse
    222 E. Weber Ave., 4th Floor
    Stockton, CA 95202
    209-468-3920
    209-468-9968 (FAX)
    E-mail: info@sjclawlib.org
    www.sjclawlib.org

40. San Luis Obispo County Law Library
    County Government Ctr.
    1050 Monterey Street, Room 125
    San Luis Obispo, CA 93408
    805-781-5855
    805-781-4172 (FAX)
    E-mail: slolawli@rain.org
    www.rain.org/~slolawli

41. San Mateo County Law Library
    710 Hamilton Street
    Redwood City, CA 94063
    650-363-4913
    www.smcll.org

42. Santa Barbara County
    McMahon Law Library
    Courthouse
    1100 Anacapa
    Santa Barbara, CA 93101
    805-568-2296
    805-568-2299 (FAX)
    www.countylawlibrary.org

    Santa Barbara County Law Library
    Santa Maria Branch
    312 E. Cook Street
    Santa Maria, CA 93454
    805-346-7548
    805-346-7692 (FAX)
    countylawlibrary.org/SantaMaria.htm

43. Santa Clara County Law Library
    360 N. First Street
    San Jose, CA 95113
    408-299-3567
    sccll.org

44. Santa Cruz County Law Library
    County Government Center
    701 Ocean Street, Room 070
    Santa Cruz, CA 95060
    831-457-2525
    www.lawlibrary.org

45. Shasta County Law Library
    Courthouse
    1500 Court Street, Basement Room B-7
    Redding, CA 96001
    530-245-6243

46. Sierra County Law Library
    100 Courthouse Square
    Downieville, CA 95936
    530-289-3269

47. Siskiyou County Law Library
    Courthouse
    311 - 4th Street
    Yreka, CA 96097
    530-842-8390

48. Solano County Law Library
    Hall of Justice
    600 Union Ave.
    Fairfield, CA 94533
    707-421-6520

49. Sonoma County Law Library
    Hall of Justice, Room 213J
    600 Administration Drive
    Santa Rosa, CA 95403
    707-565-2668
    707-565-1126 (FAX)
    E-mail: solawlib@sonomacountylawlibrary.org
    www.sonomacountylawlibrary.org

50. Stanislaus County Law Library
    1101 - 13th Street
    Modesto, CA 95354
    209-558-7759
    209-558-8284 (FAX)
    www.stanct.org/courts/lawlibrary/lawlib.htm

51. Sutter County Library
    750 Forbes Ave.
    Yuba City, CA 95991
    530-822-7137

52. Tehama County Law Library
    Courthouse, Room #38
    633 Washington Street
    Red Bluff, CA 96080
    530-529-5033

53. Trinity County Law Library
    Courthouse
    101 Court Street
    P.O. Box 1258
    Weaverville, CA 96093
    530-623-1201

54. Tulare County Law Library
    221 S. Mooney Blvd.
    Visalia, CA 93291-4582
    1-559-733-6395
    www.co.tulare.ca.us/government/public_protection/law

55. Tuolumne County Law Library
    68 N. Washington Street
    Sonora, CA 95370
    209-536-0308

56. Ventura County Law Library
    800 S. Victoria Ave.
    Ventura, CA 93009
    1-805-642-8982
    1-805-642-7177 (FAX)
    E-mail: vcll@rain.org
    www.infopeople.org/ventura/vclaw

57. Yolo County Law Library
    204 Fourth Street, Suite A
    Woodland, CA 95695
    530-666-8918
    530-666-8618
    www.yolocounty.org/org/library/law.htm

58. Yuba County Library
    303 Second Street
    Marysville, CA 95901
    530-749-7380

Appendix P

Law Reviews or Journals Issued by
California's ABA-Accredited Law Schools

The first review listed under each institution is the main review for that institution. Other reviews, if any, are then listed in alphabetical order. The www addresses are given for those reviews that have them. Some www addresses take the user directly to full text issues of the review. Others simply provide a link to a catalog description of the publication. The USC law library www page contains a list of all law journals on the www: *lawweb.usc.edu/library/journals/journals.html.*

Researchers may also want to check Appendices F and G for the LexisNexis and Westlaw law review holdings. Back issues of many of the titles may be purchased in microform from the William S. Hein Company.

California Western
California Western Law Review
*http://www.cwsl.edu/main/default.asp?nav = journals.asp
&body = journals/law_review.asp*
California Western International Law Journal
*http://www.cwsl.edu/main/default.asp?nav =
journals.asp&body = journals/intl_law_journal.asp*

Chapman University
Chapman University Law Review
http://www.chapman.edu/law/students/lawreview/default.asp

Golden Gate University
Golden Gate University Law Review
http://internet.ggu.edu/law_library/LRindex.html
Golden Gate University Ninth Circuit Survey
http://internet.ggu.edu/law_library/LRindex.html
Environmental Law Journal
http://internet.ggu.edu/law_library/LRindex.html
Golden Gate University Intellectual Property Journal
http://internet.ggu.edu/law_library/LRindex.html

Golden Gate University Forum on Law and Social Change
http://internet.ggu.edu/law_library/LRindex.html
Golden Gate University Annual Survey of International and Comparative Law

Loyola Law School
Loyola of Los Angeles Law Review
llr.lls.edu
Loyola of Los Angeles Entertainment Law Review
elr.lls.edu
Loyola of Los Angeles International and Comparative Law Review
ilr.lls.edu

McGeorge School of Law, University of the Pacific
McGeorge Law Review (formerly Pacific Law Journal)
www.mcgeorge.edu/academics/experiential_learning/law_reviews/
mlr.htm
Transnational Lawyer
http://www.mcgeorge.edu/academics/experiential_learning/
law_reviews/ttl.htm

Pepperdine University School of Law
Pepperdine Law Review
http://law.pepperdine.edu/current/academics/law_review/
Journal of the National Association of Administrative Law Judges
http://law.pepperdine.edu/current/academics/naalj/
Pepperdine Dispute Resolution Law Journal
http://law.pepperdine.edu/current/academics/pdrlj

Santa Clara University
Santa Clara Law Review
www.scu.edu/lawreview
Santa Clara Computer and High Technology Law Journal
www.scu.edu/techlaw

Southwestern University
Southwestern University Law Review
www.swlaw.edu/cocurricular/lawreview.htm
Southwestern Journal of Law and Trade in the Americas
www.swlaw.edu/cocurricular/journal.htm

Stanford Law School
Stanford Law Review
http://lawreview.stanford.edu/

Stanford Agora: An Online Journal of Legal Perspectives (formerly Stanford Journal of Legal Studies)
http://agora.stanford.edu/sjls/home.html or *http://agora.stanford.edu/agora/index_main.shtml*
Stanford Environmental Law Journal
http://elj.stanford.edu/
Stanford Journal of International Law
http://sjil.stanford.edu
Stanford Journal of Law, Business and Finance
http://sjlbf.stanford.edu
Stanford Law and Policy Review
http://slpr.stanford.edu
Stanford Technology Law Review
stlr.stanford.edu/STLR/Core_Page/index.htm

University of California at Berkeley
California Law Review
www.law.berkeley.edu/journals/clr
African-American Law and Policy Report
http://www.boalt.org/ALPR/
Asian Law Journal
http://www.boalt.org/ALJ/main.html
Berkeley Business Law Journal
http://www.boalt.org/bblj/
Berkeley Journal of Employment and Labor Law (formerly the Industrial Relations Law Journal)
http://www.boalt.org/BJELL/
Berkeley Journal of International Law
http://www.law.berkeley.edu/journals/bjil/
Berkeley Women's Law Journal
http://www.boalt.org/bwlj/
California Criminal Law Review
http://www.boalt.org/CCLR/
Ecology Law Quarterly
http://www.law.berkeley.edu/journals/elq/
Berkeley Technology Law Journal
www.law.berkeley.edu/journals/btlj
La Raza Law Journal
http://www.boalt.org/LRLJ/

University of California at Davis
UC Davis Law Review

http://www.law.ucdavis.edu/lawreview/index.htm
Environs
http://www.law.ucdavis.edu/environs/
U.C. Davis Journal of International Law and Policy
http://www.law.ucdavis.edu/jilp/
Journal of Juvenile Law and Policy
http://www.law.ucdavis.edu/jjlp/default.html

University of California at Los Angeles
UCLA Law Review
http://www1.law.ucla.edu/~lawreview/
Asian Pacific American Law Journal
http://www1.law.ucla.edu/~apalj/
UCLA Journal of Law and Technology
www.lawtechjournal.com
Chicano-Latino Law Review
http://www1.law.ucla.edu/~cllr/
Entertainment Law Review
http://www1.law.ucla.edu/~elr/public_html/
Journal of International Law and Foreign Affairs
http://www1.law.ucla.edu/~jilfa/
Journal of Islamic and Near Eastern Law
http://www1.law.ucla.edu/~jinel/
Pacific Basin Law Journal
http://www1.law.ucla.edu/~pblj/index.html
UCLA Journal of Environmental Law and Policy
http://www.law.ucla.edu/students/studentorgs/elj/
Women's Law Journal
http://www.studentgroups.ucla.edu/wlj/

University of California, Hastings College of the Law
Hastings Law Journal
www.uchastings.edu/hlj
Hastings Communications and Entertainment Law Journal (Comm/Ent)
www.uchastings.edu/comment
Hastings Constitutional Law Quarterly
www.uchastings.edu/clq
Hastings International and Comparative Law Review
www.uchastings.edu/hiclr
Hastings Women's Law Journal
www.uchastings.edu/womenslj
West-Northwest: Hastings West-Northwest Journal of Environmental

Law and Policy
www.uchastings.edu/wnw

University of San Diego
San Diego Law Review
www.sandiego.edu/SanDeigoLRev
California Regulatory Law Reporter
Journal of Contemporary Legal Issues
www.sandiego.edu/jcli
San Diego International Law Journal
www.sandiego.edu/sdilj/welcomeilj.html

University of San Francisco
University of San Francisco Law Review
www.usfca.edu/lawreview
University of San Francisco Maritime Law Journal
http://www.usfmlj.com/

University of Southern California
Southern California Law Review
http://www-rcf.usc.edu/~usclrev/index.html
Southern California Interdisciplinary Law Journal
http://www-bcf.usc.edu/~idjlaw/
Southern California Review of Law and Women's Studies
www-rcf.usc.edu/~rlaws

Western State University College of Law
Western State University Law Review

Whittier Law School
Whittier Law Review
http://www.law.whittier.edu/academic_programs/wlr/wlr.asp
Whittier Journal of Child & Family Advocacy
http://www.law.whittier.edu/academic_programs/wjcfa/thejournal.asp

Appendix Q

California Supreme Court Justices

Anderson, Alexander	1852–1852
Angellotti, Frank M.	1903–1921, C.J.
Arabian, Armand	1990–1996
Arguelles, John A.	1987–1989
Baldwin, Joseph G.	1858–1862
Baxter, Marvin R.	1991–present
Beatty, William H.	1889–1914, C.J.
Belcher, Isaac Sawyer	1872–1874
Bennett, Nathaniel	1849–1851
Bird, Rose Elizabeth	1977–1987, C.J.
Brown, Janice R.	1996–present
Burke, Louis H.	1964–1974
Broussard, Allen E.	1981–1991
Bryan, Charles H.	1854–1855
Burnett, Peter Hardeman,	1857–1857
Carter, Jesse Washington,	1939–1959
Chin, Ming W.	1996–present
Clark, William P.	1973–1981
Conrey, Nathaniel Parrish	1935–1936
Cope, Warner Walton	1859–1869, C.J.
Crocker, Edwin Bryant	1863–1864
Crocker, Joseph Bryant	1868–1880
Currey, John	1864–1868, C.J.
Curtis, Jesse William	1926–1944
DeHaven, John Jefferson,	1891–1895
Dooling, Maurice T.	1960–1962
Eagleson, David N.	1987–1991
Edmonds, Douglas Lyman	1936–1955
Field, Stephen Johnson	1857–1863, C.J.
Finlayson, Frank Graham	1926–1926
Fitzgerald, William F.	1893–1895
Fox, Charles Nelson	1889–1890
Garoutte, Charles Henry	1891–1903
George, Ronald M.	1991–1996
	1996–present, C.J.
Gibson, Phil Sheridan	1939–1964, C.J.

(Pub. 64620)

Grodin, Joseph R.	1982–1987
Harrison, Ralph Chandler	1891–1903
Hastings, Serranus Clinton	1849–1852, C.J.
Henshaw, Frederick William	1895–1918
Heydenfeldt, Solomon	1852–1857
Houser, Frederick Wilhelm	1937–1942
Kaufman, Marcus M.	1987–1990
Kaus, Otto M.	1981–1985
Kennard, Joyce L.	1989–present
Kerrigan, Frank H.	1923–1924
Langdon, William Henry	1927–1939
Lawlor, William Patrick	1915–1926
Lennon, Thomas J.	1919–1926
Lorigan, William George	1903–1919
Lucas, Malcolm M.	1987–1996, C.J.
Lyons, Henry A.	1849–1852, C.J.
Manuel, Wiley W.	1977–1981
McComb, Marshall Francis	1956–1977
McFarland,Thomas Bard	1887–1908
McKee, Samuel Bell	1880–1887
McKinstry, Elisha W.	1873–1888
Melvin, Henry Alexander	1908–1920
Moreno, Carlos R.	2001–present
Morrison, Robert F.	1880–1887, C.J.
Mosk, Stanley	1964–2001
Murray, Hugh C.	1851–1857, C.J.
Myers, Louis Wescott	1923–1925, C.J.
Myrick, Milton Hills	1880–1887
Newman, Frank C.	1977–1982
Niles, Addison C.	1872–1880
Norton, Edward	1862–1864
Olney, Warren, Jr.	1919–1921
Panelli, Edward A.	1985–1994
Paterson, Van R.	1887–1894
Peek, Paul	1962–1966
Peters, Raymond E.	1959–1973
Preston, John White	1926–1935
Reynoso, Cruz	1982–1987
Rhodes, Augustus Loring	1864–1880, C.J.
Richards, John Evan	1924–1932
Richardson, Frank K.	1974–1983
Ross, Erskine M.	1880–1886
Sanderson, Silas W.	1864–1870, C.J.
Sawyer, Lorenzo	1864–1870, C.J.

Schauer, Benjamin Rey	1942–1964
Searls, Niles	1887–1888, C.J.
Seawell, Emmett	1923–1939
Shafter, Oscar Lowell	1864–1867
Sharpstein, John R.	1880–1892
Shaw, Lucien	1921–1923, C.J.
Shenk,John Wesley	1924–1959
Shurleff, Charles Allerton	1921–1922
Sloane, William A.	1920–1923
Sloss, Marcus Cauffman	1906–1919
Spence, Homer R.	1945–1960
Sprague, Royal T.	1868–1872
Sullivan, Jeremiah Francis	1926–1927
Sullivan, Matthew Ignatius	1914–1915
Sullivan, Raymond L.	1966–1977
Temple, Jackson	1870–1887, C.J.
Terry David Smith	1855–1859, C.J.
Thompson, Ira, F.	1932–1937
Thornton, James Dabney	1880–1891
Tobriner, Matthew O.	1962–1982
Traynor, Roger John	1940–1970, C.J.
Van Dyke, Walter	1899–1905
Van Fleet, William Cary	1894–1899
Wallace, William T.	1870–1880, C.J.
Ward, Terry W.	1922–1923
Waste, William Harrison	1921–1940, C.J.
Wells, Alexander	1852–1854
Werdegar, Kathryn Mickle	1991–present
White, Thomas P.	1959–1962
Wilbur, Curtis Dwight	1918–1924, C.J.
Works, John Downey	1888–1891
Wright, Donald R.	1970–1977, C.J.

(Pub. 64620)

Appendix R

Bar Associations in California[1]

In addition to the State Bar of California, discussed in Chapter 12, there are many other associations for attorneys. Membership in the State Bar is mandatory: in order to practice in California, an attorney must be a member of the State Bar. Membership in other bar associations and lawyer organizations is voluntary. There are regional bar associations, county and city bar associations, and organizations devoted to practice specialties. In addition, many national bar associations have chapters in California.

Below are some of the many voluntary attorney associations listed in alphabetical order. The State Bar's web site maintains links to many of these organizations.

Academy of California
  Adoption Lawyers
16255 Ventura Boulevard,
  Suite 704
Encino, CA 91436
818-501-8355
http://www.acal.org/

Alameda County Bar
  Association
610 Sixteenth Street, Suite 426
Oakland, CA 94612
510-893-7160
510-893-3119 (FAX)
www.acbanet.org

Amador County Bar
  Association
35 Court Street

Jackson, CA 95642

Asian Pacific Bar Association
  (APABA)
12021 Wilshire Blvd. #603
Los Angeles, CA 90025
http://www.apabala.org/

Asian Pacific Bar Association
  of the Silicon Valley
http://www.sccba.com/apba/
  welcome.htm

Association of Business Trial
  Lawyers
http://www.abtl.org/
  welcome.htm

---

[1] This appendix was revised for this edition by Laura Cadra, Reference Librarian, Hugh & Hazel Darling Law Library, UCLA School of Law.

(Pub. 64620)

Association of Certified Family
Law Specialists
1884 Knox Street
Castro Valley, CA 94546
510-581-3799
http://www.acfls.org/

Association of Southern
California Defense Counsel
888 South Figueroa Street,
16th Floor
Los Angeles, CA 90017-2516
213-683-3050
213-489-5387 (FAX)
http://www.ascdc.org/

Bay Area Lawyers Network
1800 Trousdale Drive
Burlingame, CA 94010
650-366-5800
650-682-7085
http://www.baln.org

Bar Association of San
Francisco
465 California Street, Suite
1100
San Francisco, CA 94104
415-982-1600
http://www.sfbar.org/

Bay Area Lawyers for
Individual Freedom (BALiF)
1800 Market Street, Suite 407
San Francisco, CA 94102
415-865-5620
http://www.balif.org

Berkeley-Albany Bar
Association
P.O. Box 107
Berkeley, CA 94701
510-841-5000
510-524-3270 (FAX)

Beverly Hills Bar Association
300 South Beverly Drive,
Suite 201
P.O. Box 7277
Beverly Hills, CA 90212
310-553-6644
310-284-8290 (FAX)
http://www.bhba.org

Black Women Lawyers
Association of Los Angeles
P.O. Box 8179
Los Angeles, CA 90008
213-538-0137
*http://
www.blackwomenlawyersla.org/*

Burbank Bar Association
2219 W. Olive Avenue
PMB 100
Burbank, CA 91506-2526
818-843-0931
818-843-5852 (FAX)

Butte County Bar Association
P.O. Box 3927
Chico, CA 95927

Calaveras County Bar
Association
116 Court Street
P.O. Box 1818
San Andreas, CA 95249
209-795-0217

California Association of
Certified Family Law
Specialists
1884 Knox Street
Castro Valley, CA 94546
510-581-3799
http://www.acfls.org

California Attorneys for
Criminal Justice

1225 Eight Street, Suite 150
Sacramento, CA 95814
916-448-8868
916-448-8965
http://www.cacj.org/

California Judges Association
1700 Broadway, 7th Floor
Oakland, CA 94612
916-325-9999

California Lawyers for the
Arts
Fort Mason Center, C-255
San Francisco, CA 94123
415-775-7200
415-775-1143 (FAX)

1641 18th Street
Santa Monica, CA 90404
310-998-5590
310-998-5594
http://
www.calawyersforthearts.org/

California Minority Counsel
Program
465 California Street, Suite
1100
San Francisco, California
94104.
415-782-8990
415-477-2391 (FAX)

California Public Defenders
Association (CPDA)
3273 Ramos Circle
Sacramento, CA 95827
916-362-1686

Century Coast Trial Lawyer's
Association
P O Box 12938
San Luis Obispo, CA 93406
805-541-0300

Century City Bar Association
P.O. Box 67189
Los Angeles, CA 90067
310-358-3330

Colusa County Bar
P.O. Box 968
Colusa, CA 95932

Consumer Attorneys of
California
770 L Street, Suite 1200
Sacramento, CA 95814
916-442-6902
916-442-7734 (FAX)
http://caoc.com/

Consumer Attorneys
Association of Los Angeles
3435 Wilshire Blvd. #2870
Los Angeles, CA 90010
213-487-1212
213-487-1224 (FAX)
http://caala.org

Consumer Attorneys of San
Diego
3633 Camino del Rio South,
Suite 100
San Diego, CA 92108
619-696-1166
619-696-1294
http://www.casd.org/sa

Contra Costa County Bar
Association
704 Main Street
Martinez, CA 94553
925-686-6900
925-686-9867 (FAX)
http://www.cccba.org/

Culver Marina Bar Association
11100 Washington Blvd.
Culver City, CA 90230-3988
310-838-1151

310-559-8648 (FAX)

Del Norte County Bar
Association
P.O. Box 38
Crescent City, CA 95531

Desert Bar Association
45-025 Manitou Drive
Indian Wells, CA 92201
760-772-4277

Eastern Alameda County Bar
Association
http://www.eacba.org/

El Dorado County Bar
550 Main Street, Suite A
Placerville, CA 95667

Foothills Bar Association
P.O. Box 1077
El Cajon, CA 92022
619-588-1936
619-442-8060
http://www.foothillsbar.org/

Fresno County Bar Association
1221 Van Ness Avenue, Suite
300
Fresno, CA 93721-1720
559-264-2619
559-264-8726 (FAX)
http://www.fresnocountybar.org/

Glendale Bar Association
P O Box 968
Glendale, CA 91209-0968
818-956-1633
http://www.glendalebar.com/

Glenn County Bar Association
134 S. Sycamore
Willows, CA 95988

Harbor South Orange County
Bar Association
23412 Moulton Pkwy., Ste 120
Laguna Hills, CA 92653
949-829-8184

Hemet/Mt. San Jacinto Bar
Association
950 N. State St. Suite C
Hemet, CA 92543
909-929-6969
909-652-7102 (FAX)

Humboldt County Bar
Association
P.O. Box 310
Eureka, CA 95502

Imperial County Bar
Association
P.O. Box 43
El Centro, CA 92244

Inyo County Bar Association
106 S. Main Street #201
Bishop, CA 93514

Kern County Bar Association
1675 Chester Avenue, Suite
220
Bakersfield, CA 93301
661-344-4700
http://www.kernbar.org/

Kings County Bar Association
P.O. Box 330
Hanford, CA 93232

Korean-American Bar
Association of Northern
California
http://www.kabanc.org/

Korean-American Bar
Association of Southern

California
http://www.kabasocal.org/

La Jolla Bar Association
P O Box 1831
La Jolla, CA 92038
858-454-1839
http://
www.lajollabarassociation.com/

Lake County Bar Association
255 North Forbes Street
Lakeport, CA 95453

Lassen County Bar Association
707 Nevada Street, Suite 1
Susanville, CA 96130

Lesbian & Gay Lawyers
  Association of Los
Angeles
P.O.Box 480318
Los Angeles, CA 90048
213-637-9834

Los Angeles Arab American
  Lawyers Association
P.O. Box 260403
Encino, CA 91426-0403
818-787-2116

Los Angeles Intellectual
  Property Law Association
386 Beech Avenue, Suite 4
Torrance, CA 90501-6203
http://www.laipla.org/

Lawyers' Club of Los Angeles
  County
P.O. Box 862170
Los Angeles, California 90086
(213)624-2525
http://www.lawyersclub.org

Los Angeles County Bar
  Association

261 S. Figueroa Street, Suite
  300
Los Angeles, CA 90012
213-627-2727
213-896-6500 (FAX)
http://www.lacba.org

Marin County Bar Association
30 North San Pedro Rd., Suite
  140
San Rafael, CA 94903
415-499-1314
http://www.marinbar.org/

Mariposa County Bar
  Association
P.O. Box 1580
Mariposa, CA 95338

Mendocino County Bar
  Association
110 S. Main Street, Suite C
Willits,CA 95450

Merced County Bar
  Association
P.O. Box 3382
Merced, CA 95344

Modoc County Bar Association
200 S. Caldwell Street
Alturas, CA 96101

Monterey County Bar
  Association
P.O. Box 1371
Salinas, CA 93902-1371
831-663-6955
http://
www.montereycountybar.org/

Napa County Bar Association
P.O. Box 447
Napa, CA 94559
707-252-7122

707-255-6876 (FAX)

National Lawyers Guild—Los
  Angeles Chapter
8124 West Third Street, Suite
  201
Los Angeles, CA 90048
323-653-4510
323-653-3245
http://www.nlg-la.org/

Nevada County Bar
  Association
411 Colfax
Grass Valley, CA 95945
530-274-1821
530-272-8517

Newport Harbor Bar
5140 Birch St., Suite 100
Newport Beach, CA 92660
949-261-6333

Northern San Diego County
  Bar Association
760-758-5833
http://www.bansdc.org/

Orange County Bar
  Association
P.O. Box 17777
Irvine, CA 92623-7777
949-440-6700
949-440-6710 (FAX)
http://www.ocbar.org/

Pasadena Bar Association
301 E Colorado Blvd, Suite
  524
Pasadena, CA 91101
626-793-1422
http://www.pasadenabar.org/

Placer County Bar Association
P.O. Box 4598

Auburn, CA 95604
916-557-9181
www.placerbar.org

Plumas County Bar
  Association
522 Lawrence Street
Quincy, CA 95971

Queen's Bench Bar
  Association
816 E. 4th Avenue
San Mateo, CA 94401-3317
415-440-1002

Riverside County Bar
  Association
4129 Main Street, Suite 100
Riverside, CA 92501
909-682-1015
909-686-0106 (FAX)
http://
  www.riversidecountybar.com/

Sacramento County Bar
  Association
901 H Street, Suite 101
Sacramento, CA 95814
916-448-1087
916-448-6930 (FAX)
http://www.sacbar.org/

San Benito County Bar
  Association
Court House, Room 206
Fifth & Monterey Streets
Hollister, CA 95023
831-637-2585

San Bernardino County Bar
  Association
555 North Arrowhead
San Bernardino, CA 92401
909-888-6791
909-889-0400

*http://www.sbcba.org/lawyers/
referral.html*

San Diego County Bar
  Association
1333 Seventh Avenue
San Diego, CA 92101-4309
619-231-0781
619-338-0042 (FAX)
http://www.sdcba.org/

San Fernando Valley Bar
  Association
21300 Oxnard Street, Suite
  250
Woodland Hills, CA 91367
818-227-0490
818-227-0499 (FAX)
www.sfvba.org

San Francisco Trial Lawyers
  Association
225 Bush Street, #357
San Francisco, CA 94104
415-956-6401
415-956-6680 (FAX)
http://www.sftla.org/

San Gabriel Valley Bar
506 N Garfield Avenue, Suite
  280
Alhambra, CA 91801
626-282-2126

San Joaquin County Bar
  Association
6 S. El Dorado Street, Suite
  504
Stockton, CA 95202
209-948-0125
http://www.sjcbar.org/

San Luis Obispo County Bar
  Association
P.O. Box 585

San Luis Obispo, CA 93406
805-541-5930
www.slobar.org

San Mateo Bar Association
303 Bradford Street, Suite A
Redwood City, CA 94063
650-363-4230
650-368-3892 (FAX)
http://www.smcba.org/

Santa Barbara County Bar
  Association
123 W. Padre Street, Suite E
Santa Barbara, CA 93105
805-569-5511
805-569-2888 (FAX)
http://www.sblaw.org/

Santa Clara County Bar
  Association
4 North Second Street, Suite
  400
San Jose, California 95113
408-287-2557
408-287-6083 (FAX)
http://www.sccba.com/

Santa Cruz County Bar
  Association
340 Soquel Avenue, Suite 209
Santa Cruz, CA 95062
http://santacruzbar.org/

Santa Monica Bar Association
854 Pico Blvd.
Santa Monica, CA 90405-1325
310-450-9289

Santa Ynez Valley Bar
  Association
2963 Grand Ave
P.O. Box 809
Los Olivos, CA 93441
805-688-9226
805-688-5774 (FAX)

http://firms.findlaw.com/
SYVBarAssn/

Shasta-Trinity Counties Bar
Association
P.O. Box 991874
Redding, CA 96099-1874
530-224-0770
http://www.stcba.com/

Siskiyou County Bar
Association
744 Empire Street #110
P.O. Box 3524
Fairfield, CA 94533
707-422-5087

Solano County Bar Association
744 Empire Street
P.O. Box 3524
Fairfield, CA 94533
707-422-5087

Sonoma County Bar
Association
37 Old Courthouse Square,
Suite 100
Santa Rosa, CA 95404
707-542-1190
707-542-1195
http://
www.sonomacountybar.org/

South Bay Bar Association
230 Glover Ave, Suite I Chula
Vista, CA 91910
310-543-9773
310-543-3273 (FAX)

Southern California Chinese
Lawyers Association
P.O. Box 861959
Terminal Annex
Los Angeles, CA 90086-1959
http://www.sccla.org/

Southwest Riverside County
Bar Association
PO Box 1775
Temecula, CA 92593
909-296-1291
http://www.swrbar.org/

Stanislaus County Bar
Association
914 13th Street
Modesto, CA 95354
209-571-5729
209-529-6130 (FAX)

State Bar of California
180 Howard Street (Main
Office)
San Francisco, CA 94105
415-538-2000

1149 South Hill Street
Los Angeles, CA 90015
213-765-1100

1201 K Street, Suite 720
Sacramento, CA 95814
916-442-8018
www.calbar.ca.gov

Tahoe-Truckee Bar
P.O. Box 2614
Truckee, CA 96160
530-584-1134
http://www.tahoetruckeebar.org/

Tehama County Bar
P.O. Box 8189
Red Bluff, CA 96080

Tulare County Bar Association
208 W. Main Street #2
Visalia, CA 93921
209-732-2513
209-732-3016

Tuolumne County Bar
 Association
14570 Mono Way #L
Sonora,CA 95370

Ventura County Bar
 Association
4475 Market Street, Suite B
Ventura, CA 93003
805-650-7599
805-650-8059 (FAX)
http://www.vcba.org/

West Orange County Bar
 Association
17111 Beach Blvd. Suite 102
Huntington Beach, CA 92647
714-841-3131
714-841-2789 (FAX)

Western San Bernardino Bar
 Association
10630 Town Center, Suite 119
Rancho Cucamonga, CA
 91730
909-483-0548
909-483-0553

Whittier Bar
13215 East Penn Street, Suite
 411
Whittier, CA 90602-1781
562-698-0468
562-698-0469 (FAX)

Wilshire Bar Association
725 S. Figueroa Street, Suite
 3750
Los Angeles, CA 90017

213-612-9900
213-612-9930 (FAX)

Women Defenders
110 Grayson Street, Suite 1
Berkeley, CA 94710
510-525-0995

Women Lawyers of Alameda
1970 Broadway, Suite 1200
Oakland, CA 94612
510-835-5568
510-835-5310 (FAX)

Women Lawyers of Santa
 Cruz County
P.O. Box 1822
Santa Cruz, CA 95061-0737
831-426-8484
831-423-2839

Women Lawyers Association
 of Los Angeles
634 S. Spring Street, Suite 617
Los Angeles, CA 90017
213-892-8982
213-892-8948 (FAX)
http://www.wlala.org/

Yolo County Bar Association
P.O. Box 1903
Woodland, CA 95776
www.yolobar.com

Yuba-Sutter County Bar
 Association
7726 Kent Avenue
Live Oak, CA 95953
916-323-0335
916-323-6882 (FAX)

APPENDIX S

Selected Secondary Sources and Practice Guides[1]

In 1981 Bethany J. Ochal compiled a bibliography of California practice materials for the Law Library Journal.[2] Readers who used that bibliography might notice that a few of those old standards are included in the current bibliography below, which is designed to give practitioners a short list of current key practice materials in each subject area.

Administrative Law

California administrative hearing practice, 2nd ed. (CEB) 1997–.

California administrative mandamus, 3rd ed. (CEB) 2003–.

Arbitration

California ADR practice guide, 2 vols. (Matthew Bender) 1992–.

California practice guide. Alternative dispute resolution. (Rutter Group) 1992–.

California arbitration and mediation practice guide. (Lawpress) 2003–.

Bankruptcy

Personal and small business bankruptcy practice in California. (CEB) 2003–.

Business Law

Business buy-sell agreements. (CEB) 1991–.

California legal forms: Transaction guide, 36 vols. (Matthew Bender) 1968–.

California business litigation. (CEB) 2002–.

---

[1] This appendix was written by Jennifer Lentz, Reference Librarian, Hugh & Hazel Darling Law Library, UCLA School of Law.

[2] Ochal, Bethany J. California Current State Practice Materials: An Annotated Bibliography. 74 *Law Library Journal* 281–297 (1981).

(Pub. 64620)

Financing California businesses, 2nd ed. (CEB) 1995–.

Selecting & forming business entities. (CEB) 1996–.

Civil Procedure

California civil procedure before trial, 3rd ed. 3 vols. (CEB) 1990–.

California forms of pleading and practice annotated, 56 vols. (Matthew Bender) 1962–.

California points and authorities, 24 vols. (Matthew Bender) 1965–.

California practice guide. Civil procedure before trial. 3 vols. (Rutter Group) 1983–.

California practice guide. Federal civil procedure before trial. 2 vols. (Rutter Group) 1989–.

California procedure, 4th ed. (Witkin Legal Institute) 1996–.

California trial guide, 7 vols. (Matthew Bender) 1986–.

California trial practice: civil procedure during trial, 3rd ed. 3 vols. (CEB) 1995–.

Deskbook on the management of complex civil litigation. (Matthew Bender) 2000–.

Matthew Bender® Practice Guide: California Civil Discovery. (Matthew Bender) 2003–.

Matthew Bender® Practice Guide: California Pretrial Civil Procedure. 3 vols. (Matthew Bender) 2003–.

Commercial Law

California legal forms: Transaction guide, 36 vols. (Matthew Bender) 1968–.

Secured transactions in California commercial law practice, 2nd ed. (CEB) 2001–.

Construction Law

California construction contracts & disputes, 3rd ed. 2 vols. (CEB) 1999–.

California construction law, 16th ed. (Aspen Law & Business) 2000–.

California mechanics' lien law and construction industry practice, 6th ed. 2 vols. (Matthew Bender) 1996–.

California mechanics' liens and related construction remedies, 3rd ed. (CEB) 1998–.

Corporations

Ballantine & Sterling California corporation law, 4th ed. 7 vols. (Matthew Bender) 1962–.

California practice guide. Corporations. 2 vols. (Rutter Group) 1984–.

Forming and operating California limited liability companies. (CEB) 1995–.

Marsh's California corporation law, 4th ed. 4 vols. (Aspen Law & Business) 2000–.

Organizing corporations in California, 3rd ed. 2 vols. (CEB) 2001–.

Selecting and forming business entities. (CEB) 1996–.

Criminal Law and Practice

Appeals and writs in criminal cases, 2nd ed. 2 vols. (CEB) 2000–.

California criminal defense practice, 7 vols. (Matthew Bender) 1981–.

California criminal law, 3rd ed. 6 vols. (Witkin Legal Institute) 2000–.

California criminal law forms manual. (CEB) 1995–.

California criminal law procedure and practice, 6th ed. (CEB) 2002–.

California white collar crime: civil remedies and criminal sanctions, 2nd ed. 2 vols. (Michie) 2000–.

Condominiums

Advising California common interest communities. (CEB) 2003–.

California common interest developments: law and practice. 3 vols. (West Group) 2003–.

California condominium and planned development practice. (CEB) 1984–.

Court Practice

Bancroft Whitney's California civil practice. 35+ vols. (West Group) 1992–.

California civil appellate practice, 3rd ed. 2 vols. (CEB) 1996–.

California civil writ practice, 3rd ed. (CEB) 1996–.

(Pub. 64620)

California forms of pleading and practice annotated, 56 vols. (Matthew Bender) 1962–.

California practice guide. Civil appeals and writs. 2 vols. (Rutter Group) 1989–.

California practice guide. Civil trials and evidence. 3 vols. (Rutter Group) 1993–.

California points and authorities. 24 vols. (Matthew Bender) 1965–.

California trial guide, 7 vols. (Matthew Bender) 1986–.

California trial practice: civil procedure during trial, 3rd ed. (CEB) 1995–.

Deskbook on the management of complex civil litigation. (Matthew Bender) 2000–.

Damages

California damages: law & proof, 5th ed. (Matthew Bender) 1996–.

Debtor/Creditor

California practice guide. Enforcing judgments and debts. 2 vols. (Rutter Group) 1988–.

Debt collection practice in California, 2nd ed. 2 vols. (CEB) 1999–.

Discovery

California civil discovery. 2 vols. (Matthew Bender) 1996–.

California civil discovery practice, 3rd ed. 2 vols. (CEB) 1998–.

California deposition and discovery practice. 3 vols. (Matthew Bender) 1958–.

Employment/Labor

Advising California employers, 2nd ed. 2 vols. (CEB) 1996–.

California employment law. 4 vols. (Matthew Bender) 1989–.

California employment litigation: strategies and tactics, 3rd ed. (LEXIS Publishing) 1999–.

California law of employee injuries and workers' compensation, 2nd rev. ed. (Matthew Bender) 1966–.

California practice guide. Employment litigation. 3 vols. (Rutter Group) 2001–.

California workers' damages practice, 2nd ed. (CEB) 2001–.

Employment law compliance for new businesses. (CEB) 1997–.

Labor and employment in California: a guide to employment laws, regulations, and practice, 2nd ed. (Michie) 1997–.

Wage and hour manual for California employers, 8th ed. (Castle Publications) 2001.

Wrongful employment termination practice, 2nd ed. 2 vols. (CEB) 1997–.

Environmental law

California environmental law and land use practice, 6 vols. (Matthew Bender) 2001–.

California water law and policy, 2 vols. (Matthew Bender) 1995–.

Practice under the California Environmental Quality Act. 2 vols. (CEB) 1993–.

Estate Planning

California decedent estate practice. 3 vols. (CEB) 1986–.

California estate planning. 2 vols. (CEB) 2002–.

California family tax planning. 2 vols. (Matthew Bender) 1963–.

California probate practice. 5 vols. (Matthew Bender) 1991–.

California wills and trusts. 3 vols. (Matthew Bender) 1991–.

Estate planning practice. 2 vols. (CEB) 1987–.

Evidence

California courtroom evidence, 5th ed. (Matthew Bender) 2000–.

California evidence, 4th ed. (Witkin Legal Institute) 2000–.

California evidentiary foundations, 3rd ed. (Michie) 2000–.

Effective introduction of evidence in California, 2nd ed. (CEB) 2000–.

Jefferson's California evidence benchbook, 3rd ed. 2 vols. (CEB) 1997–.

Family Law

California community property law. (West) 2004.

California community property; with tax analysis. (Matthew Bender) 1985–.

California family law practice, 15th ed. 3 vols. (California Family Law Report, Inc.) 2000–.

California family law: practice and procedure, 2nd ed. (Matthew Bender) 1994–.

California marital settlement & other family law agreements, 2nd ed. (CEB) 1997–.

California practice guide. Family law 1. 3 vols. (Rutter Group) 1982–.

Practice under the California family code: dissolution, legal separation, nullity. (CEB) 1994–.

Forms

California civil litigation forms manual. (CEB) 1980–.

California forms of pleading and practice annotated, 56 vols. (Matthew Bender) 1962–.

California forms of pleading and practice annotated: Judicial Council forms, 3 vols. (Matthew Bender) 1962–.

California legal forms: transaction guide. (Matthew Bender) 1968–.

California points and authorities. 24 vols. (Matthew Bender) 1965–.

California transaction forms. (West Group).

West's California Judicial Council forms. (West Group) Annual.

Insurance

California automobile insurance law guide. (CEB) 1973–.

California insurance law & practice. 4 vols. (Matthew Bender) 1986–.

California liability insurance practice: claims & litigation. 2 vols. (CEB) 1991–.

California practice guide: insurance litigation. 3 vols. (Rutter Group) 1995–.

California uninsured motorist law, 6th ed. 2 vols. (Michie) 1999–.

California uninsured motorist practice, 2nd ed. (CEB) 2001–.

Jury Instructions

California forms of jury instruction. 6 vols. (Matthew Bender) 1985–.

California jury instructions, civil: book of approved jury instructions, 9th ed. (BAJI) 2 vols. (West Group) 2002.

California jury instructions, criminal (CALJIC), *7th ed.* 2 vols. (West Group) 2003.

Judicial council of California civil jury instructions. 2 vols. (LexisNexis Matthew Bender) 2003–.

Juveniles

California juvenile court practice. 2 vols. (CEB) 1981–.

Landlord/Tenant

California eviction defense manual, 2nd ed. 2 vols. (CEB) 1993–.

California landlord-tenant practice, 2nd ed. 2 vols. (CEB) 1997–.

California practice guide. Landlord-tenant. 2 vols. (Rutter Group) 1989–.

Land Use

California zoning practice. (CEB) 1969–.

Curtin's California land use and planning law. (Solano Press) 1997–.

Longtins California land use: planning, zoning, building, subdivision, environmental law, 2nd ed. (Local Government Publications) 1987–.

Legal Ethics/Professional Responsibility

California compendium on professional responsibility. (State Bar of California) 1983–.

California practice guide: professional responsibility. 2 vols. (Rutter Group) 1997–.

Real Property

California foreclosure: law and practice. (West Group) 1991–.

California mortgage and deed of trust practice, 3rd ed. (CEB) 2000–.

California practice guide. Real property transactions. 2 vols. (Rutter Group) 1995–.

California real estate law and practice. 17 vols. (Matthew Bender) 1973–.

California real estate finance practice. 2 vols. (CEB) 2000–.

California real property sales transactions, 3rd ed.(CEB) 1997–.

California water law and policy, 2 vols. (Matthew Bender) 1995–.

Miller & Starr California real estate, 3rd ed. 12 vols. (West Group) 2000–.

Real property exchanges, 3rd ed. (CEB) 2002–.

Partnership

Advising California partnerships, 3rd ed. (CEB) 1999–.

Probate

California practice guide. Probate. 2 vols. (Rutter Group) 1986–.

California probate practice. 4 vols. (Matthew Bender) 1991–.

California probate procedure, 6th ed. 2 vols. (Matthew Bender) 1998–.

California probate workflow manual revised. 2 vols. (CEB) 1980–.

California trust and probate litigation. (CEB) 1999–.

Securities

Practice under the California securities laws, Rev. ed.. 3 vols. (Matthew Bender) 1973–.

Style Manuals

California style manual: a handbook of legal style for California courts and lawyers, 4th ed. (West Group) 2000–.

Taxation

California small business guide: formation, operation and taxation. 3 vols. (Matthew Bender) 1987–.

California tax reporter: state and local, all taxes, all taxables. (CCH). 1948–.

Taxing California property, 3rd ed. (West Group) 1988–.

Torts

California government tort liability practice. 2 vols. (CEB) 1999–.

California practice guide, personal injury. 2 vols. (Rutter Group) 1984–.

California products liability: law and practice, 2nd ed. (LEXIS Publishing) 1999–.

California products liability actions. (Matthew Bender) 1975–.

California tort damages, 2nd ed. (CEB) 2002–.

California tort guide, 3rd ed. (CEB) 1996–.

California torts. 6 vols. (Matthew Bender) 1985–.

Trials

California trial objections, 9th ed. (CEB) 2002–.

California trial guide. 5 vols. (Matthew Bender) 1986–.

Effective direct and cross-examination. (CEB) 1986–.

Persuasive opening statements & closing arguments. (CEB) 1988–.

Trusts

California trust administration, 2nd ed. 2 vols. (CEB) 2001–.

California wills and trusts, 3 vols. (Matthew Bender) 1991–.

Drafting California irrevocable trusts, 3rd ed. 2 vols. (CEB) 1997–.

Drafting California revocable living trusts, 4th ed. (CEB) 2003–.

Wills

California will drafting, 3rd ed. 3 vols. (CEB) 1992–.

California wills and trusts, 3 vols. (Matthew Bender) 1991–.

Workers' Compensation

California law of employee injuries and workers' compensation, 2nd ed. 3 vols. (Matthew Bender) 1966–.

California workers' compensation law, 6th ed. 2 vols. (Matthew Bender) 2000–.

California workers' compensation law and practice, 6th ed. 2 vols. (James Publishing) 2002–.

California workers' compensation practice, 4th ed. 2 vols. (CEB) 2000–.

California workers' damages practice, 2nd ed. (CEB) 2001–.

INDEX

[References are to sections and appendices.]

(Pub. 64620)

[References are to sections and appendices.]

[References are to sections and appendices.]

[References are to sections and appendices.]

[References are to sections and appendices.]

[References are to sections and appendices.]

[References are to sections and appendices.]

[References are to sections and appendices.]

[References are to sections and appendices.]

[References are to sections and appendices.]

[References are to sections and appendices.]

[References are to sections and appendices.]

[References are to sections and appendices.]

[References are to sections and appendices.]

[References are to sections and appendices.]

R

RANHARTER, KATHRYN . . . . . .
Appendix K

RECORDER . . . 10.04[4]

THE RECORDER . . . 6.03[1]

RECORDS
Assembly Office of Research . . . . . .
   4.02[6][b]
Legislative Open Records Act . . . . .
   4.01[3]
1996 Public Records Retention Legislation
   . . . 4.01[4]
Public records access (See PUBLIC RE-
   CORDS ACCESS)
Senate Office of Research . . . .
   4.02[6][a]

REFERENDUM
Generally . . . 5.02[3]

REGULATIONS (See PRIMARY
SOURCES)

REPORTS
Agency reports . . . 8.05[5]
Attorney General . . . 11.01[1]
Bibliography on case reporting . . 6.10
California Constitution Revision Commis-
   sion . . . 2.02[3][a]
Committee reports and analyses (See
   COMMITTEE REPORTS AND ANAL-
   YSES)
*Executive Agency and Commission Re-
   ports* . . . 4.03[2][c]
Joint Rules Committee report . . . . . .
   2.03[6][c]
Official reports . . . 6.07[6][a]
State Bar of California . . . 12.05[5]
Unofficial reports . . . 6.07[6][b]

*REPORTS OF CASES DETERMINED
IN THE DISTRICT COURTS OF
THE STATE OF CALIFORNIA* . .
6.03[3]

RESEARCH PROCEDURES
Generally . . . 1.04[1]
Ballot measures . . . 5.06
List of California legal research guides
   . . . App.K

RESEARCH PROCEDURES—Cont.
Secondary sources (See SECONDARY
   SOURCES)
Sources and finding aids . . . 4.04[1]

REYNOLDS, OSBORNE M., JR. . . .
   9.06[5]

RILEY, BENNETT . . . 2.01[2]

RLIN
Generally . . . 1.04[2][c]

ROBINSON, WILLIAM W. . . . . .
   12.06; 14.02; Appendix J

RODMAN, WILLOUGHBY . . . . .
Appendix J

ROSE, CAROLINA . . . 8.06

*ROSTER, CALIFORNIA STATE,
COUNTY, CITY AND TOWNSHIP
OFFICIALS* . . . 4.04[6]

RULES OF COURT (See COURT
RULES)

RUTTER GROUP
Generally . . . 10.02[3]

S

SACRAMENTO NEWSLETTER . . .
   4.04[1]

SALVATO, GREG M. . . . 5.07

*SANDALL MEMBERSHIP DIREC-
TORY* . . . 14.04

SAN FRANCISCO DAILY JOURNAL
   . . . 6.03[1]; 10.04[4]

SAN FRANCISCO LAW JOURNAL
   . . . 6.03[2]

SARGENT, NOEL . . . 2.03[9]

SATO, SHO . . . 9.06[5]

SAUNDERS, MYRA K. . . . 2.03[9];
   6.02[1]

SCALL
Generally . . . 14.03; 14.04

[References are to sections and appendices.]

[References are to sections and appendices.]